THEOLOGICAL TRACTATES

Cultural Memory
in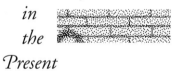
the
Present

Mieke Bal and Hent de Vries, Editors

THEOLOGICAL TRACTATES

Erik Peterson

Edited, Translated, and with an
Introduction by Michael J. Hollerich

STANFORD UNIVERSITY PRESS

STANFORD, CALIFORNIA

Stanford University Press

Stanford, California

English translation ©2011 by the Board of Trustees of the Leland Stanford Junior University. All rights reserved.

Introduction ©2011 by the Board of Trustees of the Leland Stanford Junior University. All rights reserved.

Theological Tractates was originally published in German in 1951 under the title *Theologische Traktate* ©1994 Echter Verlag Würzburg.

Printed in the United States of America on acid-free, archival-quality paper

Library of Congress Cataloging-in-Publication Data

Peterson, Erik, 1890-1960, author.

  [Theologische Traktate. English]

  Theological tractates / Erik Peterson ; edited, translated, and with an introduction by Michael J. Hollerich.

        pages cm.--(Cultural memory in the present)

  "Originally published in German in 1951 under the title Theologische Traktate." Includes bibliographical references and index.

  ISBN 978-0-8047-6967-9 (cloth : alk. paper)--ISBN 978-0-8047-6968-6 (pbk. : alk. paper)

  1. Theology. I. Hollerich, Michael J., editor, translator. II. Title. III. Series: Cultural memory in the present.

  BR85.P4813 2011

  230'.2--dc23   2011023765

Typeset by Bruce Lundquist in 11/13.5 Adobe Garamond

To the memory of
George Huntston Williams
(1914–2000),
esteemed historian, teacher,
and man of the universal Church
M. J. H.

Contents

Introduction

At the time of his death fifty years ago, the name and work of Erik Peterson (1890–1960) were known primarily to two sets of readers: an aging cohort of German Catholic intellectuals who remembered him as one of a number of brilliant Protestant and Jewish converts to Catholicism in the postwar turbulence of the Weimar Republic; and academic experts in the study of Christian origins. The former group would have been mainly acquainted with essays and articles written for a general readership and published in leading Catholic publications like *Hochland*. The latter group would have included specialists in the study of liturgy, asceticism, and apocryphal Jewish and Christian literature.

Within a few years of his death, a third set of readers emerged in the heated political climate of the 1960s and 1970s. They knew Peterson through *Monotheismus als politisches Problem*, his classic study of ancient political theology. Its rejection of "any such thing as a Christian political theology" was a frequent point of departure for Christian theologians who wanted to think that Peterson's argument applied to someone else's political theology but not theirs.

There probably wasn't much overlap among these groups. Someone who happened upon collections of his papers republished in the 1950s might not have realized that the author of the theological essays in *Theologische Traktate* was the same person who wrote the erudite technical articles in *Frühkirche, Judentum, und Gnosis*.[1] Peterson's eclectic readership reflected fractures that marked his life and thought from beginning to end.

Peterson was born into a secularized Lutheran family in Hamburg, but a conversion experience at the age of twenty brought him into the Pietist revival movement that flourished in the pre–World War I generation of German university students. In midlife, after years of agonized hesitation, he converted to Roman Catholicism, attracted by its authoritarian dimensions: the foundation in dogma and tradition, the centrality of canon law and magisterial authority, and even the Church's one-time reliance on state power to enforce orthodoxy and repress heresy. Then, after living in Rome as an underappreciated lay scholar in a Church where theology was a clerical enterprise, he became openly disenchanted with the bureaucratic centralization of the modern papacy. The man who in 1919, sickened by the bellicose nationalism of churches and theologians, wrote a brilliant satire of militarized Christianity ("The Heaven of the Military Garrison Chaplain"), also defended the providential conversion of the Roman Empire. A lifelong foe of modern Christianity's *embourgeoisement* who scorned not only liberal democracy but also pacifism and socialism, he could still say at the age of fifty-eight that the sight of Christian mediocrity was enough to induce "an existential heart attack."[2] Although he had attacked Karl Barth's dialectical theology as a Protestant theologian, because it did not recognize Church and dogma, as a Catholic, Peterson wrote little that looked like dogmatic theology. His theological essays and historical scholarship were devoted to asceticism, celibacy, and martyrdom, but at age forty-three, he married a young Italian woman and fathered five children. Barth, who knew Peterson well, rightly foresaw that he would always be a *Randgestalt*, a person on the margin.[3]

Theologische Traktate continued to find readers long after it fell out of print. That was partly due to the revival of political theology in the 1960s. More recently there has been the outpouring of scholarship on Carl Schmitt, with whom Erik Peterson formed an intense friendship, which profoundly shaped both men's thinking. Jacob Taubes, who made perceptive observations about the Peterson-Schmitt relationship, and who had his own contorted dealings with Schmitt, is said to have prized his copy of *Theologische Traktate* and to have carried it everywhere, along with Walter Benjamin's works.[4] Peterson and Benjamin are a suggestive pairing. In his book *Beyond the Border: The German-Jewish Legacy Abroad* (2007), Stephen Aschheim refers to the "iconising" of the generation of German-Jewish intellectuals that included Benjamin, Hannah Arendt, Gershom Scholem, Theodore Adorno, and others. All of them hunted for a lost transcendence that they could no longer believe in. Erik Peterson, though an ardent Christian, had something in common with their restless dissatisfaction with the world as it is. Like Scholem and Benjamin, in particular, he was launched on a search in ancient texts for a world that was not so much lost as still beyond us.

Theologische Traktate has always had Protestant readers, especially those who saw the same failings in Protestantism that he did.[5] Roman Catholics respected his learning and were pleased to have won such a prestigious convert, but were not always comfortable with Peterson's blunt judgments, his rigorous historical scholarship, and his deep sense of eschatological provisionality. Nevertheless, he found numerous sympathetic readers, not just in Germany but also, remarkably for the interwar and postwar generations, in France as well. Theologians like Yves Congar and Jean Daniélou saw that he could be a guide for the "return to the sources" animating theological renewal prior to the Second Vatican Council. Though he died before the council and would probably have had mixed views of its work and of its implementation, his legacy may yet offer a means for speaking to—and against the grain of—some of the entrenched divisions in the post-conciliar Church.

The time thus seems ripe for an English language version of *Theologische Traktate*. Except for a 1964 translation of *Das Buch von den Engeln* under the title *The Angels and the Liturgy: The Status and Significance of the Holy Angels in Worship*, now out of print, and a translation of Peterson's correspondence with Adolf von Harnack, none of the other pieces in this collection has previously appeared in English. French and Italian editions are also now out or about to appear. We have not only the magnificent resource of Barbara Nichtweiß's intellectual biography of Peterson at our disposal, but also the collected edition of his previously published and also unpublished works, *Ausgewählte Schriften*, which is now appearing under the energetic editorship of Nichtweiß and a team of collaborators.[6]

Education and Career

After completing his youthful education in Hamburg, Peterson studied "Evangelical" theology (in German *evangelisch* simply means Protestant or Lutheran, not "born again") at several German universities in the years leading up to World War I. His studies were interrupted by military service in October 1914, though he was discharged just three months later after a total breakdown.[7] Following his recovery, he returned to academic work in the fall of 1916 at the University of Göttingen, where he worked on his dissertation with the Church historian Nathanael Bonwetsch, a respected patristics scholar who shared Peterson's Pietist convictions. But he did not avoid liberal theologians on principle, enlisting Walter Bauer, for example, as a dissertation reader. Peterson was also drawn to the Göttingen faculty's celebrated "History of Religions School" of interpretation, which treated early Christianity, in rigorously historicist and comparative fashion, as one among many ancient religions. He was especially impressed with Richard Reitzenstein, the school's leading light at that time, whose ideas and methods exerted a major influence on Peterson's dissertation. His preference for positivist or empirical scholarly methods sat rather awkwardly with some of his deeper theological commitments. They are another indication of the splits referred to above.

His dissertation, *"Heis Theos": Epigraphische, formgeschichtliche und religionsgeschichtliche Untersuchungen* (*"Heis Theos"* [One God]: Epigraphic, Form-Historical, and Religious-Historical Investigations), was completed in 1920 and eventually published in revised and expanded form in 1926.[8] It studied the "One God" formula in late ancient inscriptions and texts. Peterson concluded that the formula, which was known to have apotropaic functions, originated in the shouted acclamations used in political assemblies, from which secular usage a variety of ancient religions then adapted them, for exorcism formulas, liturgical speech, and conciliar practices. The dissertation, a vintage product of the History of Religions school, was notably non-theological in its comparative and positivist methods. The reliance on key words would remain a feature of Peterson's scholarship. It left its mark on *Monotheismus als politisches Problem* and led to the near-legendary collection of citation cards that in his biographer's estimate had swollen to the hundreds of thousands by the time he died.[9] The prominent role Peterson gave to popular acclamations anticipated—if it was not already a product of—the kinship he would enjoy with Carl Schmitt when the two were colleagues at Bonn.[10]

Heis Theos launched Peterson's academic career. Doubling as his *Habilitation*, it earned him a post at Göttingen, where he served from 1920 until 1924 as *Privatdozent* for Church history, with lecturing responsibility also for Christian archaeology. Of prime importance during Peterson's four years at Göttingen was the contentious friendship he formed with Karl Barth, who got his first university appointment a year after Peterson's arrival. Besides their common debt to Søren Kierkegaard, they shared the marginality of those at the lower rungs of the professorial ladder, a marginality that in both cases was heightened by polemical temperament, high intelligence, and grandiose sense of mission. Initially, Barth was the junior partner. Peterson's learning impressed him, whereas he himself, fresh from his years as a pastor, was scrambling to catch up to the university norm. But the positions would soon be reversed as Barth's star rose in the theological firmament.

In the winter semester of 1924, Peterson was called to Bonn as ordinary professor of Church history and the New Testament. He stayed there five years, for the last of which he was also dean of the Faculty of Evangelical Theology. During that time his long-standing reservations about Protestant Christianity came to a head and impelled him to leave the Evangelical Church and become a Roman Catholic. In October 1929, he requested leave from his position and the following March, he petitioned for emeritus status. Later that year (October 1930), he was given a position as *Honorarprofessur* in the Philosophy Faculty, but he took repeated leaves. He lost the position in 1936, and it would not be restored to him until after the war. In a reprise of what happened with Barth at Göttingen, at Bonn, Peterson discovered another intimate friend with whom his intellectual and religious development would be entangled, though this time a Catholic and a non-theologian, Carl Schmitt, professor of law at Bonn from 1922 until his move to Berlin in 1928: "the only reasonable man in Bonn."[11] Peterson's Bonn years were the most settled period of his life. He enjoyed a rich social life, mostly with Catholic colleagues rather than with fellow Protestants. None of those Catholic friendships approached the intellectual depth and intensity of the bond he formed with Schmitt, however. The influences were reciprocal—Peterson's biographer speaks of a "permeable intellectual membrane" between them—and extended to every aspect of Peterson's thinking on the public character (*Öffentlichkeit*) of Christianity. Peterson even stood as a witness to Schmitt's second (and non-canonical) marriage in 1926, and later lobbied on his behalf for an annulment. The friendship deteriorated and never really recovered after Schmitt's dalliance with the Nazi dictatorship.

Peterson was received into the Catholic Church at St. Peter's Basilica in Rome on December 22–23, 1930. His conversion to Catholicism meant an abrupt derailment of his academic career. Despite the efforts of his friends in Germany, he was not able to find another university appointment. For a while he considered becoming a Catholic priest, and he actually began a fast-track seminary program in Munich. That plan apparently foundered, because in the spring of 1932 he broke off his priestly studies. For several years after his conversion, he alternated between living in Munich and in Rome. During one of his Roman stays, he met and fell in love with a young Italian woman named Matilde Bertini (1910–1993), the daughter of an editor of *L'Osservatore Romano*, the Vatican newspaper. His biographer reports that upon meeting her, he was so swept away that his other plans evaporated. They were married on June 1, 1933. Five children quickly followed.

In Rome, Peterson experienced great frustration in trying to find an academic position appropriate to his stature. The struggle to support his family left him with a bitterness he did not try to hide. Anti-clericalism, he once said to his Benedictine friend Thomas Michels, was more likely to come from moral than from dogmatic objections. From 1937 on, he had a precarious hold on a lectureship in the Papal Institute for Christian Archaeology, finally upgraded ten years later to an Extraordinary professorship. In 1956, he received a *nihil obstat* to be an Ordinary professor at the Institute, but the appointment was never realized. By that time his energies were sapped, and he was in declining health. He died on October 26, 1960, in a Hamburg hospital, after a stroke following surgery for prostate cancer. He had wished to be buried in Rome in the Campo Santo Teutonico, the venerable German cemetery adjacent to Vatican City. In a final and emblematic snub, the German religious confraternity to which he belonged denied burial rights to the family.[12] Instead he was interred in the city cemetery of Rome, in the family plot of his Italian in-laws.

Writings

Heis Theos is Peterson's only real book-length publication, and even it gives the impression of a mosaic of specialized studies. His published work consisted mostly of essays in general-interest journals, such as *Hochland*, and specialized studies on aspects of ancient Christianity and related subjects, dense with footnotes and untranslated Greek and Latin.[13] Among possible reasons for this rather crabbed production, two stand out. One is Peterson's lifelong preference for close, even minute study of individual texts. He was by nature skeptical of big-picture syntheses and doubted whether "history" in the sense of a coherent narrative was even possible. This stemmed from his acute sensitivity to the eschatological, and also from habitual intellectual restraint. His avowal of dogmatic theology did not include theological system-building, which in his view was a very different enterprise. "Discontinuity" is a theme in his diaries from early manhood to old age: "'We know in part' [1 Cor. 13] means that there is no 'systematic' or even comprehensive knowledge of God and his mysteries."[14] In today's jargon, we would say he did not believe in grand narratives.

The other explanation for his reticence is circumstantial. In mid-career, he was forced to become a virtual itinerant. And the Church he joined was not very interested in fresh theological initiatives from a lay-man, and a convert to boot. His precarious status in Rome did not recom-mend boldness. Whatever other benefits he got from becoming a Catholic, encouragement and stimulation as a writer weren't among them. The un-published writings that are now appearing enrich our appreciation of his achievement. But they mostly come from his university lectures on the New Testament, Christian origins, Church history, and related subjects. They precede his conversion. It is true that most of the articles translated here were first published in the 1930s. But even they owe a good deal of their substance to work he did in the previous decade. When they were collected and republished in 1951, Peterson had contentious negotiations with the publisher, Kösel Verlag, over how to characterize the author's re-lationship to his Protestant past. By mutual agreement, the following care-fully worded preface was added:

With the consent of the author, we present a collection of some important writ-ings and essays of Erik Peterson's, which were previously published in various places and for the most part are now out of print. No changes in the texts were envisioned, although the author today takes a critical view of many of his earlier writings, especially the articles "What Is Theology?" and "The Church," which both stem from his Protestant period. We believe that the writings collected here still have a significant role to play in contemporary theological discussion, and that reprinting them, in individually unchanged form, therefore appears justified.

The essays are presented here in the chronological order of their orig-inal publication, covering slightly more than a decade (1925–1937).[15] They make an excellent composite portrait of Peterson's thinking during the de-cisive years of his career. Readers whose main interest is in *Monotheismus als politisches Problem* (translated here as "Monotheism as a Political Prob-lem: A Contribution to the History of Political Theology in the Roman Empire"), and who are otherwise unfamiliar with Peterson will find the other papers illuminating in the way they fill out the political dimension of his theology, for his celebrated repudiation of "any such thing as a Christian political theology" was in no way a denial of the political character of the Church and of Christianity.

"What Is Theology?" (1925)

The essay *Was ist Theologie?* is unique in *Theologische Traktate* in being framed exclusively in Protestant terms.[16] The vocabulary, the issues, and the protagonists all belong to the years when the dialectical theology of Karl Barth and his allies was in the ascendant. But differences in the movement were already starting to emerge. Peterson recognized—even before the principals themselves were fully aware of it—that Barth and the New Testament scholar Rudolf Bultmann disagreed about the place that philosophy should play in theology. In this sharply worded, controversial piece, Peterson attacked the "dialectical" method by denying that it could be called knowledge at all.[17] True theological knowledge depended on the Incarnation, not as a paradox, but as a fleshly and hence partially knowable reality. The claims to "concreteness" actually avoided the concrete obedience that a concrete revelation should claim: "Dialectical reference to God leads to the non-binding character of a mythical narrative but not to theology, for which obedience is required." The description of dogma as the *Elongatur*, or extension, of the revelation of the Logos pointed both to Peterson's concern for the objectivity of revelation and to the insight that the sacraments as well were such an extension. As such they imposed "a positive legal claim of God . . . which concretely touches every one of us"— an assertion whose juridical and coercive implications he did not shrink from endorsing, to the dismay of readers then and now.

Correspondence with Adolf von Harnack (1928–1929) and an Epilogue (1932)

In the summer of 1928, Peterson exchanged a series of letters with the Church historian Adolf von Harnack, the aging patriarch of liberal Protestantism.[18] The subject was Harnack's recent assertion that the apostolic teaching office had relativized the authority of Scripture and thereby given "biblicism" a healthy and needed corrective. That claim subverted a basic axiom of traditional Protestantism, the sole sufficiency of Scripture (*sola Scriptura*). Peterson endorsed Harnack's thesis in order to illuminate the crisis that, he believed, the constitution of the Weimar Republic posed for traditional Protestantism. The Weimar Constitution derived sovereignty not from God but from the people (Art. 1), a principle that contradicted the biblical sanction for the state: "the powers that be are ordained of God" (Rom. 13:1). The abdication of the German princes deprived the provincial Protestant churches of the civil authorities who had been their traditional governors (*summi episcopi*, "chief overseers") ever since the Reformation. This reopened the question of authority in the Church. While the new constitution preserved many features of state support for the established provincial churches, it offered similar support to every denomination and even to non-religious clubs or associations devoted to a particular world-view. The effect was to undercut the established churches' privileged and public identification with the state and the nation. At the same time, the prestige of theology in the universities had declined since the war. Among theologians themselves, the previously dominant liberal theology of the prewar period was being subjected to savage critique by the Barthian insurgency.

Two years after Harnack's death, Peterson, by then a Catholic, secured his widow's permission to publish the letters, with an epilogue as commentary.[19] In his article Peterson asserted that the new situation deprived Christianity of its public character (*Öffentlichkeit*, the leitmotif of *Theologische Traktate*). The Church was reduced to being merely one voluntary society among others, while its dogmas were being dissolved by rationalism, "mysticism" both spiritual and secular, and social activism. Barth's dialectical theology was only a pretend solution, because it failed to grant the Church its proper authority. In a letter to Barth, Peterson described his epilogue to the correspondence as an "indirect communication" (in the Kierkegaardian sense) of some of the reasons for his conversion. He compared his path to Cardinal Newman's, in that he had taken "the indirect way of the 'Difficulties of Protestantism' [quoted in English]," that is, through the weaknesses of Protestantism's own presuppositions.[20]

"The Church" (1928–1929)

This short, programmatic article originated as a lecture Peterson gave in the Netherlands in the fall of 1928. It was an intentional bookend to the correspondence with Harnack, for whom he said he had written it.[21]

But he certainly had Karl Barth in mind as well, for "The Church" served equally well as a sequel to "What Is Theology?"[22]

"The Church" marked a decisive turning point in Peterson's life and career and will therefore receive a commentary out of proportion to its brevity. Not only did it signal unambiguously to Protestants that its author was en route to Rome, but it had the simultaneous, if unintended, effect of unsettling Catholics as well. The essay took as its point of departure Alfred Loisy's celebrated dictum: "Jesus proclaimed the Kingdom, and it was the Church that came." That was the bomb that a generation ago had set off the Modernist crisis in the Catholic Church, with Loisy's excommunication as one of its consequences. In 1902, in his brilliant little book *L'Évangile et l'Église* (The Gospel and the Church), Loisy, then a Catholic priest and a New Testament scholar, had defended the integrity of the Church's tradition against Harnack's historical critique. Whereas Harnack had tried to detach Jesus from the later beliefs and practices of the early Christian Church, Loisy turned Harnack's developmental critique on its head. Appealing to Cardinal Newman's theory of the development of doctrine, Loisy proposed that the true meaning of the Christian revelation could only be grasped in the light of its full development, just as the meaning of the seed could only be grasped once it had grown into a mature tree.[23] Harnack's "primitivism" privileged origins in a classically Protestant way. But in seeking to free the historical "kernel" of the true message of Jesus from the husk of ecclesiastical tradition, Harnack failed to see that there was no other historical access to Jesus except *through* the tradition, which could not simply be peeled away as an accretion. "Whatever we think, theologically, of tradition, whether we trust it or regard it with suspicion, we know Christ only by the tradition, across the tradition, and in the tradition of the primitive Christians," Loisy asserted.[24] Loisy identified the true message of Jesus as the proclamation of the Kingdom to Israel; Jesus did not in any literal sense found the Church, which had originated after Easter with the faith in the Resurrection.

Modern accounts of this thesis sometimes overlook the fact that Loisy considered it to be a legitimate and necessary development of Jesus' message, not a distortion. But after his excommunication in 1908, Loisy's apologetic came to be regarded in retrospect as a Trojan horse for Modernism. The 1907 papal decree *Lamentabili* condemned as a Modernist error the thesis that "It was foreign to the mind of Christ to establish the Church as a society that would last on earth throughout the long duration of the ages; but rather that it was in the mind of Christ that the kingdom of heaven together with the end of the world would come soon."[25]

Given this background it is not surprising that Peterson's essay aroused suspicion among some Catholic theologians and churchmen.[26] Even an early admirer and sponsor like Jacques Maritain had reservations. Yves Congar tried for years to get a French translation authorized; none appeared until 1953. His advocacy was eventually vindicated by Cardinal Joseph Ratzinger (now Pope Benedict XVI), who in 1991 acknowledged that Peterson was "the first . . . to adopt [Loisy's thesis] and take it in a Catholic direction."[27] At the time, however, critics were troubled by the very use of historical-critical methods on such a sensitive dogmatic subject as Jesus' foundation of the Church. Peterson frankly admitted there was no direct and immediate connection between Jesus and the Church, its offices, and its sacraments, though the purpose of his argument was to explain that this did not mean there had to be a separation or a gap between them.

He was not unaware of the misgivings. In the summer of 1930, he consulted with Catholic acquaintances in Rome about the precise mean-ing of the proposition "Jesus Christus instituit ecclesiam" (Jesus Christ founded a/the church). In a letter to Carl Schmitt, he reported the reassur-ance which he had received from Reginald Garrigou-Lagrange, "the most famous Roman theologian": "It is supposed to mean: Jesus Christ had the intention that there should be a Church. It is not supposed to mean that Christ founded an association with the pope as its chairman."[28] The same letter to Schmitt mentioned the possibility of a book on the Church. Though he worked on it on and off for six years, the book never appeared, perhaps because Peterson became skittish about slipping on the "slick ice" of Catholic theology. He subsequently avoided such dangerous dogmatic terrain.[29] Despite hints that he should do so,[30] however, he never changed what he had written in "The Church," saying only that he had used "a for-mulation that admittedly lent itself to various misunderstandings."[31]

There was also uneasiness about the interpretation Peterson gave to the Jewish people's rejection of Jesus.[32] Some dogmatic theologians ob-jected to seeming to treat the Church, and even the Crucifixion, as histori-cal contingencies rather than necessary and intended instruments in God's salvific plan. And there was criticism about the distinction Peterson made between the Church and the Kingdom of God. The distinction was nevertheless crucial to his argument, which posited that the continuity between the two lay in the persons of the Twelve, called by Jesus in the flesh to be the nucleus of a restored Israel, and called by the risen Christ and the Spirit to be the Twelve Apostles.

Today we would say that a greater problem has to do, not with what Peterson said about Jesus or the Church, but what he said about Judaism. In "The Church," the sharp cleavage between Jesus' public ministry and his risen state (to use Christian theological language) at least had the merit of recognizing frankly that his ministry, and that of the Twelve, was indeed in the first instance to Israel. The problem lay with the absoluteness of the cleavage, which consigned Jewish Christianity, and apparently everything having to do with primitive Christianity's Semitic origins, to historical desuetude and divine cancellation. In his later career, to be sure, Peterson's perspective changed, and Jewish Christianity became one of his favorite areas of research.[33]

The other notable feature of "The Church" was its emphasis on the political aspect of the Church as an *ekklēsia*, a self-designation that Peterson insisted should be understood in the first instance as the citizen assembly of the Hellenistic polis (rather than as the Septuagint's equivalent for the *qahal*, the religious congregation, of the Hebrew Bible). The assembly was empowered to make binding decrees, which the people endorsed by acclamation. This stress on decision-making capability is certainly an echo of Peterson's intellectual fraternizing with Carl Schmitt, but it is more than just that: it goes to the heart of his sense of the Church as a quasi-political reality:

True, the Church is not the Kingdom. But something of the Kingdom clings to the Church, both of the political desire of the Jews for the Kingdom of God, as well as of the claim to sovereignty of "the Twelve" in the Kingdom of God. It is true, to be sure, that a certain ambiguity attaches to the Church. She is not in a univocal sense a religious-political entity such as was the messianic Kingdom of the Jews. But she is also not a purely spiritual entity, in which such concepts as politics and sovereignty may not, as such, appear, as though she were restricted to "service."

"The Church from Jews and Gentiles" (1933)

Die Kirche aus Juden und Heiden ("The Church from Jews and Gentiles") was Peterson's first separate publication as a Catholic.[34] He dedicated it to "the Roman Church, in which the blessed apostles Peter and Paul confirmed the calling of all, both from the Jews and from the Gentiles, by the shedding of their blood."[35] His biographer says it was intended to advance theses first launched in "The Church" and to deflect criticisms from the Protestant side that he was prone to a "subjective Romanticism."[36] It originated as three lectures given in Salzburg in the summer of 1932, which were adapted from Peterson's unpublished university lectures on Paul's letter to the Romans,[37] chapters 9 to 11, in which Paul considers God's election of Israel and the calling of the Gentiles.

With anti-Semitism on the rise, the topic was controversial. A year later, Peterson would publish a long article in *Hochland* on the new national Protestant Church that had come into being in the wake of the Third Reich.[38] The article deplored the new Church's cooptation by the radically anti-Semitic *Deutsche Christen* (German Christians), who were protesting the Church's Jewish heritage and clamoring for the Church to recognize race and nationhood as orders of creation. At Salzburg, Peterson argued forcefully that "Israel alone is and remains the chosen people." No other people could seek to play that role. At the same time, because election was now understood in what Peterson called "eschatological time" and not secular time, "Jews *and* Gentiles belong to the chosen Israel, as it is now constituted in the Ekklesia."

To a certain extent, then, "The Church from Jews and Gentiles" may be admired for defending the integrity of the revelation to Israel, and that is how some have regarded it.[39] A less complimentary reading will note unhappy features of its attitude to Judaism and to Jews. In this piece and in others in *Theologische Traktate*, Peterson firmly endorsed the traditional representation of the *synagoga caeca*, the blindfolded synagogue, which failed to recognize Jesus as Messiah. In his view, "the Jewish problem" (*sic*) was essentially *theological* and in the hands of God, and was therefore incapable of political and social solution, either by the neutrality of the liberal state or by *völkisch* racial theory. Anti-Jewish stereotypes crop up here and there. That they were standard fare for the time doesn't make references to Jewish wealth, to "a certain hysteria [that] marks the metaphysical character of the Jewish people," to "the famous Jewish cleverness," and so on, any less obnoxious. An article or monograph on Peterson's theology of Judaism would be a welcome contribution.[40] It would have to distinguish carefully between his specifically theological judgments, his historical scholarship, and his personal prejudices.

"Monotheism as a Political Problem" (1935)

The landmark treatise *Monotheismus als politisches Problem: Ein Beitrag zur Geschichte der politischen Theologie im Imperium Romanum*, a synthesis of two earlier articles, has had an immense and controversial influence.[41] All we can do here is summarize Peterson's purpose, mention some objections to his thesis, and provide some context on his relationship with Carl Schmitt.[42]

As is well known, Peterson posited the existence of a widespread ancient political theology that legitimated monarchical rule on earth by the cosmic rule of one god in heaven. His thesis was that the triumph of orthodox Nicene Trinitarian theology over Arian heresy (which subordinated the Son to the Father) spared Christianity from subjugation to such a political theology by making its ideological presupposition impossible. Not only that, Peterson went on to say, it thereby established that *any* such thing as a Christian political theology was impossible. (It is sometimes forgotten that his proof actually had two components, the other being the victory of Augustine's eschatology of deferral over the readiness of other Christians, such as Eusebius of Caesarea, to see the Constantinian settlement as a harbinger of the peace of the messianic age.)

Readers unfamiliar with *Monotheismus als politisches Problem* ("Monotheism as a Political Problem") may be surprised to find themselves mired in chains of quotations from ancient authors with whom they have little acquaintance. Peterson says nothing at all about the present, aside from a final note. But contemporaries recognized that this short book was "a warning against a new Arianism," as his friend Alois Dempf said in his eulogy for Peterson.[43] "Arianism" was a cipher for the political theology of Christians who had been bewitched by Hitler and his regime in its early days. It was certainly his intention, Peterson later said, "to take a poke at the *Reichstheologie*" (theology of the Reich), particularly at the version being propagated by conservative Catholics, some of whom were his friends, for whom National Socialism (briefly) held out the hope of turning back the tide of secularization.[44] Peterson shared many of their assumptions about the right ordering of society and state, but recognized immediately that the Nazis were mortal enemies and could not be tamed.

Objections to the thesis are many. Some appeal to matters of fact, such as the long history of the Christian Church's establishment in the

Roman Empire, in which it was often a creature of the government. (A re-buttal might point out that Peterson was talking about *theology*, not about history.) Others hold that the thesis dictated the evidence. They think that Peterson's construction of Arianism was more fiction than historical reality, a template on which to project contemporary conflicts. He has met even stronger resistance to his broader rejection of Christian political theology altogether. One school of critics has objected that Peterson limited himself to conservative political theology that legitimated the existing order, while ignoring other political theologies that served a critical function. That was a favorite theme of leftist-oriented political theologians in the 1960s and 1970s. A different criticism, more historicist in nature, denied that a single case study of a particular time and place could possibly have the universal validity Peterson claimed.

That last critique came from none other than his close friend Carl Schmitt, who is referred to by name in the monograph's final note, which credits Schmitt's 1922 book *Politische Theologie* for introducing the concept into modern discourse. The note is perhaps intentionally vague as to whether Peterson approved of Schmitt's work. Schmitt thought he did not and much resented it, though he said nothing about it until ten years after Peterson's death, when he published a sequel to *Politische Theologie* that was aimed directly at *Monotheismus als politisches Problem.*[45] He argued that the definition of what was political and what was not was itself an inescap-ably *political* decision, the argument that he had put forward long before in his book *Der Begriff des Politischen* (1927; translated as *The Concept of the Political*). There was no theological sanctuary in which Peterson could sequester himself and pretend he was immune to political claims and re-alities. Furthermore, it flew in the face of human experience, and also of Christian faith, to say that political events, political structures, and the like were somehow to be imagined as exempt from religious reflection and di-vine validation.

This is not the place to respond on Peterson's behalf,[46] but this much should be said: Schmitt (willfully?) misunderstood Peterson to be claiming to inhabit an apolitical space. That was not his view at all. Rather, Peterson was asserting the *superiority* of the religious to the political: the supranational kingship of Christ admitted of no merely national rival, and genuinely im-perial rivals had ceased to exist in the modern world. The Church's claim to exercise a *potestas indirecta* ("indirect power"—the phrase is Cardinal Robert Bellarmine's) in matters political definitively separated a Christian from a pagan conception of politics.[47]

"The Book on the Angels" (1935)

Das Buch von den Engeln ("The Book on the Angels") is sometimes called Peterson's most finished theological work, even though, like other treatises in this collection, it is actually a composite of previous publications.[48] It was certainly his most widely read book, with Italian, French, and Spanish translations appearing during his lifetime and an English version shortly after his death.[49] It may also have been his favorite. According to Heinrich Schlier, who later held Peterson's New Testament chair at Bonn (and who eventually also followed him into the Catholic Church), it was a book "written from his heart."[50]

The book presents itself as a contribution to angelology, a theological field of study that Peterson takes seriously and refuses to treat as an antiquarian exercise. What his biographer calls his "mythical" realism, his refusal to distance himself intellectually from the spiritual and demonic world of the New Testament, no doubt has several explanations, including the influence of phenomenology on Peterson's reading of ancient religious texts.[51] Ultimately, perhaps, it stems from Peterson's own religious sensibility, which was acutely and even painfully aware of the world as both provisional and somehow transparent. For him the existence of angels and also demons was not open to doubt.

"The Book on the Angels" was written to explain the angels' spiritual function, which revealed itself most fully in worship and in mysticism. An ethereal triad of angels, liturgy, and mysticism may seem like an unpromising platform from which to expound on the public character of Christianity. And yet that is what Peterson does. The angels' role in worship and prayer has a public and even a political character. The heavenly worship of the angels—and therefore implicitly of the Church on earth as well—has, he says, an original relationship to the political world, a thesis he demonstrates first in his reading of chapters 4 and 5 of the book of Revelation; then via a rich array of ancient liturgical texts; and finally, on a cosmic scale, in mystical experience. When the hymnody of the universal Church's earthly liturgy is joined with the hymnody of the heavenly liturgy, it transcends all national hymnody, an assertion in which we can hear an implicit rebuke of the blaring nationalistic anthems beloved of the Nazis. And when he says that "the knowledge of the Church, which stands behind its worship and hymnody, [is] a 'final' knowledge, because it has subordinated every other knowledge, such as for example *that derived from the political situation of a people* [emphasis added]", he is attacking a central thesis of the Nazified political theology of the day. Here is his peroration:

The preceding exposition has perhaps shown that it was not arbitrary or pointless for us to have given our attention to the meaning of the doctrine of the angels. There is an immediate implication for the doctrine of the holy Church: the Church is more than just a human religious society, because the angels and the saints in heaven also belong to it. Seen from this perspective, then, the Church's worship is never a merely human affair: no, the angels, like the entire cosmos, take part in it. To the Church's singing corresponds heavenly singing, and, just like the participation in the heavenly singing, so too is the Church's inner life linked. The angels demonstrate that the Church's worship is a public worship that is offered to God, and because the angels possess a relationship to the religio-political world in heaven, through them the Church's worship also acquires a necessary relationship to the political sphere. Lastly, the angels in their singing are linked with the Church not only in those "like the angels" and in the "people," they are also at the same time the awakeners of the mystical life in the Church, which only finds its fulfillment when humanity, joined with the choirs of angels, begins to praise God from the depths of its creatureliness.

Peterson's political reading of the liturgy ironically put him in bad odor at Maria Laach Abbey, the center of the liturgical renewal movement, whose chief theoretician was the Benedictine scholar Odo Casel.[52] He and Peterson fell out over Casel's account of the Christian sacraments as answers to the pagan mysteries. Casel bridled at Peterson's emphasis on the *Öffentlichkeit* of the sacraments and their legal-cultic character. For his part, Peterson (trained, remember, in the History of Religions School, but by the mid-1920s skeptical of Reitzenstein) insisted that the Christian sacraments could only be understood in eschatological terms, as the figural breaking in of the New Age, which would not be fully realized until the End. They were not a personal *experience* of salvation in Christ but its proleptic realization. (It should be noted that Peterson's difficulties with Maria Laach may also have had to do with his critique of the *Reichstheologie*, which was favored by the abbot, Ildefons Herwegen.)

"Christ as Imperator" (1936)

"Christus als Imperator," a dense little gem of an article on ancient ruler cult, first appeared in a Catholic periodical.[53] A year later, it was tacked onto *Zeuge der Wahrheit* ("Witness to the Truth") when that was first published in 1937, and then reprinted in *Theologische Traktate*. They share similar themes and were written in the same circumstance: the tightening grip of the National Socialist dictatorship. Within its scholarly carapace, "Christ as *Imperator*" (I am leaving the imperial title untranslated) leaves no doubt about its contemporary relevance as a critique of absolute power and a call to Christian resistance. When Peterson quotes Vergil's famous line "imperium sine fine dedi" ("I have given empire without end," *Aeneid* 1.278f.), and then shows how Christians adapted it to mean that the *imperium Christi* was the real empire without end, the allusion to the thousand-year Reich is unmistakable. When he says of the oath taken in the imperial cult that it raised the question of whether a Christian could recognize an un-Christian historical and political "worldview" (the Nazis were always vaunting their *Weltanschauung*), he is reminding readers of the loyalty plebiscite and the army and civil service oaths of 1934. His analysis of the political and religious situation that gave rise to the imperial cult mirrored Peterson's view of how the situation in Germany enabled the dictatorship: local institutions had withered in the face of imperial expansion, the masses were ungovernable without an absolute ruler, and traditional religion was in decline. As a result, he says of Augustus and his successors, "the *princeps*, the leader, had to unify all power in himself." This was precisely what Peterson thought was happening in Germany, where Nazi *Gleichschaltung* (regimentation) was crushing competing institutions, a new ruler cult was being created, and secularization was hollowing out the nation's Christian heritage. In such an extreme situation, early Christian eschatological urgency was once again relevant:

Then we shall understand how Christ can be praised in hymn as king of the world to come, but how *even now* [emphasis in original] majesty and power are ascribed to him in the acclamations of the Church, how the historical and political world-picture of this Aeon, which makes the *princeps* the executor of *Tychē* [Fortune] is overcome in bloody conflict by the martyrs, how the Eucharistic banquet that the Church celebrates is not only a *mysterium* but already has something of the eschatological banquet in it, which the Lord will celebrate with his own upon his return (Luke 19:30).

"Witness to the Truth" (1937)

"Witness to the Truth" (*Zeuge der Wahrheit*) makes a fitting coda to the collection, steeped as it is in themes of witness, eschatological division, suffering, and ultimate triumph.[54] Once again we are dealing with a composite work assembled from previous essays. Familiar biblical texts dominate. From the gospels we have both Jesus' preaching of the Kingdom in Matthew (the Sermon on the Mount, the commissioning of the disciples) and the trial scene with Pontius Pilate in John. Above all we again meet the book of Revelation, which held an enduring not to say obsessive fascination for Erik Peterson, and about which he recalls a vivid childhood memory. Liturgical references abound, including the new feast of Christ the King, established by Pope Pius XI in 1925. And the title is taken from Søren Kierkegaard, who appears here less as lonely knight of faith and more as a Savonarola to a complacent Christianity: "If there is anything that is the opposite of the spirit of bourgeois comfort, it is primitive Christianity, which in the mouth of the martyr in Revelation blasts us like some fiery breath."

Martyrdom, Peterson tells his readers, is not just a historical memory but once again a real possibility, indeed, a mark of the Church: "A Church that does not suffer is not the apostolic Church." The martyr's witness is emphatically public: "The martyr demonstrates the public claim of the Church of Jesus Christ." In the eschatological age inaugurated by Christ, *neutrality is no longer possible and a decision, for or against, must be made.* That is the message of "Witness to the Truth." It has consequences both in the intellectual and the political sphere. Just as one cannot escape the necessity to decide by hiding behind the shield of (alleged) scientific objectivity, so the political order can't dodge it by suspending judgment on matters metaphysical. "Because human thinking is never independent of the *hic et nunc* of a political order of some kind, it inevitably stands either under the power of the Antichrist or the power of Christ."

That is a very strong claim. Peterson is not only saying that the regime of the Antichrist forces a decision on us, one that may require us to pay in blood. *Any* regime that does not recognize Christ is ipso facto in the service of Christ's enemy. Behind that claim is a critique of "pluralism" long popular with Christian conservatives hostile to the fragmentation imposed by modernity (popular sovereignty, capitalism, social emancipation, specialization of knowledge, etc.). Peterson ratchets up the urgency of the critique by framing it eschatologically in the phenomenon of martyrdom: "For the revelation of Christ also makes visible for the martyr *the metaphysical disorientation that marks the false political order* [emphasis added]: the political, whose plane of activity is in the world of pluralism, is always tempted to abandon the ultimate metaphysical orientation and to seek its gods in the world of the pluralistic."

By orienting *his* critique to the coming New Age rather than to a disappearing and irretrievable past, Peterson freed himself from the temptation of nostalgic Catholic conservatives to seek a rapprochement with the National Socialists, whom he saw with the mask stripped away: "[The martyrs] must conquer because the Antichrist wages war against the saints, because he forces a decision on them *by making the political symbol a cultic object* [emphasis added]." In 1937, the relevance of that was clear for those who had eyes to see.

What it has to say to those of us who live today, with middling contentment, in the shambling structures of liberal democracy is less clear. "Witness to the Truth" is certainly a powerful summons to resistance. But who will its audience be? Radical Christians living on the edge of a society they think has lost its soul? Conservative if not reactionary Christians obsessed with the so-called culture of death? Melancholy contemplatives? What is the prospect for a Christian politics that appears to regard as illegitimate "every political system that does not let itself be limited by the kingship of Christ"?

Although unsure of the answer to that, I am pleased to present this collection of Erik Peterson's essays, as the provocative legacy of a gifted and idiosyncratic critic of the spirit of the age, someone who frankly described himself in St. Paul's pungent phrase "as one born out of due time" (1 Cor. 15:8).[55] The Greek word St. Paul uses of himself here, *ektrōma*, literally means a premature birth, a miscarriage, or even an aborted fetus. In keeping with Erik Peterson's own refusal to seek closure before its time, let us leave it to the future to decide whether he was born too early—or too late.

Michael Hollerich
St. Paul, Minn.

Abbreviations

CSEL   *Corpus Scriptorum Ecclesiasticorum Latinorum* (Vienna, 1864–)

PG   *Patrologiae cursus completus. Series graeca*, ed. J. P. Migne (Paris, 1857–1866)

PL   *Patrologiae cursus completus. Series latina*, ed. J. P. Migne (1844–1864)

THEOLOGICAL TRACTATES

1

What Is Theology?

"As theologians, we are supposed to talk about God. But we are also human beings, and as human beings we are not able to talk about God. We are obliged to be aware of both our 'Ought' and our 'Cannot', and in so doing, to give God the glory," Karl Barth asserts.[1]

In arguing this thesis, he goes on to say that the theologian has to represent humanity, the human being as such, who is shaken by the question of God. Theology is "the distress signal of an embarrassment," "in which humanity, simply as humanity, finds itself." If theology is thus an expression of a situation facing every human being, it is still true that the theologian is not in a position to say something about God. For "to speak about God would mean to speak God's word, the word that can come only from him, the word that God becomes man." Certainly we can say that God becomes man, but we cannot say it in such a way that it becomes existential truth. Theology's task, according to Barth, is and remains the demand both to let be and to give expression to this paradoxical state of affairs: that we must speak about God and yet are unable to speak. Whenever we do this, then we are theologians and we give God the glory.

In these sentences an answer is apparently given to the question "What is theology?" *The* answer, namely, that theology only exists insofar as there is no theology. But let us not deceive ourselves; this answer is not a concrete answer to a concrete question. For the theology that only exists insofar as there is no theology is precisely not a theology but only a repetition of the question: is there theology? Of course Barth tells us that it belongs to the nature of theology that the question should always remain a question, and precisely to the degree that it remains a question is it an answer—to which corresponds, on the other hand, that the answer is no answer, but an answer only insofar as it remains a question. In this dialectic of question and answer, reference is given to God: who upholds the dialectic, thereby gives God the glory.

Barth's theology thus seems to be much more serious than any theology that has ever existed, for it does not take the trouble of first asking concretely and answering concretely. Instead, right off the bat, it refers us dialectically to God *in* every question and *in* every answer, and insofar as it does this, it gives its question and answer. What progress appears to have been made here, when there is no longer a concrete question but only "the question as such," and where there is no longer a concrete answer, but only "the answer as such," and where there is furthermore no longer concrete humanity but only "humanity as such" who is asking, or—to use Barth's terminology—the humanity that *is* question![2] And what progress too has been made in talk about God! We can say nothing definite, nothing concrete, nothing objective about God—only God himself can do that—we can only "speak as such." Speech in the dialectical form of an indefinite reference to God. But what am I saying? To "God"? How undialectically would that be thought! No, "to God as such"! To the possibility of God as such.

Nevertheless, the apparent seriousness of this type of dialectic is only a sham seriousness. It is just as much a sham as the dialectical question is a sham and the answer of the dialectician is a sham and as God himself in this dialectic is only a dialectical possibility. All dialectic gets to no higher seriousness than that of a dialectical seriousness, than that of a possible taking-seriously (*Ernstnehmen*). It is a dialectical possibility to take God seriously so that one is ready, like Abraham, to sacrifice Isaac,[3] but still just a dialectical—a mythical—possibility, alongside which stands, in similar seriousness, the writing of the diary of the seducer.[4] *This is the nemesis that plagues every dialectician: he has not become serious before his alleged taking-seriously.* Would that every reader of Kierkegaard's religious discourses would ponder that statement! Every effort at dialectic can lead to no higher seriousness than to some possible *taking* seriously. Since the dialectic evidently fails to arrive even at a real *human* seriousness, it is even less able to arrive at the seriousness of *God* in its dialectic. But as it pertains to God to transcend every human dialectic, so too it pertains to the seriousness of God that he transcends every dialectical *taking* seriously. For it pertains precisely to the seriousness of God that he is concretely visible and that he exists wholly undialectically—exists, for instance, in the form of the Last Judgment, as the Christian faith confesses. And that is how the seriousness of the dialectician is distinguished from the seriousness of God: the seriousness of God really *exists*, whereas the seriousness of the dialectician only *mythically* exists, in the form of a taking-seriously of all possibilities—that is, in a more sober sense is understood not to exist *at all*.[5]

When dialectic had transformed everything into mere appearance and possibility, then it pleased God, by his revelation, to make dialectic itself into mere appearance. Hence the truth of St. Ambrose's saying "Non in dialectica complacuit Deo salvum facere populum suum" (Not by dialectic did it please God to save his people). From the time of Adam to Christ, the archetype of all dialectical questioning had as its motto the question of the serpent in Paradise: is God supposed to have said you were not to eat from any type of tree in the garden? But from the time of Christ's first coming until his return, this is what counts: "Truly *I* say to you," and "Heaven and earth will pass away, but *my* words will not pass away." In the time from Adam to Christ, the seductiveness of all dialectical possibilities weighs on us, for the seductiveness of the serpent's question lay not in its content but in its dialectical form.

But for the time between Christ's first and second comings, this type of seduction by the possibility of the dialectical is ruled out. By what law? By the law of faith—insofar, namely, as the full stop of faith has taken the place of all dialectical questioning. Faith, whose essential quality is obedience—an obedience that belongs just as essentially to faith as disobedience belongs to the essence of dialectic. An obedience that furthermore belongs to faith not in the sense of some accidental quality, say in the sense that to some purely theoretical assent of faith there would be subsequently be added an act of the will, nor in the sense that faith itself was a voluntaristic act, but rather in the sense that to the act of faith an act of obedience is metaphysically and ontically subordinated, that it is just as metaphysically subordinated as was Eve to Adam and as the seduction of Eve was subordinated to the fall of Adam.[6] But that is of the utmost significance for the knowledge of the essence of Christian theology. For while in the time *before* Christ, the attempt to do theology could only happen in a form in which thought would dissipate itself in myths of dialectical possibilities, while life slipped ever more deeply into undisciplined and anarchic disobedience, since the coming of the Lord all myths of dialectical possibilities have now been blown away like dust, and the indiscipline that was the correlative of myth has been transformed into the obedience of faith.

The difference between theology and myth is grounded in three presuppositions: that there is revelation; that there is faith; and that there is obedience. At the same time, this means that theology cannot exist in the form of dialectic. Dialectical reference to God leads to the nonbinding character of a mythical narrative but not to theology, for which obedience is required. Essential to myth is its *narrated* character—as, for example, Kierkegaard narrates the story of the sacrifice of Isaac.[7] But essential to theology is not narration but the asking of concrete questions to which concrete answers are given. It is the essence of myth that when its story is told, everything still remains open. In Homer's narratives about the gods, for example, *moira* [fate], which stands *above* the gods, may always intervene. For theology, on the other hand, it is essential that within its appropriate presuppositions nothing in principle is left open, and that, whereas myth a priori leaves everything open, that is, repudiates all claim to knowledge, in theology the possibility of a real, even though limited, knowledge is presupposed. There is an inherent connection between Kierkegaard's mythic dialectic and his theory of the paradox of the Christian revelation, just as theology only exists intelligibly if the real possibility of knowledge is presupposed.

That does not mean that theology has to take a position in the philosophical controversy between realistic and idealistic theorists of knowledge, in the sense of a human dogmatizing in favor of the realists, but rather that the realistic character of theological knowledge is consistent with the real character of revelation. Only on the assumption that God has become man, and thereby enabled us to participate in the *scientia divina*, only under this presupposition does it make sense for theology to speak of a real, even if only analogical, knowledge of God. But a verdict is thereby pronounced on all the attempts of nineteenth-century Protestant theology to tie dogmatics tightly to the idealism of classical German philosophy. All of these attempts failed, and today they must still fail, although an incomprehensible blindness seldom lets this be recognized. They must fail because, as the realization of all of these attempts has shown, they have entered upon a path that leads at best to a religious-philosophical "system of Christian teaching," but never to a theology, for which it is precisely essential that it does *not* culminate in the form of a system.[8] Idealism must be kept separate from theology not because it is in some abstract sense theoretically false, but rather because idealism cannot concede the fact that God has become man, without thereby surrendering its own principles. As a possibility, as a dialectical possibility, the idealism of Hegelian and Barthian speculation wants to permit the validity of God's becoming man. But to speak of the Incarnation as if of a dialectical possibility is in truth not to speak of it at all. And that is exactly what Barth does. When he then says that the impossible *itself* becomes the possible, *death* becomes life, *eternity* time, God becomes man—in all of these various assertions, again and again, he has said fundamentally the same thing: nothing at all.[9] Thesis and antithesis are joined to one another in a totally formal and totally empty synthesis, in which *everything* and yet nothing is said.

When we said previously that there is a threefold presupposition in theology—namely, that revelation exists, faith exists, and obedience exists—now we can complete that assertion with the further statement that theology also presumes that revelation, faith, and obedience in some way involve a participation in the divine Logos. But that means that theology exists only if revelation contains within itself a relative degree of intelligibility. If, on the other hand, revelation is a paradox, then there is also no theology. In which case, then, we further observe that if revelation is a paradox, there is also no revelation. For a revelation that cannot to a certain extent be known is not even a revelation. Faith too, if it is only a blind feeling, a vague trust, or an obscure experience, can never be an effective presupposition for theology. Faith must be seen as a type of knowledge, at least in a relative sense. To be sure, referring to faith as a type of knowledge does not entail an empirical and psychological analysis of the soul's capacities—as though reason, feeling, and will were all to be lined up and scrutinized in terms of their proportionate participation in the act of faith. Saying that faith is a type of knowledge means, rather, that believing involves knowing only because faith exists in the domain of the revelation of the Logos of God or, to put it differently, because the condescension of God is also a revealing. Obedience too is a functional presupposition in theology only to the extent that it stays under the sway of the divine Logos—that a concrete authority is thereby presupposed.

When Barth says that our knowing that we have to speak of God, and yet can't speak, is "giving the glory to God," he is completely wrong.

For all dialectical knowing, which is also always a not-knowing rooted in the nature of this dialectic (and not, to be sure, in the empirical sense, not knowing), all dialectical knowing—let me repeat it yet again—that is also always a not-knowing, is precisely in its not-knowing *not* to give God the glory. Or to put it differently: every kind of knowing, insofar as it is in the form of dialectical knowing, by its very nature *can't* give God the glory. Precisely because this kind of knowing is not concrete knowing of a concrete authority, it can't presuppose a concrete obedience. Kierkegaard's Abraham is not obedient in the sense of concrete obedience, but rather merely in the mode of obedience as such [*überhaupt*]. Or we could also say: Kierkegaard the dialectician to be sure is not obedient; what he is, is melancholic. His melancholy, which is not concrete melancholy—that would just be grouchiness, as Kierkegaard says—but melancholy as such, this melancholy of his *is* his obedience. And this perpetual swimming over a depth of 70,000 fathoms, the labor and suffering of such a spiritual existence, precisely this and *only* this *is* his obedience. And yet it is now very easy to see that, even if the existence of the dialectician presents itself as obedience, nevertheless it can't of its very nature be obedience, and for the simple reason that obedience is an act, not an existence. But precisely here lies the deceptive factor in all of Kierkegaard's talk about "the existential" and existential being in the truth—that here, namely before an allegedly spiritual existence, one does not arrive at obedience. And that is the reason why Kierkegaard contends so passionately with dogmatic truth, for precisely insofar as he wants existentially to *be* the truth, he actually withdraws his obedience *to* the truth, because obedience is presupposed in the meaning of what dogma is.

Knowing and yet also (dialectically speaking) not knowing that I am supposed to speak of God, and yet also (dialectically speaking) am unable to speak of God, is *not* to give God the glory. Instead, the only thing that has actually been expressed is the aporia that is the universal metaphysical condition. But the knowledge that human beings exist in a state of need, precisely insofar as it is knowledge of a universal human predicament, is not also *theological* knowledge. If not only theologians—a very specific class of human—but human beings in general also know something, it is not theological knowledge. It is *not* true that one becomes a theologian through knowledge of the kind that Baudelaire, Strindberg, and Dostoevsky already grasped far more intensely than the dilettantism of a theological journalism derived from such sources. Instead, despite being in this knowledge and with this knowledge and expressing this knowledge, one nevertheless remains essentially what those just named were, and also what Kierkegaard himself was, namely, *writers*.[10] But the writer, who unlike the theologian is not a member of a special order [*Stand*], is the sociological correlative to the religious dialectician. Just as in dialectical knowing there can't be any concrete knowledge, in the same way, someone who knows in the form of the dialectic can't belong to a concrete order. But the fact that he belongs to no order makes him dangerous; should it ever be suspected, even for a moment, that he has no order, then it will surely be supposed that he has a vocation—a calling from God. Then people will believe that here perhaps is "the one who is called"—until it is eventually discovered that the person in question is neither one who has been called nor a prophet, but merely a writer or a journalist. In the present situation it must be said emphatically that, just as theology is not mythology, so it also is not simply authorship. On the contrary: the theologian stands in total contrast to the writer. And if there is anything that can excite suspicion against a theologian—and on this score Luther himself may be implicated—it is the size of his authorial and his linguistic legacy.[11] I have no hesitation in holding that Luther essentially speaks as a theologian only in places where he offers arguments. There is no theology in which argumentation does not play an essential role. But today it seems as though for us, this simple assumption, which was once part of theology, is supposed to vanish altogether. In a recent [1925] article of [Rudolf] Bultmann's entitled "Welchen Sinn hat es, von Gott zu reden?" (What Does It Mean to Talk of God?),[12] it is taken for granted as self-evident, without further ado, just as in Barth's lecture, that the task of theology is to *talk* of God. But it is just as little theology's task to talk about God as it is to write about God. It is an interesting feature of the spiritual and intellectual situation in which we live that Barth and Bultmann treat talking "*about something*" quite naïvely as the sole religious and intellectual possibility of the human person.

The ecclesiastical and theological situation of the nineteenth century and of the present could perhaps be summarized like this, but it would seriously distort the truth of the matter. For we should never forget one thing: a real speaking *of* God exists meaningfully only with Christ. Only with him does the usage to speak "*of*" [*von*] God have that decisive ambiguity, in which it expresses not only that he says something "*about*" God,

but that when he says something "of" God, what is said of God is at the
same time said *by* God. But not even the prophets *speak* "of God," rather
the word of God comes to them and then they *pronounce* God's word.
Saying God's word in the sense of the prophets is far from the same thing
as talking *of* God. It is of the greatest importance that these distinctions be
kept in mind.[13] For only if the difference is forgotten, can something like
what is said in Bultmann's article become possible. Bultmann, who forgot
that only Christ can speak "of" God and who yet takes seriously Barth's
demand that we all must speak "of" God, manages to conclude that we are
able to speak "of" God if in our free action God's "must" defines our person, by which he means that for us there is a possibility of speaking "*from*"
[*aus*] God. The assumption that we could speak *from* God—and for Bultmann that is a real assumption, not a merely dialectical possibility—leads
to the further result that we necessarily confuse ourselves with Christ.
In various places in Bultmann this gets expressed with disturbing clarity.
Thus in this sentence: "If our existence is grounded in God, that is, *is not
present outside of God*[14]—who would not think here of the eternal being of
the Son with the Father?—then to grasp our own existence indeed means
grasping God." And the corollary of this is—as Bultmann consistently
says—that real talk of God must always at the same time also be talk about
us. And yet this statement is correctly said only of Christ, for only of him
is it true that that his talk of God is at the same time talk of himself. But
Bultmann's errors were already fundamentally anticipated by Kierkegaard:
Kierkegaard's assertion that subjectivity is the truth is only applicable in a
meaningful way to Christ. "Christ *is* the truth, Christ *is* the appropriation
(i.e., the way), and Christ *is* the life, but to apply this Johannine saying to
the individual means either that one is not a Christian, or pretends that
one is Christ. But both are an expression of despair and at the same time
an offense to faith."[15] I said previously that the prophets spoke God's word
and that Christ—who *is* the Word of God—spoke *of* God. To us the word
of God does not come as it came to the prophets, and we do not speak
of God because we are not, like Christ, the Word. Everything that we are
able to say stands under the presupposition that God's word was spoken
by the prophets and that the Word of God has spoken *of* God. But that
means: theology is not the saying of the Word of God—that would mean
to forget that the prophets appeared—and theology is also not a speaking
of God—for that would forget that Christ has been revealed. Theology is

therefore not grounded in the authority that the prophets had, by virtue of which they spoke God's word, nor is it grounded in the authority that Christ not only had but that he *was*, by virtue of which he spoke of God as the Word of God. Rather theology exists only under the presupposition of the authority of the prophets and of the authority of Christ—in other words, *the authority that is manifested in theology is a derivative authority*.

The Bible is not, of course, in this sense a derivative authority. As inspired scripture it is the primary authority. Therefore the Bible does not belong to the Church in the way that dogma belongs. The Bible says [*sagt*] God's word as inspired scripture.[16] And yet since it is the holy *Scripture*, it *says* nothing. That distinguishes it from the prophets. But from another point of view, the Bible is also not God's word. For God's word *is* only the Logos. If the Bible does not *say* God's word and also *is* not God's word, then it follows that the Bible only says God's word insofar as the Bible itself is "said." To the Bible as God's word thus belong the prophets, now the interpreters of the word, and necessarily so. The prophets of the word of Scripture—their existence is only intelligible since the prophetic office of the Old Covenant has ceased, in that God's Word has spoken and in Christ has become flesh—the prophets of the word of Scripture, I said, are fundamentally to be distinguished from the Old Testament prophets. The prophets of the Old Covenant prophesy the future, the prophets of the New Covenant prophesy out of the past. Therefore allegorical interpretation is also an essential feature of their exegesis.[17] For only through allegorical interpretation can an actual retrospective prophecy come into being. But it seems that this kind of New Testament prophetism scarcely exists in our time—instead of which we are blessed with the secularized form of the New Testament prophet, the historian! His existence is a constant proof that the idea of the New Testament prophet is no phantom, though it hardly ever appears within the Church. Is the New Testament prophet, the exegete in the sense just described, who brings to life the prophetic saying of the word of God, is he a theologian? Only in a manner of speaking. Only insofar as the saying of the prophets is a preparation for the speech of the Logos. Only insofar as exegesis is also a preparation for theology. But according to its proper primary function, spiritual exegesis belongs not to theology but to the cultus, where it is then actualized in the form of the sermon. As prophecy in the Old Covenant had only existed in the form of the charismatic, so Old Testament prophetism functions in the prophecy of the New Covenant only in a spiritual exegesis and a type of charismatic homiletic proclamation.[18] I just said "in a *type*" of charismatic proclamation. For although Old Testament prophecy was charismatic, exegesis and preaching as an extension of this prophetic activity are not themselves charismatic but only bear a resemblance to the charismatic. Is New Testament prophecy, as it appears in exegesis and preaching, then theology? No; rather it is, as I have already indicated, in a certain sense only a preparation for theology. What then is the ultimate reason why New Testament prophecy is not theology? Why is biblicism wrong when it wants to make the Bible the sole ground and norm for theology? Why does the authority of the dogmas exist in addition to the authority of the Bible, and dogmatics in addition to exegesis? Because exegesis and preaching are only the lineal continuation of Old Testament prophecy, but not the continuation of the fact that the incarnate Word of God has spoken. So too it becomes understandable why the Jews, who to be sure accepted the prophetic writings but not the Word of the incarnate Logos, know exegesis and preaching, but not theology. That is of decisive significance for an answer to the question "What is theology?" There *is no* theology among Jews and pagans. Theology *exists* only in Christianity and only under the presupposition that the incarnate Word of God has spoken. Though Jews may practice exegesis and pagans study mythology and metaphysics, theology in the genuine sense has only existed since the Incarnate One spoke about God.

If prophets and exegetes are not theologians, are apostles and martyrs then perhaps theologians? No, even apostles and martyrs are not theologians. For the apostles proclaim and the martyrs bear witness. To proclaim the gospel and to bear witness to it does not yet mean to practice theology. Or to put it the other way around: to practice theology is not to proclaim or to bear witness. But are the apostles then only preachers, aren't they also teachers, and insofar as they are teachers, aren't they also theologians? I do not believe so, for catechetical teaching is not yet theology, though catechetical questions may presuppose that theological inquiry has occurred. Thus theology is also not instruction. But if theology is neither writing about God nor talk about God; if it is not prophecy, nor exegesis, nor preaching, nor proclamation, nor witnessing, nor instruction, what then is it? Answer: theology is the continuing realization, in forms of concrete argumentation, of the fact that the Logos-revelation has imprinted itself in dogma. The genuine meaning of this argumentation is defined by the *quo jure* of the divine revelation. Theology is the concrete *actualization* of the fact that the Logos of God has spoken concretely of God, so that there is thus concrete revelation, concrete faith, and concrete obedience. Precisely because theology still lies in the *elongatur* of the revelation of the Logos, as proclamation is still located in the *elongatur* of the prophetic, for that very reason, it cannot be tied essentially to any of the various human intellectual acts, such as speaking, writing, preaching, and so on; only revelation itself can ultimately define the genuine *essence* of theology.[19] But this also means that theology exists only in the time between Christ's first and second comings, and that, just as certainly as Christ assumed a body for his coming, in order to engage the human world concretely, so now the revelation of God has also concretely pressed hard on humanity.[20] Dogma is the objective and concrete expression of the way in which God in the Incarnation has physically moved in on humanity. It is so exactly right an expression for this state of affairs that every turn against the dogma, such as, for instance, that which a heretic undertakes, fittingly has its consequence as a punishment imposed on the *body* of the heretic. The *teacher of error*, who unlike the heretic does not violate the dogma, but simply teaches falsehood, cannot appropriately like a criminal be punished in his body; one can banish him as a disturber of the peace of the land, but that is something quite different from the punishment of a heretic. And this at the same time expresses how "teaching" does not at all achieve the same measure of concrete specificity as dogma. Precisely because in the teacher of error's banishment from the land, it is not the whole body that is actually affected but only the tongue, which ought no longer speak, or the hand, which ought no longer write, precisely for that reason is it also clear that it is not doctrine but dogma that is genuinely the concrete continuation of Christ's assumption of a body. It is in dogma that Christ continues to press hard on humanity. The Gospel is not good news that is directed "at everyone"—otherwise, how could it distinguish itself from the Communist Manifesto?—but a positive legal claim of God, from the body of Christ, which concretely touches every one of us,[21] and that *jure divino*. It is a *positive* legal claim, grounded in the factual accomplishment of the death and resurrection of Christ and continued henceforth in dogma and sacrament. There is no meaningful theology that would not be an expression of the fact that the legal claim of God on every human being—which is a corollary of revelation—had been continued in the form of dogma and sacrament.[22] Dogma and sacrament are a continuation of the Incarnation and address of God's Logos, just as exegesis and preaching are a continuation of prophecy. And dogma and sacrament now stand in *the* place where the prophetic address continued in exegesis, namely, in the speech of the Incarnate Logos, while on the other hand to the continuation of exegesis in preaching, there corresponds further the continuation of dogma and sacrament in theology. Prophecy could not continue in dogma and sacrament, because prophecy, as the speaking of the word of God, cannot achieve the same measure of concrete closure and validity as does the revelation of Christ. Only when the Word of God had become flesh and had thereby sealed all previous prophetic saying of God's word, only when the Word of God had found its endpoint in speaking about the word of God *as* God's Word, only since then are there also dogma and sacrament, both of them intelligibly so. For as Christ is not only the Incarnate One but also the one who as the Incarnate has spoken about God, so the Incarnation of the Logos is continued, not only in the sacraments, but also in the speech of the Logos in dogma. Or to put it the other way: because in the prophets the Word did not become flesh, therefore the prophetic proclamation also did not have sacrament as its consequence. And because—as I have shown—the prophets to be sure spoke God's word but did not talk *about* God, therefore too dogma could not be an entailment of their speech. Dogma thus does not consist of an extension of the human act of faith (that is the business of the confession, but the confession has essentially nothing to do with dogma);[23] rather, dogma consists of the extension of Christ's speaking about God. And on that account the authority of dogma is not the authority of some human being, who confesses, or some human sociological formation, which confesses, but rather is the authority of Christ, which is here articulated. Nevertheless it is not the authority that Christ has and Christ *is*, but rather the derived authority of Christ. The sacrament indeed does not directly continue the Incarnation, but rather in such a way that it is *instituted*. And dogma indeed does not directly continue Christ's talk of God, but rather in such a way that there exists a teaching power transferred by Christ to the Church, in which dogma emerges. I just said: in the teaching power transferred by Christ to the Church, in which dogma emerges. That is not supposed to mean that all Church teaching is thereby already dogma, but only that which can be traced back to Christ's speaking. Dogma belongs to the speech of Christ in exactly the same way as exegesis belongs to the speech of the prophets. Because dogma *belongs* to the speech of Christ,[24] a further point is given:

dogma is *not* grounded primarily in the authority that Christ is and has, but in the way that authority is bestowed *by* Christ. That is something worthy of note: there is an authority of Christ which is, so to speak, "loaned out." Why is that so? When Christ walked on earth and preached, he had an authority that made people say of him that he spoke like one who had authority. When he had risen, he spoke to his disciples and said of himself: all power in heaven and on earth has been given to me. But after his ascension to heaven, neither others nor he himself spoke of his authority, because he had bestowed his power on the Church, which has represented him since his ascension.[25] Earlier I said that theology exists only for the time between Christ's first and second comings. Now I can be more precise. For just as dogma and the Church have existed only since the ascension, so too theology has existed only from that time forward. It is impossible to answer the question "What is theology?" if we forget that the Word of God has become flesh and has spoken about God. But it is also impossible to answer the question "What is theology?" if one furthermore forgets that Christ has returned to heaven and that dogma exists. The one is just as important as the other. It belongs to the fantasies of contemporary thought to construct a theology without dogma. That construction is a delusion. Not because human beings—as one often hears said in threadbare apologetics—necessarily "have to use dogmatic expressions," especially when they want to act. Christian dogma is not a concession to the human propensity to dogmatize. On the contrary: precisely because dogma is what we have just explained, it declares war against every human form of dogmatizing. A theology that is not *essentially* defined by dogma is all the more a fantasy because it does not give concrete expression to the revelation in Christ. Even though it is only concerned with details of this revelation, every theology that seriously presupposes that Christ has ascended to heaven must let itself be defined by dogma. Only through dogma is theology freed from its bondage to the most dubious of disciplines, the so-called human sciences [*Geisteswissenschaften*], from keeping company with world history, literary history, art history, *Lebensphilosophie*, and all that ilk. Only through dogma can it be lifted up to a sphere in which a *man* can live. Only through dogma does it become evident that obedience belongs to revelation. For in the obedience that dogma requires, obedience to Christ is realized. Though Christ has freed us from the law, he has not freed us from obedience. The moment that dogma fades away, in that same moment we succumb again to the law. I confess that if I had to choose whether I wanted to obey the law of human prejudices and the academic opinions of the professors, or the dogma of the Church, without much hesitation I would opt for the latter. Thank God, however, that we don't *need* to choose. We don't need to choose since there *is* dogma, even if the Church no longer knows anything of it and if human incomprehension assails the dogmas. We so often complain about the disinterest other circles have in theology. There is a simple remedy for that. Were we to have the courage to live again in the sphere in which dogma has its place, rest assured that interest in theology would be renewed, as once those in the marketplaces of Constantinople were interested in the strife over *homoiousios* (of a similar substance) and *homoousios* (of the same substance). People have no interest in our theological schools of thought and private convictions—and they do well not to!—but they are passionately interested in every genuine dogma, even if only to protest against it and to be enraged over it. That is because in dogma, every person is concretely affected. Therefore, because in dogma every person is concretely affected, theology too exists and presupposes dogma in a totally concrete, embodied way, such that theologians and theology exist in the form of an order,[26] and theological science in the form of a disciplinary specialization. And yet not in the form of just one discipline among others, but rather in the form of a discipline of all other disciplines. Theology is the *first* science. That is not said in a posture of human arrogance, but from the fact that dogma has subordinated all human knowing.

We are all familiar with medieval representations of the crucifixion. At the foot of the cross lie the bones of the dead Adam. That can be a symbol of the nature of theology. Adam *is* dead, and with him has passed away the age of all merely human questioning about God and all merely human talk about God. God *has* spoken in his Son. That is what dogma says, and by which alone theology lives.

Correspondence with Adolf von Harnack and an Epilogue

In 1928, a monograph by Adolf von Harnack entitled "Das Alte Testament in den Paulinischen Briefen und in den Paulinischen Gemeinden" (The Old Testament in the Pauline Letters and in the Pauline Communities) appeared in the proceedings of the Prussian Academy of Sciences. In conclusion, it asserted that "the merely relative validity of the Old Testament when juxtaposed with the New Testament" did not permit "unconditional worship of the letter [*Grammatolatrie*] in relation to the Bible as a whole. Biblicism receives its healthy corrective in the authority of *the apostolic teaching*, which organizes and delimits the authority of 'Scripture.'"[1]

In thanking Harnack for sending me this monograph, I added that I agreed with him, but that we were also in agreement that he had expressed, not the Protestant, but the Catholic principle in these observations on the relationship between Scripture and its interpretation.

I

Reichenhall, June 22, 1928

Esteemed colleague!

It is a truism that the so-called formal principle of traditional Protestantism is a critical impossibility, and compared to it, the Catholic version is, *formally* speaking, better; but in *material* terms, the Catholic principle of tradition is much more destructive of history (both as spontaneous growth and under the pruning shears of the magisterium), because by happy chance the N[ew] T[estament] actually comprises the best sources. The Barthian reversion to biblicism—even Calvin did not retreat this much—is scholarly and religious naïveté, which enjoys its current success only in times like ours, when chaplains big and small cast doubt on reason and scholarship.

With best wishes,
Yours, von Harnack

II

Bonn, June 24, 1928

Excellency!

Permit me to take up your recent remarks. If I understand you rightly, the fact of the matter is that, as a dogmatic theologian ("formally"), you approve of the Catholic position, but as a historian ("materially") you deny it. In this solution I see a double difficulty. (1) Judgment on historical issues is relative, as your own treatise shows. It can only reach conclusions on a case-by-case basis. (2) The twofold way of considering the matter (as historian and as dogmatic theologian) always commits us to an assumption of a twofold truth. Examples: [Hans] Lietzmann maintains that the Lord's Supper in Paul is a sacrificial meal, [and] thus in the final analysis a Mass.[2] The dogmatic theologian today teaches the opposite. Or [Karl] Holl asserts that the primitive community in Jerusalem had ecclesiastical law.[3] Evangelical canonists maintain that the assumption of an ecclesiastical law is unbiblical. In the most recent issue of the *Zeitschrift für die Neutestamentliche Wissenschaft*, [Wilhelm] Mundle demonstrates that apostolic succession is universally presumed in the Acts of the Apostles.[4] In the Evangelical Church, however, the concept of apostolic succession is denied from the pastor on up to the general superintendent.

In the long run this is an intolerable contradiction, which is not removed when one abandons the traditional Protestant scriptural basis without introducing a new dogmatic authority in its place. I too consider the Barthian return to a scriptural basis to be impossible. It must logically lead back to a doctrine of strict verbal inspiration. But without any dogmatic authority there can be no church and, what is worse, no church activity.

I am often approached by doctors, jurists, economists, and politicians about the standpoint of the Evangelical Church on questions relevant to their areas of expertise. I have always been forced to state that the Evangelical Church couldn't take a position on relevant questions, because a "standpoint" was impossible given the lack of a dogmatic basis. All that remained was the nonbinding character of a general moral exhortation (compare the Stockholm Message [the public declaration of the Universal Christian Conference on Life and Work, a formative event in the modern ecumenical movement, which met in Stockholm in 1925.—Ed.]).

I see clearly that the Evangelical Church submits itself to every influence, but in the process gives itself away. The Church ceases to be a "public" [*öffentliche*] entity when it repudiates a dogmatic foundation. I am certain that we cannot return to the position of the sixteenth century—not least because the dogmatic supplement of a "Christian magistracy" is absent, in which case it should be even more necessary to seek a dogmatic foundation.

With warm greetings,
Your very devoted
Erik Peterson

III

Reichenhall, June 28, 1928

Esteemed colleague!

"All that remains" to be sure is only "the nonbinding character of a moral exhortation." That is the nature of modern Protestantism, which in general is a legitimate development of traditional Protestantism. But the "to be sure" that I have inserted above is incorrect, or rather would only be correct if there were no possibility of a religious community apart from the assumptions either of Catholicism or of traditional Protestantism, that is, if the idea of an *absolute, formal* authority were essential to every religious community. I dispute that. Instead I am of the opinion that *actual* religious community in the Christianity of all periods came into being exclusively through the "nonbinding character of a moral exhortation," that is, through the experience and faith-witnessing of inspired persons evoking resonance and light in other persons. This witness exists in all churches in spite of its monstrous encumbrance with alien material and requirements; in my view it exists more powerfully in the Protestant churches, because it lies less heavily on us; but their tendency to shape themselves into imitations of the Catholic Church must be resisted at all costs. Protestantism must confess frankly that it does not want to be and cannot be a church in the manner of the Catholic Church, that it repudiates all formal authorities, and that it depends exclusively on the response provoked by the message of God, the father of Jesus Christ and our father.

The difficulty lies in catechetical instruction in schools; for dogmatic theology in the university is simply catechetical instruction (contemporary practical theology); but in my view it is not an unhappy development for every catechetical instructor in Protestantism to go his own way. The *concordia discors* (discordant concord) that has prevailed here for four centuries has nevertheless always remained a *concordia* in itself and over against Catholicism, because in the final analysis it relies on great common experiences.

In *scholarly* terms I know no other way to articulate the essence of Christianity than the method I have applied in my lectures on *The Essence of Christianity*, however imperfectly. Naturally there is nothing of the Absolute here; but there are statements and intimations that possess the power of the Absolute.

> With best wishes,
> v. Harnack

IV

Bonn, July 1, 1928

Excellency!

Pardon the persistence of my questions. My concern is to get straight from your mouth the understanding of what weighs so heavily on me. If Anabaptism is "the legitimate result of the Reformation," [and] if Pietism is "the legitimate result of Lutheranism," then I also want to acknowledge that modern Protestantism is the legitimate successor of traditional Protestantism. Luther spoke out against the first claim; Albrecht Ritschl against the second. Can you blame me if I have reservations about accepting the third assumption?

The "community" of which you speak is the "community" of the Community Movement [*Gemeinschaftsbewegung*].[5] I do not dispute that it is "religious community," but I hold that it is meaningful only under the assumption that there is a church. One cannot resolve the problem of the church with reference to the conventicle. Luther sought to create a church, not a large conventicle. What you require is a return to Congregationalism [*Independentismus*] as the true result of the Reformation. Historically considered, German Church history would thereby coalesce with Anglo-Saxon. It is clear that in Germany, too, a high church would emerge alongside Congregationalism. The beginnings of this development in both respects are already recognizable. I can only regard this development as a political misfortune for Germany, because it subjects our national autonomy vis-à-vis the Anglo-Saxon—already endangered by the outcome of the war and the Dawes Plan—to an even heavier burden. That this solution must also break down in the face of Russian ideas, I mention only in passing. Today we cannot solve our Church problem without being clear that we are hemmed in between America and Russia. That the temporary solution cannot last is certain to me, because the current solution still lives completely in the past. Spiritually and sociologically, the Evangelical Church corresponds approximately to the spiritual and sociological status of the German National People's Party [Deutschnationale Volkspartei, or DNVP, the leading right-wing party in the Weimar Republic—Ed.]. As this necessarily had to collapse, so too Evangelical ecclesiastical life must collapse in the future. When you describe theology as catechetical instruction, you merely express with this paradoxical formula the fact that, when we talk of theology, yes, even of catechetics, we are still basically living off the capital (Catholic and traditional Protestant) of the past. For theology—particularly in a university setting—always depends on the assumption that it is more than catechetical instruction, and catechetics in turn is meaningful only under the assumption that there is dogma, or at least pure doctrine (thus a formal authority).

Were your thesis to be taken seriously, the theological faculties would have to be abolished. That this has already happened to catechetical education is known to me from the Rhineland. It would thus only be consistent also to do away with theology in the university as catechetical instruction. You recently lamented, not without justification, the disdain for reason and scholarship in contemporary theology. But can we count on interest in the *history* of dogma, once dogma has been expunged, once the formal authority of dogma has been discarded in the Church? What kind of interest can one still have in the *history* of the Church, when there is no longer a Church?

The disdain for history in the theology of the contemporary Church is, in part, simply a consequence of the initial realization in Germany of the churchly ideal that you have recommended. I see the mentality of American denominations and American seminaries emerging in our student body. I feel deeply troubled by this development in theology and the Church. I see clearly how the Church becomes a sect, how the formation of the ecclesiastical (even of the liberal) sphere contrasts with the formation of the world outside the Church, how, in a word, standards in the Church are sinking. It is incumbent on me, as the younger party, to share with your excellency my deep concerns.

> With sincere respect
> Your very devoted
> Erik Peterson

V

Reichenhall, July 7, 1928

Respected colleague!

Behind the following aphoristic responses to your letter there lies a complete and strong sympathy for the concern that you have expressed for theology and Church. I have harbored these concerns for more than fifty years; though overcome theoretically for decades now, naturally they linger on in a practical sense, because no one can anticipate the future.

Perhaps I can best express the commonality of this concern in this manner: *Rebus sic stantibus,* there are only two alternatives in relation to the Church (in the old meaning of the word): either to lead Protestantism back to Catholicism (be it of the Greek or Roman variety), or to ground it in an absolute biblicism.

But both alternatives are closed off, closed off *because they stand in contradiction to our historical knowledge,* not to speak of other reasons, which consist in the religion itself and also in the original establishment of Protestantism, imperfect though it was.

With the old concept of the Church gone, so too is the old concept of dogma and therefore of dogma as such; for a dogma without infallibility means nothing. This was already settled by Luther's position at the Leipzig Disputation, although Luther himself never fully realized the implication of his assertions, nor was he ever clear about the unsatisfactory character of his inconsistent substitute through a partial biblicism. It was splendid for him to retreat into his living faith; but the objective deficit thus created remained unfilled, and there is nothing with which it can be filled! This is why already in the first edition of my *History of Dogma* [1885], I located the fall of dogma in the sixteenth century.

Anabaptism, Pietism, Enlightenment Lutheranism, Schleiermacherism, at one and the same time, they're all legitimate and illegitimate children of Protestantism. They're legitimate in the sense that they continue consistently the enlightened and subjective-religious line of Protestantism, and illegitimate in that they either drop or transform the ancient Catholic element of traditional Protestantism.

As you correctly say, there can only be community once there is no longer a Church; for there is theoretically no third choice between community and Church. Practically, however, mixed types will continue for a long time.

What position should one adopt (1) as an Evangelical theologian, and (2) as a member of the Evangelical Church community? On (1): By an Evangelical theologian I understand a scholar who not only studies the Christian religion like other religions, but also shares the conviction that mankind and *this* religion belong together, that the one is suited for the other, and *that by historical demonstration and ethical and philosophical consideration, the basic ideas of the Gospel can be placed in a bright and convincing light.* If I didn't believe this, I would never have become a theologian, nor would I be one today. But because I do believe it, and at the same time am convinced that this is a matter of the most extreme relevance to mankind, I am filled with joy and confidence, and do not concern myself at all with the forms in which the future will unfold itself. Whether theological faculties will continue to be independent, or to exist at all (though I should be sad were they to disappear), how the churches of the future will relate to them, etc., etc., are questions whose development I calmly disavow. The task of Evangelical theology is so certain and so necessary, that in one form or another it will always remain; and if in one of my previous letters

I described the prevailing dogmatic theology as "catechetical instruction," this requires the further comment that alongside it I obviously hope for a free Christian philosophy of religion (or as you call it, "Christian meta-history"), and I see in it the crowning achievement of theological work.

On (2): What will become of the Evangelical Church, I do not know; but, as you correctly state, I can only *welcome* the development that leads more and more to independence and a purely intentional community [*Gesinnungsgemeinschaft*] in the sense—I do not shrink from this—of Quakerism and Congregationalism. It makes no difference to me how we express and distinguish ourselves in relation to Catholicism, Americanism, Russian culture, etc. We shall indeed find a way and forms free of *ecclesiastical* absolutism (absolutism only has a place in a lively spirit), [although] of course in the meantime we are still severely dependent on the remains of Catholic tradition among us, as it were, on the aroma of an empty bottle, and I am also not of the opinion that we should intentionally hasten the process, which will proceed slowly but surely, of its own accord. My motto is: "I have always chosen the next step. A distant goal has thus animated me."

But without becoming a petty reactionary and yearning for the ancient fleshpots of Egypt. They are lost; one would have to turn around and go back to Egypt.

> With best wishes
> your v. Harnack

Epilogue

The preceding statements of Harnack are published here, because they transcend the individual occasion and address the objective problematic of Evangelical theology and the church. Harnack's statements need to be put in a wider context if they are to be evaluated properly. Considered in isolation, they can evoke among many a false impression. Harnack has not spoken for Protestantism as a whole. On the contrary, as he himself indicates (letter no. 5), he speaks only for the groups that consistently maintain "the enlightened and *subjective*-religious tendency of Protestantism." He has thus made himself the spokesman of a movement that, at present, is on the defensive within the Evangelical Church, although by no means defeated.

The tendencies of contemporary Protestantism are moving instead in the opposite direction; they want to consistently maintain the *objective*-religious tendency of Protestantism, but that is to say they are moving, consciously or unconsciously, in the direction of what Harnack calls "the ancient Catholic element of traditional Protestantism." This movement has taken control simultaneously of theology and the Church. Its reaction against the old cultural liberalism has perhaps been expressed more strongly in theology.[6] The Church has been more concerned with the practical necessity of dealing with the altered status of the Protestant Church within the state, brought about by political transformations. The movement's differing point of departure in theology and Church is the reason why the development in the Church and the development in theology have proceeded independently of each other, with the result that the theologian shakes his head at "the man of the Church," because he has no connection at all with theology, and "the man of the Church" at the theologian, who confronts the concrete tasks of the Church so uncomprehendingly.

This opposition has led to a falling out, during a controversial exchange, between Karl Barth, one of the main spokesmen of contemporary theology, and General Superintendent [Otto] Dibelius, the theoretician of the modern Church movement. Like most such struggles, the controversy was played out in pamphlets and journals, without resolution. The futility of this exchange is not to be attributed to the failure of the participants, but lies in the final analysis in the character of Protestantism itself, whose presuppositions make it possible for ecclesiastical life to exist without serious relation to dogma and theology, and which can, on the other hand, evolve a theology that ignores the concrete dogmatic problem of a "state church."[7]

Within Protestantism, nothing in principle has changed in the relationship between "theology" and "Church." As in the past generation it was possible to do a theology whose historical-philological procedures were mainly untouched by the present fact of a state Church, so today it is possible to do dialectical theology with no reference to that problematic entity known as the Protestant Church, whose distinctive life perpetually escapes the comprehension of Protestant theology. Barth and Dibelius share a common interest in the public character of theology and the Church. Just as, contrary to Harnack, Dibelius would take issue with converting the Prussian state church into a private, voluntary society in the sense of the Quakers, so Barth would doubtless consider Harnack's definition of dogmatic theology as "catechetical instruction" impermissible. Dibelius tends to demonstrate the public character of the Church by intensified activity, whereas Barth wants to establish the public character of Protestant theology by a return to dogma and dogmatic theology.

Both of these attempts seem to me to be doomed in advance. No amount of activity can demonstrate the public character of the Church if it lacks a public character. But the Prussian state church, as a religious corporation under public law (in the sense of the Weimar Constitution), is not in dogmatic terms a public body, since the Baptist and Methodist churches, and so forth, are also religious corporations in this sense. The Protestant state church has only two possibilities of becoming public. It can claim for itself either the civil or the specifically ecclesiastical (the cosmic-religious) meaning of public character. The first possibility would mean a return to a system of legal establishment. At present this path is prohibited by the constitutional separation of church and state. The second possibility would entail a return to the Catholic understanding of the Church and to Catholic ecclesiastical law, and for that reason this path is likewise closed off to the Protestant churchman.

Regarded from the point of view of this dilemma, Harnack's repudiation of the Church as such and his opting for a voluntary association as the true outcome of the Reformation is not as incomprehensible as it at first sight appears. Harnack realized that, after the abolition of the system of legal establishment, that is, of Christian sovereignty, the Protestant Church can, qua church, no longer dogmatically be a public entity. Something similar may also be said of Barth's attempt to establish the public character of Protestant theology.[8] If one goes the route of *civil* legality, the state would be obligated to watch out for the confessional status of the Prussian state church and the orthodoxy of its theological faculties. But even before the collapse of the established Church regime, Protestantism no longer knew "pure doctrine" in this sense, and it is incapable of knowing it now, because in Germany there are no longer confessional boundaries in the original sense.

Now if one seeks refuge in the concept of a specifically *ecclesiastical* public identity, then the imperative of a dogmatic formation in the Catholic sense, and of a dogmatic magisterium in the Church, is necessarily raised, which in turn is precluded by Protestant presuppositions. But if there is no dogma in the strict sense in the Protestant Church, then no theology is possible, either. For there is no theology without dogmatics and no dogmatics without dogma. Accordingly, I would like to acknowledge Harnack on this point, too, when he says that Protestant theology cannot be theology in the genuine sense. But that means that Protestant theology will always remain more or less the private concern of professors of theology; and thus nothing is actually affected by the greater or lesser degree of an individual's church affiliation.

The foregoing considerations show that the confusion of the Evangelical Church in Germany caused by the abolition of the system of legal establishment—which to be sure simply brought to a close a centuries-long development that has now reached an acute stage. On the Protestant side, one occasionally laments the purely political loss of power that the Evangelical Church has suffered as a result of the constitutional changes. But to my way of thinking, much more serious than this damage to the Church's power, which could even perhaps be recouped, is the dogmatic deficit, if I may so call it, for it touches on the heart of Protestant church life and Protestant theology. To be sure the traditional Protestant Church had no church law in the authentic sense, but at least it presumed the right of the territorial prince within the Church, which in principle distinguished the state church from a religious voluntary society. To the state it owed the fact that as a state church it could be described with the dogmatic predicate of church, while on the other hand, it was again the state that attached the dogmatic stigma of sectarianism to a voluntary religious association.

Admittedly, the traditional Protestant Church had no dogma, for it lacked that teaching authority that ought to be attributed to the determinative power over dogma *jure divino*. And yet the Protestant Church possessed a kind of quasi-dogma in its various confessional documents, which had a dignity analogous to that of dogma, to the degree that, and so long as, the state guarded the binding legitimacy of these confessions. With the end of legal establishment and the introduction of the new constitution of the Evangelical provincial churches in Germany, the public character of the Protestant Church and Protestant theology has *in principle* been extinguished.

I just wrote "in principle," because awareness of the extent of what has happened has yet scarcely entered the consciousness of the mass of the faithful. But it should not be forgotten that the character of the Church, which in earlier centuries the territorial regime impressed upon the state church, is not a *character indelebilis*. In connection with the territorial and political changes in Germany (think of the so-called *Reichsreform*), it can fade faster than we think,[9] and then the call for theological reflection, as Barth raises it, will perhaps no longer die away so vainly in the Protestant provincial churches. But in that case it will be necessary not only for Protestant theology but also the Protestant Church to revise its perception of the Catholic Church and of the relation of the Protestant Church to the Catholic Church in Germany.[10]

On this point traditional Protestantism seems to me to be essentially different from the Protestantism of the contemporary period, because it saw its relation to Catholicism differently than is today the case. Traditional Protestantism had an awareness of a fundamental, dialectical kinship with the mother church; even in the worst exaggerations of confessional polemics, it remained bonded to the old church. But it was not only polemics that bound it to the Catholic Church, not only the legal succession that created a historical connection between the Protestant state bishop and the bishops of the Catholic era, not only the law of the liturgical heritage that bound Protestant worship to the Roman mass; it was also the awareness of a common dogmatic basis with the old Church in all articles of faith that were not confessionally disputed.

A consciousness of a common faith affiliation in the fundamental dogmatic truths found its realization in the common structure of the one Christian Roman Empire of the German Nation [the Holy Roman Empire]. The *Formula of Concord* of 1580 still expressly repeats the Protestant confession of the Apostles, the Nicene, and the Athanasian Creeds, and vigorously rejects "all heresies and doctrines that have insidiously been introduced into the Church." And the Protestant attitude to Catholic *theology* corresponds to this attitude to the *dogma* of the old Church. Traditional Protestant orthodoxy was "scholastic" and was linked in the closest manner with the problems of Aristotelian and Jesuit scholastic theology, as modern research has shown repeatedly.[11] But it was also ascetical and mystical as defined in its piety, not only by medieval but also by Catholic mysticism of the Counter-Reformation and of the baroque era.[12]

It seems at first sight one of the most astonishing features of modern Protestantism that it stands in alienated, uncomprehending opposition, not only to Catholicism—which at least makes psychological sense—but to its own past in traditional Protestantism, and, let it be noted, not just in "liberal" circles, but today quite generally, even among those of the so-called positive theology. The only way to grasp this incomprehension is to realize that the ontological basis of Protestantism has changed. The civil and public character of the Protestant Church and theology, which was essentially definitive for traditional Protestantism, has vanished with the extinction of the Christian state, that is, of a confessionally defined territory. Along with it, the dialectical relationship to the Catholic Church and to Catholic theology with its authentically ecclesiastical public character has been dislodged. As I see it, a good part of the development of the Protestant Church makes sense in light of this slippage in the foundations.

A decisive development in modern Protestantism's conception of Church and theology appears to me to be the attempt to develop a public character of Church and theology, which is now threatened on the political side by other presuppositions. One way to replace the loss of pure doctrine, which traditional Protestantism owed to the civil authorities of the confessional territory, leads to reason. Universal truths of reason were supposed to take the place of dogma in the status of pure doctrine. This is the path toward the "free Christian philosophy of religion" in which Harnack in his last letter saw the "crowning achievement of theological work." The second way, which sought to save mystical experience, threatened by the loss of dogma, degenerated into mere feeling. This is the path toward spiritualism and secularized mysticism. "[A]bsolutism only has a role in a lively spirit," Harnack writes in the same letter. The third way to salvage the public character of the Protestant Church, even after the repudiation of the Christian state, leads to activism. The practical proof for the truth of the Church's proclamation was supposed to be found in the works of neighborly love.

These were the three alternatives of a Church and a theology in danger of losing their public character, and with it an essential component of the very concept of the Church.[13] All three of them are still today zealously championed, but it needs no great perceptiveness to realize that none of them necessarily are conducive to the goal of Evangelical Church life and theology, and that they may even stand in opposition to the Reformation's original impetus. That Luther never intended to replace dogmatic verities with universal truths of reason needs no proof. More important, the path that leads to spiritualism and secularized mysticism is blocked by the struggle of Luther and traditional Protestantism against religious ecstatics [*Schwärmer*].[14] But even works of fraternal service, of the domestic and foreign mission, of the Gustav-Adolf Association and other organizations, can't serve to guarantee the public character of Evangelical Church life; they are not derivable from the dogmatic presuppositions of traditional Protestantism, in which faith and works are fundamentally separate, and the practical means of a religious institution like a Church are completely inadequate for such projects.

That these three alternatives, which have not been undertaken spontaneously but under the pressure of changed presuppositions, contradict the original presuppositions of Evangelical faith and Evangelical Church life, is an insight that is beginning to spread only very slowly in contemporary Protestantism. It was so much easier to enter upon one of the three paths and seemingly to slip by the difficulties of a confrontation with the Catholic faith and the Catholic Church. It was so much simpler to project, say, universal truths of reason into history and then to explain, as a historian, on the strength of our historical awareness, that a reversion to Catholicism was impossible. It was so much simpler to take refuge in the religion of experience, or the rhetoric of existential seriousness of that individual who sees through all the deceptive fraud of the church. It was so much simpler to appeal to foreign and domestic missions and to see in them the proof that the Protestant Church is really a church.

And yet this resolution of the problem, which tends toward the elimination of "the old Catholic element,"[15] is only a sham resolution. The same Harnack who explains that a return to Catholicism is impossible because of our historical knowledge, has done more than anyone to open such a return.[16] This has not been a merely personal and private concern of Harnack's; rather, it is a substantial preoccupation that runs through the work of *all* Protestant historians. Just suppose (as I attempted to do in my 1929 essay "The Church," specifically written for Harnack) that the modern construction of the history of primitive Christianity by Protestant historians is correct. Then try to deduce the theological conclusions from the same, without changing anything essential in the historical construction. You will be astonished how close you come to the Catholic conception.

Or try the path of Pietism, without which the edifice of modern Protestant Church life is unthinkable. Wasn't Albrecht Ritschl right to cite the systematic-typological connection between Pietism and Catholicism in his history of Pietism?[17] The concept of "indwelling grace" seems to me to be essential to Pietism. But that is a specifically Catholic concept, except that the Pietist seeks in the psychological sphere what the Catholic finds in the sacramental sphere.

Or try the third path of works. Don't we immediately encounter the problem of Catholicism here, too, for example, by comparing Evangelical deaconesses, in their dress, to Catholic sisters?[18] Of course there is no mistaking the difference here, insofar as the phenomenon of Evangelical deaconesses (admittedly unknown to traditional Protestantism) is much more problematic than that of Catholic sisters, and necessarily so, because the relation between faith and works is more uncertain in the dogmatic theology of Protestantism than in Catholicism.

Let us now try to draw some conclusions from the preceding considerations. It seems to us that since the dissolution of the confessional territorial regime and the repudiation of the Christian state there has no longer been a Protestant *Church* with which the Catholic Church could engage in discussion in Germany. Naturally it is possible that the political authorities in Germany could again adopt the idea of a confessional territory and also of a Christian state as the instrument of the political struggle. In that case, something that looks like a discussion between a Protestant and a Catholic *Church* would arise.[19] But we should not deceive ourselves that the original meaning of Protestant Church life and Protestant theology is ever to be resurrected intact. The result will simply be a *Kulturkampf*, in which the opportunity for an actual debate between a Protestant and a Catholic *Church* will be missed.

Finally, is the only possibility for the Catholic Church to engage in a dialogue with the three paths through which Protestantism is trying to regain its character as church? I think that here too a real argument is impossible. Quite apart from the fact that none of these alternatives represents the whole,[20] each of them in its presuppositions maintains such a dialectical relationship with Catholic truth that apologetics or polemic from the Catholic side has an inevitably confusing effect. It seems to me that only prayer and patience are possible in a situation in which every attempt at direct confessional exchange in the present circumstances of Protestant Church life must necessarily founder.

3

The Church

Prefatory Note

It has become quite common for contemporary historians of theology to develop ideas that are consistent with scriptural texts, but of which they then take no further notice as theologians. This appears to me to be an untenable compromise. One cannot maintain along with [Karl] Holl, in his celebrated Academy lecture "Der Kirchenbegriff des Paulus in seinem Verhältnis zu dem der Urgemeinde" (On Paul's Church Doctrine in Relation to the Early Christian Community), that the primitive community in Jerusalem was "catholic," that it had church law, and so on, and then not draw theological consequences (I would like to acknowledge explicitly that I am deeply indebted to Holl's arguments). One cannot argue along with [Wilhelm] Mundle that the apostolic succession is everywhere presumed in The Acts of the Apostles and then polemicize against the idea of the apostolic succession. One cannot say along with [Hans] Lietzmann that the [Last] Supper was a sacrificial meal, [and] thus in the final analysis a Mass, and then as a dogmatic theologian take no notice of that. Finally, one cannot—as happens everywhere—consider the New Testament as the depository of the ecclesiastical tradition and then turn around and play the New Testament off against the ecclesiastical tradition. I urge that acknowledgement of the present state of affairs in New Testament studies not remain separated by so great a gap from dogmatic assertions. Otherwise, the danger exists that, with the increasing gap between itself and the New Testament, the Protestant Church in Germany will become a sect.

Looking at this development from a different angle, we see that the danger it poses is today much more at hand than is widely recognized. One can perhaps acquiesce in the separation of Church and state and thereby renounce a public character that the democratic state cannot possibly grant the Church. But if so, one cannot at the same time also renounce the Church's right still to make dogmatic decisions. The Church ceases to be a "public" entity when it renounces the capacity to make a dogmatic definition. But with this renunciation of "public character" in the concept of the Church, the Church also loses the potential for a "public field of activity." The political and national consequences of such a development for Germany should not be underestimated.[1]

.   .   .

According to [Alfred] Loisy's famous dictum, "Jésus annonçait le Royaume, et c'est l'Église qui est venu" ("Jesus proclaimed the kingdom, and it is the church which came"). A central theological problem lies concealed behind Loisy's skeptical assertion. Consider this possibility: had the Jews become believers in the first period after Christ's death, would there then have been a Church? I do not believe so. Then the Son of Man would have returned and the messianic kingdom would have broken in, in which the Jews would have assumed the most important place; but the gentiles, the nations of the world, would have lived in the shadow of this messianic kingdom. The messianic Kingdom that Jesus proclaimed did not come. Why didn't it come? Because the Jews as a people did not believe in the Son of Man.

From this fact follows the meaning of our first thesis: *There is [a] "Church" only under the assumption that the Jews, as the people chosen by God, did not come to believe in the Lord. It belongs to the concept of the "Church" that it is essentially the Church of the Gentiles.* Once we have tried to become clear about this fact, several important conclusions immediately follow.

1. Since it is conceived of as the Church of the Gentiles, the Church is under no theoretical necessity to preserve Hebrew or Aramaic. With the rejection of Hebrew, however, the rejection of Semitic forms of thought in general is also theologically justified.[2] The contrast between Greek and Jewish thought that has become common in contemporary theology,[3] and the emerging preference for the Jewish or Semitic mind-set, is a theological error, for gentile Christians cannot and ought not to become Jews. Just as they ought not to have themselves circumcised, no more ought they to

adopt the Jewish linguistic mind-set. God willed the Hellenizing of Christianity and of the Church just as much as He did the calling of the Greeks.[4]

2. Because the original recipients of the proclamation of Jesus and the apostles hardened in unbelief, all conceptions of the Gospel in its projection upon another field must necessarily also experience a break. In the order of salvation, Gentiles and Jews are essentially different, for God truly spoke to Moses on Sinai and the election of Israel is irrevocable (Rom. 11:29). But with the refusal to make Gentiles into Jews, the Gospel must necessarily adopt the Gentile mode of being and existence. I do not mean this in the sense of a practical missionary adaptation, but, much more seriously, that the Gentile's different mode of being and existence, over against that of the Jew, must also be really recognized and taken seriously. Now the proclamation of Jesus was eschatological, indeed concretely eschatological, being eschatologically related to the Jews in particular.[5] The Church, however, in its existence is precisely a demonstration against the concrete-eschatological, the Jewish-eschatological. The Church is the Church of the Gentiles. And so we come to our second thesis: *There is a "Church" only under the assumption that the coming of Christ is not immediately at hand*, in other words, that a concrete eschatology is excluded and in its place the "doctrine of the Last Things" has appeared.

I want to explain something further about this important point.[6] The Apostle Paul says explicitly in Romans 11:25 that once the ordained number of Gentiles has entered in, then all Israel will also be saved. After that the end will come. The second coming of Christ is therefore linked intimately with the conversion of the Jewish people. One can conclude directly that the Jews are delaying the return of Christ by their unbelief. But insofar as they delay the return of Christ, they prevent the coming of the Kingdom and necessarily promote the continued existence of the Church. What Paul presents in Romans 11 is no longer concrete eschatology, but rather a "doctrine of the Last Things," as it can necessarily be only in the Church of the Gentiles. The replacement of concrete eschatology by the "doctrine of the Last Things" in the Church is no deviation from the preaching of Jesus, but rather the transposition of concrete eschatology into the new situation, namely, that now Gentiles and not Jews believe; that at present there is only the Church and not the Kingdom of God.

I would like to clarify what I have just said with an example. Jesus is known to have said, "Whoever lowers himself will be exalted." This saying was originally meant in a concrete eschatological sense. By means of deeds that far transcend those of the Scribes and the Pharisees, it is possible to gain an eminent place in the Kingdom of God. But now in the Church, this pronouncement must immediately lose its concrete eschatological meaning. In its place the moral meaning appears. From the eschatological project of "humbling oneself" in order to become exalted in "the Kingdom" comes the moral demand for humility and for ascetical self-renunciation. The moralizing of concrete eschatological concepts is only the necessary consequence of the fact that the coming of Christ is no longer immediately at hand, and that the Jews are no longer called to the Kingdom, but the Gentiles to the Church.

It cannot be said emphatically enough that this does not constitute a falsification of the original proclamation of Jesus, but only a necessary consequence of the preaching of the Gospel no longer to the Jews but to the Gentiles. Only Jewish Christians could protest that this was a falsification of Jesus' message. We, however, who are not Jewish but Gentile Christians, have not the slightest right to such a reproach. It is known that Jewish Christians hesitated for a long time over the new situation. Exactly when they finally repudiated the privilege of Israel and "the Kingdom" is not clear. At first, indeed, the Twelve remained in Jerusalem. The choice of Matthias in place of Judas shows that for a certain period of time the number twelve was seen as necessary, in fact as a truly constitutive factor. According to a saying of Jesus, the Twelve are supposed to "judge" the twelve tribes of Israel (Matt. 19:28). Since from ancient times the concept of "judging" and of "ruling" were virtually synonymous, the Twelve are therefore supposed to rule along with Jesus over the twelve tribes of Israel. From the fact that Matthias was chosen in Jerusalem as the twelfth apostle, it therefore appears that they were still thinking in terms of the Kingdom of God rather than the Church. It was in Jerusalem, more exactly in the temple in Jerusalem, that the coming of the messianic Kingdom and the return of the Son of Man was expected. Therefore the Twelve too do not leave "the Holy City," for the earthly Jerusalem is supposed to become "the Eternal City" of the messianic Kingdom.

So long as this belief was preserved by the Twelve, the Church did not actually exist. The question of when the decision in favor of the Church was passed admits of different answers. We may say that no decision was passed so long as the Twelve were linked to Jerusalem. At the

Apostolic Council, the Twelve, or at least the "pillars,"[7] seem still to abide in Jerusalem. In addition, the whole controversy over the circumcision of the Gentiles only has meaning if people at that time still reckoned seriously with a conversion of the Jewish *people*, but regarded the conversion of the Gentiles as merely an episode. When Paul writes 1 Corinthians, he knows that the Apostles, indeed even Jesus' brothers and Cephas, "wander."[8] By that time the ties of the Twelve with Jerusalem had thus apparently ceased. Then when Paul visits Jerusalem for the last time, only James is still there.[9] So if we wanted to evaluate The Acts of the Apostles in its reports merely as a *historical* source, we would have to assume that the decision took place between the Apostolic Council and the composition of the First Letter to the Corinthians.[10] Now it is highly characteristic—and this works against our assumption that Acts is a work of history in our profane sense—that the most important event in the development of primitive Christianity, the break of the Twelve with Jewish Christian eschatology, is not reported by Acts in the context of a historical development, but in a completely different and surprising way, in the form of the Pentecost narrative. The prophetic character of this narrative, placed at the beginning of Acts, is unmistakable. If we wanted to believe that the pouring out of the Holy Spirit had immediate "historical" results, the remainder of Acts would contradict us. The tongues miracle is intended to mean that the Apostles are destined for all the peoples of the earth. And yet the Twelve still stay in Jerusalem, even after the tongues miracle. According to Acts 1:4, they are supposed to wait in Jerusalem only until the outpouring of the Holy Spirit. In actuality, according to the account in Acts, they stay there for a much longer time.

It is my view that every interpretation of the Pentecost narrative that ignores its prophetic and proleptic character gets trapped in considerable difficulties.[11] But that is hardly the most important thing. What is truly significant is the meaning of the Pentecost narrative itself. Through a special mediation of the Spirit, the language of every nation is imparted to the Twelve. In the *languages* of the nations, the path to the nations themselves is being indicated—and thereby the path to that which we call the "Church." There is good sense in the Church's tracing of its origin back to the Pentecost narrative. The gift of tongues represents the repudiation of Hebrew as the holy language;[12] it marks the departure from the elect people and at the same time indicates, in the creation-act of language, the beginning of a new creation, that of the Church. What Loisy said is true: "Jésus annonçait le royaume" ("Jesus proclaimed the Kingdom").

I am thus led to my third thesis, which holds: *There is a "Church" only under the assumption that the twelve Apostles have been called in the Holy Spirit and have arrived at the decision, on the basis of the Holy Spirit, to go the Gentiles.*

Let us briefly note the consequences of this third thesis.

First, it follows that Jesus himself neither directly founded the Church nor himself instituted the offices in the Church.[13] Jesus preached the Kingdom to the Jews, but he did not preach the Church to the Gentiles. It has never been asserted in the Church, not even in the Catholic Church, that Jesus appointed bishops, ordained priests, and so forth. Rather, the hierarchy of the Church traces itself back to the work of the Holy Spirit in the twelve *Apostles*, and not to Jesus himself.[14] With my third thesis I have for the first time used the expression "Twelve Apostles." For there was not yet a Church so long as people in Jerusalem hoped for the conversion of Israel and waited for the return of the Son of Man. There was at that time only "the Twelve," *hoi dōdeka*, who were residing in Jerusalem. The expression "the Twelve Apostles" shows, on the contrary, the new thing, the turn to the Gentiles.[15] "The Twelve" belong to the messianic Kingdom, but "the Twelve Apostles" belong to the Church. "The Twelve" exist on the basis of a calling by the Son of Man, while he sojourned on this earth in the flesh, but the "Twelve Apostles" only exist in the glorified body of the "Lord," by virtue of a calling of the Holy Spirit. "The Twelve" have received their power immediately from Jesus, on the basis of a juridical delegation, but "the Twelve Apostles" by virtue of their reception of the Holy Spirit. The problem of the Church is resolved in this decisive fact: "the Twelve" are identical with "the Twelve Apostles." In and of itself, that did not need to be so. One could imagine a construction such as the following: "the Twelve Apostles" might have stayed among the Jews, since they had originally been destined for the Jews. They would then naturally have disappeared with the Jewish Christians. But the Church would have been built on the Apostles who had not belonged to the circle of the Twelve, thus in the first instance on the apostles Paul and Barnabas. The latter conclusion is a perception that prevails widely in Protestant circles, though without acknowledgement. And yet it is false. The Church is built on "the Twelve" and not on the apostle Paul. According to Matthew 16:18, Peter, thus the leader of the Twelve, is the rock on which the *ekklēsia* is built.[16] According to Revelation 21:14, the names of the apostles are preserved in the foundation walls of the heavenly Jerusalem. Paul does not belong to "the Twelve," a fact that marks the limit of his apostolic legitimacy, though not of his apostolic activity. And that is the reason why the apostle Paul's standing in the Church is so different from, say, Peter's.

In the canon of the New Testament letters, Paul may occupy the central place. This literary significance of his, however, is but the flip side of the fact that the Church is not actually built on him but is constructed on Peter and the Twelve. Directly connected with this is the fact that to my knowledge, there is no episcopal succession that traces itself back to Paul; because Paul lacks legitimacy, he is incapable of giving legitimacy.[17] That "the Twelve" are identical with "the Twelve Apostles" is the effect of the Holy Spirit on them. If the Twelve had not trusted in the activity of the Holy Spirit, they would have remained among the Jews and not accepted the Gentiles. Then there would have been no Church but only a Gentile Christian sect, for whom, as perhaps for Marcion, Paul and Jesus had been blended into an unrecognizable unity.[18] But because the Twelve *did* believe in the Holy Spirit, they established the link between the "Kingdom" and the Church, between "the Law" and the Holy Spirit.[19] If it was justified for the twelve judges of the tribes of Israel to become, by the power of the Holy Spirit, the twelve apostles of the Gentile Church, then it was also justified for them to bring the Gentiles the Old Testament as the holy Book, without imposing the literal fulfillment of the Mosaic Law on them.[20] Then it was also theologically permissible for them to transmit the Jewish-Christian Palestinian tradition of the earthly life of Jesus along with the collection of the Lord's words to the Gentile Church, without acquiescing in a merely pneumatic Christ. The characteristic transposition of all primitive Christian concepts, of which I spoke earlier, is only the reflection of this fundamental fact that "the Twelve" dared—at the direction of the Holy Spirit—to leave Jerusalem and to go to the Gentiles.

In this specific situation of "the Twelve," from which the Church has emerged *genetically*, is grounded at the same time the fact that there is a faith relationship to the Church: the Church—though visible—is even today still an object of faith. It is not the invisible Church that is an object of faith but the visible Church, she who is compelled, like the Twelve Apostles, still today—on the basis of the Holy Spirit—to render decisions and to demand faith where these decisions are concerned. Since the days of the Apostolic Council, the formula *edoxe tōi pneumati tōi hagiōi kai hēmin* (It has seemed good to the Holy Spirit and to us)[21] has been the sign by which the Church has been recognized. For the true Church exists only where both of these things are found: the legitimacy, in legal succession to "the Twelve," that is derived directly from the Lord; and a faith that, as with "the Twelve Apostles," is compelled on the basis of the Holy Spirit to make independent decisions. Neither of these two characteristics may be lacking, neither the legal legitimacy nor the spiritual freedom. Only the linking of these two features makes the Church explicitly into the apostolic Church, and thereby into the Church as such.

I am therefore of the opinion that a Church without apostolic Church law, and without the capacity to make dogmatic decisions, cannot as such be regarded as the Church. We cannot evade the situation of "the Twelve." We can neither revert to Jewish Christianity nor can we transcend "the Twelve," in the fashion of Marcionite Paulinism. We are bound to precisely the same spot in which "the Twelve" also had to make their decision. To be sure, the Church has never again been faced by God with such a grave decision as it was when "the Twelve" had to decide whether or not they were willing to leave Jerusalem and go to the Gentiles.[22] Let me say it one more time: the Church, regarded historically as well as theologically, is grounded in this decision of "the Twelve." For that reason, the Church's task can only be to maintain and to repeat the decision of "the Twelve" in all future situations of the Church. The decision of "the Twelve" is not maintained if legitimacy, Church offices, and Church law are repudiated. Nor is the decision of "the Twelve" upheld by those who claim that there are no dogmatic decisions in the Church, and that Holy Scripture alone has determined the articles of the faith. Rather, in the Church's capacity to make dogmatic decisions is reflected precisely the freedom that stems from the Holy Spirit.

The formula of the Apostolic Decree, *edoxe tōi pneumati tōi hagiōi kai hēmin,* is patterned after the resolution formula of the ancient polis: *edoxe tēi boulēi kai tōi dēmōi* (It seemed good to the Council and to the People). As a claim to sovereignty stands behind the ancient resolution formula, so also behind the Apostolic Decree. The eschatological power of the apostles, seated on twelve thrones, necessarily has to change into a new form of *exousia* (power) in the transposition into the Church of the Gentiles. But the claim to sovereignty does not thereby cease.

The modification in the claim to sovereignty of "the Twelve" becomes evident in the way that the alienation from Judaism and the Jews' conception of the Kingdom necessarily entails a movement toward the polis concept of the ancient world. This change is also the context for understanding the distinctive linguistic usage that promoted the word *ekklēsia* to a technical term for the concept "church."[23] The secular *ekklēsia* of antiquity is familiar to us as an institution of the polis. It is the assembly of the fully enfranchised citizens of a polis, gathered together to perform legal acts. In an analogous fashion, one could call the Christian *ekklēsia* the assembly of fully enfranchised citizens of the heavenly city,[24] gathered together to perform particular cultic transactions.[25] The worship it celebrates is a public worship and not a celebration of the mysteries;[26] it is an obligatory public work, a *leitourgia*, and not an initiation dependent on a voluntary judgment. The public-legal character of Christian worship reflects the fact that the Church stands much closer to political entities like kingdom and polis, rather than voluntary associations and unions. In addition, the leaders of the worship assemblies were authorized by the apostles through the laying on of hands. The bishops or presbyters who were ordained by the apostles had to receive something of the apostles' fullness of power. For the apostles who consecrated them were the same men to whom Jesus had once promised that they would sit on thrones, judging the twelve tribes of Israel. When so much power had been bestowed by Jesus, there was necessarily much power to be inherited.

This one example is adequate proof that Loisy's statement on the relationship between Kingdom and Church, though at first apparently dazzling, nevertheless oversimplifies the problem. True, the Church is not the Kingdom. But something of the Kingdom clings to the Church, both of the political desire of the Jews for the Kingdom of God, as well as of the claim to sovereignty of "the Twelve" in the Kingdom of God.

It is true that, along with all of that, a certain ambiguity attaches to the Church. She is not in a univocal sense a religious-political entity such as was the messianic Kingdom of the Jews. But she is also not a purely spiritual entity, in which such concepts as politics and sovereignty may not, as such, appear, as though she were restricted to "service."

The ambiguity that attaches to the Church must be explained in terms of the blend of Kingdom and Church. The occasion for this ambiguity, which has always provoked a moralist like Nietzsche against all Christian concepts, is the unbelief of the Jews. So long as they remain obdurate,[27] the return of the Lord and the coming of the Kingdom will also be delayed. But in ourselves we overcome the ambiguity that attaches to the Church only insofar as we commit ourselves to the development that led "the Twelve" from Jerusalem to the Gentiles, and with "the Twelve," under the working of the Holy Spirit, believe in the *one* apostolic Church, to which God has called the Gentiles, so that, when their number is full, all Israel too will be blessed, and after that will come the End.

4

The Church from Jews and Gentiles

*To the Roman Church, in which the blessed apostles Peter
and Paul confirmed the calling of all, both from the Jews and
from the Gentiles, by the shedding of their blood.*

Prefatory Note

*The following exposition is the almost unchanged printing of three lec-
tures delivered during the Salzburg Hochschulwochen of 1932. Out of respect
for the audience, the exposition was presented in as accessible a manner as possible. I chose the path of biblical exegesis in order to present the patristic legacy,
which has largely fallen into neglect, from the perspective of Revelation. The
notes that have now been added for publication are meant to illustrate the exposition. It was not my intention at all to give a historical account of the rich
patristic tradition.*[1]

. . .

"What limitless power, what sweet goodness, what fervent love of
divine virtue exceeding every work, which angels marvel at and choirs
of all the saints exalt with uplifted voices and constant praise, is it that
the Lord the Virgin, that the King the poor, that the Eternal the mortal through assumption of the flesh, that King Jesus Christ is married to
the Church under the title of a spouse!" With these words a fifth-century
Christian, Aponius, in the introduction to his commentary on the Song
of Songs, offers his praise of the holy Church.[2] How are we to understand

the pathos of these sentences? Is it a merely subjective mood that is straining after the sublime images of the Song of Songs for its sentiments? Or is the Church itself something that evokes such a pathos? Does the Church in its essence contain a mystery that, when it is disclosed, provokes the observer to astonishment, wonder, and praise of God? We do in fact believe that the Church possesses such a mystery in its innermost being. We can approach this mystery of the church from very different directions. Think perhaps of what [Matthias] Scheeben in his *Die Mysterien des Christentums* (The Mysteries of Christianity),[3] or the Dominican [Humbert] Clérissac in his little book *Le mystère de l'église* (The Mystery of the Church),[4] has to say about it. Let us approach the mystery of the Church by the path Saint Paul took: through the theme, as described in my lectures, of the "Church from Jews and Gentiles." Let us try, once again, to think the thoughts of Saint Paul in the context of the Letter to the Romans, chapters 9 to 11, so that we too can at the end join in with the words of the apostolic laudation, "Oh the depth of the riches and wisdom and knowledge of God! How unsearchable are his judgments and how inscrutable his ways! 'For who has known the mind of the Lord, or who has been his counselor?' 'Or who has given a gift to him that he might be repaid?' For from him and through him and to him are all things. To him be glory for ever. Amen."[5]

Chapters 9–11 in Romans constitute a large conceptual unity. Its subject is the relation of Israel to the Gentiles, who are now becoming believers, the relationship of the synagogue [i.e., the Jewish communion] to the [Christian] *ekklēsia*.[6] How could the people whom God had truly chosen no longer be the chosen people? That was the problem. In the development of the ideas, 9:26–29 expounds God's plan, and in 9:30–10:21, Israel's guilt is made clear. Then in 11:1–32, Israel's conversion at the end of time is presented, and 11:33–36 concludes by praising God's wisdom.

Letter to the Romans: Chapter 9

[1] I am speaking the truth in Christ, I am not lying; my conscience bears me witness in the Holy Spirit, [2] that I have great sorrow and unceasing anguish in my heart. My sorrow is great and there is unceasing anguish in my heart.

Paul begins his exposition with a solemn oath and a passionate reference to his anguish. He, who as apostle to the Gentiles stands compromised a thousand times over, testifies with an oath, with his guarantee that he is not lying, with his conscience illuminated by the Holy Spirit, as to the truth of his sorrow, yes, of his anguish. In the sorrow and the anguish is expressed his awareness of a decision that has in fact already been made, but whose reality is once again experienced, through the sorrow and the anguish, as an ideal possibility.

[3] For I could wish that I myself were accursed and cut off from Christ for the sake of my brethren, my kinsmen by race.

The pathos reaches its greatest intensity, the sorrow and the anguish seek their final expression. Paul would have it that the anathema be imposed on him, for the sake of his brothers, his kinsmen after the flesh, who are Israelites. He outdoes himself in finding terms for them. The richness of his vocabulary shows how completely tender is his link with them. Yes, I am your brother, you are flesh of my flesh, you are Israel and therefore have the name that God gave Jacob, the name to which the blessing is attached. We perceive how the apostle knows himself bound to his people in his total moral, physical, and religious being. For Paul the relationship of the synagogue to the *ekklēsia* is thus posited as an existential problem. Only in this way can we understand how he can wish to be cursed for the sake of his "brothers." His readiness for this sacrifice stems from the depth and totality of his bond with the Jewish people, with the Israel of God.

[4] They are Israelites, and to them belong the sonship, the glory, the covenants, the giving of the law, the worship, and the promises; [5] to them belong the patriarchs, and of their race, according to the flesh [sarx] *is the Christ, who is God over all, blessed forever. Amen.*

The fullness of Israel's wealth, as contained in Scripture, is here laid out, is spread once again, as it were, under the eyes of the Jews, before it passes into the possession of the Gentile Church. "Thus says the Lord: Israel is my firstborn Son" (Exod. 4:22); but now the title of "Son" is passing from the synagogue to the Church. The glory of God dwelt in Israel, the visible sign of the divine sovereignty in the Temple in Jerusalem, and when the prophet Isaiah had seen this glory in the Temple, he thought he would have to die.[7] But now the glory of God is taken from them, in order to dwell in the *ekklēsia* of the Gentiles and to be witnessed to in the Thrice-Holy call of its liturgy. The covenants that God had struck with Abraham, Isaac, Jacob, and Moses are shown as functioning only for the Gentiles. The Jews no longer inherit anything from him who alone is rich. The Law given to Israel is fulfilled in agape, in the "love" of those whose "justice" exceeds that of the Pharisees and the Scribes.[8] The cult in the Temple of Jerusalem is cancelled by the spiritual worship of those who know a sacrifice that is more than animal sacrifice.[9] The promises given to the fathers, which applied the fullness of God's blessing to earthly life, are received by the Church, to which is promised not only the present but also the future life.[10] Abraham, Isaac, and Jacob no longer belong to the Jews but to the Church. Abraham becomes the father of all the faithful;[11] Isaac illustrates that not the firstborn but the second gets God's promise: Jacob comes to exemplify divine election by grace. And finally, Christ, the Messiah: he descends, so far as his flesh is concerned, from Israel. It is true "that salvation comes from the Jews" (John 4:22). It comes from the Jews because Israel is God's chosen people.[12] The Messiah comes neither from Athens nor from Rome. For that reason, Christ was sent to the Jews, and for that reason too, he did not preach to the Gentiles. "Salvation comes from the Jews," but this statement now receives a deep and frighteningly ironic sense at the moment when the Messiah of the Jews is believed by the Gentiles but rejected by his people. *Who is over all—God, blessed be he forever.* We grasp this singular benediction only in the context of Paul's singular situation. "Who is over all"; for he is believed in by the Church, to which all are called. Who is "God" and not merely Messiah by virtue of his fleshly origin in the Jewish people—"blessed be he forever." It is shocking how Paul once again uses the Jewish benediction formula after having pronounced utterances—"Who is over all" and "God"—that were intolerable to the unbelieving Jew. For according to Jewish opinion, the Messiah is only a Messiah of Israel and not of the Gentiles, not of the world. And he is a human being, a Jew, and not God or of a divine nature. No, "he is over all," he is "God—blessed be he forever."[13] So speaks St. Paul, the Jew who took the step from the synagogue to the Church. The doxology in this verse testifies by its distinctive verbal stamp that Paul's opening statement of his sorrow and anguish was no mere expression, that no clever political calculation lay behind it but rather a problem: synagogue and Church were a genuine, a personal problem, which he takes hold of in a current linguistic formulation, and which he likewise takes hold of—let us also not forget this—in his existence as an apostle of Jesus Christ. For his apostleship does not just mean his being sent to the Gentiles; on the contrary, it always means being sent from the *Jews* to the Gentiles.[14]

There now follows a pericope consisting of verses 6–13 and deal-ing with the question of whether the election of Israel includes the whole people.

[6] But it is not as though the word of God had failed. For not all who are descended from Israel belong to Israel.

God has spoken. According to his words, Israel would be the chosen peo-ple. But was not God, like so many speakers, perhaps mistaken? From "Israel, his firstborn son," today have come the "children of Israel," whom people mock. From the glory of God, this image of the divine sovereign-ty in a free people, has come the hatred of all glory of a divine sovereignty in an oppressed people. Instead of having their inheritance from God's covenants, they inherit from all the covenants of this world a wealth that nevertheless yields no blessing, because this earthly abundance lacks the mystical promise of the heavenly inheritance.[15] From the Law has come the Talmud; the sacrificial cult has ceased. The blood of the animals no longer flows, since the blood of Jesus has been shed on the earth. The pa-triarchs: Abraham, Isaac, and Jacob, what are they but half-mythical per-sonages from the history of the Near East, of interest to scarcely anyone, whose problematic "morality" occasionally still stirs the anger or mockery of the Gentiles? Finally, the Messiah after the flesh, what is he any longer but one of the various toy constructs of political ideology and utopianism? Not without interest for the sociologists as a type for a particular political conception of utopia, but precisely as an ideological concept, its impover-ished character is transparent.

God never chose Israel, or, if he is supposed to have chosen it, this election has passed away with the origin of the Church. Historical life knows only the coming into being and passing away of the world's vari-ous religions. But we are Christians and have no need to trouble ourselves about the election of Israel.[16] The apostle, however, is of a different opin-ion: *Not as though the word of God had failed.* The apostle takes the elec-tion of Israel seriously, and with him, the Church as well. For the Church, to which we belong, is the *apostolic* Church, the Church of those apostles who went from the Jews to the Gentiles. But when they went to the Gen-tiles, they took with them the Holy Scripture of the Old Testament, and therefore we have not only the New but also the Old Testament in the canon of our sacred scriptures. When they went to the Gentiles, they told them about Jesus as the Christ, as the Messiah of the Jews, and therefore the Church of the Gentiles too now confesses not only Jesus and not only God, but rather Jesus Christ, who as Messiah after the flesh came from Israel, and yet now is "God" over all, "blessed forever. Amen." When the apostles went to the Gentiles, they also took along the election of Israel, and that is what the closing words of verse 6 indicate: "For not all who are descended from Israel belong to Israel," which is expounded further in the following verses.

[7] And not all are children of Abraham because they are his descendants; but "Through Isaac shall your descendants be named." [8] This means that it is not the children of the flesh who are the children of God, but the children of the promise are reckoned as descendants. [9] For this is what the promise said, "About this time I will return and Sarah shall have a son."

It is not fleshly descent, Paul wants to say, that makes for a true descendant of Abraham. But the Jews, in their insistence on legitimacy, demand a proof from Sacred Scripture. Paul produces one from Genesis 21. When Sarah has borne Abraham a son, Isaac, she demands of Abraham that he drive away his son Ismael, born of Hagar, along with his mother. Abraham resists. God then appears to him and says, "Do everything that Sarah has said to you, for in Isaac shall seed be named for you." Though the consequence is not explicitly stated, it is nevertheless clear. Physical descent from Abraham does not yet mean being the seed of Abraham in the sense of the divine promise;[17] rather, Abraham's children are those to whom the name of "child" is granted. Verse eight first repeats the idea of the preceding verse, but then expands it by the concept of "child of God" and by introducing the concept of the promise. Why is Isaac, the one born later, preferred to Ismael? The answer is, because he is the son of the promise (Gen. 18:10,14). Genuine sonship only exists only where a promise is posited. According to the natural order, there are no children of Abraham, no children of God. But by virtue of the promise, descent from Abraham and being a child of God are removed from the natural sphere and raised to something supernatural, something spiritual.[18] How marvelous was Isaac's birth! It happened on the basis of a promise. All of the natural conditions that marked the birth of Ismael were lacking. Abraham was a very old man, and Sarah was barren. And yet now Isaac is born. What can that testify but that a miracle, a spiritual event, has occurred? In Galatians 4:21–31,

Paul demonstrates that Isaac is the prototype of the Christians. They are children of the promise, not the sons of the slave woman but of the free one. One understands everything once one realizes that Paul's concern is to emphasize the difference between the spiritual and the natural order. Ismael belongs to the natural order, Isaac to the spiritual. Thus Isaac can be a type of the person who has become a believer in Christ, but Ismael a type of the Jews, who boast of their fleshly descent from Abraham. Like Isaac, we are children of the promise, but they are the fleshly children, who along with Ismael and Hagar are sent into the wilderness. Is it saying too much to contend that this has been fulfilled as the destiny of the Jewish people? Have not the Jews been sent into the wilderness? Do they not fill the whole world with the restlessness of their sojourn in the wilderness?

But let us also hear the warning that is put to us, we who live not in the wilderness but in the City of God, namely, that only the children of the promise are also truly children of God. There is a danger that people will hold the children of Christian parents already to be children of God by virtue of their physical descent. The holy Sacrament of Baptism raises a protest against such an idea. Holy Baptism says to us that we become children of the promise only through the Holy Spirit, only through the Pneuma. The apostle goes from the Jews to the Gentiles. He takes along with him the consciousness of belonging to the people of Israel. But this people to whom he belongs no longer comes forth from the one womb of Sarah, but from the one womb of the baptismal font. All the concepts of marriage, of begetting, and of offspring, which play so great a role in Judaism and there appear marked by a divine promise—all of these concepts, I say, pass over to the Church and now acquire their authentic, new, transparent, and spiritual meaning. Thus from Jewish marriage we get the mystery of the marriage of Christ with the Church[19] that is celebrated in Baptism; from Jewish begetting the spiritual begetting in the baptismal water, as it is perhaps expressed most starkly in the ritual consecration of the baptismal water;[20] and the concept of descent from Abraham is thus changed into the concept of being a child of God. What we meet here in the dogma, language, and ritual of the holy Church does not arise from some arbitrary projection, but rather has been prefigured for the Church by Israel. That we find the *Trishagion* [the "Thrice Holy" hymn of praise known to Catholics as the Sanctus—Ed.] in the holy Mass and that the symbol of the generating and bearing power of the baptismal water appears in the ritual for the blessing of the baptismal water should be understood neither as elegant liturgical inventions nor as the products of some so-called historical development, but rather only becomes theologically intelligible on the basis of the *mysterium* of the Church from Jews and Gentiles. Because God's word did *not* fail, because Israel has truly been chosen, therefore even today is seed raised up for Abraham in holy Baptism.[21] Hence too there is sonship in the Church, hence God's glory in the Church, hence the covenants of God, the Law, the cultus, the patriarchs, and also the Messiah after the flesh.[22]

[10] And not only so, but also when Rebecca had conceived children by one man, our forefather Isaac, [11] though they were not yet born and had done nothing either good or bad, in order that God's purpose of election might continue, not because of works but because of his call, [12] she was told, "The elder will serve the younger." [13] As it is written, "Jacob I loved, but Esau I hated."

To advance his argument, Paul again goes back to the history of the holy patriarchs.[23] Against the previous example, one could object that the presence of two different mothers, Hagar and Sarah, naturally made possible a different treatment of the offspring. But against Jacob and Esau, this objection is not possible. Both came from one and the same mother, [they] were even twins, and yet it is now shown that God accepts the one and rejects the other. One cannot object that the one was accepted because he had done good and the other was rejected because he had done wrong; no, the decision on God's part had already been settled when they were both still in their mother's womb and so did not yet have the chance to do good or evil.

Let us first of all be clear about a fundamental point for understanding this verse, which is not about the problem of the election of individual persons: rather, it concerns the election of a people—of the "true" Israel—for not all who are from Israel, as was said earlier, are also "Israel." Why is the *ekklēsia* preferred to the synagogue? Why must Esau serve Jacob, the elder the younger?[24] The answer is: because God only acts on the basis of election. But what then does the concept of "election" mean? Nothing more than what had previously been affirmed about the concept of the promise, namely, that God acts on the basis, not of the natural order, but of the supernatural. *Children of God are not born but reborn.* They are born on the basis of "promise" or "election." The "People of God," the "true Israel," the *ekklēsia*, is thus not, like the synagogue, an entity that constitutes itself from the natural order. The fathers of the Church had already identified this distinction between *synagoga* and *ecclesia* in their vocabulary: the *synagoga* is for them a *congregation*, the community a *grex* (flock), thus in the final analysis a naturalistic entity. In the *ecclesia*, however, they perceived the *ekkalein*, the *evocatio*, the calling forth from the world with its natural orders and natural sociological creations.[25]

Saint Paul means the same thing when he says that God has chosen his people on the basis of election. But hadn't the Jews too spoken of his election of Israel? Is there then any difference between the Jews' concept of election and that of Saint Paul? When Israel confessed that God had chosen his people from all the peoples of the world, the natural condition of the world was apparently unaffected, so to speak, by this election. The expression for that was that the people, once chosen, could now believe only on the basis of its natural continuation that it was forever to be the chosen people. The only danger that could threaten its conviction was seen in the threat to its natural continuation. On this one point everything depended. One understands what weight the "fleshly" sphere now had to acquire in the eyes of Jews.[26] Celibacy has no promise, and sterility is a source of shame.[27] I call this entire sphere among the Jews the sphere of "fleshliness." We ought not to confuse this concept with that of sensuality. The Jew is fleshly. The pagan is sensual. Those are two quite different states of affairs. For the Jews this sphere of "fleshliness" is unavoidable, because their concept of Israel's election ultimately remains bound to the natural sphere. Here is the point where they can have something fundamentally in common with pagans—where for a time even an alliance between pagans and the Jews, against the Church, can come into being.

To the fleshly Israel now stands in contrast the spiritual Israel in the *ekklēsia*. The fleshly Israel can only understand and interpret the sonship, the glory, the covenants, the legislation, the cultus, and the promises, in a fleshly way, in accordance with its fleshly being. But the *ekklēsia* will understand and interpret everything spiritually, in accordance with its spiritual being. The whole spiritual exegesis of the Old Testament by the holy Church, its allegorical and typological interpretation as we find it already in the apostle Paul, can only be seen as a makeshift solution to a dilemma, if the Church itself is a makeshift solution to a dilemma over against Judaism. But if the Church and not the synagogue is the true Israel, then too is the interpretation of Sacred Scripture by the *ekklēsia* the true interpretation over against the exegesis of the synagogue. That is doubtless most decisively shown in the interpretation of the "Law," for the Jew will ultimately understand the fulfillment of all the commands of the Law in a fleshly way. That God loves Jacob and hates Esau is something that he will ultimately only be able to grasp in terms of the deeds of both, of the "works" accomplished in fulfillment of the commands of the Torah. But that this interpretation of the patriarchal narratives is false is obvious; for God already loved Jacob and already hated Esau, when both were still in their mother's womb. It is almost an inevitable misunderstanding of the Jew, who is bound to his fleshly existence. In contrast, Paul senses that that, if fleshly descent from Abraham already defines being a child of God, then God is drawn into the generational sequence. And if we then consider the works accomplished in fulfillment of the commands of the Torah, God himself is no longer able to escape this doubled moral and physical pressure. Then God himself loses all freedom, and all talk of election on his part must cease. From this standpoint, the distinction of a spiritual from a fleshly Israel seems even to be a necessity, if the concept of God is to remain pure. If God is bound to the generational sequence of the children of Abraham or to the fulfilling of the Law of the fleshly Israel, it is then possible for the Jewish magician to exercise his power. The great role played by Jews in the magical practice of antiquity and the Middle Ages is scarcely to be understood as a mere accident, but is grounded ultimately in the false understanding "of the God of Abraham, Isaac, and Jacob" by the "fleshly" Jews.

[14] What shall we say then? Is there injustice on God's part? By no means!

This objection, too, which Paul has framed for himself, again only applies to the question of the calling of the two peoples. Is God perhaps unjust, if he now validates his election? If he loves Jacob in the Church and hates Esau in the synagogue? The answer is no, and the proof is adduced in the following verse:

[15] For he says to Moses, "I will have mercy on whom I have mercy, and I will have compassion on whom I have compassion." [16] So it depends not upon man's will or exertion, but upon God's mercy.

God's election is rooted in his mercy and compassion. God is merciful because he is free. So too is the *ekklēsia*, the Jerusalem above, "the free one." She is the mother of us all.[28] In her we too are called to freedom. But when one sets up works before God, when it is a matter of the will and of winning, when one contends as if one were in a stadium, then God abandons his freedom and his mercy. God is not unjust in hating Esau and loving Jacob. His justice is made known precisely in his love and in his mercy. God would be unjust if he let himself be bound, whether through the fleshly descent of the children of Abraham or through their fulfilling of the commandments of the Torah. God is therefore not unjust if he appears to prefer another people besides the one he had elected; actually, he remains ever the same. His election of a people always grows out of his love. He does not let the Jews prescribe conditions for his election. For that reason God is also not bound to the *ekklēsia*. No one becomes a Christian in it by natural descent, but only by being reborn in the Spirit in Baptism. Nor does the new people, unlike the synagogue, know a Law that it is able to fulfill by willing and engaging in a race. Only where the *natural order* of the people is determinative, as it is in Judaism, is there any conception of the possibility and necessity of a fulfillment of the Law. But the natural order of the people and the natural possibilities that go along with that do not define the *ekklēsia*, but rather the spiritual order and the supernatural possibilities that arise from the Pneuma. Therefore in the Church there, too, there is no Law in the character of a natural order, but only the spiritual law, "the Law of the Spirit that has made us free" in Christ Jesus.[29] As people who have been made free, we have a share in the freedom of God, and when his freedom expresses itself in mercy, so we, too, urged on by the love of Christ, can express our freedom only in love. In other words: in the new, spiritual order of the people of God, love is the fulfillment of the Law, as in the old natural order of the people it was the formal activity of the "willing and racing."

Thus we see that God is free in the *ekklēsia*. For in the *ekklēsia*, the law of physical belonging to the people of God does not prevail, but rather the spiritual rebirth that first makes us members of the spiritual Israel. Nor does there prevail in the *ekklēsia* the *nomos* [Law] of the natural order of the people, through whose fulfillment God is as it were compelled to declare who is righteous. Instead, it is the spiritual law of love that prevails in the *ekklēsia*. And because we have become children of God in Baptism and in love fulfill the Law, God remains free in the *ekklēsia* and acts toward it on the basis of "promise," "election," and "mercy." God is, on the other hand, bound in the synagogue; and not only God—the synagogue itself is bound. As the "heavenly Jerusalem" is "the free one," "the mother of us all," so the synagogue is the "unfree one," who leads all of her children into bondage. For that reason as well [on the basis of 2 Cor. 3:15: "whenever Moses is read a veil lies over their minds"], the figure of the synagogue is shown blindfolded in medieval art.[30] The Jews lead a life of bondage and constraint in both an external and an internal sense.[31] Israel too is therefore forever led into servitude;[32] for "the elder shall serve the younger," the fleshly Israel the spiritual one, until Israel too becomes free along with the whole Creation, until God too will redeem "the prisoners of Zion."

[17] For the scripture says to Pharaoh, "I have raised you up for the very purpose of showing my power in you, so that my name may be proclaimed in all the earth." [18] So then he has mercy upon whomever he wills, and he hardens the heart of whomever he wills.

In contrast to the mercy shown toward Moses, the rejection of Pharaoh is now named, because only in the two acts of mercy and rejection taken together does God's full freedom find its ultimate expression.

[19] You will say to me then, "Why does he still find fault? For who can resist his will?" [20] But who are you, a man, to answer back to God? Will what is molded say to its molder, "Why have you made me thus?" [21] Has the potter no right over the clay, to make out of the same lump one vessel for beauty and another for menial use?

Who is it that objects in verse 19? It is the Jew, who is no longer disputing with Paul there, but with God, as verse 20 shows. That the Jew slips unwittingly from disputing with a human being to disputing with God is, for Paul, provocative. In this move the fundamental position of the fleshly Jew, who appropriates God into the human, indeed the Jewish sphere, is documented. Also substantively documented is a specifically Jewish objection, insofar as the Jew, as the man of the Law, understands God's freedom only as itself a law, as determinism, instead of seeing in it the source of divine mercy.

[22] What if God, desiring to show his wrath and to make known his power, has endured with much patience the vessels of wrath made for destruction, [23] in order to make known the riches of his glory for the vessels of mercy, which he has prepared beforehand for glory.

The period that begins with verse 22 is an anacoluthon. The answer to the rhetorical question runs: naturally, God can do what he wants. But notice the progress of the ideas! Verse 22 speaks of the "patience" of God, and verse 23 of the "preparation beforehand for glory." This clearly shows that we find ourselves in an eschatological train of thought. That means too that the concept of election, previously the subject, belongs to the eschatological sphere.[33] The separation of the two peoples, the calling of the spiritual Israel into the Church and the rejection of the fleshly Israel in the synagogue, is not something that takes place in worldly time but in God's time, in the eschatological age.[34] The Jews' physical concept of election, which changes nothing in the natural sphere, is realized in natural time, in secular time. The Church's spiritual concept of election, however, which is defined by the sphere of the spiritual-supernatural, affects the concept of natural time, of secular time, of historical time, and replaces it by the concept of eschatological time. The concept of God's patience, discussed in verse 22, only gets its authentic meaning in the eschatological age. God puts up with the vessel of his wrath—the fleshly Israel—just as the Master in Jesus' parable permits the tree that he really wants to cut down to remain standing.[35] The "this year also" [of Luke 13:8] is eschatological time, God's time, the time of God's patience with the Jews. That the Jews have not yet perished, that today the synagogue still exists, that is a sign of the eschatological patience of God, who is still always waiting "this year" for the conversion of the fleshly Israel. No power of this world will be able to eliminate Judaism. Not even the Jews can eliminate themselves, so long as God's patience is still putting up with the vessels of his wrath "this year." On the other hand, verse 23, which speaks of the richness of glory that shall be made known to the vessels of mercy, shows that the Church too still awaits a final apotheosis through divine glory. We are all indeed waiting for the *ecclesia triumphans.* Thus, through the distinction between the synagogue and the *ekklēsia*, no definitive decision is yet given. Rather synagogue and *ekklēsia* belong together until the Last Day,[36] and that is also why they are depicted next to one another in our medieval churches. God is always waiting for the conversion of the synagogue: but the *ekklēsia*, although predestined for glory, yet lacks its final apotheosis through the richness of God's glory. In this way, then, a problem is indicated that Paul will treat extensively in chapter 11.

[24] even us whom he has called, not from the Jews only but also from the Gentiles?

The verse shows clearly that for Paul the whole preceding exposition on the question of the calling, the election, the hardening, and the mercy, involves problems that have nothing to do with individuals. What concerns him exclusively is the question about the Church from Jews and Gentiles, about the relation of the *ekklēsia* with the synagogue. To the predestination of the Church to glory corresponds the fact that that Jews and Gentiles are invited to the *ekklēsia*. With the calling of the Gentiles to the people of God, the *Jewish* distinction between Jews and Gentiles is thus transcended. Also transcended is the Jewish concept of election, which knows that God has chosen *one* people in contrast to the other peoples of the world. The transcendence of the "fleshly" concept of election is demonstrated by the fact that now Jews *and* Gentiles are called to the *ekklēsia*. The calling of the Gentiles to the people of God is not simply a quantitative expansion, which would be imaginable were one to become "liberal" and admit the Gentiles as well to the people of God. No! The calling of the Gentiles presumes the transcending of the Jewish concept of election. But this transcending of the concept of election can only take place in the eschatological age.[37] In worldly time, Israel alone is and remains the chosen people, and none of the peoples of the Gentiles can be accepted into the people of God or even make the attempt to once more play the chosen people. But the age of the Church is the eschatological age, which begins with the calling of the Gentiles to the people of God. That is a point that is not always clearly recognized. Precisely because Paul believes firmly that the word of God has not failed, the election of Israel has also not become void. But election must now be understood in a spiritual and not a carnal sense, eschatologically and not secularly. But then it will become clear that Jews *and* Gentiles belong to the chosen Israel, as it is now constituted in the *ekklēsia*. For just as not all belong to Israel who stem from Israel, so can— this is now the necessary consequence—they belong to Israel who are not born Israelites. Because not fleshly birth but rather the second birth incorporates one into the spiritual Israel, therefore Gentiles too are able to be called to the *ekklēsia*. Indeed, it is more than a mere "potential" that is being expressed here. It is just like the parable in the Gospel of the great Supper, to which guests are invited, all of whom then decline, until the Master hauls the guests from the highways and the byways.[38] That little word "and" between Jews and Gentiles, who are called to the *ekklēsia*, sounds so irenic, and yet concealed behind this apparently innocent copula lies the whole tragedy and pathos of the unbelieving synagogue. Even the scriptural verses with which Saint Paul confirms the calling of the Gentiles, breathe something of the divine bitterness.

[25] As indeed he says in Hosea, "Those who were not my people I will call 'my people,' and her who was not beloved I will call 'my beloved.'" [26] "And in the very place where it was said to them, 'You are not my people,' they will be called 'sons of the living God.'" [27] And Isaiah cries out concerning Israel: "Though the number of the sons of Israel be as the sand of the sea, only a remnant of them will be saved; [28] for the Lord will execute his sentence upon the earth with rigor and dispatch." [29] And as Isaiah predicted, "If the Lord of hosts had not left us children, we would have fared like Sodom and been made like Gomorrah."

A concluding argument follows, which speaks of the guilt of Israel.

[30] What shall we say, then? That Gentiles who did not pursue righteousness have attained it, that is, righteousness through faith; [31] but that Israel who pursued the righteousness which is based on law did not succeed in fulfilling that law. [32] Why? Because they did not pursue it through faith, but as if it were based on works. They have stumbled over the stumbling stone, [33] as it is written, "Behold, I am laying in Zion a stone that will make men stumble, a rock that will make them fall; and he who believes in him will not be put to shame."

God has laid a stumbling-block in Zion. It lies in Jerusalem, in the center of the Holy City. Of this stone had Isaiah prophesied that it would become a rock of offense for Israel. And that has now come to pass. For the rock is Christ. On his account have the Jews taken offense and been scandalized. Jesus is not bound to Israel merely in the sense of an external descent. No, he is the center of Israel, the rock in Zion, on which the Temple cult and the worship mandated by the Law are built. On this foundation stone the Jews have stumbled. On that account they have come to their ruin. They have come to their ruin by means of their own foundations. They thought that they would achieve their righteousness on the basis of works. And yet Isaiah already says: Whoever *believes* in this rock of offense will not be put to shame. The Jews did not pay attention to that. They thought only of what was built on the foundation: the Temple and the Law. But they forgot the foundation: faith.

Earlier we observed that the Jewish concept of election did not affect the natural condition of the world. Paul says the same thing. Only he expresses himself much more perceptively, when he says that the Jews had not thought of the stone in Zion, the foundation became their doom. It is the blindfold over the eyes of the synagogue that keeps it from seeing the foundation, the supernatural, and from recognizing the eschatological age. The Jew sticks to the Law and his works, as though both did not have their presuppositions! In a certain sense the Gentiles have it easier than the Jews. They do not have the Mosaic Law, and therefore they also don't strive for a righteousness based on the Law. They, who are without the Law, can more easily discover the presuppositions of the Law—faith, and the rock in Zion. So what did Israel actually get from all its chasing after the righteousness of the Law? It did not at all succeed in fulfilling what the Law required. But the Gentiles did achieve righteousness, a righteousness that comes from the foundation, from faith. And yet it is precisely the calling of the *true* Israel that requires faith. Where a spiritual Israel is called, that does not boast of its fleshly descent from Abraham, the foundation of the true Zion cannot be the natural fulfillment of the Law, but only supernatural faith. It is the *ekklēsia*, founded on the sacred rock of Christ, that knows that it does not bear its foundation in itself, not in fleshly descent from Abraham, and not in the natural fulfillment of some type of legal prescriptions, which knows that it is not a piece of the natural order of historical time, though it itself be an elect part of this natural order—which knows rather that it is called through God's mercy and promised through the mouth of the prophets for that last age, in which everything presses forward to God's decision in wrath and love, in hardening and mercy. But this decision has still not come down. God's patience is still putting up with "the vessels of his wrath." The sorrowing synagogue still stands next to the *ekklēsia*. The holy Church still prays on Good Friday for the conversion of the *perfidi Judaei* ("perfidious Jews").

Chapter 10

[1] Brethren, my heart's desire and prayer to God for them is that they may be saved.

The Church's prayer for the conversion of the Jews is thus an apostolic prayer. Saint Paul prepared the way for this prayer of the Church.

[2] I bear them witness that they have a zeal for God, but it is not enlightened.

The zeal for God is one of the most typical features of Jewish piety. Even the unbelieving Jew is always a zealot. Perhaps today as a socialist he is zealous for justice, perhaps as a pacifist zealous for a peace that comes not from God but from men. But the zeal of the fleshly Israel for God is without insight, at that time and today as well.

[3] For, being ignorant of the righteousness that comes from God, and seeking to establish their own, they did not submit to God's righteousness.

The Jews are zealous for the righteousness of God. The correctness of this assertion is confirmed especially clearly by the zeal for righteousness of the unbelieving Jews. But this zeal for the righteousness of God now lacks the inner detachment from oneself. The Jew who is zealous for God will by an inherent necessity always seek his own righteousness. He thinks he is zealous for God, but in the end he is only zealous for himself, he has become "*over*zealous." Here too he has failed to leave the natural sphere and natural time. Thus the Jew's zeal for righteousness will always be realized in the natural sphere and in secular time. This is why Jews are heavily involved in politics, in socialism, in pacifism, and in public intellectual life. Here too he remains the fleshly Jew, lacking deeper insight. He takes offense at the stone laid in Zion and stumbles over it. For God's righteousness, he is zealous.

But that God's righteousness is the prerequisite of all zeal for justice, this he does not realize. He overlooks the foundation, and thus fails due to the presuppositions of his own concepts. He does not recognize that in his zeal for God's righteousness, he has not for one moment left the natural sphere, and that he has in this way bound the righteousness of God to his own natural zeal for this righteousness. He has not really answered to the assumption of his faith, to the concept of the righteousness of *God*, he has not put himself *under* the righteousness of God, he was not subjected to the righteousness of God.

[4] For Christ is the end of the law, that every one who has faith may be justified.

It is no accident that in this verse, the name of Our Lord Jesus Christ is named, but grows out of the progression of the ideas. The fleshly Jew, who is zealous for the righteousness of God, has not left the natural sphere. That the concept of God's righteousness belongs to the supernatural sphere is something he has not recognized. But now in Christ the end of the Law has appeared, so far as the Law is understood as an entity of the natural order. And in Christ, so too has all natural zeal for righteousness found its end. He is the righteousness of God for everyone who believes.

In what follows, Paul uses scriptural citations to contrast the Jewish and the Christian concepts of righteousness. The Jewish perception is rehearsed in verse 5.

[5] Moses writes that the man who practices the righteousness which is based on the law shall live by it.

The Christian perception is stated in verse 6.

[6] But the righteousness based on faith says, Do not say in your heart, "Who will ascend into heaven?" (that is, to bring Christ down) [7] or "Who will descend into the abyss?" (that is, to bring Christ up from the dead). [8] But what does it say? The word is near you, on your lips and in your heart (that is, the word of faith which we preach).

The last verses draw on Deuteronomy 30:11–14, where Moses demands the daily fulfillment of the Law. To coax the Jews, he says: The commandment is indeed not in heaven, nor beyond the sea, no one needs to get it for you first, you already have it, it is in your midst. Yes, says Paul, that is true. The commandment, no—so he revises Deuteronomy—the *word* is in your midst. You don't need to climb up to heaven in order to bring the word—meaning Christ—from heaven. You don't need to travel over the sea—and again he makes a change—no, you don't need to descend to hell in order to raise Christ from the dead, for the word of God is present for believers in the preaching of the apostles. This is how the Jews had understood the passage from Deuteronomy. The commandment of God is near, namely, where the teacher in the houses of instruction interprets the commandment. We don't need to look for the commandment in heaven or beyond the sea. It isn't there. We have it in the synagogue. Does Paul say the same thing as the Jews? Is the word of God perhaps present in a Christian synagogue? No, Paul is asserting something quite different. In the synagogue, the *commandment* is near, because it is *not* in heaven and *not* beyond the sea. In the *ekklēsia*, the *word* is near, because it is in heaven and because it is in the abyss, and is preached as such by the apostles. In the synagogue, the commandment is thus present, but in the *ekklēsia* is the word, the Logos, who is in heaven and in hell, and who is preached as such by the apostles. But why is all of this being argued? Because the righteousness of God is not present in the schools as a commandment that can be known and learned, but rather is present in the cosmos for believers as *the* word, as *the* Logos.

In this way we again see inscribed, now in a new form, the fact that God's righteousness exists not in the natural but only in the supernatural sphere, not in the natural order of the synagogue or the school, but in the supernatural order of the *ekklēsia*; that God's righteousness is thus not communicated through the instruction of teachers to those who seek knowledge, but through the kerygma of the apostles, to those who believe. The kerygma of the apostles also possesses in its elements the confession of Christ's descent into hell and ascent into heaven.

[9] because, if you confess with your lips that Jesus is Lord and believe in your heart that God raised him from the dead, you will be saved. [10] For man believes with his heart and so is justified, and he confesses with his lips and so is saved.

The word for the faith that is contained in the proclamation, in the kerygma of the apostles, is the word of the Lord, of the *Kyrios* Jesus, as he is called in the Greek. Jesus is the Kyrios because God raised him from the dead, because he descended into hell and ascended into heaven, because in heaven and in the abyss he is the "word." Jesus is the Kyrios because he is the Lord in the cosmos, and not merely the teacher in the synagogue. Whoever now "confesses" with his mouth that Jesus is this Kyrios—here we are meant to think of the confession of Jesus in the baptismal confession—and who believes with his heart in this Kyrios Jesus, he is saved, yes, he is justified. Saint Paul speaks of "being saved." This shows once again that we are not dealing with natural time, with worldly time, but with time as defined by the supernatural, with God's time, with eschatological time. That is important for our understanding of the justification of those who believe. The believer is justified not in worldly time but in eschatological time, and not through his own works of the Law in the natural order of the synagogue; he is saved in the supernatural order through faith in the kerygma of the apostles and through the confession linked with baptism.

[11] The scripture says, "No one who believes in him will be put to shame."

What the Apostle has just proclaimed is something that he knows was prophesied by the prophet Isaiah (28:16). For Sacred Scripture is transparent. The prophecies of the Old Testament are not meant to be understood according to the natural time of this world, but must be read according to the point of view of supernatural, of eschatological time. Paul has slightly altered the citation from Isaiah. His version says, *"No one who believes in him will be put to shame,"* whereas in Isaiah it merely says *whoever* believes in him will not be put to shame. The insertion of "no one" again calls to mind the larger context of ideas, and the next verse explains to whom this refers.

[12] For there is no distinction between Jew and Greek; the same Lord is Lord of all and bestows his riches upon all who call upon him.

That no distinction exists between Jews and Greeks should not be understood in a liberal sense, such as on the basis of an equality of human nature. No, in the natural order, the distinction between Jews and Greeks is not cancelled, as Paul will later repeat with emphasis. Not the unity of *human* nature but rather the unity of the grace of the Kyrios alone cancels the distinction between Jews and Greeks. Thus the Catholic understanding that the distinction between Jews and non-Jews no longer exists, grounded in the supernatural, has not the slightest thing to do with the liberal viewpoint, with the natural denial of this difference.

The one Kyrios of all those, in heaven and on earth and under the earth, who with their tongues profess the Kyrios Jesus, makes all rich who bend the knee before him and call upon his name.

[13] For, "every one who calls upon the name of the Lord will be saved."

Not only was faith prophesied—that was just expounded in verse 11—no, according to verse 13, the calling upon the name of the Lord, which is expressed in the baptismal confession, that too has been prophesied by the prophet Joel (3:5).

[14] But how are men to call upon him in whom they have not believed? And how are they to believe in him of whom they have never heard? And how are they to hear without a preacher? [15] And how can men preach unless they are sent? As it is written, "How beautiful are the feet of those who preach good news!"

Not only faith, not only the baptismal confession of the Kyrios, no, the proclamation, the kerygma of the apostles, that too has been prophesied. Saint Paul applies the statement "How beautiful are the feet of those who proclaim good news!" (Isa. 52:7) to the good news of the *euanggelion*, the kerygma of the apostles.

[16] But they have not all obeyed the gospel; for Isaiah says, "Lord, who has believed what he has heard from us?"

Like faith, unbelief too has been prophesied. Because faith does not take place in worldly time but in eschatological time, it is as such capable of being prophesied. And because the unbelief of the Jews likewise does not take place in worldly time but in the critical, eschatological time that for the Jews began with the appearance of Jesus in the synagogue of Nazareth, the unbelief of the Jews was likewise prophesied by the prophets. All the prophecies that Paul here adduces would be a mockery if the belief and unbelief of which he speaks took place in historical time. But if Saint Paul intended not natural but supernatural faith, as demanded by the time of salvation, and was thinking of the unbelief of evildoers ripe for destruction, though tolerated by God with unfathomable patience, it is understandable that both, belief as well as unbelief, appear as prophesied by the prophets.

[17] So faith comes from what is heard, and what is heard comes by the preaching of Christ.

Verse 17 is merely a transitional comment to link up with verse 18.

[18] But I ask, have they not heard? Indeed they have; for "Their voice has gone out to all the earth, and their words to the ends of the world."

Faith, confession, kerygma, yes, unbelief itself, had been prophesied. Now there was only one possible rational explanation for Israel's unbelief. Perhaps they had not heard the kerygma as such? No, that possibility too was excluded. That Israel had heard the kerygma was also prophesied, as Psalm 18:5 shows. The proclamation of the Kyrios of the cosmos was perceived throughout the entire cosmos: "Its sound is heard over all the earth, and to the ends of the world its words." Because of the cosmic-universal character of the apostolic kerygma, there was no possible basis for supposing that Israel had heard nothing of the kerygma. There was no Jew who knew nothing of Christ, had heard nothing of the Church's kerygma.

[19] Again I ask, did Israel not understand? First Moses says, "I will make you jealous of those who are not a nation; with a foolish nation I will make you angry." [20] Then Isaiah is so bold as to say, "I have been found by those who did not seek me; I have shown myself to those who did not ask for me." [21] But of Israel he says, "All day long I have held out my hands to a disobedient and contrary people."

The answer to the question of whether Israel had perhaps not understood had to be: Oh, Israel understood very well what this was all about. But Israel was disobedient. Yet its disobedience too had been prophesied.

So once again, let us ask: what lay behind Paul's opinion that belief *and* unbelief, confession *and* disobedience, had been prophesied? The answer has to be: the faith of the *ekklēsia* and the unbelief of the synagogue are not phenomena within historical time, they are not natural, historical processes, but events that occur in revelatory time, in eschatological time, and as such were prophesied by the prophets.

Chapter 11

[1] I ask, then, has God rejected his people? By no means! I myself am an Israelite, a descendant of Abraham, a member of the tribe of Benjamin.

If the unbelief of Israel was prophesied, that could create the impression that God had rejected his people. And there were in fact many Christians in the *ekklēsia* of the Gentiles who consciously or unconsciously shared this opinion. Yet it was false. According to Psalm 113:14, God had promised: "The Lord will not reject his people." God stands by his word. He is not a human being who does not keep his promise. God has not rejected his people; that is already proven by the Jews who are converting. That is proven by Paul in his own person. He is still an Israelite, of the seed of Abraham and the tribe of Benjamin. Not for one moment does he hide his Jewish ancestry, not even before the Gentile Christians in Rome, with all their possible anti-Semite instincts. Even inside the Church, in the natural sphere, the distinction between Jews and Gentiles, between *Jewish* Christians and *Gentile* Christians, is entirely possible. In Jerusalem, for example, all the bishops were Jews down to the time of Hadrian.[39]

[2] God has not rejected his people whom he foreknew. Do you not know what the scripture says of Elijah, how he pleads with God against Israel? [3] "Lord, they have killed thy prophets, they have demolished thy altars, and I alone am left, and they seek my life." [4] But what is God's reply to him? "I have kept for myself seven thousand men who have not bowed the knee to Baal." [5] So too at the present time there is a remnant, chosen by grace.

That God has not rejected his people is made clear through the "remnant" that exists in the Church on the basis of election by grace. The converted

Jews within the Church are the remnant promised by God and typologically foreshadowed in the story of Elijah. As God at that time preserved 7,000 men, so now he also has chosen a remnant. In the concept of the "remnant," we once again see an expression of the fact that God's election is always an election by grace.

[6] But if it is by grace, it is no longer on the basis of works; otherwise grace would no longer be grace.

Although the distinction between Jewish Christians and Gentile Christians within the Church is intelligible in terms of the natural order, Jewish Christianity, which understands itself as the holy remnant, presumes that it is the remnant promised by God only on the basis of a divine election by grace. But that means that Jewish Christians cannot make their claim to be the remnant on the basis of their fulfillment of the commandments of the Mosaic Law.

[7] What then? Israel failed to obtain what it sought. The elect obtained it, but the rest were hardened.

Only the Jews who have become believers in Christ have found *that*, which was the goal sought by *all* Jews. But the unbelieving Jews were stubborn, hardened, obdurate. They put their hands over their ears, as they had done when Saint Stephen gave his testimony before them. Although all Jews know about Christ, they play dumb, as though they hadn't understood the Church's witness.[40]

[8] as it is written, "God gave them a spirit of stupor, eyes that should not see and ears that should not hear, down to this very day." [9] And David says, "Let their table become a snare and a trap, a pitfall and a retribution for them; [10] let their eyes be darkened so that they cannot see, and bend their backs for ever."

The stubbornness of Israel was prophesied by the prophets. That they walk into the trap that they themselves had set was also prophesied. All the images of snare and trap are pertinent in a specific sense only to Israel. The concept of the pitfall in the theological sense is an inadequate translation of this notion of a trap into which the people of Israel had fallen. This trap existed only for the chosen people. Jesus, the crucified Christ, became a trap for the Jews, for Gentiles nothing but foolishness (1 Cor. 1:22). With this reference to the trap, at the same time the limit of the famous Jewish cleverness is indicated. They don't recognize the trap laid for them, that is, the dialectic of their own theological concepts has not become clear to them; therefore they stumble over the stone laid in Zion. They are doubtless superior to the Gentiles, yet the presuppositions of his faith make every Catholic Christian superior to a Jew, however intelligent he may be.

[11] So I ask, have they stumbled so as to fall? By no means! But through their trespass salvation has come to the Gentiles, so as to make Israel jealous.

The Jews have been caught in the trap. That does not yet mean that they are lying on the ground. They have indeed taken a false step, they have stumbled and trespassed. Paul's meaning is clear. The unbelief of the Jews does not yet mean that they have become definitively unbelieving. Their trespass even has a meaning, for it becomes the possibility of bringing the Gentiles to salvation. And it also has a meaning for Israel. For when Israel sees how the Gentiles are entering the Church, that will make them jealous. The notion of Israel's jealousy is a specifically Jewish concept. Israel knows that its relationship with God is that of a wife, indeed a legitimate wife. But if God prefers another wife to Israel, then she will become jealous. God has now preferred the virgin, the *ekklēsia*, to Israel, his wife. Is it any wonder that since then a certain hysteria has marked the metaphysical character of the Jewish people?[41]

[12] Now if their trespass means riches for the world, and if their failure means riches for the Gentiles, how much more will their full inclusion mean!

Israel's prerogatives could not be expressed more strongly than in this verse, which—let us not forget!—is in a letter directed to Romans. The trespass Jews means riches: universal riches, riches for the Gentile world. But if their trespass means riches, how much more the moment of their inclusion. In this way, the ultimate conversion of the Jews is anticipated. Their conversion will have a still greater meaning for the cosmos and for the Gentiles.

[13] Now I am speaking to you Gentiles. Inasmuch then as I am an apostle to the Gentiles, I magnify my ministry [14] in order to make my fellow Jews jealous, and thus save some of them.

Once more the concept of the jealousy of Israel appears. In his apostolate to the Gentiles, Paul is not only pursuing his intention to preach the Gospel to the Gentiles, but he wants at the same time also to make the Jews jealous. If he is in the first instance an apostle to the Gentiles, nevertheless he continues to keep the Jews in mind. The conversion of individual Jews is not a matter of indifference to him.

[15] For if their rejection means the reconciliation of the world, what will their acceptance mean but life from the dead?

If the temporary rejection of Israel resulted in the reconciliation of the pagan world with God—for the Gospel, the word of reconciliation with God, is being preached to the Gentiles—what can their reacceptance mean but life from the dead? What does Paul mean by "life from the dead"? If we consider that, according to Paul, Israel's ultimate conversion will result in a heightening of God's dispensation of grace, then it seems to me most likely that we should understand the phrase about life from the dead in its literal and not in a metaphorical sense. Then Paul would be saying: the final conversion of Israel is followed by the general resurrection of the dead and the end of the world. To put it in reverse terms, Israel's unbelief would forestall the end of the world, the general resurrection of the dead, and the revelation of the full richness of God's glory.

[16] If the dough offered as first fruits is holy, so is the whole lump; and if the root is holy, so are the branches.

This verse has been understood in various ways. Some say that the first fruits are the Jewish Christians. Through them the whole loaf, that is, all Israel, is made holy. By the first fruits, or the root, others understand the holy patriarchs, especially our father Abraham.

[17] But if some of the branches were broken off, and you, a wild olive shoot, were grafted in their place to share the richness of the olive tree, [18] do not boast over the branches. If you do boast, remember it is not you that support the root, but the root that supports you.

Israel is the rich olive tree. The rich roots are the patriarchs, Abraham in particular. Some branches have been broken off the olive tree. They are the Jews who did not convert to Christ. On the other hand, there are branches from a wild olive tree that have been grafted onto the olive tree of God. They are the Gentiles. They stem from the wild olive tree, for they do not by nature belong to the people of God like the Jews; they are grafted onto God's olive tree. The adherence of the Gentiles to the *ekklēsia* thus never comes off without a certain violence, never without the skillful act of grafting on. That is rooted in the nature of the Gentiles, whose characteristic trait one can indicate as wildness. The Gentile by nature belongs to the wild olive tree. The act of the Gentiles' conversion is accordingly in every instance an act of taming or domestication. Here originates a genuine and necessary connection between Church and culture.—The Gentile as Gentile has no reason to boast in comparison with the Jew, whether converted or unconverted. He is finally just a grafted branch, while the Jews are the natural branches. He can't forget that he is carried by the root and not the other way around. The roots are Abraham and the fathers. They were Jews and not Gentiles.

[19] You will say, "Branches were broken off so that I might be grafted in." [20] That is true. They were broken off because of their unbelief, but you stand fast only through faith. So do not become proud, but stand in awe. [21] For if God did not spare the natural branches, neither will he spare you.

"Branches were broken off so that I might be grafted in."—That is the typical answer of the Gentile, who, in the Church, is unaware of the *mysterium* of the Church from Jews and Gentiles, for whom there is only the "historical" succession of Judaism and Christianity. Paul says: Not on your account were the branches broken off, but rather because they did not believe. You have nothing but faith. You do not belong by your nature to the children of Abraham. If you lose your faith, you are less than a Jew. If you lose your faith, you sink back into the barbarism of your pagan roots. If as a Gentile you lose your faith, God will spare you even less than Israel. The Gentile who loses his faith is nothing at all. The Jew who does not believe in Christ belongs nonetheless to the noble olive tree of God. The words of Saint Paul are experiencing a fearful confirmation in the present. The Christian peoples who are losing their faith succumb in fact to a measure of barbarism and loss of substance that is impossible for Jews.

[22] Note then the kindness and the severity of God: severity toward those who have fallen, but God's kindness to you, provided you continue in his kindness; otherwise you too will be cut off.

The concept of the kindness of God is a correlate to Gentile Christianity. It is the "dear" God, whom the Jewish Christian in this sense will never know.

[23] And even the others, if they do not persist in their unbelief, will be grafted in, for God has the power to graft them in again. [24] For if you have been cut

from what is by nature a wild olive tree, and grafted, contrary to nature, into a cultivated olive tree, how much more will these natural branches be grafted back into their own olive tree.

Israel's unbelief is temporary. If the Jews give up their unbelief in Christ, they will be regrafted onto the olive tree.

[25] Lest you be wise in your own conceits, I want you to understand this mystery, brethren: a hardening has come upon part of Israel, until the full number of the Gentiles come in, [26] and so all Israel will be saved; as it is written, "The Deliverer will come from Zion, he will banish ungodliness from Jacob"; [27] "and this will be my covenant with them, when I take away their sins."

What Paul has repeatedly pointed out is now in the form of a mystery solemnly shared with the Gentiles, namely, that the part of Israel that experienced hardening should last only so long as it took for the full number of the Gentiles predestined by God to enter the kingdom of God. When the full number of the Gentiles has become believers, then all of Israel will also be saved. Paul shares with the Gentiles this mystery—which could not be warranted by a natural insight into the historical process—because he does not want them to be content with their natural capacity to understand.

[28] As regards the gospel they are enemies of God, for your sake; but as regards election they are beloved for the sake of their forefathers.

The Jew is an enemy of God because he is disobedient to the Gospel; he is that for our sakes, for the sake of the Gentiles. But he is beloved of God for the sake of the election of his fathers. So his entire existence is ambiguous, and the ambiguity of this Jewish existence will only cease when all Israel becomes believers and Our Lord will have returned from heaven.

[29] For the gifts and the call of God are irrevocable.

At the end of his exposition, Saint Paul returns once again to his initial thesis. The word of God has not failed and also will not fail. The gift of grace and the calling by God cannot be revoked.

[30] Just as you were once disobedient to God but now have received mercy because of their disobedience, [31] so they have now been disobedient in order that by the mercy shown to you they also may receive mercy. [32] For God has consigned all men to disobedience, that he may have mercy upon all.

The word "all" has a heightened meaning in Christianity. "All" does not mean all in the sense of the *Communist Manifesto*, which is directed to "all." All always means concretely: Jews and Gentiles, and indeed in this heightened meaning, that *not only* Israel, *but also* the Gentiles are called to the chosen people, and that not only the Gentiles but also the Jews are included under disobedience, so that God can have mercy on all, Gentiles as well as Jews. Again we recognize here the heightened meaning of the concept of the divine mercy. It is not a timeless beneficence of God that Jews and Gentiles share in equal measure, but rather a divine superabundance, that draws Gentiles and Jews to one another in its circle. Only on the basis of this hyperbolical act of God, then, do we grasp how Saint Paul can let his exposition ring out with this act of praise:

[33] Oh the depth of the riches and wisdom and knowledge of God! How unsearchable are his judgments and how inscrutable his ways! [34] "For who has known the mind of the Lord, or who has been his counselor?" [35] "Or who has given a gift to him that he might be repaid?" [36] For from him and through him and to him are all things. To him be glory for ever. Amen.

I began my essay with the question of whether Aponius' exalted praise of the holy Church was objectively grounded or only sprang from a subjective pathos. Now we recognize the deeper meaning of the exaltation with which our holy Church is praised. The heightening of the language that we repeatedly found in Saint Paul has its ultimate basis in the exalted action of God himself, as expressed in the calling of Jews *and* Gentiles to the people of God. The mystery of the Church from Jews and Gentiles is the mystery of the divine mercy.

Monotheism as a Political Problem: A Contribution to the History of Political Theology in the Roman Empire

To St. Augustine

Pride has a certain hunger for unity and omnipotence, but in the primacy of natural things, all of which are as transient as a shadow.

Habet ergo superbia quendam appetitum unitatis et omnipotentiae, sed in rerum naturalium principatu, quae omnia transeunt sicut umbra.

ST. AUGUSTINE, *De vera religione* (On True Religion) 45, 84 (*PL* 34: 160)

Prefatory Note

The European Enlightenment preserved nothing of the Christian belief in God except "monotheism," a result as dubious in its theological substance as in its political consequences. For Christians, political involvement can never take place except under the presumption of faith in the triune God. This faith transcends Judaism and paganism, "monotheism" and "polytheism." The internal problematic of a "political theology" based on "monotheism" needs to be brought to light. May St. Augustine, whose impact has been felt in every spiritual and political transformation of the West, help with his prayers the readers and the author of this book!

.   .   .

"Beings do not want to be governed badly; 'the rule of many is not good, let one be ruler.'"

With this well-known citation from the Iliad (2.204f.), Aristotle concludes the twelfth book of his *Metaphysics*,[1] the one that we are accustomed to call his "theology." Werner Jaeger has established that book 12 of the *Metaphysics* constitutes an individual lecture written for a particular occasion.[2] As Jaeger demonstrates, it is not Aristotle's intention "to conduct school exercises, but to carry the listeners along through the massed force of the grand overall conception." When he addresses the Platonic dualists with the words of Agamemnon, "the rule of many is not good, let one be ruler" (*ouk agathon polykoiraniē, heis koiranos estō*), the impact of the conclusion is provocative.[3] Jaeger has also convincingly proven (233f.) that the final part of the twelfth book of the *Metaphysics* has a corresponding passage in book 14 (N 3, 1090b.13ff.). In contrast to Speusippus, who posited several fundamental principles with no intrinsic connection, Aristotle wants to show in both passages that Nature is not composed of a series of episodes like a bad tragedy.[4] If at the end of the twelfth book the citation from the Iliad is now introduced after the tragedy metaphor, a new image has not simply been added alongside an old one (perhaps the old one no longer seeming suggestive enough, as proposed by Jaeger, 235), but the final illumination of the concept of metaphysical unity is now found in a political metaphor that transcends a merely aesthetic one. Thus by an inner necessity the theological exposition of the twelfth book concludes with an image drawn not from the aesthetic but from the political sphere.

Aristotle's quotation from the Iliad stands in opposition not only to the metaphysical pluralism of Speusippus but to the entire Platonic tradition of a duality of principles (Λ 10, 1075a.25ff., parallel to N 1, 1087a.29ff.; see Jaeger, 235). In contrast to the dualism and pluralism of the Platonists, the Aristotelian doctrine of the self-contemplating Mind, which, as the highest principle, stands independently over against the world, is grounded in a "strict monarchism" (Jaeger, 236). While it must of course be stressed that the word "monarchy" (*monarchia*) does not yet occur in Aristotle in this context, it is nevertheless there in substance, and indeed in a double sense: in the divine monarchy, the single rule (*mia archē*) of the ultimate single *principle* coincides with the actual hegemony of the single ultimate possessor of this rule (*archōn*).

Jaeger holds the opinion that Aristotle's propositions on theology reached their full development around the beginning of the Christian era (159 n. 2), but perhaps one should say more cautiously that only at this point do they again become visible to us in the tradition,[5] though in characteristically changed forms, as we shall see now in the pseudo-Aristotelian treatise *De mundo* (On the World) and in Philo.

The treatise *On the World* shows Aristotelian features in its concept of God (chap. 6).[6] According to the unnamed author, God disposes of a power resident (*hidrymenē dynamis*) in heaven, which is the primary cause for the maintenance of everything (*sympasin aitia sōtērias*). It is not appropriate to think of God in Stoic fashion as an all-pervasive power. Even with human beings, men who have positions of leadership, for example, a general or the leader of a city or a household, do not undertake every type of work whatsoever. We can imagine the governance of God after the manner of the Persian Great King. He lives, invisible, in a palace, separated by many antechambers and surrounded by a large retinue. Just as it would be improper to assume that Xerxes himself directed everything, still less worthy would it be to believe that of God. God dwells instead in the highest sphere, while his power (*dynamis*) penetrates the whole cosmos, sets the sun and moon in motion, directs the whole heavenly realm, and so is also the primary cause for the preservation of earthly things.

Two things immediately become clear when one reads these statements: first, that the author has used Aristotelian ideas and that he has taken them from the tradition.[7] But the other thing immediately obvious is that the Peripatetic material is no longer seen in its old context;[8] rather, the engagement with the Stoic concept of God is what actually interests the author. One may rightly suppose that the author took the substance of the royal metaphor from the conclusion of the twelfth book of Aristotle's *Metaphysics*.[9] But note what has become of it: in his version, Homer's heroic king has been transformed into the Persian Great King![10] The shift in the metaphor has its origin in the shift in the definition of the problem that was caused by the encounter with Stoicism. In book 12 of the *Metaphysics*, God is the transcendent goal (*telos*) of all movement, and only in that sense king, only in that sense monarch. "The tactical movement of the soldier in the army who carries out the plan of the invisible commander in chief, is the happy metaphor that Aristotle has superbly fashioned for this conception of the world" (Jaeger, 415).

In the treatise *On the World*, on the other hand, God is a puppeteer (*neurospastēs*) who evokes the entire diversity of the world's motions just by pulling on a single string. For the author of the treatise *On the World*, the cosmos evidently has a monarchical constitution. In the institutional realization of this monarchy, God, by virtue of his function as monarch, keeps the entire institution in operation. The picture of the divine monarchy is now defined, not by the question of whether there are one or more principles (*archai*), but by the question of God's participation in the powers at work in the cosmos. The author wants to say that God is the presupposition of the fact that "power" (he says *dynamis*, in Stoic terminology, but he actually means Aristotelian *kinēsis*)[11] is active in the cosmos, but precisely for that reason, he is not himself a "power" (*dynamis*). "Le roi règne, mais il ne gouverne pas." (The king reigns, but he does not govern.) For Aristotle the cosmic monarch is the one who appears in the conflict of the principles (*archai*) as alone contrary and creative.[12] For the author of the treatise *On the World*, on the other hand, the monarch does not appear at all, but remains concealed in the chambers of his palace; he remains hidden and unseen, like the director of a puppet theater.[13] Only the power (*dynamis*) that is active in the world is visible, but the agent that stands behind it is invisible.

The differences that have just been described are instructive, not only as the expression of different ages and different political contexts, but because at the same time, they show that the ultimate formulation of the unity of a metaphysical construction of the world is always co- and predetermined by a decision for a particular political conception of unity.[14] But a second thing also immediately becomes clear: the distinction between "power" (*potestas, dynamis*) and "principle" (*archē*), which the author of the treatise *On the World* expounds in relation to God, is a metaphysical-political problem. If God is the presupposition for the existence of *potestas* (*dynamis*), then the One God becomes the bearer of *auctoritas*. That makes monotheism the principle of political *auctoritas*, as expressed, for example, in the *Pseudo-Augustini quaestiones* (Questions of Pseudo-Augustine); but if, on the other hand, the distinction of power (*dynamis*) from principle (*archē*) is conceived of in the sense of Platonic dualism, then the category of king (*basileus*) is contrasted with that of world-creator (*dēmiourgos*), as Numenius demonstrates.[15] Moreover, from the thesis that God reigns as king but does not actually rule may be drawn the Gnostic conclusion that the sovereignty of God is truly good, but the regime of the Demiurge (or demiurgic "Powers," usually seen as officials) is bad: in other words the regime is always wrong.[16]

I have spoken of a "monarchy of God" in Aristotle and the author of the treatise *On the World*, but neither of these uses the word "monarchy" in this context. Among philosophically educated theologians, it is Philo who first does so. One attempt at an interpretation might go like this: In the Isis Hymn of Andros, there is mention of the monarchy (*monarchia*) of this goddess.[17] It has been stated that this is a "striking appearance" of the goddess for such an early period, even before Serapis.[18] One might then argue that if Philo speaks of the monarchy of the God honored by the Jews, he is contrasting his monarchy with the monarchy of Isis. This terminology would thus be a function of the particular relationships spawned by religious competition in Egypt.

To this approach, however, we must object that it is inappropriate to take the word "monarchy" so seriously in a hymn.[19] The language of prayer[20] and hymnody[21] has its own laws. Linguistic formulations found[22] in these literary genres[23] in themselves offer no reason to posit a counter-formulation in prose. It would therefore not be advisable to adopt this hypothesis.

A characteristic example of Philo's usage is found in *De specialibus legibus* (On the Special Laws) 1.2, where he says we must now give our attention to the individual laws, and first and foremost to those "that have been decreed concerning monarchy."[24] The interpretation of the "individual laws" begins with the first commandment, which forbids the veneration of other gods in Israel. But why does Philo say "the laws that deal with monarchy [*hoi peri monarchias nomoi*]"? One would expect at least for him to say "the laws that deal with *divine* monarchy." But the modifier is missing;[25] that "monarchy" is divine in Israel is apparently understood as self-evident. Israel is a theocracy, the *one* people is ruled by the *one* divine monarch. *One* people and *one* God, that is indeed the Jewish arrangement.[26] Because Philo interprets the sacred legislation of Israel after the fashion of the secular legislation of an ideal polis, he puts the interpretation of the constitution, and that is the monarchy, at the beginning of an interpretation of all the particular laws. Now according to Philo's own statements (cf. *De spec. leg.* 2.224; *De decalogo* [On the Decalogue] 51) the monarchy of God addressed by the first commandment is certainly a monarchy that is also active in the cosmos, while the other particular commandments appear to refer primarily to Israel; but because the *one* God is not just the monarch of Israel but also of the cosmos, therefore the one people ruled by this cosmic monarch—"the people most beloved of God" (*De Abrahamo* [On Abraham] 98)—become priests and prophets for the whole human race (ibid.).[27] Their "prayers and feasts and first fruits" are, as Philo says, for example, in *De spec. leg.* 2.167, offered "for the whole human race"; and if Israel worships "the only true" God, then that is done not for the people but for all of humanity (ibid.). In fact, the Jewish High Priest gives thanks (*De spec. leg.* 1.97) not only "for the whole human race" but for the whole universe. Precisely because the monarchy of God is not restricted to Israel but extends to humanity and the universe, everything that the *one* people, who correspond to the *one* God, accomplishes, becomes full of meaning for humanity and for the universe. The political-theological results of this transformation of Jewish monotheism into a cosmic "monarchy" are obvious: they perforce make the Jewish people priests for "the whole human race."[28]

If we examine the section in *De spec. leg.* 1.13–31 that discusses the "monarchy" more closely, we immediately notice that the keyword "monarchy" itself is no longer used. The word here, as in other places (*De decal. 51*, etc.), is only stuck before the whole like a label. The second thing that becomes evident is that Philo has adapted Peripatetic material. God is the "King of kings" (*basileus basileōn*), thus to be compared (§18) with the Persian "Great King";[29] in relation to him, the astral deities (*theoi*) are assigned only the rank of subordinates (*tēn hyparchōn taxin*).[30] One is supposed to adhere to the worship of "the oldest cause of all things" (*tou presbytatou pantōn aitiou*) and not "worship the subalterns and gatekeepers in place of the king" (*tous hypodiakonous kai pylōrous pro tou basileōs therapeuein*) (§31). Similarly, in *De decal.* 61: just as it would be stupid and dangerous to render to the subordinates, the satraps, the honor owed to the Great King, so too would it be in relation to God.[31] Philo's account clearly implies a Peripatetic source that, like the treatise *On the World*, described the court of the "King of kings" in heaven, together with his subordinates (*hypodiakonoi*)[32] and gatekeepers (*pylōroi*).[33]

But it seems that Philo has modified this Peripatetic material in order to make use of it in Jewish theology. One point concerns the assertions about God. When it says in §20 that God is "not only the God of the intelligible and the sensible divinities, but also the Creator of all" (*ou monon theos theōn esti noētōn te kai aisthētōn, alla kai pantōn dēmiourgos*), this mention of the demiurgic activity of the highest God quite consciously transcends Peripatetic views.[34] A second point concerns the polemic against a polytheistic construction of the concept, a polemic necessitated by the use of the Peripatetic picture of the Great King with his court:[35] one does not honor the servants instead of the king (§31, also *De decal.* 71).[36] The argument that underlies this polemic is not consistent in every respect. If, for example, we take the relationship of the monarch to the servants in the sense of an "emanation" (*aporroia*), that is, that the authority (*archē*) of the supreme Divinity is source and "emanation" of all other authority or sovereignty, then we could thereby legitimate both religious veneration of astral deities as well as that of political authority figures. We find this theory of "emanation" of the divine authority, for example, in Aelius Aristides, according to whom the race of the gods is an emanation of "Zeus, the Father,"[37] as also the Hermetic Corpus teaches us that the Archons are an "emanation" of the King.[38]

The particular mode and manner in which Philo speaks of the divine monarchy show that he is interested neither in the question of the unity or multiplicity of metaphysical principles, in the Peripatetic sense, nor in the question of the relationship between "initial cause" (*archē*) and "power" (*dynamis*) in the cosmos, in the sense of the author of the treatise *On the World*. For him the theological-political problem is set against the background of his Judaism. The concept of the divine monarchy therefore has a pedagogical function for him, with the help of which the approach to Jewish monotheism is made more comprehensible to the proselyte.[39] From this perspective the divine monarchy is expounded according to all of its possible political correlations. The divine monarchy stands in opposition to the assumption of a divine "polyarchy" (*polyarchia*),[40] "oligarchy" (*oligarchia*),[41] or "ochlocracy" (*ochlokratia*) [mob rule].[42] As a result the metaphysical problem of whether there are one or more principles (*archai*) is no longer actually discussed; the decision even in the metaphysical world seems to have been arrived at from a political perspective.

A passage in *On Flight and Discovery* is evidence for this sort of interpretation: Jacob is the symbol of those "who have said that Mind [*nous*] has come in order to put everything in order and to change the disorder in existence, which stems from multiple dominions, into the order of a dominion based on law, meaning the dominion of kingship."[43] In this sense, says the text, Jacob is the adherent of the true Monarchy.[44] Philo's idea is that after the dominion of the mob ("ochlocracy"), God reestablishes the order (*taxis*) of a legally based dominion (*archē nomimos*), but this order is now that of kingship, monarchy, and not, say, that of democracy. It actually is a surprise to read this, for Philo is a passionate friend of democratic ideals,[45] yet it is clear that Jewish religious faith kept him in this context from speaking of a metaphysical, divine democracy. In the passage just cited, Philo is basing himself on Plato, who says in the *Timaeus* (30A) that the Demiurge creates order out of disorder.[46] But it is characteristic that he turns the creative work of the Platonic Demiurge into a political act, of the type performed by Augustus, who in Philo's words (like the Platonic Demiurge) also transformed "disorder into order" (*Legatio ad Gaium* [Embassy to Gaius] 147).[47] This political transformation of the activity of the Platonic Demiurge could take its departure from an ambiguity in the Greek word for order (*taxis*), which can be used to mean the "constitution" (*politeia*) of the state.[48] It is clear that Philo, as he himself also says (*hoi . . . ephasan*), has adopted this allusion to the act of restoring political order in the cosmos from literature. For Philo, it clearly refers not to Homeric kingship or to the Great King in Persia, but to Hellenistic monarchy or to the Principate of the Roman imperial period, as the truly authentic image of monarchical order in the cosmos.

It thus becomes clear that, while it was indeed possible on the basis of paganism to speak of a divine monarchy, which first constituted itself in a struggle against the cosmic powers of disorder, this could not be done from the presuppositions of the Jewish concept of God and of creation. On the basis of the metaphysics of paganism, however, it was possible to draw a parallel between the lordship of Zeus, which had been instituted only after mythical struggles, with the construction of a new political order. In fact this was frequently done. Especially impressive in this connection is Aelius Aristides' speech on Rome, in which he explains that before the sovereignty of Zeus everything had been filled with strife and revolution, but after he became sovereign, the Titans had slunk away to the deepest folds of the earth. It was the same with the Romans' domination. After they had assumed power, order (*taxis*) in everything and radiant light had come into being, and universal security had been won.[49] This idea of drawing a parallel between the lordship of Zeus and political hegemony is widespread—see, for example, Callimachus's *Hymn to Zeus*,[50] or Lucan

De bello civili (On the Civil War) 1.33ff.,[51]—indeed, it was so suggestive that the relation of Zeus to the political world became a theme of Greek thought in every age.[52]

It may be suspected that Philo had already encountered both the word and the idea of the divine monarchy in the school tradition of Hellenistic Judaism in Egypt.[53] It is noteworthy that Josephus, hence a representative of Palestinian Judaism, nowhere speaks of a divine monarchy, whereas by contrast 3 Maccabees, which originated in Egypt,[54] knows the prayer invocation "O monarch" (*monarche*, 2:2), as does the Jewish Sibyl (book 3 and fragment 1), which comes from Alexandria. And one may further suspect that this tradition, which preceded Philo, worked with a Peripatetic model. This is shown by the fact that Philo, in *De confusione linguarum* (On the Confusion of Languages) 170, cites the Iliad verse, *ouk agathon polykoiraniē, heis koiranos estō*, exactly as at the end of the twelfth book of Aristotle's *Metaphysics*. Philo says that the verse can be used of God and the world with at least as much right as of the state and human beings, for there is "One ruler and leader and king, for whom alone it is permitted to control and to administer the universe" (*heis archōn kai hēgemōn kai basileus, hōi prytaneuein kai dioikein monōi themis ta sympanta*). The formulation shows that the concept of Homeric kingship has no longer found linguistic expression here; rather, the title of king stands somewhat artificially alongside that of the official titulature of the Greek polis, which has been transferred to God. We find such a transfer of official titulature to God in Hellenistic literature, for example, in Dio Chrysostom[55] and often in Aelius Aristides;[56] it derives from the Stoic conception that the world is a city (polis), which is administered by God as the highest official. If we are inclined to find in Philo too a Stoic pantheism that appears to concede to God only the "administration," we should note how the passage in Philo continues: it speaks of the heavenly powers (*dynameis*)* of the angels that stand at the disposal of the divine Lord of the host. This shows that Peripatetic material has determined the choice of the Iliad verse and the elaboration of the image—while by contrast the transfer of the official titulature of the polis to God has the affective flavor more of "respect" (*timē*) than of a conceptual statement.[57]

---

* It is wrong to define the plural *dynameis* as "the representation of power" in psychologizing fashion, as does Grundmann, s.v. *dynamis*, in [Gerhard] Kittel [et al.], *Theologisches Wörterbuch zum Neuen Testament* (Stuttgart, 1933), 297.17f. Moreover, the heavenly *stratia* (army) is not only a Jewish symbol, but a Platonic and a Peripatetic one as well.

After Philo, the use of the concept of the divine monarchy first becomes evident again in the literature of the Christian Apologists. It seems
that this is not accidental; it would have suggested itself to the Apologists
in their defense of Christianity in the same degree to which Philo applied
it to make Jewish monotheism intelligible to proselytes. We first find the
term "monarchy" in Justin's *Dialogue with Trypho the Jew* 1.3 (ed. Good-
speed, 91 = ed. Otto, 4 = ed. Archambault, 4). Justin, tellingly, puts the
word "monarchy" in the mouth of the Jew. As though the expression were
something totally self-evident, he has Trypho say that the philosophers undertook investigations (*zēteseis*) "on the monarchy . . . and on providence"
(*peri monarchias . . . kai pronoias*).** This usage testifies to the ultimately
philosophical school (more precisely, Peripatetic) origin of this concept. It
is interesting that, exactly like Philo, Justin writes "on the monarchy," not
feeling it necessary to say "the monarchy *of God*." This shows the traditional origin of the concept and that this tradition did not come to an end
in the early Christian Church. We know from the catechetical lectures of
Cyril of Jerusalem that the preaching of the "monarchy of God" was a fixed
component in Christian baptismal instruction (*Catecheses* [Catechetical
Lectures] 6.36, to be compared with 7.1f., 4.6, and 17.2). Would it not be
easy to assume that the early Christian "teachers"—and that is what the
Apologists were—stand in a tradition that goes back to Jewish religious
instruction?[58] From Eusebius's *Church History* 4.18.4, we also know that
Justin wrote a treatise on "God's monarchy," which he compiled not only

---

** One may reasonably consider *Peri monarchias . . . kai pronoias zēteseis* (Inquiries
Concerning Monarchy and Providence) as an integral phrase, i.e., the scholastic discussion (*zēteseis*) of problems *peri monarchias* and *peri pronoias* presumes that the two have an
inherent connection with each other. On this compare, e.g., Minucius Felix *Octavius* 18:
"quoniam de providentia nulla dubitatio est, inquirendum putas, utrum unius imperio an
arbitrio plurimorum caeleste regnum gubernetur [because there is no doubt about providence, you think there is need to ask whether the heavenly kingdom is governed by the
command of a single authority or by the judgment of many]." The question of the extent
to which the *monarchia* of God allows free play for the rule of *tychē* (fortune) (or *genesis*
[coming into being]) is framed as a problem by a viewpoint that lets God reign but not
govern. On the reproach that Aristotle does not recognize "providence," cf. A.-J. Festugière,
L'idéal religieux des Grecs et l'Évangile (The Religious Ideal of the Greeks and the Gospel)
(Paris, 1932), 225ff., 228 (the absence of the word *pronoia* in Aristotle). On the scholastic
discussion of this problem, see Festugière, ibid., 231; reproach for Aristotle's denial of *pronoia* by Origen, 254, by Eusebius, 258, by Gregory of Nazianzus, 260.

from the scriptures that we use but also from books of the Greeks."[59] It is commonly agreed today that the treatise extant under this title does not actually belong to Justin. Whether that opinion is justified may remain unexplored here.[60] On the basis of Eusebius's data, however, Justin's genuine treatise can scarcely have looked much different from the one we have under this title. This suggests that it will also have stood in some kind of connection with that Pseudo-Hecataeus, who in the pre-Christian era in Egypt forged a collection of verses of Greek poets that were supposed to testify to Jewish monotheism.[61] I consider it very probable that this collection already used the concept of the "monarchy" for Jewish monotheism and that the knowledge of this key word in Philo goes back, even if not to Ps.-Hecataeus himself, at least to the ambience of Alexandrian Judaism, from which Ps.-Hecataeus emerged. The significant thing is that here, too, in the derivation of the "monarchy" concept from Greek poetry, the connection between Christian and the older Jewish conversion literature again becomes clear. The "monarchy" concept of Alexandrian Judaism was in the final analysis a politico-theological concept, intended to justify the religious superiority of the Jewish people and their mission to paganism. When Justin takes up the concept and continues the Jewish tradition, he not only demonstrates here again the close link between Christian and Jewish instruction, as I believe I have already shown in explaining the connection between Jewish proselytizing and Christian baptismal instruction, but also clarifies how Christian conversion literature, like Jewish, uses the politico-theological concept of the divine monarchy in order to justify the superiority of the "people of God" who assemble in the church of Christ, as compared to the polytheistic beliefs of "the peoples" (*ethnē*, pagans).

There are two passages in the *Apology* of Justin's student Tatian to be examined for the use of the word "monarchy." In chapter 11, he speaks of "the monarchic character of the universe" (*tōn holōn to monarchikon*) (ed. Schwartz, 30.11). In chapter 14, he says: "You Greeks . . . are more used to pluralism than to monarchy, and hold that we ought to follow the demons, as though they were strong" (ibid., 15.9f.).[62] This last cited text shows that it was right to juxtapose the concept of the divine monarchy with the Iliad citation in Aristotle's *Metaphysics*, for the "pluralism" (*polykoiraniē*) of which Tatian speaks is certainly an allusion to the celebrated verse from the Iliad, which we subsequently encounter again and again in the apologetic literature, be it in Pseudo-Justin's *Cohortatio ad gentiles* (Exhortation to the

Gentiles) 17 (ed. Otto, 64), in Theodoret's *Graecarum affectionum curatio* (Cure of Greek Maladies) (ed. Raeder, 68.7ff.), or in the apologetic chapters of the literature on the martyrs (Eusebius of Caesarea, *De martyribus Palaestinae* [On the Martyrs of Palestine] [ed. Schwartz, 907.21]; *Martyrium Sancti Codrati* (Martyrdom of St. Codratus) 3, in *Analecta Bollandiana* 1 [1882]: 451).[63]

The last of the Greek Apologists who makes rich use of the metaphysical monarchy concept is Theophilus of Antioch. In *Ad Autolycum* (To Autolycus) 2.4, we find the word used in a doxographical paragraph. He reports that the Platonists maintain that matter is "unoriginated" (*agenētos*), but says that if there are two things that are "unoriginated" (*agenētos*), "then the monarchy of God cannot be proven" (*oude mēn monarchia theou deiknutai*, ed. Otto, 54). Here the concept of the divine Monarchy has been expressed in contrast to Platonic dualism, as was the case with Aristotle. But the justification does not move along Aristotelian paths; instead, it takes its orientation from the concept of the omnipotence of God, in the sense of Christian dogmatics.[64] In 2.18 (ed. Otto, 74) reference is made to the contradictions of the Greek poets in their assertions about God. Some assume a single god,[65] others—inspired by demons—discover a plurality of gods;[66] when they grow sober, however,[67] they speak, like the prophets, "of the Monarchy of God and of the Judgment."[68] That is a notable statement: the doctrine of the Monarchy of God is an index of spiritual sobriety, whereas polytheistic utterance is the expression of a "possession" of the soul of the poet. In poetic enthusiasm, a metaphysical pluralism is articulated that in the final analysis is of demonic origin.

There is also a treatment of the demonic origin of polytheism in Theophilus's *Ad Autol.* 2.28. Had not the serpent in Paradise said, "You will become like gods?" When Adam knew his wife after their expulsion from Paradise (Gen. 4:1), then he experienced "the mystery of the Monarchy of God," namely, that there was no metaphysical pluralism or dualism, in the sense perhaps that one God had created Adam and another God had created Eve; rather, it became known to him that Eve had been shaped from his side. In Theophilus, the concept of the divine Monarchy is not only a formula and a slogan, but receives speculative elaboration. Theophilus, who since [Friedrich] Loofs's monograph [cited n. 71] has become more understandable as a deep, spiritually rich theologian, has with great cleverness emphasized the concrete circumstances in human life in which the temptation to a metaphysical dualism becomes articulated. It is poetic enthusiasm and womanhood that can seduce us to this error, although both temptations can be overcome. The poetic high can change into sobriety, the woman can be "known," that is, the experience of her formation from the side of Adam is changed into the knowledge that *one* God has created them both. To be sure, it is clear in Theophilus that the Monarchy concept, precisely because it is addressed in the individual concrete situation, cannot metamorphose into the political, which in its conception of unity necessarily always transcends the individual situation.

The passage on the "knowledge" of Eve just discussed was likely formulated by Theophilus out of a quite particular motive. If we consider that the concepts of the divine Monarchy and of sexual intercourse have been linked with each other, we cannot avoid the impression that the purpose was to polemicize against a position that denied the divine Monarchy of God and intercourse. That would indicate that Theophilus's target was Gnosticism. Now we know that Theophilus wrote a (lost) work against Marcion, who taught dualism and described intercourse as evil and dirty.[69] It would therefore be reasonable[70] to say that in the deliberations of *Ad Autol.* 2.28, one can perceive an echo of the earlier work[71] against Marcion.[72] In that case it would also be granted that the word "monarchy" in Theophilus took its specific meaning in opposition to Gnostic dualism. If we furthermore recall from Eusebius (*Church History* 5.20.1) a text of Irenaeus's called *On the Monarchy, or That God Is Not the Author of Evil* (*Peri monarchias ē peri tou mē einai ton theon poiētēn kakōn*), which Loofs has shown was strongly dependent on Theophilus, we shall see that the usage and concrete application of the "monarchy" concept by Irenaeus in this writing has preserved Theophilus's orientation against Gnostic dualism. The work was directed against a "Valentinian" named Florinus, about whose expressly Gnostic doctrine we are relatively well informed from an Arabic source.[73]

It is worth noting that in his great book *Against Heresies*, Irenaeus does not to my knowledge make use of the word "monarchy." That is all the more remarkable in that the sources from Asia Minor in Irenaeus's work continue to bear witness to the "monarchy" concept, while elsewhere we find that it was precisely people from Asia Minor who, according to the traditional interpretation, so exaggerated the divine Monarchy in Rome that they produced what is known as the "Monarchian" heresy in Christian dogmatic history. When the sources for the history of so-called "Monarchianism" are examined, it is striking that in his treatise *Against Noetus*, Hippolytus avoids the term "monarchy" altogether. In his *Refutation of All Heresies*, he uses the word a single time in the controversy with Noetus, but he gives absolutely no indication that he saw it as a key term among the heretics clustering around Noetus (*Refutatio omnium haeresium* 9.10.11 [ed. Wendland, 244.23]).[74]

The situation is different with Tertullian.[75] In *Adversus Praxean* (Against Praxeas) 3 he says of his opponents: "They say, 'We hold to the Monarchy,' and they voice the very sound of the Latin so loudly and with such exaggeration that you would think they actually understand the monarchy which they are pronouncing" ("Monarchiam", inquiunt, "tenemus" et ita sonum ipsum vocaliter exprimunt Latini et tam opifice, ut putes illos tam bene intellegere monarchiam quam enuntiant [ed. Kroymann, 230.29ff.]). Tertullian also speaks in chapter 10 of "those most vain Monarchians" (*vanissimi isti Monarchiani*, 240.18). On the basis of our earlier study of the use of the word "monarchy," it is clear that the term itself was universal in the Church. Why would one now suddenly make an issue of the word? Why use the expression with such passion that it becomes the name of a particular group in both Rome and Carthage? When Praxeas and his circle—thus possibly not Noetus—adopt the term, that is linked with the identification of Christ with God, which Praxeas had proposed. It appears that Praxeas applied the traditional ecclesiastical term "monarchy" to what he regarded as the logically necessary identification of Father and Son, in order thereby implicitly to polemicize against the ecclesiastical teaching. Praxeas seems to have been the first to apply the concept of the "monarchy"—albeit polemically—to the relationship of the Son to the Father, whereas the term previously had found expression only in the cosmological sphere.

What, in contrast, is Tertullian's understanding of the monarchy of God? To the logic of Praxeas the "grammarian,"[76] who identified the Father and the Son, Tertullian, like a legal scholar, opposed a constitutional construction.[77] He says (*Adv. Praxean* 2 [ed. Kroymann, 230.24ff.]): "I know that 'monarchy' signifies nothing else but 'singular and sole rule,'[78] although the fact that monarchy belongs to one person does not keep the one to whom it belongs from having a son, or from adopting a son for himself, or from administering his monarchy through whomever he wishes" (monarchiam nihil aliud significare scio quam singulare et unicum imperium, non tamen praescribere monarchiam ideo, quia unius sit, eum, cuius sit, aut filium non habere, aut ipsum se sibi filium fecisse aut monarchiam non per quos velit administrare). It is therefore not ruled out that the Monarchy "might be governed through other intermediate persons, whom it should appoint as its officials" (non etiam per alias proximas personas administraretur, quas ipsa prospexerit officiales suos, 231.4f.). If the monarch has a son,[79] that does not mean that the Monarchy is divided "and ceases to be a Monarchy, if the son should also be appointed to participate in it, but is principally his by whom it was shared with the son; and so long as it is his, it is still a monarchy, which is held jointly by the two as united" (et monarchiam esse desinere, si particeps eius desumatur et filius, sed proinde illius esse principaliter, a quo communicatur in filium, et dum illius est, proinde monarchiam esse, quae a duobus tam unitis continetur, 231.7ff). There follows a reference to the fact that the *monarchia* does not cease to be Monarchy just because it uses many legions and hosts of angels in its service. Nor does it destroy the Monarchy if a second and a third rank are accorded to the Son and the Holy Ghost,[80] but only if "another hegemony, with its own foundation and proper status," (alia dominatio suae condicionis et proprii status, 231.24) is ascribed to a creator god different from the Highest God, as the Gnostics do, such as Valentinus and Prodicus.[81]

If we recall the previous history of the *monarchia* concept, it is clear that the image of the divine Monarchy and its development in Tertullian's treatise *Against Praxeas* are traditional in most respects. That is not unimportant for the judgment of the whole work, which is not so much an original theological speculation as a polemic written for the occasion and using traditional material.[82] The only thing actually new is the development of the image of the divine Monarchy from the legal relationships of the Roman Imperial period: the relationship of Christ to God is understood on the basis of the Roman double principate. But in reality even this attempt to make the relation of the Son to the Father intelligible had already been made earlier in the apologetic literature, as chapter 18 of the *Apology* of Athenagoras (ed. Schwartz, 20.7ff.) shows (also see J. Geffcken, *Zwei Griechische Apologeten* [Two Greek Apologists] [Leipzig, 1907], 197, who to be sure sees only a "facile comparison" in Athenagoras).

So far as the substantive content of Tertullian's image is concerned, it is curious that the same argumentation that Tertullian uses to define the relation of the Son and the Holy Spirit was used outside of the Church as a justification for polytheism. We discovered the image, which was native to Peripatetic-Platonic school tradition,[83] in the treatise *On the World*, and in Philo. But this does not exhaust the documentary evidence. One may think of the orator Maximus of Tyre, who speaks of God as "the Great King," who "has many visible and invisible gods as sharers in dominion, of which part stand at the door to make announcements"; others are kings who as "akin" to him eat with him and are his guests, while others are their servants, and yet others, even lower than these.[84] According to Maximus, the perception was universal among both Greeks and barbarians that "*one* God is the king of all, and that many gods exist in addition, children of the gods, such as rule along with God."[85] According to Aelius Aristides, Zeus gave the four regions to the gods as "subordinates and satraps."[86] Similarly, Celsus compares the demons with satraps and servants, and in the Pseudo-Clementine *Homilies*, the following is presented as pagan teaching: "just as there is one emperor who has under him viceroys, governors, prefects, leaders of a thousand, of a hundred, of ten, so too does the *one*, great God, have the gods under him as subordinate powers, which stand under him but rule over us."[87] Finally, Tertullian himself bears witness to the wide-spread character of this idea,[88] writing that "very many construe divinity in such a way that they suppose the *imperium* of supreme power is in the hands of one, but his duties are in the hands of many" (sic plerique disponunt divinitatem, ut imperium summae dominationis esse penes unum, officia vero eius penes multos velint).[89] Time and time again, it is the same idea: "Le Roi règne, mais il ne gouverne pas." The gods are kings, satraps,[90] viceroys, "friends of the King,"[91] or officials;[92] actual *imperium* belongs to the highest God, who is compared to the Roman emperor or the Persian Great King.[93] We have already met with a polemic against this theory by Philo: one must not honor the servants in place of the master. Philo's objection recurs constantly in tireless fashion in patristic literature.[94] Tertullian, for example, takes it up in chapter 24.4 of his *Apology*: "And yet what crime does he [i.e., a Roman citizen] commit who transfers his efforts and his expectations [away from subordinate imperial officials] for the sake of greater favor with Caesar, and does not allow the title of God, just as that of emperor, to be bestowed on anyone but the *princeps* himself, since it is judged a capital offense to call anyone Caesar or to hear them so called, besides Caesar himself?" (Et tamen quod facinus admittit qui magis ad Caesarem promerendum et operam et spem suam transfert nec appella-tionem Dei ita ut imperatoris in alio quam principe confitetur, cum capitale esse iudicetur, alium praeter Caesarem et dicere et audire?) Now it is astonishing that Tertullian, who, as the exposition in his *Apology* shows, was familiar with this image from the pagan defense of polytheism, should nevertheless dare to employ the same thing to define the Trinitarian relationships. Perhaps the weight of the Roman constitutional construction of the double principate, which posited a *participatio imperii* (a sharing of command),[95] kept him from seeing that it was impossible simply to transfer pagan theology's secular monarchy concept to the Trinity, which requires its own conceptual development.[96]

In contrast to the Jewish-Christian dictum that one may not honor the servants in place of the master, nor the gods in place of God, Celsus objected—under the influence of the model of the heavenly bureaucracy: "Is it not true that the satrap and governor or praetor or procurator of the King of the Persians or the Romans, also too the possessors of lesser domains, offices, or ministries, can inflict great harm on one if they are neglected? But could the satraps and ministers in the heavens and on earth impose only slight harm if they are treated disrespectfully?" (Origen *Against Celsus* 8.35; see Keim, *Celsus' wahres Wort*, 126, also Glöckner, ed., *Celsi Alēthēs Logos*, 65.24ff.) The objection is skillfully formulated, because it shifts the political content of the image of the divine Monarchy toward a political polemic against the Christians. But the polemic against the monotheism of the Christians did not always take on a political character. Frequently, people will simply have asserted, in opposition to the Jewish-Christian objection that one must not worship the gods alongside God, that on the contrary, one must recognize [them] and pay homage. A passage in Philostratus leads us to suspect such an attitude. In a fragment from his treatise *On the Sacrifices* (Porphyry in Eusebius, *Preparation for the Gospel* 4.13; on the tradition from Porphyry, see Ed. Norden, *Agnostos Theos* [Leipzig, 1913], 344), Philostratus says that we owe veneration to the First God, the One, who is separate from everything else, but we also have to acknowledge the rest [of the gods] (*meth' hon gnōrizesthai kai tous loipous anagkaion*). Eduard Norden, who has drawn attention to this text in his *Agnostos Theos*, 39, is doubtless correct when he sees in it a polemic against monotheism. In common with Eduard Zeller,[97] he has further pointed to the polemic of the so-called Onatas, who objects to monotheism on the grounds that the adherents of this faith could not see the actual worth of the divine sovereignty, which consisted in the fact that one should rule and be the leader of *similar* beings and should stand above the others (*to gar megiston axiōma tās theias hyperochās ou syntheōreunti, legō dē to archen kai kathageesthai tōn homoiōn kai kratiston kai kathypterteron eimen tōn allōn* (for they do not grasp the greatest status of the divine sovereignty: ruling over and leading similar beings, and being omnipotent and preeminent over the others), in Stobaeus *Anthologium* 1.39 (ed. Wachsmuth, 1: 49.7–9). Norden has also expressed the opinion (*Agnostos Theos*, 40 n.) that the well-known passage in Plotinus *Enneads* 2.9.9, in which he protests against Christian monotheism, is "nothing but a repetition of that Pythagorean polemic." I consider that wrong where Plotinus is concerned, for Plotinus's argument runs in another direction. On the contrary, Norden has overlooked the fact that we find exactly the same argument as in Onatas in the critique of Christianity, preserved in Macarius Magnes, by a pagan, who asserts: "The 'monarch' is not the one who alone *is* but who alone *rules*" (Macarius Magnes 4.20 [ed. Blondel, 199]). Just as Hadrian only ruled over those who possessed the same human nature (e.g., he didn't rule animals), God is likewise a monarch only insofar as he rules over beings that have the same divine nature. In this fashion, polytheism sprang as a logical consequence from the premise that monarchical rule could exist only over beings of like nature. The concluding portion shows that the inventor of this argument was a philosopher and not a mere rhetorician. The initial dictum, "The 'monarch' is not the one who alone *is* but who alone *rules*," shows, in its polemical juxtaposition of concepts of being and rulership, that we are dealing with a mind actively engaged in polemical exchange with the Jewish-Christian concept of the divine Monarchy. I have no doubt that the pagan quoted in Macarius Magnes was the philosopher Porphyry.[98] In addition to everything else we know about him, it fits that he has adopted in great measure the Pythagorean tradition. It was Porphyry, as we have seen, who preserved Philostratus's critique of monotheism, and it is certainly not too bold to suspect that the thought of the Pythagorean Onatas, according to which rulership could exist only over beings of like nature and that therefore God must rule over other gods,[99] was also taken over by Porphyry from Pythagorean speculation.[100]

What was the Christian's answer to Porphyry's objection? He replied: Rulership for God means something different from rulership among men. Hadrian rules on the basis of the law that pertains to political rulership (*nomoi dynasteias*),[101] which by definition means that there can be no equality between the governor and the governed. Therefore coercion (*anagkē*) and power (*bia*) also belong to the essence of political rulership. Matters are otherwise with God, who alone has the Monarchy (here that means "rulership") and thus in the strict sense is "Lord" over all creation. It belongs to the essence of his rulership that it is exercised over what is different (*tōn anomoiōn hēgemoneuei*), and therefore he also rules not with the power of tyranny but with the firmness of love. And when Porphyry further objects that the Christians do not hold steadfastly to the Monarchy of God, for the angels are for them what the gods are for the pagans (Makarios 4.21 [ed. Harnack, frgm. 76]), the Christian replies that this too is false. The angels stand in God's light and are therefore "divinized," but in their own nature they are not divine.[102]

Our analysis has shown that the first attempts to join the traditional doctrine of the divine Monarchy with the dogma of the Trinity failed. That is as true of the attempt of Praxeas as of Tertullian. It is helpful now to see how, in the Christological discussions between bishops Dionysius of Alexandria and Dionysius of Rome, the difficulties of combining the traditional concept of the divine Monarchy with a developed Christological speculation were overcome. It is well known that Dionysius of Alexandria represented subordinationist ideas against teachings that had spread to Egypt and that held that before the creation of the world the Father was a single person with the Son (*hyiopatēr*).[103] On the contrary, replied the bishop of Rome,[104] and condemned "those who divide, mutilate and cancel the divine Monarchy, which belongs to the most revered part of the proclamation of the church of God, insofar as they [speak] of three powers and divided hypostases and of three divinities."[105] Whoever holds such a doctrine is like Marcion, who also divides and dissolves the divine Monarchy into three principles (*archai*).[106] In contrast, the pope represents the view that God has never been without the divine Logos (*theios logos*) and the Holy Spirit. Only "in this way can one preserve the divine Trinity and the holy proclamation of the Monarchy."[107] Dionysius of Rome had not, any more than Novatian, repeated the impossible attempted solution of a legal construction of the Trinitarian doctrine, which necessarily led to subordinationist ideas like those of Dionysius of Alexandria. Instead, as the parallel of the teaching of the Alexandrian bishop with Marcion suggests, he applied the philosophical interpretation of the concept of the "Monarchy" (*monarchia = mia archē* [one first principle]), which ever since Theophilus of Antioch and Irenaeus had become general in the church, to the Trinitarian relationship—to our knowledge, he was the first to do so—and in this fashion paved the way for an attempted compromise between the Monarchy concept and the dogma of the Trinity. Now it is interesting to observe that in Rome one reckons the doctrine of the "Monarchy"—like Justin and Philo, Dionysius says simply "Monarchy," without adding that this is a matter of the divine Monarchy—as a "most revered" part of the Church's proclamation, and that one speaks in this connection of a "holy proclamation" of the Church. It is likely that one could only speak this way if the ancient tradition of making Christian monotheism intelligible in catechetical teaching by means of the image of the "Monarchy" of God had been preserved in Rome. But it does not seem that this tradition had previously been known in the same measure in Alexandria. Neither Clement of Alexandria nor Origen had apparently used the word "Monarchy" with reference to God.[108] The same can be shown too for St. Athanasius.[109] Not the "Monarchy" of God but the divine Monad (*monas*) is characteristic of Alexandrian theology. However, the Pythagorean-Platonic concept of the "Monad" (*monas*) means that the concept of number, contested by Aristotelian metaphysics in its doctrine of the One Principle (*mia archē*), has now been reintroduced into theology. There is therefore an appropriate justification for turning in the direction of Aristotelian metaphysics in the study of the Monarchy concept. Nevertheless, that will not be my topic at the moment; first the political-theological question of monotheism requires further discussion.

I have in this discussion repeatedly emphasized the political meaning of the concept of the divine Monarchy. Now one could perhaps object that this construal is a modern interpretation of the state of affairs, and that this is fundamentally a matter of an "image," to which no political significance should be attributed. But the case of Celsus's polemic against the Christians shows that the political meaning of Jewish-Christian monotheism did not stay completely veiled in antiquity. According to Celsus, the Christians rejected polytheism on the grounds that one cannot serve several masters (Origen *Against Celsus* 7.68; see Glöckner, ed., 63.10). To this Celsus replied that that is the voice of revolution, the voice of those who stick to themselves and stand aloof from the rest of men.[110] Whoever speaks this way is basically projecting his own feelings onto God. Whoever, on the other hand, honors the gods thereby also honors the supreme God. Consequently, anyone who says of the divine that there is only One God is really an atheist,[111] because he brings division and revolution into the royal governance of God, as if in God there were partisanship and as if he could have an adversary of some kind (8.2 and 11). Indeed, the startling worship of Christ as the Son of God shows with how little seriousness the Christians actually take the worship of a single God to the exclusion of any other (8.12f.).

The interesting feature of these statements is that Celsus sees Christian monotheism politically as "revolt" (*stasis*). In this revolt, Celsus sees reflected the Jewish-Christian character of being a closed group apart from the rest of humanity. Because the Christians understand themselves as a faction, as the faction of the *One* God, their monotheism is itself tainted with faction and excludes the worship of other gods. The monotheism of the Christians is "revolt" in the metaphysical world, but as such it is at the same time revolt in the political order, for "the individual parts of the earth, in which the nations worship their ancestral gods, have probably from the beginning been subject to various overseers and under the care of certain dominating powers" (5.25). Whoever destroys the national cults is therefore in the final analysis also destroying ethnic particularities,[112] and at the same time attacking the Roman Empire, in which there is room for the national cults as well as for ethnic particularities. For the *One*, the highest God of Celsus, is indeed a metaphysical and not an ethnic entity, and exists impartially over against all national determinations (1.24 and 7.1; cf. also Origen *Exhortation to Martyrdom* 46). God permits the legitimacy of the traditional religions of the diverse peoples, for truly he rules but does not reign in the hearts of his worshippers.[113] That is the province of the gods of the diverse peoples, to whom, however, the Christians want to deny any worship at all. So in the final analysis it is political considerations that inspire Celsus's opposition to Christian monotheism.[114] He fears the destruction of the Empire, and if the Christians say that the *One* God whom they worship will defend the empire, Celsus invokes the fate of Jewish monotheism. Far from the Jews being lords of the whole world, not the smallest parcel of land is left to them (8.69). To be sure, it would be a remarkable development "if it were possible for Asians, Europeans, and Libyans, Greeks as well as barbarians, who are divided to the ends of the earth, to agree on a single law.[115] But whoever thinks this could happen knows nothing at all" (8.72). This short fragment betrays once more Celsus's final "pagan" conviction, bereft of any justification.[116] If it were capable of overcoming national distinctions, monotheism could be discussed, but the diverse nations will never be united in this sense of a single "law." The effect of Jewish-Christian monotheism on political life can therefore only be destructive.

The significance of Celsus's arguments is that they disclose the linkage of the problem of Jewish-Christian monotheism with the question of political life, which concretely means: with the political problem of the Roman Empire.[117]

How did Origen come to terms with Celsus's objections? Against the pagan's doubting that diverse nations could ever adopt one Nomos, Origen invokes his faith in the divine Logos, who will bring this to pass. Just as, according to the teaching of the Stoa, fire would become master of the other elements, so too the Logos will manage to transform souls (8.72). As witness to this faith, a long text from Zephaniah 3:7–13 is cited, in which it is said that God will assemble the nations on the day of judgment and in the fire of his zeal he will consume the earth (Origen equates the world conflagration of Zephaniah [cf. 1:18] with the Stoic doctrine of the *ekpyrōsis*), then the nations will receive *one* tongue and will call upon the name of the Lord, and all serve him under *one* yoke (ibid.).[118] It is telling that Origen answers Celsus's argumentation with an eschatological prophecy. National differences will cease on the last day. He compares the future to the condition that existed on the earth before the confusion of languages,[119] but he concedes that this condition cannot penetrate those who still exist in a body.[120] An interesting feature of this answer of Origen's is the general tendency to smooth out ethnic distinctions. This cancellation of final ethnic distinctions is seen under an eschatological aspect and therefore framed as "prophecy." Yet the integrity of his thinking makes him acknowledge that the elimination of ethnic differences is not yet possible, because we still live in this age and are still in this body. When Origen utters the belief that the Word of God will be Lord over every person and every thing, we should not see this as the fruit of a fantastic confidence in the power of spirit in the world. Rather, behind Origen's belief stands the knowledge that in the spread of his doctrine, Christ has shown himself to be stronger than his adversary, "than the emperor and prefect and Roman senate and all officials and nations" (2.79 [ed. Koetschau, 201.13ff.]). From an ultimately eschatological perspective and the happy consciousness that the Christian faith has spread irresistibly, he arrives at a theological interpretation of the political problem of the Roman Empire, which is found in the same treatise against Celsus (2.30). In connection with Psalm 72:7 ("In his days justice and fullness of peace have arisen"), Origen gives the following as his interpretation: the psalm's prophecy began to be fulfilled with Christ's birth. God prepared the nations for his teaching inasmuch as they existed under the one Roman emperor, so that there was no excuse about there being many states and many separate nationalities, which might have hindered the carrying out of Jesus's command to the apostles, when he said, "Go then, and make disciples of all nations" (Matt. 28:19). Now it is a matter of fact that Jesus was born in the reign of Augustus, who may be said to have brought the many nations of the earth into harmony through his sole rule. As a result, therefore, it would have been quite an obstacle to the spread of Jesus's teaching in the world if a plurality of states had existed—that would have meant the necessity on all sides of wars to protect their homelands, as was the situation before the age of Augustus. "How then would it have been possible for a peace-loving teaching such as Christianity is, which does not even allow self-defense against enemies, to make headway, if Jesus's coming had not coincided with a universal change toward a more humane existence?"[121]

This interesting text, which to be sure does not speak directly of Christian monotheism but only of Christian teaching in general, basically presumes the same problematic and tendency as is expressed in Origen's answer to Celsus's doubt about a universal monotheism. Here too the problem recurs: the negotiation of national differentiation and Christian proclamation. Everything is seen from the same perspective of the fulfillment of prophecy and the spread of Christian evangelism. The psalm (Ps. 72) that forms the point of departure for the explanation belonged to the ancient Christian proof from prophecy in doctrinal instruction from the earliest period.[122] But just as Celsus speculatively expanded what was in itself a traditional anti-Christian polemic, Origen speculatively expanded an equally traditional apologetic. We may surmise that it was through Celsus that Origen was first inspired to meditate on political-theological problems.[123] According to his original inclination, he does not seem to have been open to political problems. The text confirms the earlier assertion that faith in the eschatological cancellation of national differences leads to the tendency to declare that this differentiation can already be *seen* disappearing. And now the reference to the Pax Augusta serves this purpose. It is telling that the specific aspect of Augustus's peace (in itself capable of a variety of interpretations) that Origen chose to emphasize was the harmony it created among the nations and the way this facilitated the preaching of the gospel. That was the problem as the discussion with Celsus had posed it.

We can realize the distinctive achievement of Origen in this respect if we compare his linkage of Augustus with the gospel with two earlier such attempts. The first attempt at a parallel is found in Hippolytus's *Commentary on Daniel* 4.9 (ed. N. Bonwetsch and H. Achelis, 206.10ff.), which says:

When in the twelfth year the Lord was born under Augustus, from which point the empire grew, while the apostles summoned all nations and languages and created the faithful people of the Christians . . . then the empire of this age, which reigned at that time "according to the influence of Satan," copied this exactly and gathered for its part out of all nations the noblest and armed them for battle, calling them "Romans." (Hippolytus knows that the Romans, in contrast to the Persians, are not exactly an ethnic group; see his comments on Dan. 4:8 [204.14ff.].) And therefore the first census also occurred under Augustus, when the Lord was born in Bethlehem, so that the men of this world were enrolled and were named "Romans," whereas those who believe in the heavenly king were named Christians, and bear the sign of the victory over death on their brows.

Harnack has called this passage from Hippolytus the most drastic expression of Christian self-consciousness (*Die Mission und Ausbreitung des Christentums in den ersten drei Jahrhunderten* [*The Mission and Expansion of Christianity in the First Three Centuries*], 4th ed., 1: 278). This is wrong. What we hear expressed in Hippolytus is mistrust of an empire that claims a universality which only belongs by right to the Church. It is the same mistrust that is found in other periods of a world ruler who unites all the kingdoms of this world and who can only be the Antichrist. Gregory of Elvira will later say of the Antichrist: "He alone will have monarchical power over the whole world" (ipse solus toto orbe monarchiam habiturus est) (= *Tractatus [Ps.] Origenis*, ed. P. Batiffol and A. Wilmart [Paris, 1900], 195.13). Yet no trace of this mistrust against a world state is found in the fundamentally apolitical Origen.

The other attempt to establish an inner connection between Augustus and the gospel is found in Melito, bishop of Sardis. But Melito basically only says (in Eusebius *Church History* 4.26.7) that the Christian "philosophy" had begun under Augustus and had brought rich blessings to the Roman Empire. In contrast to the objection of pagans that Christianity had brought misfortune to the empire, he thus declares that the religion, which blossomed under Augustus, was intrinsically linked with the empire's prosperity. That is an old and widespread apologetic theme,[124] but still not an actual political-theological reflection. This we find first in Origen,[125] who was probably only pressed toward such considerations by Celsus's political theology.

What we can only discern as beginnings in Origen we find developed by his pupil Eusebius in the most diverse directions. In his *The Proof of the Gospel* (3.2.37), Eusebius takes up the prophecy in Genesis 49:10, according to which the ruler will not fail from the tribe of Judah, who is the expectation of the nations. The text had already played a role in Christian proofs from prophecy.[126] Eusebius refers this prophecy to Christ, who appeared at the time that the Jewish kingdom came to an end. That occurred when Augustus became sole ruler and Herod, who was a foreigner,[127] was established as king over the Jews. An intrinsic connection thus exists between the end of the national Jewish kingship and the monarchy of Augustus and the appearance of Christ: it is obvious that Origen's fundamental idea recurs here, namely, that the cessation of national sovereignty in the monarchy of Augustus stands in a providential relationship to the appearance of Christ.[128] The cessation of national sovereignty is documented by Eusebius—and in this respect he goes far beyond Origen—with numerous historical facts. In 3.7.30–35 of *The Proof of the Gospel*, the argument is developed as follows:

Who would not be astonished, reflecting that it cannot be human doing that it was only from the time of Jesus and not before that most of the nations of the world came under the *one* rulership of the Romans, and that simultaneously with his unexpected appearance, Roman affairs began to flourish? Namely, when Augustus first became sole ruler over the majority of the nations, at the time when the Ptolemaic dynasty came to an end after Cleopatra was taken prisoner.

But not only in Egypt, Eusebius continues, did national kingship cease, but also Judaea, Syria, and so on, which the Church historian then documents with a series of historical dates. We recognize here one of the motives for Eusebius's interest in universal history. Because national sovereignty ended providentially, the chronological course of the history of individual nations merits attention:[129]

Who will not concede that this was not accidental, that it coincided with the teaching of our Savior, considering that it would not have been very easy for his disciples to make their way everywhere had the nations been divided from one another and no communication existed between them, because every people would have maintained its own sovereignty (§33). But as things now stand, since they had lost their sovereignty, the apostles could accomplish their mission without fear and full of confidence, for the God who is over all had prepared their way and silenced the rage of the superstitious pagans, through their fear of a still greater dominion (§34). Consider, therefore, that had nothing hindered the adherents of polytheistic error from struggling against the teaching of Christ, and the superstitious had succeeded in regaining their sovereignty (§35), you would have seen civil disturbances, persecutions, and no small wars today in city and countryside alike. But as it is we see the handiwork of the superintending God, who has subordinated the enemies of his Word through the still greater power [i.e., of the Roman Emperor].

From this sequence of thought I emphasize the following: the idea that the apostolic mission was facilitated by the Roman Empire is something that Eusebius has in common with Origen. But a new feature is the usage of the "superstitious citizenry" (*tōn kata poleis deisidaimonōn*, §33).[130] This phrase, as it were, encapsulates Eusebius's theological conception of history. The polis is polytheistic because nation-statehood is pluralistic. Noteworthy, too, is the further thought that civil wars and other types of war are tied in with polytheistic nation-statehood. By contrast, the Roman Empire connotes peace.

Again and again Eusebius argues in this work that before Augustus, human beings lived in "polyarchy," dominated by tyrants or democracies, without joining in true union with one another. This is argued in great detail in *The Proof of the Gospel* 7.2.22. The results were endless wars and all the suffering that went with war. "When, then, the Lord and savior appeared, and at once with his arrival Augustus became the first among the Romans to rule over the nations, at that time multiple authorities vanished, and peace embraced the whole earth." At that time were fulfilled the prophetic predictions of peace among the nations, for example, Micah 5:4–5 and Psalm 72:7. In 8.3.13–14 of the same work,[131] he writes: "Under the new law [of Christ], peoples and nations without number, who had turned away from their ancestral gods and the old superstitious error, have been invited to the God who is over all" (§14). For this reason they are now blessed with the greatest peace, while pluralistic sovereignty and local kingship no longer exist, so that, as it says in the prophet Isaiah, now "one people does not raise the sword against another, as they once did earlier, when they were at war; instead, everyone takes his ease from his work, under his own vineyard or olive tree, for nothing any longer frightens him, as it says in the prophet (Mic. 4:4)" (§15). "But all of that only came to pass once the Romans possessed the sovereignty, from the days of the coming of our savior up to the present." There is a striking lack of exegetical tact in the way that Eusebius, without further qualification, sees the prophetic predictions of the peace among the nations as being fulfilled in the Roman Empire. In *On the City of God* (3.30), Augustine saw it differently. It is true that Eusebius's arguments in *The Proof of the Gospel* are in the service of the biblical demonstration of Christian doctrine.[132] But when Eusebius now says, "This all came to pass, once the Romans possessed the sovereignty, from the days of the coming of our Savior up to the present," this makes it clear that he has a special interest in the present—in the political present of the Roman hegemony. In the preface to book 8 of his *The Proof of the Gospel* (§3), Eusebius argues that the Sacred Scriptures have predicted a sign for the coming of Christ: peace, the cessation of political pluralism in the form of nation-states, the rejection of demonic, polytheistic worship of idols and the pious knowledge that there is only *one* creator God over all men. In principle, monotheism had begun with the monarchy of Augustus. Monotheism is the metaphysical corollary of the Roman Empire, which dissolves nationalities. But what began in principle with Augustus has become reality in the present under Constantine. When Constantine defeated Licinius, political monarchy was reestablished and at the same time the divine Monarchy was secured (Eusebius *Life of Constantine* 2.19). Constantine himself had delivered lectures (ibid., 4.29) that refuted paganism and presented the doctrine of the divine Monarchy to his listeners. But he not only gave lectures on this doctrine; at the same time, in his own monarchy, he imitated the divine Monarchy. To the *one* king on earth corresponds the *one* God, the *one* King in heaven and the *one* royal Nomos and Logos (*Tricennial Oration* 3 [ed. Heikel, 201.19f.]).***

Now it is time to pull together Eusebius's individual ideas and to establish the origin and the intention of his various themes. In a superficial sense, the first thing that strikes the eye is that Eusebius has repeated the

---

*** In this fashion an ancient Stoic ideal was fulfilled. See Plutarch, *De Alexandri fortuna* (On the Fortune of Alexander) 1.329a and 330d: *henos hypēkoa logou ta epi gēs kai mias politeias hena dēmon anthrōpous hapantas apophēnai boulomenos* (he wanted to make earthly affairs subject to a single rational standard and to a single government, and to show all human beings as a single people). Constantine thus realizes the goal contemplated by Alexander the Great. (On the same ideal in Caracalla's career, see J. Stroux, "Die Constitutio Antoniniana," *Philologus* 88 [1933]: 284 and n. 13.)

ideas just described in all of his writings, sometimes with the same expressions.[133] From this one can conclude what current significance he saw in them. What we are hearing is the voice not of a scholar but of a political propagandist. The second striking thing, but one which has an inherent connection with the first, is the strongly rhetorical coloration of the ideas. Typical of this is not merely the verbosity with which, for example, in the treatise on the *Preparation of the Gospel* or in the *Theophany*, the peaceful state of affairs is described, but also the rhetorically exaggerated contrast of the description of the situation before and after Roman domination. One could easily demonstrate in these contrasting descriptions how Eusebius the rhetorician is defined by a commonplace in the ancient panegyrics on Rome—apart from the mythological exempla—as we see, for instance, in Aelius Aristides, whose text we cited above, or in Plutarch *De fortuna Romanorum* (On the Fortune of the Romans) 317b–c.**** The literary context in which Eusebius presents his ideas is now not just the proof from prophecy in the Old Testament, but also the work of history and the encomium. In this literary expansion, we can see the way in which his point of view has moved beyond Origen. The problem of monotheism is regarded from a standpoint that is not eschatological but historical and political. The cessation of national sovereignty is documented with historical

****. . . *prin ge tēn gēn megethos labousan ek tōn synistamenōn kai pheromenōn hidrythēnai pōs autēn kai tois allois hidrysin en hautēi kai peri hautēn perischein. Houtō tōn megistōn en anthrōpois dynameōn kai hēgemoniōn kata tychas elaunomenōn kai sympheromenōn hypo tou mēdena kratein de boulesthai de pantas, amēchanos ēn hē phora kai planē kai metabolē pasa pantōn, mechri hou tēs Rōmēs ischyn kai auxēsin labousēs kai anadēsamenēs touto men ethnē kai dēmous en autēi, touto d' allophylous kai diapontious basileōn hēgemonias, hedran esche ta megista kai asphaleian, eis kosmon eirēnēs kai hena kyklon tēs hēgemonias aptaiston peripheromenēs, pasēs men aretēs engenomenēs tois tauta mēchanēsamenois, pollēs de tychēs synelthousēs.* (. . . until the earth, gaining its great size from the union of its constitutive elements, was stabilized from their addition, and somehow got its foundation in itself and around itself for the other [elements]. In a similar way, while the mightiest powers and dominions among men were being driven about as fortune would have it, and were colliding with one another because they all wanted to hold power without being under anyone else, the constant movement, drift, and change of all the nations could not be remedied, until Rome grew strong and expanded, and attached to herself not only the nations and peoples near her, but also the dominions of foreign peoples beyond the seas. Thus the affairs of this vast empire gained stability and security, since the supreme government was brought into a peaceful order and one, unshakeable circle of domination. Though every virtue was native to those who procured this [order], a great deal of good fortune also accompanied them.)

dates, but in this historical demonstration, which appears as a fulfillment of Old Testament prophecies, a choice is at the same time made politically for the Roman Empire. National sovereignty is allied intimately with polytheism, with the effect that the Roman Empire is then pressed into service in the struggle against polytheism. War is attributed either to demons[134] or to the fatalism of polytheistic nationalism—we should think here of the Hellenistic philosophy of history based on the *tychē* (fortune) of peoples—while Christianity presents itself in contrast as supportive of the peace policy of the Roman Empire. The three concepts: Roman Empire, peace, and monotheism, are thus inextricably linked with one another. But now a fourth impetus intrudes: the monarchy of the Roman Emperor. The *one* monarch on earth—and for Eusebius that can only be Constantine—corresponds to the *one* divine monarch in heaven.[135] Despite the influence of ancient philosophy and rhetoric on Eusebius,[136] there should be no mistake that the whole conception linking empire, peace, monotheism, and monarchy consists of a unity fashioned by Christians. How differently a pagan thought about the unity of the empire and the unity of worship, the example of Celsus has shown, who in the final analysis gave the incentive for the elaboration of this whole Christian ideology.

Eusebius's ideas had an enormous historical influence. One finds them echoed everywhere in patristic literature. I limit myself to a selection of a number of witnesses.[137] St. John Chrysostom, for example, writes thus in his *Address against Jews and Pagans* 3: "Christ appears at the time when there were no more Jewish rulers and they had fallen under the domination of the Romans." After which he cites Genesis 49:10 and continues: "At the time he was born and that first assessment [tax census] took place, when the Romans had become masters of the Jewish people . . ." (*PG* 48: 817). Seen in this light, then, Augustus's census appears as a work of divine providence (Chrysostom *Homily on the Birthday of Jesus Christ* 2 [*PG* 49: 353]).[138] Augustus acts under divine influence and serves, even though unwittingly, the "parousia of the Firstborn." Other Antiochene theologians, such as Diodore[139] and Theodoret,[140] are aware of these ideas. According to Diodore, God favored the Roman Empire with a special providence. After the fashion of Eusebius, Diodore describes the Pax Romana in its blessed effects, in order to draw the interesting conclusion that the Apostle Paul had in mind this divine economy toward the Romans, when he commanded in Romans 13:1, "Be subject to the authorities." The commandment of obedience to authority is thus not justified in purely positivist terms, but also derives from the special providence of God regarding the Roman Empire. It would be easy to multiply examples from the literature of the Greek fathers, but what has been cited may suffice.[141]

Nevertheless, it is relevant that the actual figure of Augustus in this speculation must necessarily seem meaningful for Christianity. In principle, Augustus inaugurates monotheism, as Eusebius's assertions make clear, and Constantine only fulfills what Augustus had begun. Political and rhetorical motifs are once again bound up with this theological construction of history. The political idea that the Roman Empire does not lose its metaphysical character when it shifts from polytheism to monotheism, because monotheism already existed potentially with Augustus, is now linked with the rhetorical-political idea that Augustus is a foreshadowing of Constantine,[142] as was customary for Roman emperors in all periods.[143]

One understands that Eusebius's timely and relevant theologoumenon had to have a great impact on the subsequent age. This influence did not remain limited to the east but subsequently also influenced the sentiments of the Fathers in the west. Prudentius, *Contra Orationem Symmachi* (Against the Oration of Symmachus) 2.583–592, wrote the following in his poetic response against the pagan prefect Symmachus:

> Do you want me to tell you, Roman, what cause it was that so exalted your labors, what it was that nursed your glory to such a height of fame that it has put rein and bridle on the world? God, wishing to bring into partnership peoples of different speech and realms of discordant customs, determined that all the civilized world should be harnessed to one ruling power and bear gentle bonds in harmony under the yoke, so that love inspired by their religion should hold men's hearts in union; for no bond is made that is worthy of Christ unless unity of spirit joins together the nations it associates . . .

> Vis, dicam, quae causa tuos, Romane, labores / in tantum extulerit, quis gloria fotibus aucta / sic cluat, inpositis ut mundum frenet habenis? / discordes linguis populos et dissona cultu / regna volens sociare deus subiungere uni / imperio, quidquid tractabile moribus esset, / concordique iugo retinacula mollia ferre / constituit, quo corda hominum coniuncta teneret / religionis amor; nec enim fit copula Christo / digna, nisi inplicitas societ mens unica gentes . . . (2.583–592)

> Such is the result of the great successes and triumphs of the Roman power. For the time of Christ's coming, be assured, the way was already prepared, the general good will of peace among us had already built it under the rule of Rome. For

what room could there have been for God in a savage world and in human hearts at variance, each according to its different interest maintaining its own claims, as once things were?

hoc actum est tantis successibus atque triumfis / Romani imperii: Christo iam tunc venienti / crede, parata via est, iam dudum publica nostrae / pacis amicitia struxit moderamine Romae. / nam locus esse deo quis posset in orbe feroci / pectoribusque hominum discordibus et sua iura / dissimili ratione tuentibus, ut fuit olim? (2.619–626)

Only through the unity of political power "does the condition of life become stable and a settled way of thought draws in God in the heart and subjects itself to one Lord" (fit stabilis vitae status et sententia certa / haurit corde deum domino et subiungitur uni [2.632–633)].[144]

About the same time St. Ambrose—in the manner of Eusebius—considered the prophetic prophecy of the peace of the nations to be fulfilled in the Roman Empire and also demonstrated the link with monotheism. In the interpretation of Psalm 46:9, "Making wars cease even to the ends of the earth, he destroys the bow and crushes weapons: and burns the shields with fire" (Auferens bella usque ad fines terrae, arcum conteret et confringet arma: et scuta comburet igni), St. Ambrose writes as follows: "And truly, before the Roman Empire was founded, not only did the kings of the various cities make war on one another, but the Romans themselves were often torn with civil wars" (Et vere antequam Romanum diffunderetur imperium, non solum singularum urbium reges adversum se praeliabantur; sed etiam ipsi Romani bellis frequenter civilibus atterebantur). There follows an enumeration of the civil wars up to the battle of Actium:

Whence it happened that weariness of civil war led to the transfer of the Roman Empire to Julius Augustus; and thus domestic strife was ended. Now it came to this pass so that the apostles could be sent immediately to the whole world, as Jesus had said: "Go and teach all nations" (Matt. 28:19). Even kingdoms closed off by foreign mountains lay open to them, like India to Thomas, Persia to Matthew. Nevertheless, because of the vast expanse of the countries that lay in their path, when the Church arose, he spread the power of the Roman Empire throughout the whole world, and calmed the minds of those at war and the borders of the lands, with the gift of peace. Living under one imperium over the nations, all men learned to confess the imperium of the one almighty God, in faithful eloquence.

Unde factum est, ut taedio bellorum civilium, Julio Augusto Romanum deferretur imperium; et ita praelia intestina sedata sunt. Hoc autem eo profecit, ut recte per totum orbem apostoli mitterentur, dicente Domino Jesu: "Euntes docete omnes gentes." Illis quidem etiam interclusa barbaricis montibus regna patuerunt, ut Thomae India, Matthaeo Persia. Sed tamen quo plura obirent spatia terrarum, in exortu ecclesiae potestatem Romani imperii toto orbe diffudit, et dissidentium mentes, terrarumque divortia donata pace composuit. Didicerunt omnes homines sub uno terrarum imperio viventes, unius Dei omnipotentis imperium fideli eloquio confiteri. (*PL* 14: 1142f.)

The substance of these arguments agrees totally with the ideas of Eusebius. We may pass over the question whether this indicates that the psalm interpretation of Eusebius, who expounded his familiar ideas on the relevant verse (see *PG* 23: 412), influenced the psalm interpretation of Ambrose.[145] The one sure thing is that [the interpretation of] St. Ambrose is not original, and that there can be no talk of his having "represented the Christian universal history" in the interpretation of Psalm 46.[146]

It is not surprising also to see St. Jerome in the stream of this tradition that ultimately goes back to Eusebius. In his interpretation of Micah 4:2 Jerome says: "Before a child was born to us, whose rulership was on his shoulder, the whole world was filled with blood, peoples contending against peoples, kings against kings, nations against nations. At last even the Roman Republic itself was torn with civil wars" (Antequam nasceretur nobis puer, cuius principatus in humero eius, totus orbis plenus erat sanguine, populi contra populos, reges contra reges, gentes dimicabant adversum gentes. Denique etiam ipsa Romana Res publica bellis lacerabatur civilibus). There follows a rhetorical description of the civil wars, as with Ambrose: "Afterwards, however, in consequence of the empire of Christ, Rome acquired sole imperium, the world became accessible to the travels of the apostles, and the gates of the cities were opened to them, and the sole empire was constituted at the preaching of the one God" (Postquam autem ad imperium Christi, singulare imperium Roma sortita est, apostolorum itineri pervius factus est orbis et apertae sunt eis portae urbium et ad praedicationem unius Dei singulare imperium constitutum est [*PL* 25: 1187D–1188A]). The final words show that the old association of monotheism with the Roman Empire still survived.[147]

It would be pointless to pile up still more citations from the Latin fathers of the Church. Let just one more author be discussed, because he once again illuminates our theme in a remarkable way: the Spaniard Orosius.[148] In the sixth book of his treatise *Against the Pagans*, Orosius develops an entire Augustus theology. It is first narrated in chapter 20 how Augustus, in year 725 after the founding of the city, returned from the Orient as victor. The day when he paraded into Rome in triumph and for the first time closed the doors of the Temple of Janus, and also for the first time was hailed as Augustus, is the day of the Epiphany, the day on which Christ appeared.[149] Orosius concludes from this that the arrival of Augustus in Rome contains a mysterious reference to the coming of Christ. In this connection, he attributes political-theological significance to the marvels that accompanied Augustus's triumphal procession, and of which earlier historians had spoken. The appearance of a solar ring is supposed to point out Augustus as the "sole and most powerful person in this world, and the only one brilliant" (unum ac potissimum in hoc mundo, solumque clarum), in whose time was to come the one "who alone has made and rules the sun itself and the whole world." Then he tells us a tale also passed on by Dio Cassius, about a spring of oil that welled up in Trastevere. This too receives a Christian interpretation. The spring of oil refers to the *unctus*, to the one anointed with oil, hence to Christ. When the oil flowed for a whole day, that symbolized the eternal duration of the Roman Empire, to which belong the ones anointed with oil, that is, the Christians.

In chapter 22, still more political-theological pronouncements follow. In the year 752 after the founding of the city, Augustus secured peace in all the parts of the world. For the third time, the doors of the Temple of Janus were closed. People then bestowed the title "Lord" on Augustus. But he rejected it, because he was only a man.[150] But at the same time, that is, when Caesar had secured through his efforts the surest and most genuine peace, Christ was born, whose coming corresponded to that peace. At his birth, men heard the angels rejoice: "Glory be to God in the highest and peace to men of good will."[151] At precisely this time, Caesar refused to let men call him Lord; he, to whom all things were subjected, did not dare it, because the true Lord of the human race was born at that time among men. In the same year, the Caesar whom God had ordained for such great mysteries decreed a universal census of every province, and commanded that all men were to be counted. That was the time when God let himself be seen as a man, that was when he wanted it to happen. Thus at that time Christ was born, who immediately after his birth was enrolled in the Roman census . . . he who had created all men let himself be enrolled among men. Since the creation of the world, no such a thing had been reserved for either the Babylonian or Macedonian kingdoms,[152] let alone smaller ones. And there is no doubt, rather, it is obvious to the knowledge and insight of the faith, that our Lord Jesus Christ by his will had increased and defended this city, which he had led to the very summit. He wished in the first instance to belong to it, when he came, in order to be named a Roman citizen through the "acknowledgement of Roman taxation." Just as for Eusebius, for Orosius, the unity of the Roman Empire and the unity of God are tied together: "The one God, who established this unity of kingship at the time when he wished to shine forth, is loved and feared by all; the same laws that are subject to the one God are everywhere dominant" (unus Deus, qui temporibus quibus innotescere voluit, hanc regni statuit unitatem, ab omnibus diligitur et timetur; eaedem leges, quae uni Deo subiectae sunt, ubique dominantur [5.2.5]). Indeed, Orosius goes so far as to attribute the foundation of Rome to the monotheistic God of the Christians, and can write with Christian feeling of Rome's foundation legend: "the one true God . . . who chose the weak things of the world to confound the strong, and founded the Roman Empire when a shepherd of the lowliest condition was raised up" (unus et verus deus . . . quae infirma sunt mundi elegit, ut confundat fortia, Romanumque imperium adsumpto pauperrimi status pastore fundavit [6.1.5]).[153] So then, for Orosius the Roman Empire and Christianity became a unity, so that he can say, "As a Roman and a Christian, I approach the Christians and the Romans" (ad Christianos et Romanos Romanus et Christianus accedo [5.2.3]).

Orosius speaks of the Pax Romana being in harmony with the patristic tradition. Twice he links peace dates from Augustus's history with sacred history. Of the character of this peace, he is in no doubt. It is a peace that does away with war,[154] and national pluralism has accordingly been abolished. "Throughout the whole world there was one peace, not by the mere cessation but by the very elimination of all wars, the twin doors of Janus were shut, now that the roots of war had not merely been crushed but torn up. That census was the first and the greatest, since the entire creation of great nations swore by this one name of Caesar and at the same time was united by the commonality of the census of the one society" (Toto terrarum orbe una pax omnium non cessatione, sed abolitione bellorum, clausae Jani geminae portae extirpatis bellorum radicibus, non repressis, census ille primus et maximus, cum in hoc unum Caesaris nomen universa magnarum gentium creatura iuravit simulque per communionem census unius societatis effecta est [7.2.16]). More than anyone else, this Spanish provincial bound the Roman Empire and Christianity together, most impressively in his linking of Augustus with Christ. In this way, he clearly Christianized Augustus,[155] and Christ, in becoming a Roman citizen, has been Romanized. The political meaning of this construction is patent. The affinity of Christian monotheism with the Roman Empire has been asserted.[156] That had already been Eusebius's theme, but the political disasters to which the Roman Empire in the fifth century had been exposed had among many—in particular among pagans—provoked the question of whether the empire's political weakness was not ultimately attributable to the loss of inner continuity, whether the Christianization of the Empire had not in the end led to its inner collapse. Orosius has not in reality given a new answer to this question. He has been content to demonstrate once again, to an extreme degree, the internal connection between Christian monotheism and the Roman Empire.[157]

In reality, however, this posing of the question had already been transcended by the development of Christian theology itself. For was it really correct to see the Christian faith simply as monotheism? The use the Arians had made of the concept of the divine Monarchy had to lead to an answer to this question. We know that the Arian Eunomius wanted "to preserve, always and everywhere, the transcendence of God and the Monarchy"[158] (Eunomius *Liber Apologeticus* [Apologetic Book] 27 [*PG* 30: 865A]).[159] That statement comes at the end of a formula of faith that, as has long been known, is connected with the confession found in *Apostolic Constitutions* 7.4.1.[160] In book 5.20.11 of the same treatise, there is a section belonging to the Arian redactor of the *Apostolic Constitutions*, in which it is demonstrated how Christ, the Son of Man, in fulfillment of the prophecy in Daniel 2:34, has become a great mountain "that has filled the whole world and has crushed the plural sovereignty of local regimes, as well as the plural deities of the godless, by preaching the only God and establishing the sole sovereignty of the Romans."[161] In these arguments, which faithfully repeat Eusebius's way of thinking,[162] the ultimate political meaning of Arianism is candidly expressed. Monotheism is a political imperative, a piece of *Reichspolitik*. At the moment that the concept of the divine Monarchy, which was only a mirroring of the earthly monarchy in the Roman Empire, was juxtaposed with the Christian Trinitarian dogma, the controversy over this dogma immediately became an openly political struggle.

For if monotheism, the concept of the divine Monarchy in the sense in which Eusebius had formulated it, was theologically untenable, then so too was the continuity of the Roman Empire untenable, and Constantine or his successors could no longer be recognized as the fulfillers of what had begun in principle with Augustus. But that threatened the unity of the still mainly pagan Roman Empire. In that case, Christianity had to appear plainly as a "revolt" in the metaphysical and political order, precisely as Celsus had already declared. We see that it was a pressing political interest that first drove the emperors to the side of the Arians, and that, on the other hand, the Arians were fated to become the theologians of the Byzantine court. Orthodox Trinitarian doctrine in effect threatened the political theology of the Roman Empire.

Even after the Arian controversies, people did not stop talking about the divine Monarchy,[163] but the phrase loses its political-theological character alongside the orthodox dogma. Gregory of Nazianzus gave it its ultimate theological depth when he declared, in his *Third Theological Oration*,[164] that there were three opinions about God: anarchy, polyarchy, and monarchy. The first two assumptions unleashed disorder and revolt in God, and ultimately dissolution. Christians, on the other hand, confessed the Monarchy of God. To be sure, not the Monarchy of a single person in the godhead, for this bore the seed of schism within itself, but the Monarchy of the triune God. This conception of unity had no correspondence in the created order. With such arguments, monotheism is laid to rest as a political problem. It is no accident that at this time the Jewish origin of monotheism was known to the fathers of the Church, and now the old apostolic front against Jews and pagans becomes discernible on behalf of the Trinitarian doctrine.[165] With this, however, the linkage of the Christian proclamation to the Roman Empire was *theologically* dissolved.

What the Greek fathers [of the Church] achieved in relation to the concept of God, St. Augustine accomplished in the west for the concept of "peace." The Augustan peace, which had served to promote a very dubious political theology, appears questionable in the eyes of St. Augustine: "For even Augustus himself waged civil wars against many, and a host of outstanding men also perished in them, among whom was Cicero" (Nam et ipse Augustus cum multis gessit bella civilia et in eis etiam multi clarissimi viri perierunt, inter quos et Cicero [*On the City of God* 3.30]).[166] And if one were to invoke the alleged fulfillment of Psalm 46:9, "Making wars cease even to the ends of the earth" (Auferens bella usque ad fines terrae), in the Pax Romana, à la Eusebius, Ambrose, and many others, compare what St. Augustine, probably in conscious antithesis, elsewhere comments on this verse:

We have yet to see this fulfilled. Wars we still have among us: among the nations, for kingship; among the sects, among Jews, pagans, Christians, heretics there are wars, wars abound; some struggle for the truth, others for error. The text is therefore not yet fulfilled, the one which says, "Making wars cease even unto the ends of the earth." But perhaps some day it will be fulfilled. Or has it perhaps been fulfilled in a manner of speaking? In certain respects it has been fulfilled: in the wheat it has been fulfilled, but not yet in the tares.

Hoc nondum videmus esse completum: sunt adhuc bella, sunt inter gentes pro regno; inter sectas, inter Judaeos, Paganos, Christianos, haereticos, sunt bella, crebrescunt bella; aliis pro veritate, aliis pro falsitate certantibus. Nondum ergo completum est, "Auferens bella usque ad fines terra": sed fortasse complebitur. An et modo completum est? In quibusdam completum est; in tritico completum est, in zizaniis nondum completum est. (*PL* 36: 522f.)

Monotheism as a political problem had originated in the Hellenistic transformation of the Jewish faith in God. Insofar as the God of the Jews was amalgamated with the monarchical principle of the Greek philosophers, the concept of the divine Monarchy at first acquired the function of a political-theological propaganda formula for Jews. This political-theological propaganda formula was taken over by the Church in its expansion into the Roman Empire. It then met up with a concept of pagan political theology, according to which the divine Monarch indeed reigned, but the national gods had to rule. In order to counteract this pagan theology, tailored to fit the Roman Empire,[167] it was asserted from the Christian side that the national gods could not rule at all, because national pluralism had been suspended by the Roman Empire. In this sense the Pax Augusta was then interpreted as the fulfillment of the Old Testament eschatological prophecies. Nevertheless, the doctrine of the divine Monarchy was bound to founder on the trinitarian dogma, and the interpretation of the Pax Augusta on Christian eschatology. In this way, not only was monotheism as a political problem resolved and the Christian faith liberated from bondage to the Roman Empire,[168] but a fundamental break was made with every "political theology" that misuses the Christian proclamation for the justification of a political situation. Only on the basis of Judaism and paganism can such a thing as a "political theology" exist. The Christian proclamation of the triune God stands beyond Judaism and paganism, even though the mystery of the Trinity exists only in the Godhead itself, and not in Creation. So too, the peace that the Christian seeks is won by no emperor, but is solely a gift of him who "is higher than all understanding."

The Book on the Angels:
Their Place and Meaning in the Liturgy

S. patri Benedicto[1]

All creatures visible and invisible have a relationship to the Church. The angels are ministers of its saving work, and through the Church there takes place the replacement of their legions lost by the desertion of Satan and his accomplices; but in this recruitment, it is not so much we who are incorporated with the angels, as it is the angels who become part of our unity, because of Jesus, our common head—and more ours than theirs.

BOSSUET, IVe Lettre à une demoiselle de Metz (fourth letter to a young woman from Metz), nr. 8 [*Les grands Écrivains de la France*, vol. 1: *Correspondance* (Paris: Hachette, 1904), p. 61][2]

Prefatory Note

This essay seeks to provide a theological understanding of the place and the meaning of the holy angels in worship. As with other theological disciplines, "pure history" almost completely dominates the study of liturgy today. As a result, the danger exists that the theological understanding of the spiritual function of the holy angels will eventually disappear. I therefore offer these thoughts for consideration.

Introduction

The Church's way leads from the earthly to the heavenly Jerusalem,[3] from the city of the Jews to the city of the angels and saints. The Church's existence between the earthly and the heavenly city determines its nature. Its character is conditioned by the fact that Christians have left the earthly Jerusalem,[4] and, because they have no lasting city on earth (Heb. 13:14),[5] like Abraham they seek one to come, whose builder is God (Heb. 11:8–10). They "have drawn near[6] to the city of the living God, the heavenly Jerusalem, and to countless angels in solemn assembly and to the *ekklēsia* of the firstborn, who are enrolled in heaven as citizens,[7] and God who is judge of all, as well as the souls of the just who have been made perfect, and to Jesus, the mediator of the new covenant" (Heb. 12:22–24). The Church, which draws near to the heavenly Jerusalem, comes to a solemn gathering,[8] in which countless angels, the citizens of the heavenly city, and the souls of the just who have been made perfect partake. It is a cultic gathering that is assembled in heaven, for the heavenly Jerusalem is not only a city but also a temple and a holy shrine, into which Christ as the heavenly High Priest has entered (cf. Heb. 9:24).

The contrast between the earthly and the heavenly Jerusalem is also expressed in St. Paul's Letter to the Galatians. Abraham had two sons, one by a slave woman and one by a free woman. That is an allegory, which the Apostle relates to the two testaments. Hagar is the mother of the slaves, that is, the Jews, who espouse the earthly city; Sarah, on the other hand, stands for the free Jerusalem "above," our mother (Gal. 4:21–27). In Philippians 3:20, Paul expressed our adherence to the heavenly city in an especially pointed way when he says that we "have our commonwealth in heaven,[9] whence we also await our *sōtēr*,[10] Lord Jesus Christ." St. John's visions of the heavenly city in Revelation are in the same vein. It is characteristic that, just as in the Letter to the Hebrews, the image of the heavenly city and of the heavenly temple are interchangeable. Revelation 21, for example, gives a description of the heavenly Jerusalem, which comes down to the earth, but in chapters 4 and 5, we are given a description of divine worship in heaven. Images from the political and the cultic spheres are thus intermingled, exactly as in the Letter to the Hebrews. The earthly Jerusalem, with the Temple cult, is clearly the point of departure for the ideas and images of early Christian literature, though this point of departure has now been left behind and Jerusalem as a political entity, city as well as place of worship, is no longer found on earth but in "heaven," to which Christians' eyes are turned. Perhaps we could also say that, just as the profane *ekklēsia* of antiquity is an institution of the polis, so the Christian *ekklēsia* is an institution of the heavenly city, the heavenly Jerusalem.[11] Just as the profane *ekklēsia* is the assembly of the citizens of the earthly polis to enact legislation, the Christian *ekklēsia* could analogously be defined as the assembly of the citizens[12] of the heavenly city for the accomplishment of specific cultic acts—and the legal enactments of the Christian *ekklēsia* are also cultic acts.[13] On the one hand, a distinction is thus made between heavenly city and *ekklēsia*,[14] while on the other hand, a connection is forged between the heavenly Jerusalem and the *ekklēsia* through the sacraments and worship as such. When St. Paul says, for example, that we are the children of the Jerusalem "above," which is "free," that should be taken to mean that by virtue of baptism, we become children of the heavenly city, indeed its citizens. And when the Letter to the Hebrews says that we have drawn near to the festal gathering, and partake with myriads of angels, citizens of the heavenly city, and souls of the just made perfect, we need to think of this cultic "drawing near" to the festival in heaven in such a way that the liturgy that the Church celebrates on earth is an actual participation in the cult celebrated by the angels in the heavenly city. The words of the Letter to the Hebrews thus take on a pregnant significance.

In short, it is clear that the view of the relationship between the *ekklēsia* and the heavenly city that is being advanced here has implications for our understanding of the nature of Christian worship. For if the Church has left the earthly Jerusalem and its Temple and is now on its way toward the heavenly Jerusalem and its temple, it will necessarily also meet with the residents of the heavenly city, those of whom Hebrews speaks: angels, citizens of heaven, and the just ones who have been made perfect,[15] in a unity mediated by the cult. All cultic acts of the Church would thus either be a participation of the angels in the earthly cult, or, to put it the other way around, all earthly worship by the Church would be understood as participation in the worship that the angels offer to God in heaven. But does this opinion admit of some degree of certitude? Does the testimony of Holy Scripture and of the Church's tradition speak in favor of such a thesis? The following explorations are intended to answer this question.

I

One of the peculiarities of the Revelation of St. John is the way in which its eschatological visions are interrupted by liturgical-hymnic "insertions." To be sure, the concept of "insertions" is not a completely accurate description of the text as it stands. Nevertheless, precisely this is what we need to discuss. Of the seven or eight "insertions" of this type, the first occurs in chapter 4 in the vision of the throne of God, and the second in chapter 5 in connection with the narrative of the opening of the seals of the book of destiny. At the beginning of chapter 4, a voice says to the Seer: "I want to show you what must happen." But then the narrative is not "what must happen" in either chapter. Instead, chapter 4 offers, as has been said, the description of the throne of God and chapter 5 the dramatic account of the opening of the seals of the book of destiny by the "Lamb," and in connection with that, the hymnic praise of the Lamb. From the standpoint of narrative economy, then, chapters 4 and 5 thus have a retarding effect. At the same time, however, that is exactly characteristic for the relationship of primitive Christianity to the eschatological events. The Seer is in no hurry to share his visions, for it is not he who will loosen the seal of the closed book of destiny but the Lamb, who alone is "worthy" to do so.[16] So too is this why Revelation is titled "the Revelation of Jesus Christ" and not "the Revelation of St. John."[17] More urgent than any communications on the eschatological events is the report on the vision of the heavenly throne room and of the heavenly divine liturgy. Or to put it otherwise, certainly, the eschatological events that the visionary sees are important. But the primary thing, over and above every eschatological world event, is the eternal God, "who was and who is and who comes" (4:8) and who in an "eternal world" is glorified unceasingly by the angels. So, then, if the Revelation of St. John is constantly being interrupted by liturgical-hymnic sections, in the final analysis that is not to be explained by resort to the notion of "insertions" but by the theological fact that every eschatological world event is grounded in God's eternal world. A portrayal of the eschatological events in the cosmos therefore has to make manifest the backdrop of an "eternal" world, and the portrayal of the terrible suffering of the eschatological time likewise has as its necessary backdrop the description of a world that has been snatched away from suffering and only knows the praise of God. Seen from this point of view, eschatology and worship are by no means opposites. Amid all the suffering of this worldly age, amid all the turmoil and demonic struggles within this Aeon, there remains eternally and unshakably that worship that the angels render to the Eternal One, in which earthly worship takes part.

The "eternal world" of which Revelation speaks is in "heaven" (4:2), where God's throne stands, which perhaps expresses the fact that it is not "the eternal as such"—or even "the eternal in man"—that is the basis of every happening, but rather that an eternal ruler stands behind the eschatological event.[18] Yet the eternal ruler is invisible—as is every true ruler—and only his throne and the brilliant shining of his dominion, jewel-like,[19] can be seen (4:3). Before the throne are seven flaming torches, which should probably be understood as representing an eternal dominion (4:5),[20] and spreading wide beyond the throne the endless crystal sea of the heavenly ocean (4:6). The actual throne seat is borne by those four living creatures which are first spoken of in Ezekiel 1. Twenty-four elders (4:4) sit around God's throne, here as the heavenly representatives of the "spiritual" Israel.[21] In the description of the four creatures, St. John blends the Cherubim of Ezekiel 1 with the Seraphim spoken of in Isaiah 6.[22] That is typical of him. What really interests him are those angels who utter the Thrice Holy. The whole description of the heavenly court finally culminates in the Thrice Holy cry of the four living creatures. The "eternal world" thus gives voice to the praise of God. It is so completely the end of the eternal world that it is perhaps not the Seraphim, which stand at some distance before God (Isa. 6), that cry out the Thrice Holy, but rather the four living creatures, who bear the throne of God and thus are much closer to him. Because it is intrinsic to the eternal world in which God is enthroned to praise him, therefore they say without ceasing, day and night, "Holy, holy, holy is God the Lord," and so on. Isaiah 6 does not explicitly say that the praise is without ceasing.[23] When Revelation emphasizes that the cry of "Holy" is uttered "day and night," that is connected with the fact that it is the angels that bear God's throne—and not the Seraphim—who, as representatives of that eternal world in which God himself is enthroned, utter the Thrice Holy in order, as it were, that their cry of "Holy" may resound eternally and without ceasing.[24]

The living creatures "give praise and honor and thanksgiving to the one who sits on the throne and lives forever and ever" (v. 9), or, as it says in verse 8: "to the almighty God, who was and who is and who is coming." To the eternal God the praise of the eternal world is fitting. But consider for a moment the richness of the expression "Praise, honor, and thanksgiving."[25] The first two terms move on the same plane. The "thanksgiving" (Greek *eucharistia*), however, is only possible when God has in some way revealed himself. The fact that the God of eternity is named as "he who was, who is, and who is coming" shows that this third designation of the praise of God is intrinsically distinct from the first two.[26] Here too the third member diverges from the first two. One expects to hear it said, "he who was, who is, and who will be," instead of which we hear "who is coming." The ontological figure of "eternity" is subverted in the third member by the phrase "who is coming." In the same way, the figure of cosmic praise is subverted by this *eucharistia*. The praise of the eternal world, which is appropriate for the God of eternity, is not simply a praise that arises from the nature of an eternal cosmos, but is also "thanksgiving," *eucharistia*. This shows how it is possible to move from praise that stems from the very being of an eternal cosmos to thanksgiving for God's will, or, to put it in other terms, the possibility of the link between the heavenly and the earthly liturgies. This link is expressed in chapter 4 of Revelation by the twenty-four elders' taking up of the praise of the throne angels. The twenty-four elders are the representatives of the spiritual Israel, meaning the Church. Thus it is not as though the angels' cry of "Holy" resounds only from within a world in which the Eternal One is enthroned; to this we must add the angelic world's knowledge of God's manifestation in creation and redemption,[27] by virtue of which their cry of "Holy" receives its character as *eucharistia*.

The twenty-four elders, before intoning their hymn, perform obeisance to the one who sits on the throne.[28] We have the impression that the setting is a heavenly throne room rather than a heavenly temple.[29] They also cast down their wreaths or crowns.[30] They are wearing crowns, therefore they are kings. On the other hand, they are also priests, as 8:5 shows. It is thus the "royal priesthood" (v. 10) that is falling down before the one who sits on the throne.[31] These royal priests sing a hymn after the Thrice Holy of the throne angels has been heard:

Worthy are you, our Lord and God,
To receive glory and honor and power,
For you have created all things,
And by your will they existed and were created.

This hymn is fundamentally an acclamation. The acclamations appear here because they are fitting for the God who, like a king, possesses his throne for eternity.[32] They are heard on the lips of the twenty-four elders because they too, insofar as they are "kings," belong to the political world. That is an important acknowledgement: the worship of the heavenly Church, and therefore implicitly too of the earthly Church's liturgy, which is joined with that of the heavenly, has an original relationship to the political world,[33] consisting in the fact that the Christians have left the earthly Jerusalem, which is at once polis and temple, in order to draw near to the heavenly temple and the heavenly polis.[34] Therefore, too, God is seen as a king, and likewise is it stressed that his priests are "royal priests." Not just "royal" in the sense that they serve a king, but in the deeper sense that they themselves are kings, sit on thrones, and wear crowns or wreaths. Now it becomes understandable why the hymn takes on the form of an acclamation, beginning from the "Worthy are you" up to the "to receive glory, honor, and power."[35] To be sure, the praise of the elders is not somehow cancelled out by the concept of an acclamation, just as little as their character as priests is cancelled by the fact that they are "kings." They are priests, too, and so the praise of the elders is not only an acclamation but also a doxology or, as here, a hymn:

For you have created all things,
And by your will they existed and were created.

It is noteworthy how in the strophes of the hymn that praise God's manifestation in creation, God's unfathomable will is also emphasized—a formulation that is meant to express the sovereignty of the king of eternity.

Chapter 5 of Revelation tells of the undoing of the seal on the scroll that lies in the hand of the eternal king. An angel asks: "Who is worthy to open the book and loosen the seals?" No one is able to open it—neither angel nor man nor demon (v. 3). John begins to weep, but an angel consoles him. "The Lion of Judah has triumphed" (v. 5). When "the Lamb that was slain" takes the book in his hand, the four throne angels and the twenty-four elders fall down in obeisance before the Lamb (v. 8). The text shows that the throne angels, who sing the Thrice Holy, are not there simply to carry the throne of God and as the bearers of the ruler of eternity to give him glory. No—for they are also devoted to the Lamb, and that makes understandable why, as I have previously explained, they also pronounce the "thanksgiving" as well as giving "praise and honor." Along with the throne angels, the twenty-four elders also fall down, for the worship of the Church in heaven, as on earth, derives from the fact that the Lamb has taken the scroll from the right hand of God and has loosened the seals. And when the angel asks the entire spiritual cosmos (v. 3) who is worthy to open the book and loosen its seals, the Church now answers him through the mouths of the twenty-four elders:

Worthy are you to take the scroll and to open its seals,
For you were slain and by your blood did ransom men for God
From every tribe and tongue and people and nation,
And have made them a kingdom and priests,
And they shall rule on earth.

The angel had said: "The Lion of Judah has triumphed." The Lamb is thus judged worthy to open God's scroll and to loosen its seals. The opening of the book is linked to the victory of the Lion of Judah. The hymn of the heavenly Church is thus a triumphal hymn (*epinikion*). No other "victor" can open the book, meaning that no purely political decision, which is tied to a "victory" on earth, is able to read the book of destiny that lies in the hand of God. Only the victory of the Lion of Judah loosens the seals of the book of history's destiny, and that is what makes the elders sound their praise. While in chapter 4, we had the elders' hymn as a sort of continuation of the "Holy" cry of the throne angels, now in chapter 5, we hear the elders' praise after the metaphysical question of the angel as to who will open the book of destiny. When the Church thus in her hymns praises the Lamb that was slain, that is because she realizes the superiority of the Lion of Judah over all the "kings of the earth,"[36] because she knows a kingship and priesthood that it superior to all other kingships and priesthoods, because it has been won from every "tribe and tongue and people and nation."[37] The Church's hymnody is the transcending of all national hymns, just as the Church's speech is the transcending of all languages. That is so because the victory of the Lion of Judah has transcended the victory of all the kings of the earth and is therefore worthy to open the book of destiny on the right hand of God. It was noted earlier that the Church's worship has an original relationship to the political world, and we are now able to grasp that still more precisely by the reference to the "victory" of the Lamb. The victory of the Lamb founds a new polis. "Cuius rex est et conditor Christus [whose (= the City of God) king and founder is Christ]," as St. Augustine says (*City of God* 17.4.2; cf. also 20.4). By his "blood" are we purchased from the "tribes, tongues, peoples, and nations," that is, we have been freed from the natural captivity to "tribes, tongues, peoples, and nations." The blood of the Lamb has created a new people, the people of the Christians, as the Church Fathers are forever saying.[38] Over against all national hymns, the hymn of the Church is thus a "final," eschatological hymn, just as the people that intones this hymn is a final "holy people."[39] And the hymn is eschatological because the Lamb that was slain transcends all human history, in that to him alone is granted the opening of the seals of the book that lies in the hand of God. But in the same measure, then, is the knowledge of the Church, which stands behind its worship and hymnody, a "final" knowledge,[40] because it has subordinated every other knowledge, such as for example that derived from the political situation of a people.[41] That the Church's hymn is a final hymn, that it is an eschatological hymn, is expressed by St. John with the words "They sing a new song" (v. 9). The "new song" is the hymn of the New Age,[42] imperishable as it itself is, while every type of ethnic singing, folk music, and national anthem eventually succumbs to its inevitable decline.

The new song of the elders does not resound alone, but an immense number of angels takes up the song and intones a loud cry:

Worthy is the Lamb that was slain,
To take power and riches and wisdom
And strength and honor and glory and blessing.

This is not actually a hymn but rather an acclamation-like doxology. The genuinely predicative content typical of a hymn is lacking. In general, the text also says that the angels, the throne creatures, and the elders all utter this cry together.[43] This already tells us that what we have here is not an actual hymn but rather a doxology. This cry of the entire heavenly spiritual world is meaningful when the new song of the elders praises the creation of the new people of the royal priests.[44] The new people, which transcends every other people, is greeted with a cry from the heavenly spiritual world, which as doxology transcends every political acclamation of the peoples of this world.

It is significant that the doxology speaks of "the Lamb that was slain" and not merely of the Lamb as such. The Lamb that was slain is probably an imperial symbol [*Reichssymbol*], a symbol of the New Age, of the final, eternal, and indestructible kingdom. It thus stands in contrast to the beasts of prey, which according to the Book of Daniel symbolize the kingdoms of this world. But it should be noticed that it is the Lamb that was slain and not simply the Lamb as such. We have to do here, not with the pacifist opposition of domestic animal and beast of prey, but with the sacrificial animal and beast of prey.

To the praise of the throne angels, elders, and angels is joined the praise of the whole cosmos, meaning the visible cosmos, which is thus linked with the praise of the heavenly spiritual world:

To the One who sits on the throne and to the Lamb,
Blessing[45] and honor and glory and power
Unto ages of ages.

The visible cosmos also utters an acclamation-like doxology, joining in so doing with the myriads of angels. The visible cosmos praises the One who sits on the throne and the Lamb. Thus the cosmos praises not simply its creator but also its redeemer, the Lamb. In this fact is grounded the possibility of a sermon to the birds and fishes, indeed the whole creation waits in yearning and longing for "the revelation of the sons of God" (Rom. 8:19).[46] And when the visible creation in all its parts has uttered its doxology, the throne creatures call out "Amen" (v. 12). It is instructive that the praise that began with the throne angels and found its end in the visible creation can only be intensified with the Amen cry of the throne angels. With this is concluded Revelation's description of the heavenly cultus in chapters 4 and 5. After the Amen only one further thing remains: the obeisance of the elders (5:14), the parting gesture, which stands as a wordless action along with the Amen of the throne angels, in order to bear witness through the expression of the body what could only appear questionable as an expression of the tongue.

This concludes the exposition of chapters 4 and 5 of Revelation. What are we to conclude from it? The first thing is this: according to Holy Scripture, in heaven God is offered worship by the angels and the blessed.[47] But in the persons of the elders, this worship is given a connection with the Church on earth. The worship of the heavenly Jerusalem, as described by Revelation, is defined by the singing of the Sanctus, of the triumph songs, of the psalms (Rev. 19:6), of the "new song" and, as chapter 19 shows, also by the Alleluia cry. Finally, the heavenly cultus still knows the Amen acclamation. We thus have to do with a liturgy, as the frequently occurring cult-formulas demonstrate.[48] My thesis that there is a worship in heaven in which the earthly Church takes part is thus confirmed by Sacred Scripture. Characteristic for this worship in heaven is the way in which political and religious symbolic expressions are thoroughly intermingled,[49] which is shown most clearly in the resemblance of the doxologies to acclamations. That the heavenly worship described in Revelation has an original relationship to the political sphere is explained by the fact that the apostles left the earthly Jerusalem, which was both a political and a cultic center, in order to turn toward the heavenly Jerusalem, which is both a city and royal court, and yet also a temple and cult site. With this is connected the further point: that the Church's anthem transcends national anthems, as the Church's language transcends all other languages.[50]

Finally, it is to be noted this eschatological transcending has as its ultimate result the fact that the entire cosmos is incorporated into its praise. This eschatological incorporation of the cosmos in divine praise has nothing whatsoever to do (if I may put it that way) with the "natural" divine praise of creation as we know it in the hymns and poetry of the many peoples (Greeks, Egyptians, Hebrews, etc.). It appears here in Christianity because the entire cosmos is affected by the eschatological events, or, as a variant of the Thrice Holy in the Letter of Clement has it, because "the whole creation is full of the divine glory" (1 Clem. 34:6).[51]

Having demonstrated that according to Sacred Scripture, the rites of the Church participate in the liturgy celebrated in heaven by the angels and the blessed, let us now seek proof of this in ecclesiastical tradition as well.

II

In the Liturgy of St. Mark, practiced by the Christians of Alexandria, we encounter the following prayer:

You are raised above every principality and power, virtue and dominion and every other name that is named, not only in this world, but in the world to come as well. Around you stand a thousand times a thousand and ten thousand times ten thousands of angels and the hosts of archangels. Around you stand the two most worthy creatures, the many-eyed Cherubim and the six-winged Seraphim, who cover their faces with two wings and cover their feet with two and fly with two. With tireless voice and with never-silent praises of God, they cry out to one another the threefold holy victory hymn, with which they sing, cry, glorify, call out and say to your great glory: "Holy, holy, holy is the Lord of Hosts, heaven and earth are full of your glory." At all times everything hallows you. So then, Lord God, accept too our hallowing, which with all who hallow you we praise and say [as the people]: "holy, holy, holy is the Lord of Hosts, heaven and earth are full of your glory."[52]

The core of this prayer derives from Isaiah 6, the vision of the prophet in the Temple. But the text is modified in the Christian liturgy in a very suggestive way. Isaiah gazes on "the glory of the Lord" in the temple, but the Christian liturgy in heaven. The gaze that is directed at the Lord thus finds its object not in the usual direction of the eye, but rather is directed on high: "You are raised above every principality and power, virtue and dominion and every other name that is named, not only in this world but in the world to come." This broadening of the Isaiah text has been expressed with words from St. Paul's letter to the Ephesians (1:21). But in the passage from Ephesians, St. Paul's words are used in connection with a mention of the ascension of Christ and his sitting at the right hand of the Father. We now understand better why the horizon has changed in comparison with Isaiah. In the liturgy, the Isaiah vision has been broadened into a cosmic dimension, because in the meantime, Christ's ascension has occurred. But Christ's ascension, for its part, is only an expression of the fact that the entire cosmos has been drawn into a suffering-with through the eschatological events linked with Christ. The ascension of Christ, his sitting at the right hand of the Father, expresses for us the utter distance of God.[53] This separation from God is so great that, while at first the angels are still named that have a function (rule, authority, power, and dominion) and are thus also capable of being named, ultimately the sphere of any type of denomination is left behind, or more precisely, the sphere of any possibility of being named: "You have been raised above every name that has been named not only in this age but also in the one to come" (Eph. 1:21). The description of God's distance appears to want to slip into negative formulations, even though the symbolic power of the prophetic vision prevents this slippage into conceptual negations. But here too, in the reappropriation of Isaiah's vision, we find a characteristic expansion in comparison with the prophet's vision. Isaiah sees only seraphim in his vision, but the Christian liturgy adds angels, archangels, and cherubim. This widening of the Isaiah vision through the enumeration of the choirs of angels is a characteristic feature of the Christian liturgy in contrast to the Jewish.[54] It is worth noting with how firm an instinct the sequence—angels, archangels, cherubim, and seraphim—of the added choirs of angels has been chosen. The conceptual elaboration that has left behind the sphere of all naming, indeed the very possibility of naming, now brings us gradations of new and ever-expanding classifications. The "thousand times a thousand and ten thousand times ten thousand of holy angels" (Dan. 7:10) still stand, as it were, on the border of the heavenly vision that first in the seraphim, as the prophet saw it, now finds its ultimate visual portrayal.

We can thus identify a double expansion in the Christian liturgy, in comparison with the vision of the prophet. First, the horizon has been expanded beyond the local, from the Temple it has become heaven,[55] and from the earthly Jerusalem, the heavenly. Second, the vision of the seraphim itself only becomes visible against the background of a hierarchically ordered angelic world. Both expansions of the vision of Isaiah show finally that the need for a transcending of the prophetic vision has been given a verbal expression. This need for a transcending of the prophetic vision remained alien to Judaism. Judaism (referring here to orthodox Judaism) knew only a military rather than an actually hierarchical structuring of the angelic world, and it never abandoned the connection between the angels' cry of "Holy" and the Temple in Jerusalem. Proof of this is the Jewish form of the Sanctus (the so-called Qedusha), which broadened the Isaiah text with the cry of the cherubim in Ezekiel 3:12: "Praised be the glory of Yahweh from his house," for through this addition is expressed the idea that "the glory" of God dwells only in the Temple of Jerusalem ("in his place"). For the Christians, however, the glory of God has its tent, not in the Temple of Jerusalem, but in the temple of the body of Jesus (cf. John 1:14), and if Isaiah once had seen the glory of God, so had he seen the glory of Jesus (John 12:41). All the details in the New Testament about the divine glory are defined by this fact and should only be interpreted on its basis.[56] Thus Saint Paul also says that the Jews had once seen the glory of God (Rom. 9:4), and Eusebius says in his *Proof of the Gospel* that the glory of God had left the city of Jerusalem in order to dwell on the Mount of Olives, where Christ ascended to heaven (6.18.23 [ed. Heikel, 278]).[57] So too it then follows that, when the glory of God moves away from the Temple of Jerusalem into the heavenly Jerusalem, the Sanctus cry of the angels, which serves the glory of God, must likewise move into the temple in heaven. But from the heavenly Jerusalem, in which the Sanctus cry echoes, as we perceived in

Revelation 4:8, the call of the angels resounds in the earthly *ekklēsia* of the Christians, who have drawn near to the heavenly city, so that the Church too joins in with the Thrice Holy of the angels.[58] Because the glory of God is no longer there in the Temple in Jerusalem but rather in the Church of Christ, when it is gathered in worship with the angels in heaven, the diction of the prophetic vision has also therefore changed: from the Temple in Jerusalem becomes "heaven and earth,"[59] which are full of the glory of God, and the seraphim too only become visible against the background of an angelic hierarchy that is known through the ascension of Christ. It is thus a mistake to say, as people constantly do, that in the liturgy the "Isaiah citation" has been variously "expanded"; that would mean treating the Christian liturgy as a literary work,[60] which it certainly is not. What we really mean is that the vision of the prophet has undergone a widening, because the glory of God no longer dwells in the Temple of Jerusalem but in the temple of the body of Christ,[61] who has risen into heaven.

It is also noteworthy that the Christian liturgy was not satisfied just to repeat the simple expression of the prophet, according to which the seraphim "cry out and say": "Holy, holy, holy is the Lord of Hosts." Instead, in strikingly full phrasing, the Christian liturgy says: "With tireless voice and with never-silent praises of God, they cry out to one another the threefold holy victory hymn, with which they sing, cry, glorify, call out and say: 'Holy, holy, holy is the Lord of Hosts, heaven and earth are full of your glory.'" In contrast to Isaiah, the eternal duration of the cry of "Holy" is thereby emphasized,[62] as we have already seen with regard to the Sanctus in Revelation 4:8. Earlier, it was noted that this stress on the unceasing praise of God by the angels is unknown in Judaism.

Perhaps in the words "For all time, everything hallows you," the liturgy is pointing us toward this idea of a ceaseless praise. For if "everything"— and that means the whole of creation—is offering its eschatological praise to God, then that praise is also offered to him "at all times." In contrast, just as the Sanctus of the seraphim is heard only in the Temple of Jerusalem, and is thus spatially confined, the praise of the angels is temporally limited to the same degree, as the witnesses cited above show. We should, accordingly, see in the idea of the unceasing praise of the angels a polemical usage over against Judaism, in which are expressed the departure from the Temple in Jerusalem and the turn toward the eschatological praise of God in the whole cosmos.

The verbal expression for "the hallowing" of God by the angels has become much more differentiated in the liturgy, as compared with Isaiah. The liturgy says: "they sing, call, glorify, cry out, and say" (cf. in the Mozarabic Liturgy, for example, "perenni jubilatione decantant adorant magnificant [with perpetual joy they sing, adore, and magnify]" [Marius Férotin, ed., *Le "Liber ordinum" en usage dans l'Église wisigothique et mozarabe d'Espagne* (*The Book of Orders* Used in the Visigothic and Mozarabic Church in Spain), Monumenta ecclesiae liturgica, 5 (Paris, 1904), 339]). This richness of expression should not be seen as simply a later liturgical development, for we already find this notable phenomenon in Christianity's beginnings. As I said earlier, the richness of expression in the liturgy corresponds to a comparable richness in the Book of Revelation, which speaks of "Praise, honor, and thanksgiving" (4:9) and "Blessing, glory, wisdom, thanksgiving, honor, might, and power" (7:12).[63] Although the individual words can be traced back to the Old Testament (in the form of the Septuagint), the frequency of substantives used synonymously with the word "glory" goes far beyond the earlier proportion.[64] We probably need to recognize here the same striving identifiable in the extension from the [Jerusalem] Temple to heaven, from the earth to the whole cosmos, and from the simple expression of praise to the ceaseless act of praising. The act of giving praise has to be transcended, just as the glory that the giving of praise serves was transcended. Thus it will not be enough to explain the differentiation of expression by saying that it is not the seraphim alone but the entire angelic world that participates in the "hallowing" of God. The "crying out and saying" (so Isaiah) is not supposed to be seen as a natural "crying out and saying," but as a "mystical" giving of praise, at once a "singing, calling out, and glorifying," meaning that through these usages the voices of the angels are supposed to be made as it were transparent. The attempt to characterize the voices of the angels runs parallel to this. According to the Liturgy of Saint James, they sing with "bright" voices (F. E. Brightman, *Liturgies Eastern and Western*, vol. 1: *Eastern Liturgies* [Oxford, 1896], 50.29f., and the liturgy of the Syrian Jacobites, ibid., 86.9), according to St. Ephrem with "the sounds of harps" (Hubert Grimme, *Der Strophenbau in den Gedichten des Ephraems des Syrers* [Strophe Construction in the Poems of Ephrem the Syrian] [Freiburg in der Schweiz, 1893], 25), according to the Slavic Enoch with "soft" voices (20:4), according to St. Ambrose: *cum suavitate canorae vocis* (with the sweetness of a melodious voice) (*in Ps.* 1:2 [*PL* 14: 965A]; cf. *canoris vocibus* (with melodious voices) in Cassiodorus, *in Ps.* 32 [*PL* 70.226D]). Examples could easily be multiplied.

I believe I have shown in the preceding discussion that all the changes in the Isaiah citation in the liturgy can be explained by a single, coherent theological principle. Because the Christians left the Temple of Jerusalem in order to draw near to the temple in heaven; because the glory of God no longer dwells in the earthly temple, but rather in the temple of the body of Jesus, who has ascended into heaven: therefore the Sanctus no longer echoes on earth, but in heaven; therefore the seraphim are seen against the background of the orders of angels; therefore the cry of the angels becomes an eternal hymn; therefore the voice of the angels becomes transparent; and therefore too heaven is full of the glory of God. That in contrast to the wording of the prophet, the changes in the Sanctus cry of the liturgy have to be interpreted in light of the Christian revelation is confirmed through its continuation in the text of the Liturgy of St. Mark in every form, where it says: "Truly are heaven and earth full of your glory by the epiphany of our Lord and God and savior Jesus Christ" (Brightman, 132.11f.). The other liturgies, and along with them the Roman Mass, give expression to the Christian understanding of the Sanctus in that they add the "Hosanna in excelsis. Benedictus, qui venit in nomine Domini" to the Sanctus.[65] That is just the final and direct statement that the Christian liturgy's cry of "Holy" is directed in a way essentially different from the prophetic version of the cry of "Holy."[66] It is arranged differently because through Christ everything has been transcended: the sites of the glory of God, as well as the position of the seraphim, their voice, and also the character of their call. This transcending signifies expansion into the cosmic dimension (heaven instead of the Temple) and incorporation into a whole (seraphim along with other orders of angels), the irruption of the eternal into the hymnody (the unceasing character of the praise), and an ineffable refinement and spiritualization of the voice of the angels (the expansive phrasing of the "hallowing").

That the Church should join in with its version of the angels' Sanctus cry is dictated by the very nature of its liturgy. In the first instance, this means that the Church's worship is not that of a human religious society whose liturgy is tied to a temple. Rather, it is a worship that permeates the entire cosmos, in which sun, moon, and all the stars take part. That is how it is put in the Liturgy of St. James, for example:

whom the heavens and the heavens of heavens and all their power praise, sun and moon and all the hosts of the stars, earth, sea, and all that is in them, and the heavenly Jerusalem, the festal assembly, the Church of the firstborn, who are enrolled as citizens in heaven, the spirits of the just and of the prophets, the souls of martyrs and of apostles, angels, archangels, etc.[67]

Or one could quote the first of the prayers of Ps.-Cyprian:

Cui angeli archangeli milia milium martyrum chorus apostolorum et prophetarum gloria exultant, cui omnes aves laudes canunt, linguae confitentur caelestium terrestrium et infernorum: tibi omnes aquae in caelo et sub caelo confitentur, te insensibilia sentient [For whom angels, archangels, thousands of martyrs, a chorus of apostles and prophets exult in glory, for whom the birds sing praises, (whom) tongues of those in heaven, on earth, and under the earth confess: you all the waters in heaven and under heaven confess, even those things without sense are aware of you].[68]

It is always the entire cosmos that participates in the praise of God, though this is something that could not be conceived of had Christ's ascension not torn open heaven. The heaven of the angels is, if I may put it this way, the most central, the most spiritual part of the cosmos. Therefore, even if the praise of sun, moon and stars, and so on, should vanish from the liturgy (as in the prefaces of the Roman Mass), the singing of the angels would never be permitted to disappear from the Church's worship, for that is what first gives the Church's praise the depth and transcendence that are called for by the character of the Christian revelation. As an eschatological cultus, the worship of the Church originates, not in the self-satisfying, self-enclosed natural order, but in a human mode of being that is transcended by the higher order of being of the angels, and that is first stimulated to its own act of praise by the praise of the spiritual world.

Humanity's act of praise is first joined with the angels' praise: that tells us that in the liturgy, humanity is seen only in a total cosmic context, and that humanity's praising is concerned specifically with this cosmic totality. So when humanity's act of praise is joined first with the angels' praise (cf. the "Cum quibus [angels] et nostras voces ut admitti jubeas, deprecamur" [With these (angels) we pray thee join our voices also] in the Preface for Quadragesima Sunday in the Roman Mass; likewise in the Preface for the feast of the Holy Cross),[69] a further inference follows: the "hallowing" of God in humanity's act of praise is not as aboriginal as the angels' praise. Humanity must first be exhorted to give praise to God in the cultus.[70] Through the [Mass of the Faithful to the Canon's] "Gratias agamus Domino Deo nostro" [Let us give thanks to the Lord our God], we are reminded of our duty, and by its "Dignum et justum est" [It is right and just], we are solemnly bound to this service.[71] Therefore we also pray in the Our Father that "hallowed be thy name," "on earth as it is" already hallowed "in heaven"—by the angels.[72] In this fact—that the hallowing of God in humanity's act of praise is not as original as the angel's cry of "Holy"—is grounded the difference between the heavenly and the earthly liturgy.

That the Church joins in with the angels' cry of Sanctus also means that the Church's liturgy is incorporated into a great order, because the seraphim too, whose song the Church takes up, are incorporated into an order of other angels. This pull toward incorporation in the Church's cultus does not originate in a human need for order, but rather in that divine will for order that entails redeemed humanity as the tenth *ordo* after the nine *ordines angelorum* (Gregory the Great *Homilies on the Gospels*, bk. 2, *Hom.* 34 [*PL* 76: 1249C]).[73] For, as St. Augustine says, "adiungitur ista Ecclesia, quae nunc peregrina est, illi coelesti Ecclesiae, ubi angelos cives habemus [that Church which is now on pilgrimage is joined with the heavenly Church, where we have the angels as citizens]" (sermon 341.9 [*PL* 39: 1500]). Christ is "totius caput civitatis Jerusalem, omnibus connumeratis fidelibus ab initio usque in finem, adiunctis etiam legionibus et exercitibus angelorum, ut fiat illa una civitas sub uno rege et una quaedam provincia sub uno imperatore, felix in perpetua pace et salute, laudans Deum sine fine, beata sine fine [the head of the whole city of Jerusalem, when all the faithful from the beginning (of time) until the end have been gathered together, and are joined by legions and armies of angels, to make that one city under one king and one province under one emperor, happy in perpetual peace and safety praising God without end, blessed without end]" (Augustine, *in Ps.* 36 [*PL* 36: 385]).[74]

The cultus of the Church thus culminates in the religio-political dimension or, to put it differently, in the *ordo* concept of a heavenly hierarchy.[75] So the thesis that the Christian cultus has an original relationship to the political sphere is confirmed once again. As this will to order excludes the arbitrariness of purely individual formulations from the liturgy, it also has an intrinsic tendency—this will immediately be clear from the preceding argument—to alter the Church's worship into a service similar to the worship of the angels. That, however, is only possible if within the cultus a song of praise is constructed that essentially resembles the song of praise of the angels—if, in other words, the number of the angelic orders is increased by the order of angel-like priests and monks. To the essential definition of a monk (in the ancient sense of the word) belongs the fact that the monk imitates the angels' way of being and thereby also imitates in the monastic order the liturgy that is tied to the angelic existence.[76] That means two things: first, that the monk in the monastic *officium* joins *freely* in the hymnic praise of the angels, while the people, in the Mass, need a summons first to join in the angels' cry of Holy. Second, it means that the monk takes part *continuously* in the hymnic praise of the angelic orders, who sing God's praise unceasingly.

Through this voluntary and continuous participation in the hymnic praise of the angelic orders, there thus appears in the Church—and that means above all in the Church's worship—the new order of the monks, and thereby also the new distinction between the people and the monastic order. The distinction between priests and people (*laos*, laity) quite obviously means something different from the distinction between the people and the monastic order. In the first case, the distinction consists in the divine institution of the priesthood; in the second case, however, [it consists in the fact that] the monk's voluntary incorporation in an order that is like [that of] the angels obliges the monk to an act of praise like that of the angels. A further inference also follows: the song of the angel-like monks must have a different significance from that of the Sanctus cry of the people. When the people join in the "Sanctus, sanctus, sanctus," what they are doing is not fundamentally a song but rather an acclamation. The people confirm and declare that it is "truly right and just" when the angels call out their "Holy, holy, holy" before the divine majesty. When, on the other hand, the monks join in the cry of the angels, their cry becomes a hymn,[77] just as the call of the seraphim in the Christian liturgy was transformed from a crying out (in Isaiah)[78] into a victory hymn (the Liturgy of St. John Chrysostom, etc.).[79] We now understand even better why the liturgy speaks not only of a "crying and saying" but also of a "singing, calling out, and glorifying." In the linguistic richness of expression of these verbs is reflected the transformation of the acclamation into the hymn (and, as we have yet to see, from the singing of psalms into the hymn). An acclamation is uttered in the *hic et nunc* of natural time, but the hymnody of the angels in the endlessness of eternity. Hence it is said of the angels that with "inexhaustible voice and never-silent laudations" they sing the victory hymn of the Thrice Holy; by the same token, a continuous participation in the liturgy of the angels can only take place in the form of recitation of the office day and night. For "quisquis caste et innocenter assidue utitur vigiliis, angelorum vitam procul dubio meditatur [whoever chastely, innocently, and tirelessly practices vigils, without doubt shares the life of the angels]" (*Augustini Sermones*, ed. Morin, 1: 458.28–30—see the whole context of this sermon).

It should now need no further explanation when we hear it said with respect to the singing of the angels, and to participation in it, that "the people," meaning the laity, no longer belong to the cosmic chain. The people remain disconnected, just as the "thousand times a thousand and ten thousand of ten thousands of angels" remain detached from the archangels, living creatures, cherubim, and seraphim. On this basis we also grasp the meaning of a passage in Origen,[80] who once made the profound remark that "the singing of psalms is the business of human beings, but the singing of hymns belongs to the angels and to those who live like the angels" (*Selections on the Psalms*, on Ps. 118:71). Behind this statement stands the Alexandrian theologian's perception that psalms are appropriate to the "practical" life (*praktikos bios*), whereas hymns are part of the "contemplative" life (*bios theōrētikos*).[81] That Origen's assertion is expressing the difference between the people's singing and the singing of the monks is at any rate clear.[82] Certainly, the people possess not only the possibility of acclamation, but also that of psalm singing, whereas the angels and those who live like angels leave behind both acclamations and psalm singing, for the order of eternity could only issue in hymn singing.[83] In this sense, we also see how a transcending of the literary genre, namely, the genre of the psalms, has occurred in favor of the genre of the hymns in the cultus of the Church—a transcending that runs parallel to the other transcendings already discussed.[84] Thereby, too, we arrive at the ultimate fact that the singing of the monks is essentially different from the singing of the people. The people sing with natural voices in the natural order of things. Nor, obviously, does any of this change if, say, a choir trained in polyphonic singing should take the place of the people. By contrast, the singing of the monks is always the singing of people whose entire existence has been raised above that of the natural order of things and who have approximated the being of the angels. And so their singing will always contain within itself something of the sounds of the cosmos and the praise of the angels.

The fact that the singing of those like the angels does not include polyphony is grounded in the angelic order, for the angels all sing "with one voice."[85] Because, furthermore, the cultus that is offered to God in heaven employs as its sole instrument the voice of the angels (if I can put it this way), without any type of mechanical musical instrument, it is also ruled out for the singing of the angel-like monks to be accompanied with musical instruments. It is well known that the early Church exerted great efforts to prohibit all musical instruments in Christian worship, even though Jewish worship in the Temple had possessed a series of musical instruments that every interpreter of the Psalter has had to deal with. The only way to understand this exclusion of musical instruments is to realize that the apostles have left Jerusalem, with its Temple music, and have drawn near to the heavenly Jerusalem, in which there are no musical instruments of any kind, and the angelic existence has become the only instrument of divine praise.[86] If the musical instruments in the Psalter are regarded from this point of view, is it surprising that Christian existence is also subjected to the same interpretation?[87] "You are trumpet, lyre, zither, tympanum, chorus, chords, and organ and beautifully sounding cymbals. You are all these things—let nothing here be thought vulgar, nothing transitory, nothing silly [Vos estis tuba, psalterium, cithara, tympanum, chorus, chordae et organum et cymbala bene sonantia. Vos estis haec omnia; nihil hic vile, nihil transitorium, nihil ludicrum cogitetur]": these are St. Augustine's words, expressed in his commentary on Psalm 150, words that also express the conviction of all the Church Fathers.

Finally, it is also not accidental that medieval treatises on music begin their expositions with reference to the harmony of the spheres.[88] Because the Church's act of praise is expressed together with the praise of the cosmos, every meditation on the role of music in the cultus of the Church must also therefore take notice of the kind of praise of the sun, moon, and stars.[89] Theological meditation on the character of Christian worship will define the resounding of the spheres and the singing of the angels and the joint singing of those like the angels. The harmony of the spheres resounds, the singing of the angels echoes, the liturgy of the Church is heard. The sun resounds, because it revolves,[90] the angel sings, because he stands, but humanity participates in the praise of the cosmos and the angels because it has been summoned to do so by the Church, through the mouth of the priest. Between the movement of the spheres and their resounding, there exists an inner connection analogous to that between the standing of the angels and their singing. The cosmos resounds in its own right and proclaims in its ordering that it does not transgress the laws of the Creator. But the angel sings, meaning that he does not resound in his own right, as does the cosmos, because he has been raised above the cosmos in order to serve God. The liturgy of the Church, finally, is expressed in "jubilation," the jubilation that once burst forth from the hearts of the disciples, "when they saw raised up to heaven the one whom they had mourned as dead. Words were incapable of expressing such joy, all that was left to them was to rejoice over what no man was able to explain."[91] It is clear that all the different specifications of being that focus on the cosmos, the angel, and humanity, likewise contain musical specifications. As the last musical specification, that of the individual human being, proves, that depends ultimately on the participation of humanity in the heavenly liturgy. One possibility for that exists in the laity's participation in popular liturgical singing; the other possibility is for humanity to be incorporated into the order of those who are like the angels, meaning the ones who participate in the monastic office. But always, the Church's liturgy means its participation in a heavenly liturgy.

This completes my analysis of the Liturgy of St. Mark. My thesis, according to which the whole earthly worship of the Church is to be understood as a participation in the worship that the angels offer to God in heaven, has been confirmed, not only on the basis of Sacred Scripture but also on the basis of the Church's tradition, as expressed in the liturgy. One may object, however, that the first part of my thesis, which speaks of a participation of the angels in the Church's worship, has yet to be proven. In what follows, I shall attempt to provide this demonstration in the form of the individual sacraments, without, of course, making any claim to completeness as a theological analysis.

Beginning with baptism: in the Christian tradition of antiquity, there are two passages in which the angelic world is brought into connection with the sacrament of holy baptism. The first point is the consecration of the baptismal water, which is brought into relationship with the angel. In baptismal homilies, the narrative about the pool in Jerusalem in the Gospel of John (5:4) was not infrequently interpreted as a type of Christian baptism.[92] This would suggest the appropriation of the angel from the Johannine *perikopē* [passage] into the prayer for the consecration of the baptismal water. The oldest witness for the linkage of the baptismal water with the angel is Tertullian, in his treatise on baptism, which says in chapter four:[93] "medicatis quodammodo aquis per angeli interventum [when the waters have in some sense been endowed with healing power by the intervention of the angel]," and in chapter six declares: "in aqua emundati sub angelo spiritui sancto praeparamur [cleansed in the water under the angel's presence, we are made ready for the Holy Spirit]," and further: "angelus baptismi arbiter superventuro Spiritui Sancto vias dirigit abolitione delictorum [by the removal of sins, the baptismal angel as witness makes straight the way for the Holy Spirit to descend from on high]." In the African church, we find a further witness for this perception in Optatus, who argued against the Donatists: "unde vobis angelum, qui apud vos possit fontem movere [how do you have an angel who is able to move the font for you?]" (*De schismate Donatistarum adversus Parmenianum* [On the Donatist Schism, Against Parmenian] 2.6 [ed. Zirosa, 43]). Then we have in the Gelasian Sacramentary a prayer for the consecration of the baptismal water, in which it says: "et super has abluendis aquas et vivificandis hominibus praeparatas angelum sanctitatis emittas, quo peccatis vitae prioris ablutis, reatuque deterso, purum sancto Spiritui habitaculum in regeneratis procuret [and may you send forth the angel of holiness on these waters, made ready to cleanse human beings and restore them to life, and once their guilt is removed, may he provide a pure dwelling place for the Holy Spirit in those have been reborn]" (ed. Wilson [Oxford, 1894], 116). Further we have, in the *Missale Gothicum*, prayers that ask as follows: "descendat super aquas has angelus benedictionis tuae [may the angel of your blessing descend upon these waters]," or "angelum pietatis tuae his sacris fontibus adesse dignare [deign to bring the angel of your piety to this sacred font]" (J. Mabillon, *De liturgia gallicana*, 3 vols. [Paris, 1685], 3: 247).[94] And the Spanish liturgy says similarly: "et ex tuis sedibus angelum tuum sanctum dirigas, qui eas sanctificet [and from your throne may you send your holy angel to sanctify these (baptismal waters)]" (*PL* 85: 466).

Besides this idea of the angels' connection with the consecration of the baptismal water, there is the related conception of the angels' presence in the actual baptism. So, for example, St. Ambrose says in his treatise on the mysteries that the renunciation of the devil takes place in the presence of the angels: "Praesentibus angelis locutus es. . . . Non est fallere, non est negare: angelus est, qui regnum Christi et vitam aeternam adnuntiat [In the presence of the angels, you spoke. . . . there is no mistaking, no denying it: it is an angel who announces the kingdom of Christ and eternal life]" (2.6). Greek authors speak similarly of how the angels are present and rejoice at the baptism, for example, Gregory Nazianzen, *Oration* 40.4 (*PG* 36: 364A) and Cyril, *in Proc.* 15. This is given poetic expression in a song by the Byzantine poet Romanos (Paul Maas, "Die Chronologie der Hymnen des Romanos," *Byzantinische Zeitschrift* 15 [1906]: 27).[95] According-ing to the *Ordo* (Order of Worship) of Jacob of Edessa, "the heavenly host stand around the baptistery in order to receive the sons who are now like God" (J. A. Assemani, *Codex liturgicus ecclesiae universae*, 15 vols. [Rome, 1749–1766], 2: 226 = Denzinger, *Ritus orientalium*, 1: 287). This in turn leads us to the idea that the person receives his guardian angel at the mo-ment of baptism. Compare Ps.-Macarius, *PG* 34: 221B, and *Le livre des mystères du ciel et de la terre* (The Book of the Mysteries of Heaven and Earth), Patrologia Orientalis, 6 [Paris, 1911], 420f.), for example.

We can pass over further ideas regarding the connection between baptism and the angels here. Suffice to say we have clearly demonstrated how the early Church saw an inherent connection between baptism and the angelic world. The same can now be shown with regard to the holy Eucharist. Here, too, we have to establish the double thesis that the an-gels are either directly involved in the action of the liturgy or are thought of as present at holy Mass. The most important witness for the first idea is the prayer in the Canon of the Roman Mass (the prayer *Supplices te*): "iube haec perferri per manus sancti angeli tui in sublime altare tuum, in conspectu divinae maiestatis tuae [command this to be taken by the hands of your holy angel to your sublime altar, in the sight of your divine maj-esty]."[96] We have parallels to the prayer for acceptance of the sacrifice by the hand of the angels in the Mozarabic Liturgy: "ut sanctificata sumamus per manus sancti angeli tui [that we may receive through the hands of your holy angel what has been made holy]" (*PL* 85: 116 and 550), or "accepta dis-currente sancto angelo tuo nobis sanctificata distribuas [what has been ac-cepted in the mediation of your holy angel, may you give to us what has been sanctified]" (ibid., 85: 590), also "huius sacrificii munera per manus angeli tui iubeas sanctificari [may you command that the gifts of this sacri-fice be sanctified by the hands of your angel]" (ibid., 85: 1031), etc.[97]

For the Gallican Mass, we have the witness of Germanus (?), who in his *Second Letter on the Common Office* says, concerning the Easter Vigil Mass: "Angelus enim Dei ad secreta super altare tamquam super monumen-tum descendit et ipsam hostiam benedicit, instar illius angeli, qui Christi resurrectionem evangelizavit [The angel of God descends on the altar as if on a monument and blesses the host itself, like that angel who announced the resurrection of Christ]" (text according to Johannes Quasten, *Expositio antiquae Liturgiae Gallicanae Germano Parisiensi adscripta* [Exposition of the Ancient Gallican Liturgy Ascribed to Germanus of Paris] [Münster, 1934], 27.19f.). Finally, we have a similar notion in the Eastern Church in the text of the Liturgy of St. Mark, with which we have become familiar. The priest prays God to accept the gifts "at his holy, heavenly, and spiritual altar in the heights of heaven, through the service performed by the archangels" (Brightman, *Eastern Liturgies*, 129.20ff.). It has been proposed that the angel in the *Supplices te* prayer in the Roman Mass can be understood on this basis. That will have to remain an open question.[98] However, "140the Masses of both East and West undoubtedly speak of an angel's intervention in the Eucharistic action.[99] Accordingly, we then have the other notion that the angels are present when the holy Eucharist is offered on the sacrificial altar.[100] When the priest steps toward the altar in order to offer the unbloody sacrifice to God, "the angels gather around the priest; the whole sanctuary and the space around the altar are filled with the heavenly hosts, to honor the one who lies upon the altar." Those are the words of St. John Chrysostom from his treatise *On the Priesthood* (6.4). And as support for his statement, he adds that these angels have been seen in a vision, "around the altar, bending down to the floor, the way that soldiers can be seen standing guard in the presence of the king."[101] We hear similar things in Western sources. According to St. Ambrose, commenting on Luke 1:12 (ed. C. Schenkl, *CSEL* 32, pt. 4 [Vienna, 1902], 4: 28.12ff.), there can be no doubt that "assistere angelum, quando Christus assistit, Christus immolatur [an angel is standing by, when Christ is standing by, (when) Christ is sacrificed]," and Gregory the Great asserts in his *Dialogues* (4.58): "Quis enim fidelium habere dubium possit in ipsa immolationis hora ad sacerdotis vocem coelos aperiri, in illo Jesu Christi mysterio angelorum choros adesse, summis iura sociari, terrena coelestibus iungi unumque ex visibilibus atque invisibilibus fieri [Who among the faithful can doubt that at the very hour of the sacrifice the heavens are opened at the word of the priest, that choirs of angels are present in that mystery of Christ, that what is humble is bound with what is highest, that the earthly and the heavenly are joined, and that seen and unseen become one?]" (*PL* 77: 428A). And the Armenian John Mandakuni says in his *Orations*: "Do you not know that at the moment when the Holy Sacrament comes upon the altar, heaven above is opened and Christ descends and is present, that angelic hosts float from heaven to earth and gather around the altar, where the Holy Sacrament of the Lord is, and that everything is filled with holy spirit?" [102]

We also see that the angels participate in the sacrament of penance. The sources do not just speak of an angel of repentance (*Shepherd of Hermas*; *Apocalypse of Adam*, ed. James, 139; Clement of Alexandria, *Who Is the Rich Man Who Is Saved* 42.18), but also of an angel who discloses concealed sins (Methodius *On Leprosy* 8; cf. also Origen *On Ps. 37, Hom.* 1). In the *Passio S. Genesii* (Passion of St. Genesius) the following is reported: "vidi [in a vision] . . . angelos radiantes super me stetisse, qui omnia peccata, quae ab infantia feci, recitaverunt de libro [I saw . . . that radiant angels had stood over me and recited from a book all the sins that I had committed since early childhood]" (T. Ruinart, *Echte und ausgewählte Acten der ersten Martirer*, 6 vols. [1832–1836], 2: 147). It is even more interesting that in the first of the pseudo-Cyprianic prayers, it is said: "continuo mittas angelum sanctum tuum, qui deleat universa commissa mea, sicut deluisti spiritum immundum a Sara [may you send your holy angel to wipe out all my sins, as you drove the unclean spirit from Sarah]" (ed. Hartel, 148.11). Thus the angel apparently participates here just as in the sacrament of baptism and in the Eucharist. We similarly see the angels taking part in the sacrament of matrimony. In Tertullian, *Ad Uxorem* (To His Wife) 2.8 (ed. Oehler, 1: 696), we read of the "felicitas matrimonii, quod ecclesia conciliat et confirmat oblatio et obsignat benedictio, angeli renuntiant, pater rato habet [the happiness of (that) marriage which the Church produces and the offering confirms and the blessing seals, which the angels proclaim and the Father holds as valid]." As far as the participation of the angels in the consecration of a bishop is concerned, the *Apostolic Constitutions* (8.4.5) state that they assist in the election of the bishop. When the people are supposed "to give testimony" to the moral qualities of the candidate, they are reminded that in this act "the Holy Spirit and all the saints and attendant spirits are present" (ed. Funk, 472.17ff.). Finally, concerning the sacrament of the dying, in the *ordo* for the *commendatio animae* (commendation of the soul), it is prayed that "In regnum tuum servum tuum suscipe. Suscipiat eum sanctus Michael . . . Veniant illi obviam sancti Angeli Dei et perducant eum in civitatem caelestem Jerusalem [Receive your servant into your kingdom. May St. Michael accept him. . . . May the holy angels of God come to greet him, and may they lead him into the heavenly city, Jerusalem]." Or, in an even better passage: "Egredienti itaque animae tuae de corpore splendidus angelorum coetus occurrat; judex Apostolorum tibi senatus adveniat, candidatorum tibi Martyrum triumphator exercitus obviet, liliata rutilantium Confessorum turma circumdet, jubilantium te Virginum chorus excipiat et beatae quietis in sinu Patriarcharum te complexus astringat [And so may a shining company of angels run to greet your soul as it leaves the body; may the senate of the apostles welcome you as [your] judge, a triumphant army of white-clad martyrs meet you, a throng of glowing confessors bedecked with lilies surround you, a chorus of jubilant virgins receive you, and the embrace of a blessed peace clasp you in the bosom of the Patriarchs]." As in antiquity the solemn entry into a city developed into a richly appointed procession,[103] so the soul of the faithful departed is brought in solemn procession into the heavenly city. Once again, the thesis is confirmed that the Church, as an entity related to the heavenly city, has a fundamental relationship to the political sphere, which is expressed in the choice of its images. It would be easy to demonstrate the conceptual content of the prayers for the *commendatio animae* in a great number of texts by early Christian authors, though that should be left for a work of its own. I merely draw attention to the fact that the grave mound too stands under the protection of the angels, according to the *Rituale Romanum*, and that it is prayed that "mittere digneris sanctum Angelum tuum de coelis, qui benedicat et sanctificet hos cineres [deign to send your holy angel from heaven, to bless and sanctify these ashes]," and so on, in the *Benedictio cinerum* (Blessing of the Ashes) (*Missale Romanum, Feria IV cinerum* and *Dedicatio ecclesiae*).

Thus we have seen that in the sacraments and blessings we must reckon with a participation of the angelic realm, indeed, that the angels even take part in various ways in the cultic actions. We should also mention that apart from the Mass the angels are thought of as present in the psalmody of the monks. In chapter 19 of the *Rule of St. Benedict*, we read: "Ubique credimus divinam esse praesentiam . . . maxime tamen hoc sine aliqua dubitatione credamus, cum ad opus divinum adsistimus [We believe the divine presence is everywhere . . . Let us especially and without any doubt believe this when we assist in the divine work]," after which Ps 137:1 is cited: "'in conspectu angelorum psallam tibi'. Ergo consideremus qualiter oporteat in conspectu Divinitatis et angelorum eius esse, et sic stemus ad psallendum, ut mens nostra concordet voci nostrae ["In the sight of the angels I sing to you." Therefore, let us think about the way in which we need to be in the sight of the Divinity and of his angels, and let us stand for our psalm singing in such a way that our mind is in harmony with our voice]" (ed. C. Butler, 51f.).[104] The best interpretation of this passage is in the *Commentarius Pauli Warnefridi in S. Regulam* (The Commentary of Paul Warnefrid on the Holy Rule) (Monte Cassino, 1880), 256, which says: "Duobus modis intelligi potest: uno modo intelligitur, quia cum psallimus Deo, assistunt ibi angeli, eo quod Deus non est sine suis nuntiis; altero modo intelligitur, quia si nos intendimus corde, quod ore dicimus, nostra intentio similis est intentioni angelorum [This can be understood in two ways: in one sense it means that when we sing psalms to God, the angels stand there too, so that God is not without his messengers; in another sense, it means that if we mean in our hearts what we say with our voices, our intention is like the intention of the angels]."[105] How realistically this perception was taken in the Middle Ages—that the monks sing the psalms in the presence of the angels—is evident from the *Regula Magistri* (Rule of the Master) 148: "Caveatur, ut qui orat, si voluerit expuere aut narium spurcitias jactare, non in ante, sed post se retro projiciat propter angelos in ante stantes, demonstrante propheta ac dicente: 'In conspectu angelorum psallam tibi' [Care should be taken so that when someone is praying, if he wants to spit or to blow mucus from his nose, he should not do so facing forward but only after turning around, because of the angels who are standing in front of him, as the prophet proves when he says, 'in the sight of the angels I sing to you']" (*PL* 88: 1009).[106] And Alcuin writes: "Fertur dixisse Bedam: Scio angelos visitare canonicas horas . . . quid si ibi me non inveniunt inter fratres? Nonne dicere habent: Ubi est Beda? [Bede is reported to have said: I know that the angels visit at the canonical hours . . . what if they don't find me there with the brothers? Aren't they going to ask: Where is Bede?]" (epistle 219, in *Opera*, ed. Froben, 1: 282).[107]

Not only the singing of the psalms, but any prayer in community happens along with the angels: "Not only does the High Priest pray along with those who pray truly, but also the angels in heaven, who rejoice," Origen writes in *On Prayer* 11, and in Clement of Alexandria, we read that the gnostic "prays with angels, as one who has already become like one of the angels . . . even when he prays alone, he has the choir of the saints, who stand there with him (Clement of Alexandria, *Stromateis* [Miscellanies]

7.12.78.6).[108] And the Armenian writer Elisha says, in his commentary on the Our Father: "You are not far from the angels, rather along with them do you enter into prayer, so that with them you praise God. As you are united with them, they become participants in your songs in prayer and praise. Open your mouth confidently and say: 'Your will be done, as in heaven, so on earth'" (trans. S. Weber, in *Ausgewählte Schriften der Armenischen Kirchenväter*, Bibliothek der Kirchenväter, 58 [Munich, 1927], 282). The Church is precisely, as it says in a Coptic homily, "the place of trust and of the gathering of the angels. The Church is the place where the Cherubim and Seraphim gather" (William H. Worrell, *Coptic Manuscripts in the Freer Collection* [New York, 1923], 356f.).[109]

From this perspective, it is a natural development in the symbolic interpretation of the cultus that reference to the angels is constantly made. The sounding-board (*sēmantron*)[110] recalls the trumpets of the angels (Ps.-Sophronius in *Spicilegium Romanum*, ed. Mai, 4: 34), and when those who are singing the psalms sing the hymn of the cherubim, that means that they are singing along with the angels on high (ibid., 4: 48).[111] The whole complex of ideas goes far beyond the belief that the Church, or rather the individual churches, have a guardian angel.[112] We have seen that a much closer relationship exists between the Church and the angels than accounts typically have us believe. The fundamental thing is to grasp clearly the role that the angels actually play in these ways of thinking. When St. John Chrysostom says that the holy angels accompany Christ in his presence in the Eucharistic celebration the way that soldiers accompany a king, then we realize why they appear in the holy Mass. They serve the purpose of making the Eucharist's *public* character clear. As the emperor demonstrates the public character of his political authority when he appears in the company of his bodyguard, so Christ demonstrates the public character of his religio-political authority when he is accompanied by the bodyguard of the angels at holy Mass. When the angels are present in the singing of the psalms, the celebration of marriage or the election of a bishop, in the renunciation of the devil in baptism or in the entry of the soul into the heavenly city, that always entails that the psalmody, marriage celebration, and episcopal election, baptism or consummation of a life, are public, officially ecclesial and not private processes. The state did not endow the Church with this *public* character [*Öffentlichkeit*]; rather, it belongs intrinsically to the Church as such, whose Lord, as heavenly king, also possesses a heavenly public nature. The relationship of the *ekklēsia* to the polis in heaven is thus, as I have repeatedly said, also a political relationship, and on this basis the angels must always be present in the cultic actions of the Church.

St. John Chrysostom's commentary on Psalm 137:1, "Before the angels will I sing psalms to you," notes: "another translator says: 'publicly [*parrēsia*], O God, will I sing to you'" (*PG* 55: 407). In this translation of "before the angels" with "publicly", we are in actuality, I believe, given an understanding of no small part of the texts that speak of the participation of the angels in the Church's worship. Early Christianity did not actually know the concept of the Church as a legal entity.[113] The Church exists whenever it assembles, be it for cultic acts or for conciliar resolutions.[114] The gathering together of the *ekklēsia* is always accompanied by the appearance of those angels who, coming from the heavenly city, endow the Church with its character as a public entity.[115] This being the case, we can also understand that when the Greek Church speaks of the intercessory prayer of the martyrs, it is appropriating for itself precisely an image from the political sphere. The martyrs are "the friends" of the king, who possess the right of an audience with him and are able to tell him everything freely [*parrēsia*].[116] The choice of so telling an image is not an accident. Rather, it arises from the fact that the prayer of the earthly as well as of the heavenly Church is a "public" [*öffentlich*] prayer, because it is the prayer of a polis that, to be sure, does not exist on earth, but in heaven as a "commonwealth."

.   .   .

The preceding exposition has shown that we can also speak with good reason of a participation of the angels in the worship of the Church. Now it is necessary to demonstrate how the angels in their praise giving, with which the praise of the Church is united, become the root cause of the mystical life of the Church.

III

It has already been pointed out that the Sanctus call of the angels in the liturgies is described as a mystical act of praise, as *theologia*. In their singing, the angels, as it were, ecstatically rise above themselves.[117] In

Clement of Alexandria, we have furthermore met with the idea that the gnostic who prays with the angels himself becomes angelic. In Diadochus of Photikē, one finds a similar thought, namely, that *theologia* illuminates our spirit with the fire of transformation, and thereby makes it the companion of the attending angel spirits.[118] Evagrius Ponticus, the oldest theoretician of monasticism, distinguished in his theory of mysticism between two types of knowledge: the "essential" gnosis, which is concerned with essences, and a lower form of gnosis, which only deals with concepts. The essential gnosis has a side that is related to mysticism; it also necessarily presumes a higher form of being for humanity—without *apatheia* (calm) it is impossible to appropriate this gnosis for oneself. The full achievement of gnosis, then, culminates in *theologia*, meaning in the praise of God.[119]

All of these details from Clement, Diadochus, or Evagrius demonstrate a connection between the mystical life and the angels, those spirits who themselves, as we have concluded from the liturgies, in mystical fashion proclaim the *theologia*, that is, the praise of God in the Sanctus. To say this means first of all that the mystical life does not stem from the order of being to which humanity rightly belongs and necessarily so, just because it is human. Rather, the mystical life involves a level of being that, like the ontological order of the angels, lies beyond the level proper to humanity. On the basis of this higher level, humanity can live and grow, and it can also on this basis have an altered relationship to God.[120] From what has already been argued, it is clear that this raising of humanity above its natural existence takes places in the cultus when the number of the choirs of angels is increased by that of the angel-like priests and monks. The origin of the mystical life in the Church is thus to be sought in the giving of praise in the holy Mass. This admission into the choir of the angel-like always means an approximation to the angels' order of being. Faith is thus not transcended by the mystical life—faith is obviously something that is common to both the angel-like and the laity—rather, the ontological presuppositions of faith are transcended. Not humanity's religious status but its metaphysical level of being is accordingly sublimated.[121]

The gnosis of Evagrius and Diadochus culminates, as I have said, in *theologia*. The term is ambiguous. On the one hand, the word *theologia* refers in ancient philosophy to knowledge of the highest principles of being. On the other hand, *theologia* also can mean not just knowledge but also the Logos, especially in the heightened diction of the poets of the archaic period.[122] In Christian mysticism, the word "theology" also has this double sense. According to the oldest monastic writers, mysticism constitutes the highest level of a gnosis that, beginning with the lower form of discursive gnosis, progresses to the intuitive gnosis of essences and ideas, and then reaches its consummation in the gnosis of the Holy Trinity. On the one hand, *theologia* as gnosis thus constitutes the highest form of knowledge; on the other hand, this mystical gnosis in a certain sense is not gnosis at all, but rather a praise of God like that of the pure spirits. The older Greek usage of the word *theologia* as poetic speech about God has thus been transformed into a way of naming the praise of the angels and the mystical glorification of God. But what in the ancient usage were only two juxtaposed meanings of one and the same word are here, in Christian mysticism, intrinsically linked with each other. The gnosis that as mystical knowledge culminates in *theologia* also entails that this *theologia* no longer remains knowledge of God, but becomes a praising of God like that of the angels.

What that means becomes clear if we consider the angels whose life and being have archetypal significance for the mystical gnostic. Admittedly, there are many different beings that are designated as angels. There are, for example, angels who are associated with atmospheric phenomena.[123] They leave the mystics cold, because they are all in some way distanced from God and have their countenances turned toward the world and its chaotic passions. It is otherwise, however, with the cherubim and seraphim, who stand before God and sing without ceasing their Holy, Holy, Holy. It is in their ranks that the one who is like the angels desires to be enrolled. And so through the gnosis he begins to rise above the world. He begins to fly and flies beyond all that is visible and invisible in heaven and on earth, into a world that is no longer involved with this perceptible cosmos and the human beings who inhabit it, but is instead oriented solely to God, as directly oriented to God as are the countenances of the cherubim. But now something remarkable begins to happen. The pure spirits whom the gnostic encounters, who in their very being are orientated toward God, are not beings who would somehow be petrified in a mute veneration before God. Their authentic being is not grounded in their immobility but in their movement,[124] which they manage with the beating of those wings that Isaiah first described with an unmatched power of perception. To this beating of wings and the wings' covering of the feet—so richly expressive in its symbolism—there corresponds a distinctive gushing forth in word, in call, in song, of the Holy, Holy, Holy. In other words, the authentic being of these angels is grounded in this overflow into word and song, in this phenomenon.

    • We should not imagine this as though—on the analogy of humanity's mode of being—a portion of the angels has been selected from the angelic world and entrusted with the task of singing something before the Lord God. That would actually be an intolerable idea, and the desire to do such a thing for all eternity does not make immediate sense. In reality, something quite different is involved here: not angels who are mainly imagined, in some totally abstract fashion, as "angels as such," and who in addition happen to sing; but angels whose angel existence consists precisely in their pouring forth the praise of the Holy, Holy, Holy in the way previously described. This call constitutes their very being, in this pouring forth, they are what they are, cherubim and seraphim. But just because they have their very being in this gushing forth of praise, in this partial movement of their wings, they are also able to claim exemplary significance for the being of the mystic. With these angels, we are dealing with angels who are pure spirits in this singing, in this hymnody, in this giving of praise. Why shouldn't the mystic, who in his being has become like the angels, also want to arrive at that supreme form of existence of the pure spirits, whose existence is essentially constituted in the streaming forth of the pure praise of God? For of what use then are all the virtues of the angels, if their praise of God, their most authentic life, that for which alone they exist, that through which their innermost form of being is set to vibrating, is not attainable by human beings? And for that reason gnosis culminates in *theologia*, for that reason from theology as the knowledge of God comes theology as praise of God, because the highest of created beings, the angels, whether cherub or seraph, exist in no other way than in the praise of God and pour forth his glorification.

    But, one may object, is it then possible for humanity to approach the angels, to become like the angels? Is it not the case that a human being must always remain a human being? No! A human being can draw near to the angels because the angel too—as its name already indicates—can draw near to humanity. Did angels not descend to the shepherds in the field and sing "Glory to God in the highest" at the birth of the Savior? Where Christ Our Lord is, there too are the angels: at his birth, at his temptation, at his resurrection and at his ascension. Because the angels are inseparable from him, they are also present with him in the holy Mass. But just as the angels descended and let their song of praise be heard in the ears of the shepherds, the song of praise for him who, before his descent was raised above all angels, so also after his ascension has been raised on high above all the angelic powers,[125] and "to whom has been given a name that is above every other name" (Phil. 2:9)—so too rises up the one like an angel, who had ascended to the ultimate orders of cherubim and seraphim and from these orders in heaven has come down again to the orders on earth, where he unites himself with priests and laity in the song of praise, listens to the holy readings, and receives the sacraments as one whose unclean lips need cleansing, as one who, becoming liable to corruption, cannot do without the nourishment of incorruptibility. Never, while living in the flesh, will anyone leave the earthly *ekklēsia* through entry into the heavenly Jerusalem; even though raised up to the third heaven, the "angel-like one" will always have to return to the earthly Church, to the earthly cult, and to those theological virtues of faith, love, and hope that are binding for him, as well as for the whole Christian people.

That justifies our understanding that the angels belong not just to Christ but also to us. And that humanity is only a part of creation and therefore is constituted in connection with other entities, among them angels and demons. We have to realize that the angel is not simply something through which our human nature was once created—but rather something through which it is constantly being created anew. And for that reason, none of the reflection that we devote to the nature of the angels is superfluous, for what the angel teaches us about itself also teaches us something about ourselves as well. The angels are more than a poetic ornamentation left over from the storehouse of popular fables. They belong to God and to Christ and to the Holy Spirit, but they also belong to us. For us, they stand for a possibility of our being, a heightening and intensifying of our being—but never for the possibility of a new, a different faith.[126] They instruct us about dark depths of our existence, in which there is movement and impulse that perhaps does not depend on us, that perhaps is never recognized as such by us or perceived as movement toward the angelic—movement that we perhaps only become aware of as an inclination toward purity of heart, or as a passion for mental clarity and an authentic existence.

There are many ways by which humanity hastens toward the angel, not as though people were actually intent on becoming angels, but because the life that they are living is only a provisional life, and because what we shall be has yet to be revealed.[127] And if we are not hastening toward the angel that stands before God, then most certainly we are hastening toward that angel who has fallen away from God; then we are drawing near to the demon. For we human beings always exist in such a way that we transcend ourselves and thereby draw near either to the angel or to the demon. The human person, who transcends himself because only in such self-transcendence does he exist, is able to climb and climb, not in a moral but in a metaphysical sense,[128] until he becomes a comrade of the angels and archangels, until he gets to the boundary at which the cherubim and seraphim also stand. There, where a halt is required of him by a boundary that neither he himself nor any archangel has set, he begins to join in with the spheres and to sing with the archangels. His singing is not simply an imitation of the singing of the angels, not a modest chiming in with the call of Holy, holy, holy that ceaselessly and majestically resounds from their lips; rather, it is at the same time something that bursts forth from his innermost being, when he arrives at the limit of all creation, which is also the limit of himself as a creature. In his singing with the cherubim and seraphim, his ascent is over, his self-realization is finished. For what else can a human being who rises up to the angels know, save that all creation praises God, praises God even in the farthest of the planets, even in the smallest blade of grass? As he once was only in a position, when he climbed and climbed and transcended himself, then still to keep climbing, because he was forever not yet there, so in the end he exists with the angels and archangels only as a song, and as a song he pours himself out before God.

What is here sung out is creation itself, which arrives at its limit and bears witness to God from its created state. And what is true of the highest levels of created being is likewise true of the ultimate levels of being of plant, animal, or inanimate thing, which stand far below the levels appropriate to humanity. In the Psalms, when the animals or mountains break forth in the praise of God, that represents no mere creative exaggeration, no poetic hyperbole, no anthropomorphic "ensoulment" of what strictly speaking has no soul, but rather something ultimately grounded, in totally realistic fashion, in the very essence of creatureliness, something that penetrates from the cherub and the seraph down to the humblest thing in the world: yes, it is the whole of creation, which as we have heard and recognized from the Gospel is full of divine glory. How remarkable that humanity—at the level of being befitting its metaphysical roots—by expressing its lowly creatureliness is able to begin to ascend and to associate itself with cherub and seraph, and then in union with them can say no more than that it is nothing at all, and that it exists only as a song of praise before God. This is why such singing—for example, the Song of the Sun of Saint Francis—neither represents a slipping of faith into the poetic nor is rooted in some type of mystical nature religion; instead, Saint Francis begins to sing—one might almost say to "resound"—because he is touched so deeply with the grace of Christ. Hence how right it is that the saint joins in brotherly fashion with sun and stars, water and death, because the grace of the Crucified has awakened the ultimate depths of his creatureliness, so that he exists, not only as that sinner who has encountered mercy, but also as that wretched creature—related to the ass—who has no other possibility but to pour forth the praise of God.[129]

Thus will the mystical life of the Church be able to unfold only in inner linkage with the cult of the Church. Only from the life of the Church, which praises God with the angels and the whole of creation, can praise be awakened, which in the cult as in the mystical life of grace gives notice that heaven and earth are full of the glory of God, since the glory of God has departed from the temple in Jerusalem, to make its dwelling in the temple of the body of Jesus in that Jerusalem that as the one "above" is the mother of us all.

· · ·

The preceding exposition has perhaps shown that it was not arbitrary or pointless for us to have given our attention to the meaning of the doctrine of the angels. There is an immediate implication for the doctrine of the holy Church: the Church is more than just a human religious society, because the angels and the saints in heaven also belong to it.[130] Seen from this perspective, then, the Church's worship is never a merely human affair: no, the angels, like the entire cosmos, take part in it.[131] To the Church's singing corresponds heavenly singing,[132] and, the Church's inner life is also organized like the participation in the heavenly singing. The angels demonstrate that the Church's worship is public worship offered to God,[133] and through them the Church's worship also acquires a necessary relationship to the political sphere, because the angels possess a relationship to the religio-political world in heaven. Lastly, the angels in their singing are linked with the Church, not only in those "like the angels" and in the "people," they are also at the same time the awakeners of the mystical life in the Church, which only finds its fulfillment when humanity, joined with the choirs of angels, begins to praise God from the depths of its creatureliness.[134] Therefore we sing in the *Te Deum*:

Te Deum laudamus, te Dominum confitemur,
Te, aeternum Patrem, omnis terra veneratur,
Tibi omnes Angeli, tibi Caeli et universae Potestates,
Tibi Cherubim et Seraphim incessabili voce proclamant:
Sanctus, sanctus, sanctus Dominus Deus Sabaoth,
Pleni sunt caeli et terra maiestatis gloriae tuae.

We praise you O God, we confess you as Lord,
You, the eternal Father, the whole world worships,
To you Cherubim and Seraphim cry out unceasingly,
Holy, holy, holy, Lord God of Hosts,
Heaven and earth are full of the majesty of your glory.[135]

Christ as *Imperator*

Along with the designation of Christ as *rex*, early Christian literature also shows that he is entitled *imperator* as well. In his exhortation to
chastity, Tertullian says, "Are we too not soldiers, in fact under an even
more stringent discipline, because we serve so great an emperor [*eo quidem
maioris disciplinae, quanto tanti imperatoris*]?" (*On Modesty* 12). And in his
writing on fleeing during a time of persecution, he says, "To me, he is a
finer soldier of Christ, his emperor, if he . . . runs away in a time of persecution" (*On Flight* 10). In Cyprian's fifteenth letter, we read: "If all of Christ's
soldiers must keep the teachings of their emperor . . ." and so on (*Letter*
15.1). The Roman confessors use the same image (*Letters of Cyprian* 31.5). In
the treatise called *De montibus Sina et Sion* (On Mounts Sinai and Zion),
wrongly ascribed to Cyprian, Christ is named *imperator* and *rex* (*De mon.
Sina et Sion* 8).[1] Also relevant here is the usage found in the *Passio Sanctorum Scillitanorum* (The Passion of the Scillitan Martyrs), in which the holy
Speratus says during his hearing, "I acknowledge my Lord, King of Kings
and emperor of all the nations [*cognosco dominum meum, regem regum et
imperatorum omnium gentium*]" (in *Ausgewählte Märtyrerakten* [Selected
Acts of the Martyrs], ed. [Rudolf] Knopf and [Gustav] Krüger, 3rd ed.
[Tübingen, 1929], 29.8). In Arnobius's apology *Adversus Nationes* (Against
the Nations), Christ is similarly named *imperator* (*Adv. Nat.* 2.65 [*CSEL*
4: 101.11, also 17.17]; cf. Joseph de Ghellinck et al., "Pour l'histoire du mot
'Sacramentum,'" [Toward the History of the Word *Sacramentum*] in *Spicilegium sacrum Lovaniense, études et documents*, fasc. 3 [Paris, 1924], 1: 226
n. 3, 230, 232). Further instructive is Lactantius's usage. According to him,

whoever practices *proskynēsis* before the emperor "should be punished like a deserter of his Lord and Emperor and father [*tamquam desertor domini et imperatoris et patris sui puniretur*]" (*Div. Inst.* 7.27.16). In *Divine Institutes* 6.8, he speaks of "God, the teacher and emperor of all [*magister et imperator omnium deus*]," and in 4.6.5, he expresses the opinion regarding an oracle of the Sibyl (see Geffcken's edition, 227 under frgm. 1): "In these verses the Son of God is predicted to be the Leader and Emperor of all [*Filium Dei ducem et imperatorem omnium his versis praedicat*]."[2] In St. Augustine's *Enarrationes in psalmos* (Explanations of the Psalms), on Psalm 36:25 (Sermon 3.4 [*PL* 36: 385]), he notes: "so that he himself would be the head of the whole city of Jerusalem, with all of the faithful assembled from the beginning until the end, joined by legions and armies of angels, and that there would be a single city under a single king and, as it were, a single province under a single emperor" (ut esset et ipse totius caput civitatis Jerusalem omnibus connumeratis fidelibus ab initio usque in finem, adiunctis etiam legionibus et exercitibus angelorum, ut fiat illa una civitas sub uno rege et una quaedam provincia sub uno imperatore).[3] Finally, Christ is called "the true Emperor" in the commentary of Aponius on the Song of Songs (ed. Bottino and Martini, 202) and in another place referred to not only as the *princes principum* but also as the *imperator imperatorum* (233).

. . .

Although one may suggest that in some of the references above, the word be translated as "general" rather than "emperor,"[4] we should be cautioned by the fact that this translation is impossible in other passages in which *imperator* stands alongside *rex*. In 1 Tim. 6:16 the Greek acclamation *hōi timē kai kratos aiōnion* (to whom be honor and eternal glory) is rendered in Latin as *cui honor et imperium*. There is disagreement as to whether this acclamation applies to God or to Christ. The case is similar in 1 Pet. 4:11 and 5:11, but in Rev. 1:6 the phrase *ipso gloria et imperium* (to him be glory and *imperium*) most probably refers to Christ. In any case, the referral of this acclamation to Christ is prominent in patristic literature. That becomes understandable when one recognizes that the *regnum Christi* can also be designated as an *imperium*. Thus in the *De laude martyrii* (On the Praise of Martyrdom) of Pseudo-Cyprian (24 [47.16]) it is said of the martyrs: "kingdoms are revealed, empires are prepared [*patent regna, parantur imperia*]" (cf. also 30, according to which the martyrs "claim empires for all time [*imperia perennis temporis tenent*]). In a Latin tomb inscription (in [Franciscus] Buecheler and Alexander Riese, eds., *Anthologia Latina* [Leipzig, 1894–1897], no. 1359.3f.), it is said: "Leaving this world, he has laid claim to the immense empire of Christ [*mundumque relinquens immensum Christi possidet imperium*]." Maximus of Turin says in a homily (*Hom.* 85 [*PL* 57: 447B]): "Pride does not enter the empire of heaven [*non enim ad imperium coelorum pervenitur superbia*]." It is thus clear that the Kingdom of Heaven has been named an empire.

The *Paschal Poem* of the fifth-century poet Sedulius (*Carmen Paschale* 2.63–66 [*CSEL* 10: 48.63–66]) even says of Christ: "whose name embraces everything in an everlasting enclosure and whose empire has no end [*cuius nomen et aeterno complectens omnia gyro imperium sine fine manet*]." In this way, Sedulius sets faith in the "empire of Christ which has no end [*imperium sine fine Christi*]" over against the promise made by Vergil to the earthly Rome: "I gave an empire without end [*imperium sine fine dedi*]" (Aeneid 1.278f.).[5] In *On the City of God* 2.22, when St. Augustine calls on the Romans to seek the heavenly fatherland and adds: "In it you will reign truly and forever [*in ea veraciter semperque regnabis*]," he too is invoking this passage from Vergil, but in place of the *imperium sine fine dedi* he has conjugated the verb in the future tense: "he *will give* an empire without end [*imperium sine fine dabit*]." The *imperium Christi* has thus taken the place of the pagan empire.[6] If we take this larger context into consideration, when reading passages in early Christian literature that speak of Christ as the *imperator*, we are justified in understanding them not in the exclusively military sense of Christ as "field marshal" of his *militia*, but at the same time in seeing in the *Christus-Imperator* the master of an *imperium* that transcends all the *imperia* of this world.

Seeing Christ in the image of the Roman emperor is thus ancient. I think this parallel was already intended in the Book of Revelation, in which Christ is praised in hymn as the "ruler [*princeps* (Gk., *archōn*)] of the kings of the earth [*regum terrae*]" (Rev. 1:5). Only in this way can we explain why the "One like a son of man" stands in heaven between two candelabra; he is thus the counterimage to the imperial portrait, which was set up between candelabra.[7] Only in this way can we understand why his feet are said to shine like burnished bronze (1:15). His feet are emphasized because homage (*proskynesis*) is paid to them, as to the feet of the emperor. Only in this way do we see why it is said that his voice resounds like waterfalls (ibid). His voice, as it were, drowns out the voice of the earthly emperor. When he holds seven stars in his hand (1:16), he is appropriating—as has long been seen—a symbol of imperial power, and when his face shines like the sun (ibid.), he becomes the counterimage of the imperial *roi-soleil* (Sun King). This also explains why his raiment is described (1:13). The representation of imperial garb as a symbol of power is here contrasted with the description of the clothing of the royal high priest in heaven, who as such is superior to the "kings of the earth." As the imperial *princeps* is greeted with acclamations, so too homage is paid to the heavenly *imperator* in acclamations.

The political counterdescription continues in chapter 4 of Revelation. First, we have a description of a throne on which sits one whose name is not given. Perhaps this reflects the Jewish avoidance of the divine Name, or perhaps the notion that veneration is being paid to an empty throne: the One who sits on the throne is invisible; only his brilliance can be seen in the precious stones, a traditional symbol of political sovereignty. The One who sits on the throne is acclaimed with the cry "You are worthy!" (*dignus es*), which also stems from the political sphere (see chapter 8 in the life of Gordian in the *Scriptores Historiae Augustae*).[8] The whole scene is a declaration of loyalty before the throne of the invisible ruler, and a striking counterdeclaration to the ruler cult and adoration of the monarch's empty throne, an originally Hellenistic practice that later came to Rome.[9]

The One who sits on the throne holds a book in his right hand (5:1). This too evokes an image from the political realm, for the emperor holds a scroll in his hand. This scroll is sealed. It can only be opened by the official to whom the emperor hands it. If Christ here represents that official, he is naturally much more than an official, for—under the symbol of the Lamb—he sits with God on the throne (though the emperor too, as emperor, remains an official in his own right, for he is also a consul). Next, it is significant that the angel calls Christ not a lamb but the "Lion of Judah," who has "conquered" (5:5). The mention of Christ's "victory" once again suggests a notion taken from the political realm. As Christ now receives the scroll in his hand, the *proskynesis* of the twenty-four elders takes place: the handing over of the scroll, described via an analogy with a political procedure, is accompanied by a political gesture. At the same time, the elders swing golden bowls filled with incense. These are probably the *turibola* that we know from the Roman imperial cult and that are particularly familiar from use in triumphs and processions, though not only there.

The opening of the scroll is followed by the description of the four eschatological horsemen in chapter 6. It is hard to avoid the impression that the opening of the scroll and the appearance of the horsemen have something to do with one another. The commentators usually note that the colors of the horses correspond to the colors of the factions in the circus. The idea of a race is also suggested by the fact that the start of the race is indicated: a voice calls out to the horses, "Come!" If the games at the circus are part of this scene, their association with the opening of the scroll may be seen in the practice of beginning a tenure in office with circus games. The emperor's assumption of his consular office at the New Year is celebrated with such games.[10] We thus grasp Revelation's association of ideas: the inauguration of the sovereignty of Christ is observed with cosmic circus games, which represent the prelude to the end of this world.

It would be easy to find more examples of the political character of the symbolism in the Book of Revelation, and the opposition in which it stands to the imperial cult. But let what has been said suffice. Clearly the juxtaposition of Christ with the emperor is not some timeless piece of symbolism but a polemical symbol of an actual struggle.[11] The polemical character of this image appears clearly in patristic witnesses to the emperorship of Christ. The *militia* of Christ, summoned to battle by the heavenly emperor, conducts a struggle for power in the person of the martyrs. This struggle can ultimately be understood only from the eschatological character of the Christian proclamation. In his well-known book *Militia Christi* (Tübingen, 1905), 10, Adolf Harnack asserts that the military element in the Christian mentality derives not from Christian apocalyptic but from moral exhortation. I consider this one of those misunderstandings of Harnack's, and of liberal theology, that show a failure of theological insight. We cannot understand the early Christian concept of the martyr without recognizing its connection with early Christian eschatology. Just reading Revelation will show these connections. Christ—who is emperor—and Christians—who belong to the *militia Christi*—are symbols of a struggle for an eschatological *imperium* that is opposed to all *imperia* of this world. This is not simply a matter of a conflict between a state and a Church that face each other as two opposed institutions, and as institutions must find a modus vivendi; rather, a *battle* (and not merely an accommodation) has now become unavoidable because the institutional basis in the empire has been lost. With the expansion of the empire, the masses can no longer be governed simply through the institutions of the polis; the *princeps*, as leader [*Führer*], has to unify all power in himself.

But the transition from traditional institutional forms into the personal dynamic of the political action of the *princeps* inevitably evoked a corresponding dislocation in the religious sphere. Though there had previously been a state cult—such as the Capitoline triad—tied to the institutions of the state, while guaranteeing a great tolerance to those outside it, with the decline of those institutions, the person of the monarch had now to become more important for the cult than the worship of the state gods. From the standpoint of the political logic of a pagan state, it was thoroughly consistent for the actual bearer of political power also to become the actual recipient of religious devotion. But as *auctoritas* gradually devolved onto the *princeps*—and was thereby ultimately canceled—so all the weight had to fall on his *potestas*, and in that way the religious veneration of the state gods had to boil down to the imperial cult. The cult of the traditional state gods could be tolerant, while the imperial cult necessarily became intolerant, because the divine had become present in the emperor and, as a *numen praesens* (present divinity), demanded to be recognized.

It is well known that the presence of the divine emperor continued above all in the imperial image, which became as it were the sacrament of the imperial cult. The imperial image was dispatched everywhere and upon its arrival in a city was welcomed in solemn procession as though it were the emperor himself. Its ubiquity expressed the omnipresence of the divine emperor in his domain. Every subject can have his loyalty tested by this image. The presence of the imperial images is thus always an obligatory presence—in contrast to the gods' images in the temple—and so it becomes unthinkable to offer sacrifice and *proskynesis* apart from the presence of the imperial images.

Because the actualization of governmental authority depends on the person of the *princeps*, his *salus* is the object of all petitions, prayers, and sacrifices for him.[12] Furthermore, because the emperor performs his tasks amid the irrationality of the realms of politics and history, his *tychē*, his *fortuna*, his *genius*, can claim the greatest importance not only for politics but also for religious life as well. People are compelled to swear by the imperial *tychē*, or by the imperial Genius,[13] because in their political life they have become dependent on them.[14] Belief in the emperor's success becomes a duty of *devotio*, for the emperor's *tychē* is what guarantees victory. Defeats are impossible. The *princeps* is always victorious, acclaimed as *semper victor*.[15] Hence arises the possibility of mythologizing the monarch's sovereignty. With the beginning of his reign, the Age of Gold breaks in, as numerous Roman imperial coins testify. The *felicitas temporum* (happiness of the ages) is promised under a new star. A new astrological world era has begun.

.   .   .

At the time of Christ's birth, kingship as an actual institution no longer existed. The national kingship of the Jews had ceased to exist long before. Herod, though king of the Jews, was a foreigner.[16] Among the Romans themselves, there was no longer a *rex* but a *Caesar*, who in his essence transcended existing institutions. When Pilate asks the Jews, "Shall I crucify your king [*regem vestrum crucifigam*]?" they answer, "We have no king but Caesar [*non habemus regem, nisi Caesarem*]" (John 19:15). This answer describes the political state of affairs into which Christ was born. The Jews have no *rex,* and the Romans do have Caesar. To Pilate's question, "So you are a king [*Ergo rex es tu*]?" Jesus answers, "You say that I am a king [*Tu dicis quia rex sum ego*]" (John 18:37). How that question is to be answered is shown in Jesus' saying, "My kingship is not of this world [*Regnum meum non est de mundo hoc*]" (John 18:36). Christ is thus king, and not emperor, of the coming aeon. As such he is the *Rex regum* and the *Dominus dominorum* (Rev. 17:14; 19:16; cf. 1 Tim. 6:15). But to the answer that Christ gives to Pilate, "You say that I am a king [*Tu dicis, quia rex sum*]," he adds: "For this I was born, and for this I have come into the world, to bear witness to the truth [*Ego in hoc natus sum, et ad hoc veni in mundum, ut testimonium perhibeam veritati*]" (John 18:37)—an addition that hardly comports with the repudiation of royal dignity. Therefore to the witness for Christ as king of the world to come, it must be added that he will become revealed in battle as an emperor, a battle that the angels fight with the powers of evil and the apostles and martyrs with the powers of this earth. In a world that has necessarily been divested of every institutional structure, because the Jews are without a king and the pagans only have a Caesar, the king of the world to come must also become something of an emperor in the struggle for the future aeon. If the Kingdom of God were something utterly supernatural, of course, that could not happen; but if the Kingdom of Heaven "suffers violence," if the apostles and martyrs together with the royal high priest offer priestly sacrifice in order to rule royally, then it is really possible for Christ's eschatological presentation to be perceived, as it were, in the sight of the witnesses, and for the heavenly Son of Man to be seen as analogous to the emperor. Then we shall understand how Christ can be praised in hymn as king of the world to come, but how *even now* majesty and power are ascribed to him in the acclamations of the Church, how the historical and political world picture of this aeon, which makes the *princeps* the executor of *tychē*,[17] is overcome in bloody conflict by the martyrs, how the Eucharistic banquet that the Church celebrates is not only a *mysterium* but already has something of the eschatological banquet in it, which the Lord will celebrate with his own upon his return (Luke 19:30).[18]

It is in this sense that the Church appropriates the words of Tertullian (*Apologet.* 50):

[W]e are willing to suffer, but in the way that a soldier wants war. No one willingly suffers, since that inevitably involves anxiety and danger. However, a man fights a battle with all his strength and, though he complained about the battle in the first place, he rejoices to conquer in battle, because he wins glory and booty. We engage in battle when we are called to trial in court, because we fight there for the truth against a capital offense. Being victorious means getting what you're fighting for. Our victory consists in the glory of pleasing God and the booty of eternal life.[19]

In this way, through the struggles of its martyrs, in the overcoming of a world in which the Jews have no king and the pagans have only Caesar, the Church regards Christ as *imperator* in anticipation of his kingship of the world to come.[20]

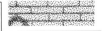

Witness to the Truth

When we enter a church and turn our gaze to the altar, we are rarely aware that the altar on which the holy sacrifice is offered contains the relics of martyrs, that it is very often built over the bones of a martyr. Nevertheless, we should take a moment to ponder this fact, for the Church's practice of offering Christ's sacrifice over the burial place of a martyr seems to express a very particular conception of the martyr's relation to the Church. When one considers this ecclesiastical custom, one is tempted to formulate the following thesis: the Church is built on the foundation of the martyrs. But no sooner is this thesis expressed than the objection immediately follows: In confessing our faith we do not say "I believe in the holy Church of the martyrs" but rather "I believe in the holy, apostolic Church." The concept of the apostle thus takes precedence over that of the martyr. Therefore, too, in the *Te Deum,* the apostles and prophets are named first, and only after them does it say,

Te martyrum candidatus laudat exercitus.

The white-robed army of martyrs praises you.

If the concept of the apostle therefore takes precedence over that of the martyr, does that perhaps mean that the apostles were not martyrs? It was not so long ago that liberal Protestant historical scholarship—in complete contrast to what Catholic tradition has passed on—expounded the thesis that only in the third and fourth centuries did the apostles become martyrs, under the influence of the cult of the martyrs, which already existed. To be sure, since then Protestant theology has revised its opinion on this as on other points. From the side of Protestant exegesis, it has been asserted that St. Paul, particularly in the letter to the Philippians, developed a theology of the martyrs;[1] and just recently a Protestant theologian has declared that the ecclesiastical concept of the martyr, and the very term itself, were created by the Johannine writings.[2]

However the details may currently be seen in Protestant scholarship, the preeminence of the martyr and the martyrological point of view in relation to the apostles is clearly recognized.[3] Thus we have a point on which modern Protestant theology, in contrast to the dogmatic prejudices of the sixteenth century, could rediscover the path to the Catholic concept of the martyr, and thereby to the Catholic cult of the saints in general, if one were prepared to draw theological consequences from one's scholarly insights—which unfortunately has yet to happen.[4]

In the address which Jesus gives to the Twelve when he sends them out, he says:

See, I am sending you out like sheep into the midst of wolves; so be wise as serpents and innocent as doves. Beware of them, for they will hand you over to councils and flog you in their synagogues; and you will be dragged before governors and kings because of me, as a testimony to them and the Gentiles. When they hand you over, do not worry about how you are to speak or what you are to say; for what you are to say will be given to you at that time; for it is not you who speak but the Spirit of your Father speaking through you . . . you will be hated by all because of my name. But the one who endures to the end will be saved. . . . A disciple is not above the teacher, nor a slave above the master; it is enough for the disciple to be like the teacher, and the slave like the master. If they have called the master of the house Beelzebul, how much more will they malign those of his household! . . . Do not fear those who kill the body but cannot kill the soul; rather fear him who can destroy both soul and body in hell. . . . Everyone therefore who acknowledges me before others, I also will acknowledge before my Father in heaven; but whoever denies me before others, I will deny before my Father in heaven. . . . Do not think that I have come to bring peace to the earth; I have not come to bring peace, but a sword. . . . Whoever loves father or mother more than me is not worthy of me; and whoever loves son or daughter more than me is not worthy of me; and whoever does not take up the cross and follow me is not worthy of me. Those who find their life will lose it, and those who love their life for my sake will find it. (Matt. 10:16–20, 22, 24–25, 28, 32–34, 37–39)

Those are perhaps the most important sentences in the great commission speech of Jesus to the Twelve (Matt. 10). To begin with, it is significant that according to the word of Jesus, the apostles and their message are not being sent to a neutrally disposed mankind that with its religious yearning might be ready receive the apostles' proclamation of the kingdom of God with open arms. No; they are sent like sheep among wolves, while, as St. Augustine has remarked in one of his sermons, it is assumed that the wolves are in the majority; and yet it is the sheep who are sent to the wolves, and not the reverse, with the wolves sent to the sheep. We look first of all to the Jews, since the Apostles are brought to the councils and synagogues of the Jews. But then they are brought to Roman governors and to kings, so that proceedings against them before the court become a testimony about the pagans. As Jesus was brought before the tribunal of Jews and Gentiles, so too the apostles. In the passion narrative of Jesus and in the trial proceedings against the apostles and martyrs, both the Jews and the Gentiles in their ultimate intentions are openly guilty before God. Therefore it makes sense for the apostles to beware of men, and specifically that means: of Jews and Gentiles. That the teaching of the apostles encounters this hostile resistance is conditioned by the fact that with the appearance of Christ, the final, critical time has broken in, bringing not reconciliation but decision, not peace but the sword. In this critical time that has broken in with the appearance of Christ, in which all natural orders are dissolved and even blood ties are no longer able to bind human beings, because on the contrary according to the words of Jesus brother delivers up brother to death and children their parents, in this time in which the end of the present age is announced, can Jesus assert: "Whoever loves father and mother more than me is not worthy of me" (Matt. 10:37). It is clear that he who brings the sword cannot predict for his disciples anything but that they will be hated by all, for his name's sake. He knows that they will mock, whip, and kill them, that persecutions will be prepared for them, and that the disciples will flee from one town to another. But if they endure to the end, whether of their lives or the world itself, they receive the promise of their salvation and happiness. Whoever "has left brothers or sisters or mother or father or children or fields, for my sake and for the sake of the gospel, will receive it back a hundredfold" (Mark 10:29–30). Indeed, whoever gives even a cup of cold water to one of these persecuted disciples, can be sure of his reward (cf. Matt. 10:42), for whoever receives an apostle, receives the one who has sent him. Thus between the apostles and Jesus a tight connection exists; one could even call it a thoroughly shared eschatological fellowship of suffering and destiny. The student will share the same fate as the teacher. If Jesus, the master of the house, was called a devil, how could one find milder words for his disciples? If Jesus was dragged before the tribunal of Jewish and Gentile judges, the same fate awaits the apostles.

But a special aspect of this fate is emphasized in Jesus' words: it is the aspect from which the word "martyr" originates. When the disciples stand before the court, they may find themselves at a loss as to what to say, how they are to respond. On the contrary, they are to give no thought to this anxiety. The Holy Spirit, the Spirit of the Father, will speak through them and transform their speech from a mere apologetic defense to a *witness* against Jews and Gentiles; they become witnesses, in Greek, "martyrs." This alone is the final command of Jesus: that his disciples publicly confess him and his name. Whoever confesses to Jesus publicly on earth, Jesus himself will confess before his Father in heaven. For in the time of decision, in the eschatological time, there are only two things: either confession of Jesus or denial of him. Playing hide and seek with a generic piety, an unclear here-and-there, is ruled out, not as a human possibility but rather through him who brings the sword and whose name—O sweet Name of Jesus!—brings with it a division, which does not stop even before the private sphere of family life, but rather separates son from father and daughter from mother (Matt. 10:35).

·   ·   ·

When one hears the words of Jesus, it is clear that the concept of the apostle takes precedence over that of the martyr—but also that, on the other hand, the concept of the martyr cannot simply be severed from that of the apostle. The sayings about persecution apply in the first instance to the Twelve, but then, almost imperceptibly, an expansion occurs. "Whoever does not take up his cross and follow me is not worthy of me" (Matt. 10:38). That is a saying that can in no way be limited to the apostles. Apostleship is a restricted reality (even down to number), but the concept of the martyrs is not restricted to the apostles, and the great number in white robes with palm branches in their hands, whom St. John sees in Revelation, is beyond counting. What does that say to our topic?

First, the general point: that the apostolic Church, which is founded on the apostles, who become martyrs, is also always the suffering Church, the Church of the martyrs. A church that does not suffer is not the apostolic Church. But because the concept of the martyr is not limited to that of the apostle, the successor of the apostle in the juridical sense is not necessarily a successor of the suffering of the apostles. The apostolic suffering can very well be repeated in a martyr who is not a successor of the apostles in a juridical sense, just as the miracles of the apostles can be performed by people who, regarded juridically, are not successors of the apostles. Martyrdom is thus a charisma and not necessarily tied to an office in the Church. It is a special grace of God that no man can produce on his own. To be sure, in the Twelve office and charisma are united, and the apostles are therefore also martyrs; in the successors of the apostles, however, office and charisma are separated. And the result is: the successor of the apostles is not a new apostle but a successor of the *only* apostles, the Twelve; otherwise today we would have in the Church not bishops but apostles as successors of the Twelve.

But a second consequence also follows: in the Church the concept of the martyr necessarily develops into an independent category alongside that of the apostle. This separation of the apostles—or, to be more precise, the successors of the apostles—from the martyrs has always given offense. Some expect that all of those who are successors of the apostles in a juridical sense must become martyrs; while others are unwilling to admit any kind of independent category of "martyr." Both opinions are mistaken because they both depend on a misunderstanding of the special situation of the Twelve Apostles in the Church. It is enough simply to bow to two facts: that the successors of the Twelve Apostles are no longer apostles and that the concept of the martyr as an independent category in the Church is necessary if the Church wants to maintain its continuity with the apostolic charisms (and that means also the suffering and martyrdom of the apostles) not only in its teaching but also in its life. Whoever expects that all who are juridical successors of the apostles must necessarily become martyrs as well, will end up in a sect. Whoever, on the other hand, rejects the independent category of the martyr in the Church by claiming that it did not yet exist in the apostolic period, will only *seem* to have preserved the apostolic teaching. In fact, rejection of the concept of the martyr eliminates suffering for the Church—though suffering is necessarily linked with the preaching of the apostles—and thereby deprives the concept of the preaching of the gospel of its original meaning. To get this point, one simply needs to read Kierkegaard's *Attack on Christendom*—which is really an attack on Protestantism—in order to understand the consequences of Protestantism's rejection of the concept of martyrdom and sainthood for the preaching of the gospel. The secularization of Protestantism, which Kierkegaard fought against so passionately and to which he opposed the concept of the "witness of the truth"—meaning the concept of the martyr—is just the inevitable result of the Protestant rejection of the cult of the martyrs and the saints.

I have thus established my first thesis: that the martyr claims charismatic status in the Church, because the concept of the martyr is different from that of an apostle, even though the apostles themselves were martyrs.

The second thesis that one can infer from the words of Jesus is that the martyr is necessary to the concept of the Church. There are certain humane types who are inclined to attribute everything that happens in the world to mere misunderstandings. If it were up to them, it would have been a mere misunderstanding whereby Christ was crucified and the apostles were killed; when the hour of martyrdom again comes to the Church, these same people are inclined to attribute it all to a misunderstanding. On the contrary: the words of Jesus now show them that not a human misunderstanding but a divine necessity makes martyrs. Jesus' saying, "Is it not necessary that the Son of Man suffer these things?" applies to all the Church's suffering. As long as the Gospel is preached in this world—and that means to the end of time—the Church will also have martyrs. If the message of Jesus had merely been a philosophical doctrine about which one had to discuss for years on end, for centuries, there would never have been martyrs. And if individual human beings died for such a philosophy of Christ—they still would not be martyrs in the Christian sense of the word. To emphasize the point one more time: not human convictions and opinions, to put it still more pointedly not even human zeal for the faith makes martyrs,[5] but only Christ himself, who issues the summons to martyrdom and thereby makes martyrdom a special grace: this Christ, who is preached by the Church in the Gospel, offered up in the sacrifice of the altar, and whose name all of those who are baptized in the name of Jesus Christ are bound in their conscience to confess. We forget so often that in this world the Gospel is preached by lambs before wolves, and that according to Jesus' own words, the message of the Kingdom of God is delivered—now as then—to an adulterous and sinful generation (Mark 8:38). How can one actually expect that the wolves won't fall on the sheep? Perhaps it is rather to be expected that the disciples of Jesus would be ashamed of him and his words before this "adulterous and sinful generation." But he who predicted Peter's betrayal reckoned with this possibility, too. Certainly, there may be times in which martyrs are fewer and times in which they are more; but to say that at certain times there are no martyrs at all would be to deny the Church's existence at that time.

But why are the disciples "hated by all" (Matt. 10:22) for the sake of Jesus' name? Who are these "all"? They are "the men" of whom the Twelve are to beware: Jews and Gentiles. These are not "human beings as such" in the sense of a mere abstraction, but men who exist concretely, in their total reality in this world, as Jews or as Gentiles. For what other possibilities are still available for those who have not received the grace of Christ? The Jews are named first by Jesus as persecutors of the Church, and of them is most said, for the Jew is in another and a more original sense than the Gentile an enemy of Christ. It is a fact that in every persecution of the Church from the time of the apostles to the present day, the Jews have taken part. But as the Gentiles once collaborated with the Jews in the condemnation of Jesus, so what happened at the trial of Jesus is still exemplary in the world of today. The Gentiles, despite their awareness of how much separates them from the Jews—recall the anti-Jewish utterances of the anti-Christian pagan Celsus—nevertheless work together with the Jews, when it serves them, to fight against God's Anointed. And so according to God's will both Jews and Gentiles became enemies of the Gospel, so that God would have pity upon both.

The third conclusion to be drawn from the words of Jesus concerns the fact that the martyr demonstrates the public claim of the Church of Jesus Christ. As it belongs to the concept of the martyr to be brought for reckoning before the public organs of the state—in councils and synagogues, before governors and kings—to be subjected to a public judicial proceeding and the penalties of the public law, so too the public confession of the name of Jesus belongs to the concept of the martyrs. But insofar as the martyr before the court, in the public realm of the state, confesses him who will return publicly in the glory of the Father in order to judge this world, both Jews and Gentiles, in this very confession the martyr leaps beyond this world's concept of "public" and demonstrates in his words the public claim of another, a coming new world. He who confesses Jesus publicly on this earth is, in the moment of his confession, confessed publicly by Jesus in heaven. The significance of the act of confession on earth is matched by Jesus' solemn confession of the name of his confessor before God and the holy angels (cf. Luke 12:8). Because it is a confession of faith and not a confession of guilt, the words that the martyr speaks before the organs of the public authority are not human words but words that the Holy Spirit of the Father in heaven speaks in the confessors of Jesus Christ. Though the world sees in the confessor's words only a confession of guilt and not a religious profession, the Church knows that in the simple confession "I am a Christian," testified before the representatives of the authority of the state, God's Holy Spirit speaks, in that the public claim of the dominion of Jesus Christ is also testified to. The Church also knows that when the martyr steps forward as a witness for Christ the heavens open, as happened at the stoning of Stephen, and the Son of Man becomes visible, he who in heaven before the angels not only solemnly confesses his confessor, but also, when he stands at the right hand of God, makes known the future tribunal, before which the judges of this world, whether Jews or Gentiles, will receive their judgment.

The final thing to be concluded from the words of Jesus is that the martyr suffers with Christ as a member of the mystical body of Christ.[6] When we say that the martyr suffers *with* Christ, we mean that his suffering is not described fully by simply saying he suffers *for* Christ. Many soldiers have died for their king. But the martyr's death differs from the soldier's death in that the martyr does not only suffer *for* Jesus, rather he is led into his own death by the death of Christ. The passion and death of Christ, because it is "the Son of Man," the one who became man, who suffers, extends over the entire Church as his mystical body. Therefore the one who confesses Jesus in baptism is baptized into the death of Jesus, and therefore too the one who gives thanks to God in the Eucharist for having sent us his son Jesus participates in Jesus, in that he eats the broken body of the Lord and drinks the cup with the blood of the New Covenant. Because we are baptized into the death of the Lord and are fed with the blood of the Lord, it is unavoidable for everyone who belongs to the Church to have a share in the suffering of Christ. To be sure, there are various ways in which the individual members of the body of Christ suffer with the head. The suffering of Christ, says St. Thomas [Aquinas] (*Summa Theologiae* 3.66.12), works in water baptism by a figural representation (*per quandam figuralem repraesentationem*), but in baptism by blood through an imitation of the act (*per imitationem operis*), and for St. Thomas there is no doubt that baptism by blood is the noblest of all baptisms.[7] This justifies us in saying that the possibility of martyrdom, which exists for all of us, is rooted in the same reality of the baptism unto death of Jesus, into which we have been baptized through baptism by water. We are all, as St. Paul says (Rom. 6:3), "baptized into the death of Christ." And this makes us realize that the possibility by which we too must sacrifice even body and blood for Christ, is grounded in the fact that the body and the blood of the Lord, in which we partake, comes to us in that cup which the Lord accepted in Gethsemane. Thus baptism by water and baptism by blood come from the same Lord, prefigured in the symbol, as Cyril of Jerusalem has shown, of the blood and water that flowed from the side of Jesus.[8]

. . .

But, someone may say, if it is true that the passion and death of Christ extend over the whole Church as his mystical body, are not we, who are anything but martyrs, perhaps outside the body of Christ? The Lord has already given the answer to this question, when in the sayings on persecution he also speaks of discipleship and of taking the cross on oneself. Not everyone can become a martyr, for martyrdom presumes a special calling; it is, as was already said, a charism in the Church. But in some sense we all can, no, we *must* follow the Lord in his passion, and therefore the cross is not only a symbol for the martyrs, but for all Christian lives in general. It is thus no accidental historical development, as Protestant historical scholarship forever is opining, but grounded in the very substance of the matter, that the "saints," who have undergone all their mortifications and sufferings, become a parallel to the martyrs. And if we do not become martyrs and do not become saints, we must all nevertheless undergo some type of asceticism.

But in Christian asceticism, for us who, to use Paul's expression, bear the *mortificatio Christi* (2 Cor. 4:10) in our bodies, there is really only a single principle, that of suffering with Christ, of mortification with him who was put to death for us.[9] The one who said, "My Father, if it is possible, let this cup pass from me" (Matt. 26:39) knows our faint-heartedness, our dread of suffering and death. He knows that we shrink from following him, that we are weak and do not want to take the cross upon ourselves, that we are afraid of poverty, scorn, revilement, blows, and death. But he who bore our weak flesh removed our faint-heartedness by his own apparent faint-heartedness, as St. Athanasius puts it.[10] Everything that happens in the Church happens under the presupposition that Christ not only died but that he rose again. Therefore it is not only the passion and death but also the power of Christ's resurrection that extends over the mystical body. We are thus not only baptized into the death of Christ but at the same time we receive the Holy Spirit in baptism. The ascetical and spiritual life of Christians is not only a mortification but at the same time an overcoming, a living, a walking in the Holy Spirit. And therefore too the physical pain, the suffering and death of the martyr are finally not the end but the victory over this world that he has won in the glory of Christ,[11] and that leads out of this world directly into Paradise. He who in action has imitated the suffering of Christ and who calls from under the altar in heaven, "How long, Lord, holy and true, will it be before you judge and avenge our blood on the inhabitants of the earth?" (Rev. 6:10), he receives from God the white robe that wins him entrance into Paradise. The attaining of Paradise, in which the martyr has an immediate share and which separates him from the rest of the faithful, is thus the power of the Resurrection that is extended to those in the mystical body of Christ who have in a real sense died with Christ. If we suffer with Christ, we will also have a share in his glory, it says in Romans 8:17. "The glory of the martyrs," as St. Augustine says, "is the glory of Christ, who has gone before the martyrs, who has fulfilled them, and who crowns them." (*Augustini Sermones post Maurinos reperti*, ed. Morin, 57.1) How unhappy the Protestant polemic against the Catholic Church's cult of the martyrs and of the saints looks in this light! In its striving to protect the glory of Christ over against the martyrs and the saints, the Protestant polemic strikes the mystical body of Christ. But how can one attack the body of Christ without at the same time striking the head, from whom comes the grace of the members?

Anyone who has read the epigrams that Pope Damasus composed in Rome in honor of the martyrs has perhaps been struck by the way they repeatedly say, when speaking of the Church's persecutions, "But when the sword passed through the Mother's heart." Because the body of Christ suffers in the martyrs, who (to use St. Paul's expression) "are fulfilling in their body what is lacking in the afflictions of Christ for the Church," therefore the Mother too suffers along with the martyrs, and therefore Mary is rightly hailed by the Church as *regina martyrum*. Now we understand when St. Peter writes: "Do not be surprised at the fiery ordeal that is taking place among you to test you, as though something strange were happening to you" (1 Pet. 4:12). No, the Church's sufferings lose all of their strangeness when they are seen in light of the suffering of Christ. They are not reason for deep unease, but rather the occasion to give thanks to God. "But rejoice insofar as you are sharing Christ's sufferings," as 1 Peter goes on to say in the passage quoted above, "so that you may also be glad and shout for joy when his glory is revealed."

Over all the suffering that recurs to the Church of Christ stands Our Lord's saying in the Beatitudes: "Blessed are you when people revile you and persecute you and utter all kinds of evil against you on account of the Son of Man! Rejoice on that day and be glad, for your reward is great in heaven" (Matt. 5:11–12).

The Book of Revelation and the Martyrs

The Book of Revelation is one of the least familiar writings in the New Testament. It is true that sectarians of all ages have gladly devoted themselves to this book, and that may have been a reason why in the Church its readers have tended to be regarded with a degree of suspicion. And it is doubtless true that this book, with its to us so often fantastic images, is frequently dark and in places incomprehensible, and to a certain extent will always remain incomprehensible. But a still further factor may explain why we avoid contact with this book. Let me illustrate this by telling about an experience I had in my childhood. As a child I once found a bible in a box of books belonging to my grandfather. When I opened it up, my eye fell on the chapter of Revelation (Rev. 6) that describes the going forth of the four horsemen of the Apocalypse. After I had read through to the end of the chapter, I fled terrified from the attic; it was as though I had peeked into a secret that was at once terrible and real, and yet which should have remained discreetly concealed. It makes sense, therefore, it may perhaps even be a good thing, that avoidance of the mystery of the Last Things keeps many from reading this book. Let us just say it point blank: this book about the Last Things is dangerous. It lets us take a look into an abyss that surrounds us, but that we are anxious to cover over, hoping that it may not be as bad as all that or that the worst may not come to pass. In another sense, this book is dangerous because of the frightening way it shows us what under certain circumstances we may be obliged to do, what God and his Christ could some day demand of us. Who does not think with a certain uneasiness about warnings that remind us of a duty that we are not sure we shall be able to fulfill?

So what God wills and what our weakness wants conspire to keep us at a safe distance from the Book of Revelation. The Church's engagement with this text—as with the various other books of the Bible—has its divinely ordained time and hour. One of these divinely willed hours came when the pagan Roman state demanded that Christians participate in the imperial cult. In the age of the persecutions, the Church of the martyrs turned to this book.[12] Another divinely willed hour came when the Roman Empire collapsed under the attacks of the peoples on its borders. That was when St. Augustine read this book in order to interpret the meaning of this event, and of history as such, in *On the City of God*.[13] But it was also a divinely willed holy hour when this book itself was written. Under the impression of the doctrine that all scriptures of the Old and the New Testament have been inspired by the Holy Spirit, we are often inclined to overlook that the Holy Spirit has its own "times and hours," or, if I may so put it, its "occasions." St. John did not, however, forget that the Book of Revelation had its "time and hour" when it was written down: "I, John, your brother, who share with you in Jesus the tribulation and the kingdom and the patient endurance, was on the island called Patmos because of the word of God and the testimony for the sake of Jesus. I was in the Spirit on the Lord's day" (Rev. 1:9–10). With these words the "occasion" of the Holy Spirit is made known. John was exiled to Patmos because he had publicly testified for Jesus. He shares the "tribulation" with other Christians but he also endures with them, and so is already with them in the kingdom of Christ. In this concrete setting of confession and martyrdom,[14] there comes to pass the "Revelation of Jesus Christ," for that is the true title of the book, not, as we often call it, the "Revelation of St. John." St. John did not have some type of "private revelation"; rather, Jesus Christ has revealed himself. Obviously not as he did in his first coming—for this occurred essentially in "secret" (in mystery)[15]—but as he will be "revealed" in his second coming. As John—in analogy to Jesus, "the true witness" (Rev. 1:5 and 3:14)—became "revealed" by his public witness, so too there corresponds to this emergence from the private into the public sphere a manifestation of Jesus Christ from the mystery of his first coming into the public reality of his second coming. Not by accident does St. John emphasize the "tribulation" that he shares with the recipients of his book, for according to primitive Christianity the "tribulation" is both participation in the "suffering" of Christ,[16] in its concealment, yet at the same time an impetus toward his "glory," his might, his power, his rule, and also his public manifestation. According to primitive Christianity, the tribulation, the suffering, is never merely individual, but always collectively experienced,[17] and the "participation"[18] in it that St. John shares with other Christians pervades the entire cosmos:[19] all of creation takes part in this tribulation (Rom. 8:19). But just as humanity rises above tribulation in hope,[20] so too creation, if I may use one of St. Paul's images in Romans 8:19,[21] raises "its head up" and waits for the "unveiling," for the "becoming revealed" of the sons of God. Suffering is universal in this world because it is a suffering with the suffering of Christ, who has entered into this world and yet has transcended this world, when he rose from the dead and ascended into heaven. But where the meaning of the suffering with Christ becomes public, that is, in the open political setting of a public trial[22]—and that is an essential precondition of the concept of the martyr—there too the glory of Christ becomes public and "revealed" in a way comparable to the public character of the state. Thus according to Acts 7:56, St. Stephen, as a martyr, does not so much see the risen Christ as the glory of the "Son of Man" standing in heaven at the right hand of God. In exactly the same way, St. John also sees in his visions in Revelation the "Son of Man" in his complete majesty in heaven (Rev. 1:22ff.). But just as the confessor must not worry about what he will say in court, because the Spirit of the Father will speak through him, Jesus says (Matt. 10:19f.; cf. Luke 21:14f.), so too in the martyr the Holy Spirit "translates," if I may put it this way, the sacramental bond and faith in the crucified and risen Christ into the showing of the Son of Man enthroned in glory.[23] It is completely clear that here everything is "grace," both the "public" confession as well as the "public" suffering and finally the revelation of the glory linked to them, the glory of him with whom they suffer and for whom they make their testimony.

·   ·   ·

The "revelation" of Jesus Christ in "glory" means that the Lord takes on a "public character" analogous to the public character of the political realm. The symbols of political sovereignty that the Book of Revelation has transferred to Christ show this clearly. The seven lampstands that surround the Son of Man in heaven correspond to the candelabra at the courts of Hellenistic and Roman rulers, their fire symbolizing the eternal length of their political sovereignty. We also meet the seven stars that Christ holds in his hand on the coinage of the Roman emperors, to indicate the omnipotence of their rule. The *proskynesis* (obeisance) which is performed before the Son of Man and the acclamations made to him all reflect an analogy to the political world before which the Son of Man becomes "revealed." In Revelation, Christ is therefore also hailed as "ruler of the kings of the earth" (1:5) and "King of kings and Lord of lords" (19:16 and 17:14). He is "the priestly king" who, as will be explained later, becomes revealed at the end of time. Here it is important to note that with the martyr not only does "the Son of Man" become "revealed" in heaven, but along with "the Son of Man" at the same time too "the human beings who live on the earth." In chapter 7, it is told how an angel comes from heaven to mark a seal on the brow of the slaves of God, the 144,000 elect. It is well known how the early Church used the expression "seal" for baptism (and confirmation). Although baptism in itself is indeed a "mystery," nevertheless through the concept of the "seal," the concealment that belongs to every mystery is cancelled. That is what is represented by the concept of the seal applied to the brow.[24] But the Book of Revelation shows us that this "revelation" through sealing stands in parallel to the "revelation" of the Son of Man, even though the sealing occurs before the disclosure of the Son of Man. In this "revelation" of the mystery of baptism as a seal there naturally lies as well the possibility of a danger to the baptized. The "sealed," those who have been sealed on their brow, become visible and can be persecuted. But not only are "the elect" sealed, so too are the followers of the Antichrist. To be sure, they do not have a seal but a mark, a brand on brow and hand (13:16). The idea is clear: in view of the revelation of Jesus Christ there is no more anonymity among human beings. All human beings are signed, either with the seal of Christ or with the brand of the Antichrist.

But not only does humanity become "known" in view of the revelation of Jesus Christ: no, the cosmos too now becomes revealed.[25] In chapter 12 it is told how a great sign is seen in the heavens: a woman clothed with the sun, with the moon under feet and a crown of stars on her head. It is she who is to give birth to the one who will shepherd all the nations with an iron rod. It is the Mother of God. But scarcely has she become visible in the heavens, before she has even given birth to her son, than the dragon now appears to devour her child after his birth. The "revelation" of Christ, expressed symbolically by his birth in heaven, has as its immediate result the "revelation" of the demonic power that rules the cosmos. The dragon too becomes visible in heaven. Admittedly, the dragon is soon afterwards cast out of heaven onto the earth; thereby he seems to have forfeited his visibility, but only apparently so, for now a beast climbs out of the sea, a beast that has received the power of the dragon (13:1). Instead of the dragon, meaning the devil, now the Antichrist is revealed, who is supposed to be symbolized by this beast. But that is not all. After him another beast climbs up from the earth; it is the false prophet, perhaps we might say, the theologian of the Antichrist. He too, like the devil and the Antichrist, only becomes visible through the revelation of Jesus Christ. That is expressed in visual terms by the image of the emergence from the sea or from the earth. It is clear that there can only be an Antichrist when Christ has appeared; but now it also becomes clear that the Antichrist becomes revealed only to the extent that Christ is revealed. In this way it is recognized that Antichrist can only exist in the Endtime. "Children, it is the last hour and as you have heard, the Antichrist is coming," it says in 1 John 2:18. But it is said in 4:1 of this same letter that many false prophets (who in 1 John 2:18 are called "antichrists") have gone out into the world. Here we clearly see that the false prophet, the heretic, the theologian of the Antichrist, is a reality that has first become visible for the martyr through the revelation of Christ. There were disputatious philosophers before Christ, but false prophets as theologians of Antichrist—in other words, heretics—just since Christ has been revealed, by whom the Antichrist and his theologians have also been disclosed. Seen from this perspective, it becomes possible to understand the passion with which the Church, in the person of its saints, has persecuted heretics. It is not simply a case of rejecting the representative of a differing opinion, a false understanding, as judged from a totally abstract, timeless, scientific or scholarly perspective; on the contrary, the false teacher is seen as standing in the service of a demonic power, as it has been disclosed by the revelation of Jesus Christ. According to primitive Christianity, the false teacher is therefore cursed (Col. 1:8) or handed over to Satan (1 Cor. 5:5; 1 Tim. 1:20)—they amount to the same thing—indeed, according to Revelation 2:23 is even slain, because he shows through his teaching that he is from Satan, in that his teaching is only a teaching about the deep things of Satan (Rev. 2:24) and not a teaching about the deep things of God (1 Cor. 2:10). Just as the revelation of Christ makes human anonymity impossible but rather has revealed all men for what they are, so too does the revelation of Jesus Christ mean that humanity's knowledge is no longer concealed but is always recognized either as a knowledge of the Holy Spirit, from the *pneuma* that searches out the "deep things of God" (1 Cor. 2:10), or as a knowledge of "the deep things of Satan." A so-called "pure knowing," seen from this perspective, would try to abstract itself from the revelation of Jesus Christ, whereas that revelation in fact means that every kind of knowing is either Christian or anti-Christian. Seen from this angle, we can see how the martyr, who has become revealed in a way analogous to Christ, has a sharp eye for the appearance of a heretic. One understands in this connection the warnings of St. John or of St. Ignatius against heretics.

It is significant that the false prophet appears in the wake of the false Christ. The Antichrist himself pursues neither philosophy nor theology; he belongs to the world of politics and therefore wages war against the "Lamb" and against "the saints." Now the thinking of the false prophet takes as its presupposition the perverted political order created by the Antichrist. Because human thinking is never independent of the *hic et nunc* of a political order of some kind, it inevitably stands either under the power of the Antichrist or the power of Christ. Recall the fifth chapter of Revelation, which relates the opening of the scroll by the Lamb. No one could open the scroll in the hand of God, no one could undo its seal. No angel, no man, no demon, but only the "Lion of Judah" who has conquered, only he is able to do it. That doubtless presumes the notion that through a victory in the political order, a kind of knowledge is also established. Thinking is determined by the political order. Because the victory of the "Lion of Judah" transcends all other "victories" in the merely political order, the thinking allied to the "victory of the Lamb" also transcends every type of thinking that emanates from a merely political order. The important point to be clear about is that the "revealing" of Jesus Christ leads to a type of reflection that, like real "knowledge," is *public* and therefore goes beyond a "wisdom" that is reserved only for initiates.

When the Book of Revelation asserts a connection between heresy and the perverted political order of the Antichrist, it anticipates the experience of many centuries in the Christian era. Every real heresy that in the course of church history has or will become prominent—we do not include here mere school controversies—stands and has always stood shoulder to shoulder with a political order of an anti-Christian stamp.[26]

. . .

Another word on the figure of the Antichrist. The cosmos, into which Christ, his saints and the martyrs are placed, is symbolized by the dragon, the beast, and the other beast, that is, through the devil, the Antichrist, and the false prophet. In light of the revelation of Jesus Christ, all three become visible for the martyrs: the devil in the metaphysical order, the Antichrist in the political order, and the false prophet in the intellectual order. As there is no longer a "pure knowing" in the intellectual order, but only either a knowledge of the deep things of Satan or a searching by the Holy Spirit of the deep things of God, so too in the time of martyrdom there is in the political order no possible concept of political activity based on alleged neutrality. In view of the revealing of Jesus Christ, the sphere of the political must also become revealed.[27] That becomes clear above all in the question of power. For power is something mysterious—who will possess it? The cosmic force of Satan, who delegates it to the Antichrist (Rev. 13:2), or God, who has given it to his Son?

And further: As a mystery, power in the final analysis demands to be worshipped. The only question is whether we are worshipping the legitimate power of the Almighty or the usurped power of the one who makes himself like God. According to Revelation, the false prophet has human beings erect a cultic image of the Antichrist (13:14). The political symbol becomes a cultic object and is even able to perform wonders (13:15). But now humanity is divided by the political symbol seen as a cultic object. Those who do not bow before the image of the Beast are either slain (13:15) or subjected to an economic boycott (13:17).

In chapter 17 we have another symbol for the public unveiling of the world of the political. Babylon appears in the person of a whore, clad in purple and scarlet and sitting on a scarlet beast. When St. John has seen the whore in her complete appearance, he is amazed. Here a woman symbolizes, as is common, the city, the *tyche*, the *fortuna* of political existence. But now this woman has been revealed as a whore who is bound to no one but gives herself away to all. For the revelation of Christ also makes visible for the martyr the metaphysical disorientation that marks the false political order: the political, whose plane of activity is in the world of pluralism, is always tempted to abandon the ultimate metaphysical orientation and to seek its gods in the world of the pluralistic. That the false political order seeks its ultimate bond in the world of the pluralistic is expressed by Revelation when it says that the kings of the world have come to commit fornication with the whore of Babylon. The ultimate metaphysical disorientation of a political order that does not receive its power from God is brought to symbolic expression when Babylon holds the cup of wine in her hand. The pluralism of the political world, which in the time of revelation can intensify to the point of a metaphysical pluralism, has become an intoxication that makes all the nations of the earth drunk (18:3).

Still another feature of the political becomes clear for the witnesses of Jesus Christ through his revelation. When Babylon, the great whore, has fallen, the merchants, traders, and shipmasters raise a great song of lament (18:11–19). It is striking with what detail this lament is recounted in Revelation. The brilliance of the political is exposed after the fall of Babel as in reality the economic profit of international commerce.

Over against the whore of Babel stands the virgin Jerusalem, ready for her marriage with the single husband, as St. Paul says (2 Cor. 11:2), or for the marriage with Christ the Lamb, as St. John here expresses it (Rev. 21). In her is symbolized a sovereignty that has overcome the temptation that consists in political pluralism. It is clear that "the virgin" does not hold the cup of wine in her hand. Where Jerusalem is, where the Church of the Martyrs is, there is sobriety, there is Logos. For the virgin who is made ready for the marriage with the Lamb knows the path that she will take. Where Jerusalem is, there is simplicity, yes, even possibly poverty, yet the splendor of the virgin is in heaven, with God and with the Lamb; she therefore has no need of a splendor borrowed from the earth, which in the final analysis can only serve to enrich international business.

Accordingly, both the whore and the virgin have become visible for the martyr. Both have become visible because the revealing of the "Son of Man" throws both humanity and the whole cosmos into bright light.

Not only does the demonic abyss of the world open before us in light of the revealing of the "Son of Man," and in the "revelation of Jesus Christ" become visible for the martyr, but also the destiny and duty of the faithful in the great hour of the "tribulation." It is not true that the faithful are spared suffering and apparent defeat because the Lamb has now "conquered." No, "the two witnesses" who according to Revelation appear in Jerusalem are overcome and slain by the beast that climbs from the abyss. "And their dead bodies will lie in the street of the great city that is symbolically called 'Sodom' and 'Egypt,' where also their Lord was crucified" (Rev. 11:8). According to 13:7, it was given to the beast, meaning the Antichrist, "to contend with the saints and to overcome them." According to 16:5f., an angel finds it justified that God punishes the world,[28] for it has shed the blood of the saints and the prophets. The revealing of those who have been "sealed" therefore occurs through their suffering. Suffering is imitation (Phil. 3:10) of the suffering of Christ, and every defeat at the hands of the demonic powers is nothing but a likeness to the defeat of Jesus, "the true witness."[29]

It is important to note that, according to St. John, in the revelation of Jesus Christ, no one stays exempt from this suffering. A fearful scene is described in Revelation 6:9ff. John sees under the altar in heaven the souls of those who "have been slaughtered for the word of God and for the testimony they had given." The martyrs who lie under the altar cry out with loud voices, "Sovereign Lord, holy and true, how long will it be before you judge and avenge our blood on the inhabitants of the earth?" And to them were given white robes, according to 6:11, and they were told to be patient yet a little longer, until the number was completed of their fellow servants and brothers, who were likewise to be killed.

"Let anyone who has an ear to hear listen: If you are to be taken captive, into captivity you go; if you kill with the sword, with the sword you must be killed" (Rev. 13:9–10). This is to be understood in connection with the endurance and the faith of the saints. In chapter 7, St. John sees in heaven a great host of those clothed in white. One of the elders asks him who these were and says, "These are they who have come out of the great tribulation and have washed their robes and made them white in the blood of the Lamb" (Rev. 7:14). With blood they have made white the robes that they wore, with the blood that they have shed, and yet this is not their blood but the blood of the Lamb. St. Paul says in Colossians 1:24 that in his own suffering he is completing what is lacking in the sufferings of Christ. Once again we have the same thought: all suffering is eschatological suffering and is endured in conformity with the suffering of Christ, and those who have suffered with Christ are therefore assured of the glory of Christ.

. . .

Against this heroic message humanity, alas so cowardly, now rebels. From the letter of St. John to Laodicea, we see the judgment of Jesus on the cowardly: "I know your works: you are neither cold nor hot. Would that you were either cold or hot! But because you are lukewarm, and neither cold nor hot, I will spit you out of my mouth" (Rev. 3:15–16), In 21:8, it likewise says, "But as for the cowardly, their place will be with the murderers and the adulterers and the rest, in the lake that burns with fire and sulfur." According to the judgment of the martyr, it comes down to one thing: to conquer, to conquer with Christ: "Whoever conquers," says the one who holds the seven stars in his right hand (cf. 2:1), "to them I will give permission to eat of the tree of life that is in the paradise of God (2:7)." "Everyone who conquers . . . will rule over nations" (2:26). "Whoever conquers will become a pillar in the temple of the heavenly Jerusalem" (cf. 3:12). "Whoever conquers as Christ has conquered, will sit with Christ and the Father upon the throne" (cf. 3:21). "Those who conquer will inherit everything" (21:7).

It is thus not true that the martyrs constitute a self-enclosed class and that the rest of the faithful can be content to think, "Thank God for the martyrs!" No, the souls of the martyrs that lie under the altar in heaven are unable to find rest, says St. John, until their brothers have followed them in martyrdom. Potentially all the faithful could thus be called to martyrdom, for all are signed with the seal of God that makes their allegiance to "the Lamb that was slain" a public reality. They must "conquer" because a battle is imposed upon them, because the dragon lies in wait for "the seed of the Woman," to whom not just Jesus but all of us belong—we are all the children of Mary (Rev. 12:17). They must conquer, because the Antichrist wages war against the saints, because he forces a decision on them by making the political symbol a cultic object. They must "conquer" in that they become "public," they become "public" in their witness for Jesus. For in this Endtime of the revealing of the "mystery of lawlessness,"[30] everyone is called to give testimony for God: the angel who declares that God is justified when he strikes the world (16:5), the altar in heaven, to which the Church's prayers are brought (16:7), and so finally, too, humanity: everyone is required to give testimony for God and against this world, in which the dragon rules and the Antichrist and the false prophet have appeared. "For none of us lives a private life and none of us dies a private death," says St. Paul in Romans 14:7f., "but if we live, we live to the Lord, and if we die, we die to the Lord, so then, whether we live or whether we die, we are the Lord's." We are always bound to the public reality of the Lord, to the public revealing of the Lord.

Living in the revelation of Jesus Christ is a life in the great tribulation. "Blessed are those who weep now, for they will laugh" (Luke 6:21). For "he will wipe every tear from their eyes," says St. John (Rev. 21:4). "Blessed are those who mourn now," it is said in the Sermon on the Mount (Matt. 5:4), "for they will be comforted." And again the martyr agrees: "Death will be no more; nor mourning, nor crying, nor pain" (Rev. 21:4). "Blessed are you," the Sermon on the Mount says finally (Luke 6:22f.), "when people hate you, and when they exclude you, revile you, and despise your name on account of the Son of Man. Rejoice on that day and leap for joy, for surely your reward is great in heaven; in like manner their fathers also treated the prophets." What else is the unveiling of the revelation of Jesus Christ, in which the martyrs take part, but the illustration of this blessing of Jesus?

When one hears the beatitudes of the Sermon on the Mount or reads the promises of the Book of Revelation, one realizes that Christianity is not a trivial matter. If there is anything that is the opposite of the spirit of bourgeois comfort, it is primitive Christianity, which in the mouth of the martyr in Revelation blasts us like some fiery breath. And yet everything doesn't simply culminate in the easing of the suffering undergone, in the fading away of the last sobbing in eternity. No; the final thing is the victory song of those who stand beside the crystal sea of the ocean of heaven, and, as the Jews did once at the Red Sea, sing the song of Moses, the Servant of God, and the ode of the Lamb: "Great and wonderful are your works, Lord God the Almighty! Just and true are your ways, King of the nations! Lord, who will not fear and glorify your name? For you alone are holy! All nations will come and worship before you, for your judgments have been revealed" (Rev. 15:3–4).

Everything culminates in the song, for the great tribulation of this world is not a dull pain but a thoroughly transformed tribulation, illuminated for the martyrs by the suffering of Christ, which fades into the exultation of the new ode. Even though Satan was unchained in the world, the martyrs utter no word against God's creation:[31] "Great and wonderful are your works, Lord God the Almighty." Even though the way of suffering—of suffering with Christ—was bitter, "righteous and true are your ways, King of the nations." Even though the abyss that opens before us in the revelation of Jesus Christ is fearful, "who does not fear you, Lord, and who does not glorify your name?" "For you alone are holy . . . and your judgments have been revealed"—they have been revealed in the suffering of Christ and in the suffering of the Church, which suffers with Christ.

Do we now have the courage to say with St. John, "Yes, come soon. Amen, come Lord Jesus"? We now know what that means, the coming of Jesus, the revelation of Jesus. Oh, that God would send us all the Holy Spirit, through whom we could say in truth and justice, "Yes, come—come, Lord Jesus." Come to us in your suffering, so that you may come to us in your kingdom!

The Martyrs and the Priestly Kingship of Christ

"When Jesus was born in Judea, in the days of King Herod, behold, wise men from the East appeared in Jerusalem, asking, 'Where is he that is born king of the Jews? For we observed his star at its rising, and have come to pay him homage.' When King Herod heard this, he was frightened, and all of Jerusalem with him" (Matt. 2:1–3). These are the verses with which St. Matthew has described the birth of the priestly king. The sequel is well known: while it is said of the Wise Men, "On entering the house, they saw the child with Mary his mother; and they fell down and paid him homage. Then, opening their treasure chests, they offered him gifts of gold, frankincense, and myrrh" (2:11), of Herod we are told that he became enraged and ordered all the children in Bethlehem and the surrounding area who were two years old or younger to be killed (2:16). When the one is born as man who in his assumed human nature will become priest and king, his dignity immediately becomes known through the actions of those who are a type of belief and a type of unbelief. The Wise Men offer gold, frankincense, and myrrh. "Gold," so it says in the Office for Epiphany, "so that his royal power should be shown"; the frankincense was to refer to the high priest, and the myrrh to the Lord's burial. The gifts of the Wise Men from the East, who are a type of the believing Church of the Gentiles, which stretches from the east to the west, demonstrate the priestly kingship of Christ in its universality, which spans the nations.[32] But the priestly kingship of Christ is also revealed in the behavior of Herod, who is a type of the unbeliever. The earthly king, in fear before the eternal king, resorts to murdering children, though the murdered children become unintentional martyrs to Christ, whom they cannot yet confess with their mouths,[33] and thereby witnesses for the priestly kingdom of "the Lamb that was slain," whom they have followed wherever it was able to go (Rev. 14:4; reading for the feast of the Holy Innocents). The earthly king is afraid that the heavenly king will take his kingdom away from him, but the hymn from the feast of Epiphany says:

Crudelis Herodes, Deum
Regem venire quid times?
Non eripit mortalia,
Qui regna dat coelestia.

Cruel Herod, why do you fear the coming of God, the King? He who gives the heavenly kingdom does not steal earthly kingdoms.[34]

And yet this misunderstanding of the kingship of Christ arises again and again. In the Gospel of John (chap. 6), it is told that after Jesus' miraculous feeding of the five thousand, the crowd wanted to take him by force to make him king. When Jesus realized this, he withdrew alone to the mountain (6:15). Neither Herod nor the Jewish people, neither the representative of monarchy nor the people [*Volk*] who yearn for a leader [*Führer*] and a king to sate their hunger, understand the Kingdom of Christ. Mary and Joseph flee with their child to Egypt from Herod; the Lord withdraws into isolation on a mountain from the people.

The question of the kingship of Christ is given expression for the last time when Jesus stands before Pilate.[35] Pilate has the Lord brought into his presence and asks him: "Are you the king of the Jews?" (John 18:33). And Jesus says, "'My kingdom is not of this world. If my kingdom were of this world, my followers would fight to keep me from being handed over to the Jews. But my kingdom is not from here.' Pilate asks him, 'So you are a king?' Jesus answers, 'You say that I am a king. For this I was born, and for this I came into the world, to testify [as a martyr] to the truth. Everyone who belongs to the truth listens to my voice.' Pilate asks him, 'What is truth?' After he had said this, he went out to the Jews again and told them, 'I find no case against him. But you have a custom that I release someone for you at the Passover. Do you want me to release for you the King of the Jews?' They shouted in reply, 'Not this man, but Barabbas!' Now Barabbas was a robber" (John 18:36–40). After the scourging of Christ, Pilate tries a second time to release him. "But the Jews cried out, 'If you release this man, you are no friend of the emperor's. Everyone who claims to be a king sets himself against the emperor'" (19:12). Pilate asks for the last time: "'Shall I crucify your king?' But the chief priests cried out, 'We have no king but the emperor.' Then he handed him over to them to be crucified" (19:15). Luke also tells how during the inquiries, Pilate had the Lord sent to Herod, who in those days was likewise in Jerusalem, and that on this account Pilate and Herod had become friends.

Not only the representative of monarchy, not only democracy, but even the representative of empire is unable to understand the kingship of Jesus. He is able to make some sense of a national kingship among the Jews, but what is a kingdom that is not of this world? What is a king who has come into the world to be a witness to the truth, yes, to translate it concretely, to appear as a *martyr*? What is truth? The skeptical question "What is truth?" is asked in response to the claim of Jesus that he had come into the world to be a witness to the truth. As an ultimate metaphysical presupposition, whether explicit or not, this skeptical question underlies every political system that does not let itself be limited by the kingship of Christ. It is deeply symbolic that to negotiate Jesus' fate, the representative of the pagan empire [Pilate] turns to the Jews—rather than to Jesus, who has just confirmed his kingship to him—after asking, "What is truth?" His skeptical question has a kind of resolution when he lets the Jews choose between Jesus and Barabbas. The robber Barabbas is a political revolutionary in whom he knows the Jews are far more interested than in the king who has come into the world to bear witness to the truth. The Jews decide for the political rebel who comes from this world, and against the kingship of Christ, which is not of this world; but it is telling that the representative of pagan imperialism also, in whose mind standing before the one who is the truth has aroused the ultimate question of what truth is, now permits people to choose in favor of the political rebel and against the king who has appeared as a witness for the truth. To be sure, he lets it be known that he has stood before the truth and that he seeks to avoid it, because he formulates the theoretical question about what truth itself is but avoids the practical decision in favor of the king who has come into the world to appear as a witness to the truth. In this way, the decision of faith, which is indissolubly linked to the kingship of Christ, is dodged through the theoretical pretext that one cannot know what the truth itself is. But the theoretical pretext cannot hide the fact that one has stood before him who came into the world as king, to bear witness to the truth. The untruthful behavior of Pilate, who against his conscience and his better knowledge hands Jesus over to the Jews and who permits the (impermissible from a Roman standpoint) decision of the Jews in favor of the political rebel over against the kingship of Christ, out of his pitiful fear that he might lose his status as a friend of the emperor, proves that he has stood before the truth, who is Jesus Christ, and has evaded it.

.   .   .

The situation of Jews and of pagans in the face of the kingship of Christ, as it is disclosed in the story of Pilate, is different. The Jews, who in their blind hatred of the kingship of Christ, which is not of this world, play off the emperor against the "king of the Jews," forget that their Messiah is supposed to be a king in Israel. With the cry "We have no king but the emperor," they not only lose every claim to await a royal Messiah in their people, but at the same time too every metaphysical and moral claim to exist as a sovereign nation. All they have left is the possibility either to live as an oppressed nation or to opt for Barabbas, as the type of the political rebel.

The situation of the pagans differs from that of the Jews. In the person of Pilate placed before the king whose kingdom is not of this world, they hand Jesus over to the Jews to be crucified and let the political agitator go free. Because they go against their better judgment and their conscience in their treatment of the king who has come into the world to bear witness to the truth, they forfeit their own political authority. Because in the political sphere they hand over the king whose kingdom is not of this world to the Jews to be crucified and release the political rebel, they not only subvert the purpose of their political office but also debase their individual relationship with Caesar in the way they privatize it and make their decisions purely according to the advantages that they can get from that relationship—Pilate does not want to lose his political status as a "friend of the emperor."

Jews and pagans thus band together to crucify the king whose kingdom is not of this world.[36] But insofar as Jesus, as the eternal high priest, now suffers on the cross and sheds his blood for both Jews and pagans, his kingship as a priestly kingship becomes ever more clearly revealed in its superiority to all "dominions and powers" of this world. It is significant that the question of the kingship of Jesus is resolved before Pontius Pilate and not before a Jewish tribunal. Mary and Joseph flee to Egypt from Herod, and Jesus withdraws into solitude from the Jewish masses that want to make him king. But the question of the kingship of Jesus cannot be taken up with the Jews, since they have proclaimed that they have no king. It can only be discussed with the Romans, who have an emperor: only to those who have a kingdom of this world can testimony be given about the kingdom that is not of this world. The testimony that the king who comes into the world makes is *public* testimony (1 Tim. 6:13). As such it presupposes the public reality of the Roman Empire; but as testimony for the truth, which can only be heard by those who are of the truth, it also transcends political reality and, in view of the pagans' surrender of the witness to the Jews, it becomes a witness against all "dominations and powers" of this world. Not by chance did the name of Pontius Pilate enter the Church's Creed.[37] It did not happen just to verify a historical recollection, but to fix forever a historically significant event for those who through their baptism make public confession to Christ—that event, namely, when the testimony of the kingship that is not of this world was rejected by the political powers of this age, when "the Lord of glory" (1 Cor. 2:8), the king who bears witness to the truth, was "crucified and buried" under Pontius Pilate, but also arose in glory to heaven under him.[38] When St. Paul speaks in First Corinthians of the wisdom of God that is concealed in mystery, which none of the rulers of this age has known, for had they known it they would not have crucified the Lord of glory, he is playing off the scene of Christ before Pilate. In that scene, Jesus appears as witness of the kingdom that is not of this world, but the divine Wisdom is not recognized by those who in this age exercise political power, and so the king of the age to come, the "Lord of glory," is surrendered by them to die on the cross (1 Cor. 2:8).

·   ·   ·

The words of St. Paul to which I have just referred give an indication of how Jesus' reply, that his kingdom is not of this world, is to be understood more exactly. Jesus' kingdom is not of this universe because it is bound not to the present age but to the one that is to come. The kingship of Christ cannot be separated from the eschatological character of the Gospel. We can best determine what that means if we cite some statements that St. John makes in the Book of Revelation on the kingship of Christ.

In Revelation 1, St. John wishes the Church in Asia "peace and grace from him who is and who was and who is to come, and from the seven spirits who stand before the throne of God, and from Jesus Christ, the faithful witness, the first-born from the dead and the ruler of the kings of the earth. To him who loves us and freed us from our sins by his blood, and made to be a kingdom, priests for his God and Father, to him be glory and dominion for ages unto ages. Amen" (Rev. 1:4–6). The assertions made about Christ are of the highest relevance here. Jesus is located in heaven, where the eternal God and the seven spirits who stand before the throne of God dwell. This Jesus, who has risen from the dead, is called both "the faithful witness" and the "ruler of the kings of the earth." The striking juxtaposition of these two concepts becomes really comprehensible only in the light of the Gospel of John, when one remembers that in the Gospel of St. John, Jesus declares before Pilate that he is a king whose kingdom is not of this world, and that he has come into the world in order to be a witness for the truth.[39] The situation of Jesus before Pilate is thus retrieved into memory in the Book of Revelation. At the same time it becomes clear that the crucifixion, which is directly linked with the witness before Pilate, sacrifices a victim whose blood has absolved us of our sins, or, as it says in Revelation: "You have ransomed" us "for God from every tribe and language and people and nation" (Rev. 5:9), so that now we have been made kings and priests (1:6 and 5:10). What the analysis of the Pilate scene in the Gospel of John has already shown is explicitly confirmed by the Book of Revelation. In the witness that Jesus makes to Pilate that his kingship is not of this world, and in the linking with that witness of the events of the crucifixion and resurrection, the kingship of Christ is actualized *in this world*, so that his death is a sacrificial offering by which human beings are freed from their sinful bondage under the "principalities and powers" of the present age and called to be participants in the priesthood and kingship of Christ in the age to come.

The acclamation "To him be glory and might unto ages of ages" (Rev. 5:13) is directed at this realization of the kingship of Christ in the present age. Nothing in the Church's prayer and worship tends to be repeated as mechanically as the doxologies. And yet they richly deserve to have their original meaning rediscovered. The doxology of the Book of Revelation, which proclaims glory and might to the "ruler of the kings of the earth," is the voiced pronouncement of, as it were, the voiced accompaniment to the enthronement of Christ, who, as the king whose kingdom does not belong to this age, is shown to be the superior of all those kings who *are* of this world. Those who know they have been called to be priests and kings in a new age now, in their acclamation, appropriate for him the glory and might that were once the property of the kings of the earth. The universality of the kingship of Christ,[40] which the fathers of the Church already found revealed in the fact that the Wise Men, who offer their gifts to the future priestly king, come from the East into the Roman Empire, is expressed emphatically in the Book of Revelation when it says that the new priestly and royal race has been "ransomed from tribe and language and people and nation" (5:9).

Yet another feature of the kingship of Christ is made clear in the following verse from Revelation: "Look! He is coming with the clouds; every eye will see him, even those who pierced him; and on his account all the tribes of the earth will wail. So it is to be" (Rev. 1:7). It not only pertains to the kingship of Christ that he has come to bear witness to the kingship that is not of this world, and to die for the sake of this witness; it not only pertains that his death has become a sacrifice, and that his resurrection, ascension, and enthronement at the right hand of God have secured his royal triumph for the Son of Man, for the Incarnate One; it also pertains that the Son of Man will return in royal glory on the clouds of heaven for judgment.

Also relevant to the theme of the kingship of Christ is the answer that Jesus gives to the high priest's question of whether he is the Messiah: "From now on you will see the Son of Man at the right hand of almighty God and coming on the clouds of heaven" (Matt. 26:64 and parallels). The Son of Man who stands at the right hand of God and of whom Jesus speaks before the Jewish high priest is also the object of the vision seen by the dying Stephen (Acts 7:56): It is Christ enthroned with God, the king who will come again in judgment, whom not only the martyr Stephen sees, but also the martyr John, who "for the sake of the word of God and of the witness for Jesus was on the island of Patmos" (Rev. 1:9). It is very relevant to the basic train of thought here to recall how St. John describes the Son of Man in heaven amid the seven golden lampstands. "He was clothed with a priestly robe that was girdled with a golden sash across the breast" (Rev 1:12). The priestly robe is supposed to represent his priestly rank, the golden sash his royal rank. The one who "created us to be a kingdom and priests for his God and Father" (1:6) is accordingly revealed for the martyr as a royal high priest, this martyr who offers priestly sacrifice with Christ so that he might rule royally with Christ. Sacrifice and dominion, priesthood and kingship are thus in the Son of Man, who came into the world to appear as a martyr/witness for the truth. In these kindred concepts, then, all of those in the Church have a share who have offered priestly sacrifice with Christ in order to rule royally with him, the martyrs in the first place and then all of the saints.

Now it is very telling that the priestly king in heaven, whose appearance St. John describes in the Book of Revelation, in the recounting of the details of his vision becomes a counterimage of the Roman emperor. In the answer that Jesus gives to the Jews, he speaks not of the king but of the Son of Man who stands at the right hand of God and who will return on the clouds of heaven. In the answer that he gives to Pilate, however, he speaks of his kingship. The words about the Son of Man are meant for the Jews, who by their own admission have no king; the word about the king is meant for the pagans, who have no king but rather an emperor, a Caesar. Note how the pagan, who has an emperor, hands over the king whose kingdom is not of this world to the Jews for crucifixion. He who serves a dominion that as mere Caesarism is wanting in true legitimacy, surrenders the crucified, who as the king whose kingdom is not of this world grants legitimacy to all the kings of the earth. For St. John, Christ rather than Caesar becomes the emperor, because Christ wants to lead the pagans, who have no king but merely a Caesar, back to the kingdom of the new age.[41]

The connection between kingship and priesthood needs even deeper consideration. The Son of Man becomes a king in that he offers himself in priestly fashion as a sacrifice to the Father. Because in their negotiations with Pilate over the kingship of Jesus, the Jews cried out, "We have no king," through the crucifixion of Jesus the Jews have forfeited not only kingship but priesthood and sacrifice. And because in the person of Caesar's representative the pagans have handed over to the Jews for crucifixion "the king who gives witness for the truth," they have not only made public the dubious legitimacy of their Caesarism, they have also rendered illegitimate (in a metaphysical sense) the alliance between principate and pontificate as it had existed since Augustus (12 BC).

Since the death of Christ and since his ascension, that is, since the Incarnate One became priest and king in his human nature, the attempt has constantly been made to unite kingship and priesthood, the highest forms of state and religious authority. It would actually be surprising if this attempt had not been made. That the medieval German emperors sought to unite *regnum* and *sacerdotium* in their own persons by appealing to the sacramental character of royal anointing is well known. But already in the eighth and ninth centuries, this effort was resisted, and ninth-century councils rightly emphasized that only Christ was *rex* and *sacerdos* in one.[42] That the unification of kingship and priesthood, of highest state and re-ligious authority, has repeatedly been attempted in itself shows that the transcending of earthly kingship by the priestly kingship of Christ requires political authority, not only to reject the usurpation of priestly author-ity, but even to exercise its political power in a way that is not heedless of the power that the Father has given to the Son. This demand has the ap-pearance of a metaphysical weakening of human power, and indeed in a certain sense it is. When St. Paul says that Christ has "disarmed the pow-ers and authorities and made a public example of them, celebrating a tri-umphal procession over them in his person" (Col. 2:15), it becomes clear (disregarding for the moment the context of this verse in the Letter to the Colossians) that the kingship of Christ has stripped all "powers and au-thorities" of this age of their demonic character. He has exposed them for public examination, insofar as the rulers of this age allowed themselves to be seduced into crucifying "the Lord of glory" (1 Cor. 2:8), whereby they but unmasked themselves. And he has made a triumphal procession with them, insofar as his ascension, his enthronement at the right hand of God, and his return in judgment, constitute the triumph of the kingdom that is not from this world over all "powers and authorities."

Since Christ is priest and king, earthly power is stripped of its de-monic character and can no longer raise the claim, as paganism once did, to be the bearer of sacramental functions. Since Christ is priest and king, priestly kingship can exist only in the people of God, which in the *ekklēsia*, the Assembly, celebrates the mysteries of the priestly king. In the Church *all* of those anointed with the holy chrism of baptism are anointed to a priestly kingship, as St. Augustine often stressed.[43] "May all of us who are proud to serve under the banners of Christ the King as his soldiers, also rule with him in the heavenly court," as the Postcommunion prayer for the feast of Christ the King has it. And yet the participation in the suf-fering and in the priesthood of Christ "via the figural representation" of the sacrament is one thing, and its "imitation in action" quite another, St. Thomas [Aquinas] says (*Summa Theologiae* 3.66.12). Participation in the glory and the kingship of Christ in the Church is also therefore diverse. The holy martyrs, who participate "via the imitation in action" in the sacrifice of the eternal high priest, have a share in the kingship of Christ in a special sense. They who have drunk the cup with Jesus are now already sitting with him on the throne to judge, not only the twelve tribes of Israel (Matt. 19:28), but even the cosmos and the angels (1 Cor. 6:2f.). The martyrs who have followed the Lamb wherever he goes (Rev. 14:4) have shown by their deaths that there is no kingship of Christ without his priesthood. And the martyrs' deaths and glory are quite simply the most appropriate form in which the priestly kingship of Christ is realized in the members of his mystical body.

Notes

Erik Peterson, *Ausgewählte Schriften*, ed. Barbara Nichtweiß et al. (Würzburg: Echter-Verlag, 1994–), is cited below as *AS*.—Ed.

INTRODUCTION

1. Erik Peterson's *Frühkirche, Judentum, und Gnosis* (Freiburg im Br., 1959; repr. Darmstadt, 1982) will be reprinted as vol. 11 of the new edition of his collected works.

2. Erik Peterson, diary entry, March 24, 1948, cited in Barbara Nichtweiß, *Erik Peterson: Neue Sicht auf Leben und Werk* (Erik Peterson: A New Look at His Life and Work) (Freiburg im Br.: Herder, 1992), 257. *AS*, 9 (2009), *Theologie und Theologen*, pt. 2: *Briefwechsel mit Karl Barth u.a., Reflexionen und Erinnerungen* (Correspondence with Karl Barth and Others, Reflections and Recollections), ed. Barbara Nichtweiß, 411.

3. Karl Barth to Erik Peterson, August 8, 1932, cited in Nichtweiß, *Erik Peterson*, 831. Three years later, following marriage and children, Barth could not resist saying, "I can . . . only marvel or lament that you wanted everything all at once: becoming Catholic *and* remaining a theologian *and* getting married *and* living in Rome" (Barth to Peterson, November 21, 1935, *AS*, 9.2: 350).

4. As told to the writer by the late Krister Stendahl in November 1992. On Taubes, see his *The Political Theology of Paul*, ed. Aleida Assmann, Jan Assmann, et al., trans. Dana Hollander (Stanford, Calif.: Stanford University Press, 2004).

5. For a recent example, see Reinhard Hütter's reading of Peterson in his *Bound To Be Free: Evangelical Catholic Engagements in Ecclesiology, Ethics, and Ecumenism* (Grand Rapids, Mich.: Eerdmans, 2004), 20–34.

6. A dozen volumes of Peterson's *Ausgewählte Schriften* (*AS*) have been published or are in preparation. Besides the Nichtweiß biography, a second edition of which appeared in 1994, see also the excellent collection *Vom Ende der Zeit: Geschichtstheologie und Eschatologie bei Erik Peterson* (On the End of Time: Theology of History and Eschatology in Erik Peterson), ed. Barbara Nichtweiß (Münster: LIT, 2001).

7. Following a long conversation with Peterson on June 5, 1931, Barth recorded briefly on an index card, found in the Karl Barth Archive in Basel, that Peterson had been discharged for "mental illness" after an attempted suicide; see *AS*, 9.2: 485–487.

8. Christoph Markschies is preparing an expanded and updated edition, to appear as volume 8 of *AS*.

9. Nichtweiß, *Peterson*, 280–282; now kept in the Erik Peterson Library at the University of Turin.

10. On the Schmitt-Peterson nexus, see Nichtweiß, *Peterson*, 727–762, and her important article "Apokalyptische Verfassungslehren: Carl Schmitt im Horizont der Theologie Erik Petersons" (Apocalyptic Constitutional Doctrine: Carl Schmitt in the Horizon of Erik Peterson's Theology), in *Die eigentlich katholische Verschärfung . . . : Konfession, Theologie und Politik im Werk Carl Schmitts* (The Authentically Catholic Sharpening: Confession, Theology, and Politics in the Work of Carl Schmitt), ed. Bernd Wacker (Munich: Wilhelm Fink, 1994), 37–64.

11. So Peterson described Schmitt to Karl Barth (November 30, 1924, cited Nichtweiß, *Peterson*, 727; now in *AS*, 9.2: 213).

12. The confraternity, the Erzbruderschaft zur Schmerzhaften Muttergottes (Confraternity of the Sorrowful Mother of God), is open to Roman residents from German-speaking lands of northern and central Europe. Peterson rarely attended its meetings, apparently because he felt alienated from much of the German community in Rome. His biographer says that failure to attend required meetings and/or to pay the outstanding balance on a grave plot were cited as reasons for the denial (Nichtweiß, *Peterson*, 875).

13. Updated bibliography now in Peterson, *Theologie und Theologen*, pt. 1: *Texte*, ed. Barbara Nichtweiß (2009), *AS*, 9.1: 659–684.

14. Diary entry from October 1954, cited in Nichtweiß, *Peterson*, 720; now in *AS*, 9.2: 423.

15. Omitted is the short essay "Was ist der Mensch?" (What Is Man?), which was published in 1948 in the journal *Wort und Wahrheit*. Although its roots go back to Peterson's 1925–1926 university lectures on the Gospel of Luke, its significantly later date of publication sets it apart from the other papers in *Theological Tractates*. It is now available, along with other short post–World War II papers of Peterson's, in *Marginalien zur Theologie und andere Schriften* (Marginal Notes on Theology and Other Writings), ed. Barbara Nichtweiß (1995), *AS*, 2.

16. *Was ist Theologie?* (Bonn: Cohen, 1925); reprinted in *Theologische Traktate*, 9–43, and *AS*, 1: 1–22.

17. Judgments differ about the effect this critique had on Barth. Bruce MacCormack, *Karl Barth's Critically Realistic Dialectical Theology: Its Genesis and Development, 1909–1936* (Oxford: Clarendon Press, 1995), 367–371, doubts it had a lasting impact. See Nichtweiß, *Peterson*, 649–655, for a different assessment; her treatment of the Barth-Peterson relationship, ibid., 499–721, is a virtual book within a book.

18. Peterson's letters to Harnack were first published in *Hochland* 30 (1932–1933), 111–124; reprinted in *Theologische Traktate*, 293–321, and *AS*, 1: 175–194.

19. Previously translated, and here reprinted by kind permission of the jour-

nal, in Michael Hollerich, "Erik Peterson's Correspondence with Adolf Harnack: Retrieving a Neglected Critique of Church, Theology, and Secularization in Weimar Germany," *Pro Ecclesia* 2 (1993): 305–344.

20. Peterson, letter dated October 15, 1932; cited in Nichtweiß, *Peterson*, 763, 835.

21. First published in 1928 (predated by the publisher as 1929); reprinted in *Theologische Traktate*, 411–429; in *AS*, 1: 245–257; and again in *AS* as the centerpiece of a supplementary volume (*Sonderband*): Erik Peterson, *Ekklesia: Studien zum altchristlichen Kirchenbegriff*, ed. Barbara Nichtweiß and Hans-Ulrich Weidemann (Würzburg: Echter, 2010), 93–104. Peterson mentions the dedication to Harnack in the epilogue to the correspondence.

22. Peterson to Barth, October 23, 1928 (*AS*, 9.2: 268; the whole exchange with Barth on "The Church," is now published in *AS*, 9.2: 267–277).

23. Alfred Loisy, *The Gospel and the Church*, ed. Bernard B. Scott (Philadelphia: Fortress, 1976), 16–17.

24. Ibid., 13.

25. See Nichtweiß, *Peterson*, 850 n. 163, 851 n. 165.

26. On the Catholic reception of "The Church," see Nichtweiß, *Peterson*, 846–861, on which I largely depend. See also her paper "'Imaginäres Vaterland': Erste Skizze der Beziehungen Erik Petersons nach Frankreich" ("Imaginary Fatherland": First Sketch of Erik Peterson's Connections with France), in *Vom Ende der Zeit*, 265–273, and the illuminating study by Giancarlo Caronello, "Erik Petersons Rezeption in Italien," ibid., 275–329.

27. Joseph Cardinal Ratzinger, *Called to Communion: Understanding the Church Today*, trans. Adrian Walker (San Francisco: Ignatius Press, 1996), 21 n. 6.

28. Nichtweiß, *Peterson*, 853 n. 190.

29. Ibid., 861.

30. Ibid., 860–861 n. 228, with references to comments from Anselm Stolz, Jacques Maritain, and Charles Journet.

31. Cf. "The Book on the Angels," chap. 6, p. 237 n. 34, in the present volume.

32. On his treatment of the "hardening" of the Jews, see the editor's footnote on the last page of "The Church."

33. See Nichtweiß, *Peterson*, 294, for the shift and for its anticipation already in his work in the 1920s.

34. "The Church from Jews and Gentiles" was originally published as *Die Kirche aus Juden und Heiden*, Bücherei der Salzburger Hochschulwochen, 2 (Salzburg: A. Pustet, 1933); reprinted in *Theologische Traktate*, 241–292, and *AS*, 1: 141–174.

35. "Ecclesiae Romanae in qua beati apostoli Petrus et Paulus vocationem catholicae et ex gentibus et ex judaeis per sanguinis effusionem confirmarunt" (cited in Nichtweiß, *Peterson*, 835).

36. Ibid., 839.

37. Now published as Erik Peterson, *Der Brief an die Römer*, ed. Barbara Nichtweiß and Ferdinand Hahn, *AS*, vol. 6 (1997).

38. Erik Peterson, "Die neueste Entwicklung der protestantischen Kirche in Deutschland" (The Most Recent Development of the Protestant Church in Germany), *Hochland* 31 (1933–1934): 64–79, 144–160; now reprinted in *AS* 9.1: 610–645. I hope to publish my translation of this article, which is a first-class piece of contemporary history.

39. Nichtweiß, *Peterson*, 548.

40. See the excellent remarks of Nichtweiß, *Peterson*, 545–549.

41. Peterson, *Monotheismus als politisches Problem: Ein Beitrag zur Geschichte der politischen Theologie im Imperium Romanum* (Leipzig: Hegner, 1935); reprinted in *Theologische Traktate*, 45–147, and *AS*, 1: 23–91.

42. On the genesis and reception of Peterson's book on monotheism, see esp. *Monotheismus als politisches Problem? Erik Peterson und die Kritik der politischen Theologie*, ed., Alfred Schindler (Gütersloh: Gütersloher Verlaghaus Gerd Mohn, 1978), and Nichtweiß, *Peterson*, 763–830.

43. Alois Dempf, "Erik Petersons Rolle in der Geisteswissenschaft" (Erik Peterson's Place in Scholarship), *Neues Hochland* 54 (1961–1962): 24–31.

44. Nichtweiß, *Peterson*, 766. On the *Reichstheologie*, see the classic study of Klaus Breuning, *Die Vision des Reiches. Deutscher Katholizismus zwischen Demokratie und Diktatur 1929–1934* (The Vision of the Reich: German Catholicism between Democracy and Dictatorship 1929–1934) (Munich: Max Hueber, 1969). See also my article "Catholic Anti-Liberalism in Weimar: Political Theology and Its Critics," in *The Weimar Moment: Political Theology, Liberalism, and the Law*, ed. Rudy Koshar and Len Kaplan (forthcoming).

45. *Politische Theologie II: Die Legende von der Erledigung jeder politischen Theologie* (Berlin: Dunker & Humblot, 1970), now in English translation as *Political Theology II: The Myth of the Closure of Any Political Theology*, trans. Michael Hoelzl and Graham Ward (Malden, Mass.: Polity Press, 2008).

46. Noteworthy here is Taubes' rejoinder in *Political Theology of Paul*, 110–113.

47. Nichtweiß, *Peterson*, 734–735.

48. Peterson, *Das Buch von den Engeln: Stellung und Bedeutung der heiligen Engel im Kultus* (Leipzig: Hegner, 1935); reprinted as "Von den Engeln" in *Theologische Traktate*, 323–407, and *AS*, 1: 195–243.

49. Jean Daniélou contributed a preface to the French edition: *Le livre des anges*, trans. C. Champollion (Paris: Desclée de Brouwer, 1954).

50. Cited in Nichtweiß, *Peterson*, 385.

51. See ibid., 340–382, esp. 376–382.

52. Ibid., 414–426.

53. First published in *Catholica* 5 (1936): 64–72; reprinted in Erik Peterson, *Zeuge der Wahrheit* (Leipzig: Hegner, 1937), 73–86; in *Theologische Traktate*, 149–164; and in *AS*, 1: 83–92.

54. First published in 1937 as *Zeuge der Wahrheit*; reprinted in *Theologische Traktate*, 165–224; and in *AS*, 1: 93–129.

55. Erik Peterson, diary entry, February 14, 1958 (*AS*, 9.2: 438–439).

CHAPTER I: WHAT IS THEOLOGY?

1. Karl Barth, *Das Wort Gottes als Aufgabe der Theologie* (The Word of God as the Task of Theology) (Munich, 1924), 156ff.

2. Ibid., 160.

3. See Søren Kierkegaard, *Fear and Trembling* (1843).

4. See Søren Kierkegaard, *Either-Or* (1843).

5. It is a misunderstanding of this type of dialectical taking-seriously when someone presumes that there is genuine moral seriousness behind it, as does, for example, Emanuel Hirsch (see *Theologische Literaturzeitung* 50 [1925]: 63). Over against God, seriousness does not exist in the sphere of intentionality. The seriousness of which Revelation speaks is neither moral nor dialectical seriousness. Even the seriousness of ethical self-condemnation leads to nothing more than the Pharisaism of failure.

Contemporary theology has misunderstood Kierkegaard twice over: once by Barth, when he tried to introduce Kierkegaard's dialectic into theology; and once by Geismar and Hirsch (as earlier by Holl), who construed Kierkegaard's dialectical seriousness as genuine ethical seriousness. It is frankly true, as even Barth explicitly admits (*Das Wort Gottes*, 167), that the dialectical path that he holds to be that of Paul and of the Reformation does not arrive at its goal. But when one tries to express that in the form of the dialectic, nothing at all is being said. And in the lecture of Barth's that we are presently examining, his protests to the contrary, nothing at all is being said. The dialectical form of the thesis of his lecture just proves this (ibid., 158). Besides, Kierkegaard himself explicitly denied that Luther was a dialectician (*Die Tagebücher* [The Diaries], ed. and trans. Theodor Haecker [Innsbruck, 1923], 2: 125) and said that making an apostle into a dialectician is simply confusion.

6. Eve could only be seduced, Adam could only fall. And yet seduction and fall now belong together, not in the sense of a temporal sequence, although the seduction had to precede the fall, but rather in the sense that Eve belongs together with Adam.

7. Theodor Haecker, writing in *Hochland* 22, no. 8 (1924–1925): 192, was the first to demonstrate that with Kierkegaard, we have to do with myths.

8. On the impossibility of the concept of a theological system, see my article "Über die Forderung einer Theologie des Glaubens. Eine Auseinandersetzung mit Paul Althaus" (On the Demand for a Theology of Faith: An Exchange with Paul Althaus), *Zwischen den Zeiten* 3 (1925): 281–302.

9. Barth, *Das Wort Gottes*, 165. The Christian dogma that God has become man is not the same as the paradox that the impossible has become possible. *The paradoxical is the surrogate of revelation.* Part of contemporary theology lives on this surrogate. When I present the "paradoxical" as the authentic meaning of rev-

elation, I might just as well say that two times two makes five and that I "believe" this religiously—and it is not going too far to say that such a belief is already widespread. As a result, just as the Professor can no longer be distinguished from the Prophet, so the Reformer, under this construal, can no longer be distinguished from the Apostle. The "paradoxical" makes its appearance in history in the moral paradox of the Stoics and then as the mystical paradox of Sebastian Franck. But to the Christian theologian that is a dubious ambience. The Stoic paradox, for example, that the wise man alone is king, is a paradoxical *statement*. But that the cross of Christ is a scandal to the Jews and foolishness to the Greeks is not at all in the same sense a statement, because the cross of Christ is itself not a "statement."

10. Kierkegaard says explicitly in his diaries: "I am without authority; I am a genius—not an apostle" (*Tagebücher*, ed. and trans. Haecker, 2: 48). Had he been a theologian, then he would not have been without authority. In general one sees in a passage like this already the fantasy in Barth's attempt to set up a pedigree consisting of the following names: Kierkegaard, Luther and Calvin, Paul and Jeremiah (Barth, *Das Wort Gottes*, 164). Kierkegaard was a writer, Luther and Calvin were reformers, Paul was an apostle, and Jeremiah a prophet. Thus we have to do with quite disparate individuals, of whom the apostle and the prophet can *never* be placed in a pedigree consisting of human orientations and intellectual possibilities. One may indeed cite the prophet Jeremiah and also, as in Hebrews 11, present him as a model of faith, but to cite him as a theological ancestor is impossible, because Jeremiah belongs as little as Paul to a series of theologians. It is truly remarkable that someone should appeal constantly to Kierkegaard and yet at the same time be unable to recognize the difference between an apostle (or a prophet) and a theology professor.

11. Luther's authorial legacy as a whole is always rated positively by a Reformation historiography oriented totally to non-theological and cultural-historical concerns. But that legacy is exactly what the theologian needs to subject to theological investigation. The foundation of Luther's pathos and rhetoric in the peculiar character of his faith needs to be shown. Luther's faith is essentially sustained *in* this pathos and *in* this rhetoric. Luther's pathos is not simply the subjective pathos of a man with a passionate sensibility, but rather is motivated objectively. It seems to me that the late medieval nominalism that underlies his concept of faith is just as significant for this pathos as the nominalism of the neo-Kantians is responsible for the pathos of Barth's writings.

12. Rudolf Bultmann, "Welchen Sinn hat es, von Gott zu reden?" *Theologische Blätter* 4 (1925): 129ff.

13. As the argument in the text will make clear, we need to make the following distinctions: the prophets pronounce or "say" [*sagen*] the word of God; Christ, as the Word of God, "talks" [*redet*] about God (think of the meaning of [the Greek] *lalein* in the Gospel of John); but the Church "speaks" [*spricht*]. The language here is making fine distinctions. It would be easy to elaborate the distinctions. There is "saying" only where someone "has something to say." That is the case with the

prophets, who had to say God's word. But Christ does not in the same way have to "say" the Word of God, because he himself is that Word, and therefore he "talks." Insofar as the Church "speaks," there is always something that suggests a judicial determination, a demand for obedience. That becomes clear if we consider that a verdict is always "spoken," but never "said" or "talked." Thus we see that Bultmann's theme [in "Welchen Sinn hat es . . . ?"] is formulated in a lexically false way. It ought not to be formulated as "What does it mean to talk [*reden*] of God?" That is in fact a meaningless question, and Bultmann's attempt to give it meaning must remain futile—rather one must ask: in what sense can we speak [*sprechen*] of God?

14. Bultmann, "Welchen Sinn hat es . . . ?" 134. Bultmann's article shows that the rejection of metaphysics is not meant as seriously as is often maintained. Only a particular form of metaphysics is rejected, but the Fichtean metaphysics is upheld that, for example, lets the "I" and God be realized in free action. The dignifying of this "action" with the word "faith" is not a new development.

In the theology of the modern period, one still "believes." But today, when the Church and theology are asked *what* they actually believe, the answer is simply: they believe. If one persists in asking the question, one is offered ambiguous or fuzzy words like revelation, paradox (Bultmann is close to saying "contingency"), the irrational, the numinous, grace, etc. If one then asks Church and theology, further, whether they believe in the Incarnation of the Son of God, one learns that the object of faith is not a particular thing, such that one ought not talk about an "object" of faith, that "faith is an attitude of the soul," and so forth. Avoiding a concrete answer to a concrete question in this way is not very honorable. The old liberalism of the nineteenth century was in this respect far more positive, because it at least said what it did not believe. Contemporary theology, which counts it as its badge of honor that the contradiction of theological orientations is almost transcended, ought to consider that it is no mark of honor to have removed strife from the world by avoiding every concrete question and concrete answer.

15. From my article "Über die Forderung einer Theologie des Glaubens," *Zwischen den Zeiten* 3 (1925).

16. The word "inspired" is understood in a very broad sense, without reference to any particular theory of inspiration.

17. Allegorical scriptural interpretation is the central kernel of prophetic exegesis. I hope to treat the subject of allegorical interpretation on another occasion. Allegorical interpretation belongs so intrinsically to prophetic revelation because it is determined neither by an interest in "understanding" the text nor by the intentionality of a human being's intellectual act, but by discerning the types and symbols that revelation itself has fostered. Allegorical interpretation is "knowledge" in exactly the same sense as is dogma, meaning that both are knowledge, not in the sense of an intentional knowledge bound to a human being, but knowledge insofar as it is given with and from revelation. Allegorical knowledge is thereby distinguished from dogmatic knowledge by the manner of revelation. Prophecy

results in the symbolic knowledge of allegory, the revelation of the Logos in the conceptual knowledge of dogma.

18. In the sense used here, I consider correct the meaning that recent Church historians attach to the "charismatic" character of the *prophētai* and the *didaskaloi* in the most ancient Christianity. Prophets and teachers are similar to the charismatics. But to equate the New Testament prophets with the Old Testament prophets is to misunderstand primitive Christianity's concept of *pneuma* and to backdate Montanism to the primitive community.

19. One can also say this: the subject of theology is not the theology professor, but primarily Christ and secondarily the Church.

20. [The German phrase "jemanden auf den Leib rücken" means to press a person hard or crowd in on them. Peterson is presenting the Incarnation as a form of divine pressure on human nature and describing that in a bluntly physical metaphor.—Ed.]

21. The misunderstanding that the Gospel is a proclamation that is directed "to all" arose from the empirical situation that we encounter the proclamation *first* (in Bible and preaching) and are then directed to the revelation of Christ. The sequence of this mediation leaves the impression that the preached and written word is the actual substance of the thing, but the *event* of revelation itself only a kind of illustration for the word. Such a perception completely mistakes the relation of the revelation of Christ to the prophetic word. That Christ has spoken (as the incarnated Logos) is something totally different from the fact that a prophet has spoken. For prophetic utterance, the Bible is a perfectly adequate medium. But for the speech of Christ, it is essentially *in*adequate to think of it as in the Bible, in that Christ has not only *said* God's Word but also *is* it. Precisely this expresses Christ's superiority to the prophets. And therefore dogma too co-exists with Christ's speech. By virtue of dogma, the risk is removed that the biblical mediation of Christ's address will make his speaking about God the equivalent of a prophetic utterance. If we remove dogma from the New Testament revelation, we reduce Christ to the level of a prophet. That statement is not only true theologically but can be verified historically and empirically a thousand times over. Only through dogma does the difference between the Old and the New Testaments really find expression. The Bible in itself, the prophetic address as such and the exegesis and preaching that are linked to it, can never by itself determine this difference between the Old and New Covenant. In other words, the fact that Christ as the *Incarnate* One has spoken of God is the reason why he cannot adequately be contained in the words of Scripture—instead, while he permeates the words of Scripture, he is incorporated into another sphere of reality. The Bible is the body of the *prophetic* word, whereas the body of the Logos of God is not the Bible but the Church, and the dogma that is fixed by the Church.

22. The terms "dogma" and "sacrament" do not derive from jurisprudence by accident. Note where legal terminology appears in sacramental contexts in the New

Testament and try to explain precisely why this is—without merely citing analogous usages from the papyri, the fashionable subaltern posing of the question. This is connected to an essential feature of the character of the New Testament revelation. Old Testament prophecy could never possess this quality of juristic exclusivity, because God's Word was never vouchsafed to just *one* prophet. It was ever in process of delivery. Only through the Incarnation did it come to a conclusion, to a conclusion that was not simply a "closure," a simple cessation of prophecy, but in its "en-closure" something that the prophetic word never was: a fulfillment. Spiritual exegesis and preaching are not at all a fulfillment in the same sense as dogma and theology. It is characteristic of exegesis that it expresses the *polymerōs kai polytropōs* (in many and varied ways) (Heb. 1:1) of the prophetic word. Allegorical interpretation therefore has to do with a wealth of types and veils. Dogma, however, in its conceptual univocity also expresses the univocal and definitive character of the revelation of the Logos, its speaking "in these last days" (Heb. 1:1).

23. On this point a misunderstanding of dogma almost always occurs. It is obvious that neither a teaching nor a confession can be absolutized for all time. But dogma is not at all in this sense teaching and confession, nor does it lie in a sphere that is prone to the human propensity to absolutize. Modern Protestantism typically interprets the dogma of the ancient Church in terms of its concept of a confession. But that is intrinsically and historically incorrect.

24. Dogma belongs to the speech of the incarnate Logos, as the body of Christ belongs essentially to his head. The body of Christ is not a subordinate *accidens* (secondary quality) that he could just as well do without, and in the same way, dogma is not something that one can put brackets around according to one's preference and leave unnoticed. The body of Christ is also not—as little as is dogma—something that is only constituted in the act of faith. If Church and dogma are only constituted in the act of faith, then they belong essentially to the human being who believes. *But the Church is not the body of belief or of believers; it is the body of Christ.* And dogma is not a concretion of the act of faith—and theology is therefore also not a statement of faith—but rather a concretion of the Logos.

25. The Church can represent Christ because Christ is absent and the Church—according to its nature—is visible, as any body is visible. Giving Christ his honor means recognizing the place of dogma, which belongs to Christ, in the objective intellectual order. And honoring the Logos in theology means participating in the Logos's speaking of God as it is mediated through dogma. But we ourselves cannot give Christ the honor, he must allow that of us, he must allow that of us in an objective manner—namely, in dogma.

26. If all the faithful are priests, then all the faithful are also theologians. If theology is no longer the task of an order [*Stand*], it succumbs to the diversity of human "callings." Then there is a theology of the worker, a theology of the capitalist, a theology of the journalist, and even a theology of the theology professors. Everyone in his particular "calling" has then become a theologian. Happy the age in which there are as many theologies as there are "callings"; just one thing is lacking: *the* theology.

CHAPTER 2: CORRESPONDENCE WITH ADOLF VON HARNACK

AND AN EPILOGUE

An earlier version of this translation appeared in *Pro Ecclesia 2* (1993). It is reprinted here with permission.

1. Adolf von Harnack, "Das Alte Testament in den Paulinischen Briefen und in den Paulinischen Gemeinden," Sitzungsberichte der Preussischen Akademie der Wissenschaften. Philos.-hist. Kl. (1928), 124–141. My thanks also to Harnack's widow for permission to quote from his letters.

2. Hans Lietzmann, *Messe und Herrenmahl: Eine Studie zur Geschichte der Liturgie* (Bonn, 1926), 227. [Translated by Dorothea H. G. Reeve as *Mass and Lord's Supper: A Study in the History of the Liturgy* (Leiden, 1953).]

3. Karl Holl, "Der Kirchenbegriff des Paulus in seinem Verhältnis zu dem der Urgemeinde," in *Gesammelte Aufsätze zur Kirchengeschichte*, vol. 2: *Der Osten* (Tübingen, 1928)], 54.

4. Wilhelm Mundle, "Das Apostelbild der Apostelgeschichte," *Zeitschrift für die Neutestamentliche Wissenschaft* 27, 1 (1928): 41. "One sees . . . how the notion of the unconditioned apostolic authority, but also the idea of the 'apostolic succession' dominates Acts' conception of history."

5. [The late-nineteenth-century *Gemeinschaftsbewegung* was a Pietist movement inside and partially also outside the Evangelical state churches. It was influenced by Dwight Moody's work in America. In the words of an early leader, it aspired to be "in the church, if possible with the church, but not under the church," as cited in Ernst Helmreich *The German Churches under Hitler* (Detroit, 1979), 33; in contemporary parlance, it was a parachurch movement.—Ed.]

6. Most strongly perhaps in the theological work of Friedrich Gogarten.

7. The struggle against the office of the bishop in the Evangelical Church is an opposition to all concerns to establish a link between Church leadership and theology.

8. One cannot, as Barth tried to, return to the theology of the sixteenth century, without also returning to the Church of the sixteenth century, and, what is still more important, to the confessional state of the sixteenth century.

9. The earlier territorial changes in Prussia have, with the creation of the Prussian Union, had portentous results for the confessional character of Protestantism. What kind of theology will arise once the Deutscher evangelischer Kirchenbund [German Evangelical Church Association, the federal association of the twenty-eight separate provincial churches formed in 1922—Ed.] has again established itself as a church?

10. Recently, Georg Wobbermin (see *Theologische Blätter* 11 [1932]: 186) has repeatedly accused Karl Barth of favoring Catholicism, and has also made him responsible for my conversion. As to the first point, Wobbermin has constructed a "catholicizing" from the fact that Barth has taken Catholicism seriously in theological terms, a substantially false judgment, I think, or else the whole of tradi-

tional Protestantism was "catholicized." As to the second point, for myself I can only quote Barth's statement that my own theological development has evolved completely independently of Barth's. Seen psychologically, Pietism and Kierkegaard have perhaps given the decisive impulse to [my] return to the Catholic faith. But in the final analysis all Protestant paths lead to Rome.

11. One thinks of the works of Ernst Troeltsch, E. Weber, P. Petersen and Karl Eschweiler.

12. Mention may be made of the important works of the elder Althaus on the history of the literature of prayer and on Wilhelm Koepp's book on Johann Arndt, *Johann Arndt: Eine Untersuchung über die Mystik in Luthertum zur Frage nach der Mystik* (Johann Arndt: An Investigation of Mysticism in Lutheranism, on the Question of Mysticism) (Berlin, 1912).

13. The beginnings of the Protestant mission movement, which traditional Protestant orthodoxy is known to have rejected, should be mentioned in this connection.

14. On this point the struggle against Schleiermacher in dialectical theology seems to correspond thoroughly to the assumptions of traditional Protestantism.

15. The "old Catholic element" in traditional Protestantism was not simply a "vestige" but had the function of maintaining the relationship of Protestantism to Catholicism as a dialectical relationship. This means that traditional Protestantism was not yet conscious of being "historically" separated from the Catholic Church.

16. This seems to me to be the deeper reason for the respect for Harnack in Catholic circles.

17. Albrecht Ritschl, *Die Geschichte des Pietismus* (The History of Pietism) (1880–1886; facsimile, Berlin, 1966). The demonstration of the systematic-typological connection in Ritschl's book is much more significant than the allied attempt to show historical-genetic connections.

18. Recall the polemic against the Kaiserswerther sisters and their dress in the Protestantism of the nineteenth century.

19. From this standpoint, one can say that to some extent, the confessional dialogue in Germany exists only on the plane of political theology.

20. It is revealing that the argument of the *Zeitschrift für Kontrovers-Theologie Catholica* (published by Robert Grosche at the Winfriedsbund Press, Paderborn) is mainly with dialectical theology. An exchange with the Protestant Church is impossible.

CHAPTER 3: THE CHURCH

1. [Karl Holl, "Der Kirchenbegriff des Paulus in seinem Verhältnis zu dem der Urgemeinde," in *Gesammelte Autsätze zur Kirchengeschichte*, vol. 2: *Der Osten* (Tübingen, 1928); Wilhelm Mundle, "Das Apostelbild der Apostelgeschichte," *Zeitschrift für die Neutestamentliche Wissenschaft* 27, 1 (1928): 36ff.; Hans Lietzmann,

Messe und Herrenmahl: Eine Studie zur Geschichte der Liturgie (Bonn, 1926). These two paragraphs appeared before the notes in the original publication of "Die Kirche" in 1928, which also contained this important addendum, deleted by Peterson when the essay was reprinted in *Theologische Traktate* in 1951: "The arguments found in this text go back to a lecture delivered in Holland in September 1928. A larger work on the Church, which should appear in the foreseeable future, will justify or develop further the ideas outlined here." That larger work never appeared.—Ed.]

2. A "holy language" (in the strict sense of the word) exists only in the stage of the prophetic revelation. But just as "the Son" is the end of prophecy, so is he also the end of "holy language." It is characteristic that the Church did not adopt a single ancient gospel in Aramaic.

3. Recall Harnack or Adolf Schlatter. On the connection between Semitic language and Semitic thought form, see Louis Massignon, "Pro Psalmis," *Revue juive* 1 (Paris, 1925). [Contemporary scholarship on Christian origins is far less ready to accept the smooth distinction presumed here between "Semitic" and "Greek," which perhaps says as much about disciplinary divisions in German university life (between classics and biblical studies) and about the pervasive anti-Judaism in Christian theology of the time as it does about first-century realities. Among many examples of modern correctives, see the work of Martin Hengel, beginning with his landmark study *Judaism and Hellenism* (2 vols.; Philadelphia, 1974). Peterson himself became far more interested in Christianity's Jewish roots than this article would suggest.—Ed.]

4. This is why Paul can make *Ioudaioi* parallel with *Hellēnes* [1. Cor. 1:22].

5. That the eschatological proclamation of Jesus was first of all *related* to the Jews does not mean that it was *identical* with the eschatological understandings of the Jews.

6. When Barth and his circle play off concrete eschatology against the "doctrine of the Last Things," they are making the inherently futile attempt to return to Jewish Christianity.

7. Gal. 2:9. "The pillars" (*styloi*) are possibly to be understood as the "bearers" of the heavenly edifice of the Endtime. The concepts "foundation stone" and "pillars" probably come from the same class of eschatological thought.

8. 1 Cor. 9:5. [Peterson reads Paul's verb *periagein* in the intransitive sense of "wander about," although the more common transitive meaning of "lead about, take someone along as company" is the translation adopted in the NRSV. See *A Greek-English Lexicon of the New Testament and Other Early Christian Literature: A Translation and Adaptation of Walter Bauer's "Griechisch-Deutsches Worterbuch zu den Schriften des Neuen Testaments und der übrigen urchristlichen Literatur,"* ed. W. F. Arndt and F. W. Gingrich (Chicago, 1952), s.v.—Ed.]

9. Acts 21:18. It is telling that along with James, the *presbyteroi* are named.

10. The ancient tradition that goes back to the *Preaching of Peter*, according to

which the twelve Apostles stayed in Jerusalem for twelve years, appears to me to be (perhaps gnostic?) *speculation*.

11. [Peterson's eschatological interpretation of primitive Christianity stressed its "proleptic," or anticipatory, character, in which the New Age was breaking in but had yet to appear in its fullness. This is important for understanding the theological reading of Acts that Peterson uses here. Consistent with German biblical scholarship of his time and afterwards—see, e.g., the standard commentary of Ernst Haenchen, *The Acts of the Apostles: A Commentary* (Philadelphia, 1971), 90–110—he tended to minimize the genuinely historical character of Acts. See Nichtweiß, *Erik Peterson*, 486 n. 191 and 489 n. 215.—Ed.]

12. Within the Church, Hebrew is the holy language only alongside Greek and Latin. The medieval theory of the three "holy languages," which is based on the *titulum* on the cross (John 19:20), has a deep meaning that should not be overlooked from the point of view of a philosophy of history.

13. [Elsewhere Peterson defended ways in which Jesus *could* be said to have founded the Church. On the basis of his early unpublished lectures on Church history, Nichtweiß cites Peterson's assessment of the role played in the formation of the canon by the Lord's sayings. The testimony of St. Paul in 1 Cor. 11:23 shows that the authority of the Lord's sayings and the authority of the Church and its decisions mutually reinforced each other—an authority that he argued went back to Jesus himself and was passed on to his followers (see Nichtweiß, *Erik Peterson*, 570 n. 305). In the same lectures on Church history, Peterson defended the authenticity of Peter's confession in Matt. 16:18; when joined with Jesus' saying about the raising up of the Temple (Mark 14:58), Jesus' promise to Peter pointed to the equation of the rebuilt "temple" with the "rock" on which he would build the Church: "Christ proclaimed his resurrection to Peter and in the resurrection of his body, the building of the *ekklēsia*" (cited in Nichtweiß, *Erik Peterson*, 858 n. 216). This correlation has been echoed in the work of such contemporary biblical scholars as the late Ben Meyer and N. T. Wright.—Ed.]

14. Cf. [André] Wilmart, "Les ordres de Christ," *Revue des sciences religieuses* 3 (1923): 305–27, esp. 322: "La stabilité de la hiérarchie n'est pas autrement fondée que par l'entremise des apôtres" (The stability of the hierarchy is not founded otherwise than through the mediation of the Apostles).

15. [Nichtweiß points out that he may later have modified this sharp distinction. In a 1948 encyclopedia article on "Apostoli," he recognized that Jesus could well have combined "apostleship" with the number twelve, since "being sent" could also reflect the Jewish institution of the *šaliaḥ* and not stem only from the post-Easter Gentile mission (Nichtweiß, *Erik Peterson*, 627 n. 299).—Ed.]

16. [Giancarlo Caronello, "Zur Rezeption in Italien," in *Vom Ende der Zeit*, ed. Nichtweiß, 313–316, shows how Peterson's understanding of the place of Peter evolved, as revealed in several small publications at the time of the controversy over the grave of St. Peter in the early 1950s. Peterson thought it was a mistake to value

the grave site itself over the theological content of the legacy of Peter in the literary remains of early Christianity, such as the report from the late second-century Roman presbyter Gaius about the "monument" (*tropaion*) to Peter on the Vatican hill (as preserved in Eusebius's *Church History* 2.25.7). In general, he emphasized the eschatological and martyrological aspects of the Petrine tradition, because he was more convinced than ever—perhaps in reaction to the apotheosis of the papacy in the closing years of the pontificate of Pius XII—that the Church's offices needed to be understood, not as "organization" but as "eschatological institution," i.e., as representation and sacrament of the coming age, not the present age.—Ed.]

17. As an "apostle" Paul is able to appear alongside the others, next to "the Twelve Apostles." But he can never be accepted into the college of the Twelve. "The apostles" belong to the charismatic order, but "the Twelve" to the legal order. The difference between Paul and "the Twelve" also becomes clear in the different ways in which the Lord appears to them. Cf. the resurrection appearances recounted in the gospels with the narrative of the appearance on the way to Damascus. In the different ways in which the Lord appears to "the Twelve" and to Paul are rooted, not only theological differences within the apostolic proclamation, but also the completely different position Paul has in the Church and in the way he lives on.

18. An especially instructive feature of Harnack's Marcion is the fact that a Protestantism that repudiates every connection with the Catholic Church will by necessity arrive at the precisely "primitive" solution of Marcion.

19. "Law" here naturally has the meaning of *ius divinum*. *Ius divinum* exists in the Church because it was the Son of God who legally delegated it to "the Twelve." In general, the recognition of *ius divinum* does not deny that there is still also a "holy law" in the Church, alongside "Church law." The punishments of Ananias and Sapphira, or of Elymas, which are reported in the Acts of the Apostles, are not Church-legal punishments so much as done in the sense of the "holy law" of antiquity. The specifically new and Christian element, to be sure, consists in Church law and not in "holy law." [*Ius divinum* should not be taken as a divine endorsement embracing everything that would be today understood by Roman Catholics as "canon law," a reality with which Peterson at that time had little acquaintance. As Barbara Nichtweiß properly cautions us (*Erik Peterson*, 619 n. 239), Peterson meant only to say that the Church has in and of itself a properly legal character that is divinely willed, and that the Church has the capability of functioning as the court of last resort in dogmatic and disciplinary cases. The distinction between "Church law" and "holy law" was important to Peterson (see esp. Nichtweiß, 628–631). The latter term reflected pagan usages and referred to cultic and sacral law. Peterson adopted it to describe binding enactments that could claim the direct authorization of the Spirit. Their character is therefore "charismatic" in the meaning normal since Sohm and Weber. St. Paul is the outstanding exemplar (see Nichtweiß, 631–637, on St. Paul as the "Apostle of the Exception"). But there is nothing

distinctively Christian about "holy law," according to Peterson; that distinction attaches only to Church law.—Ed.]

20. The Old Testament is not a Jewish residue in the Church but a legitimate inheritance. With the Old Testament, the Church has inherited the blessings of God and the promises of Israel. [On Peterson's theology of Judaism, see the introduction.—Ed.]

21. As is well known, this formula from Acts 15:28 has been repeated in conciliar decrees.

22. Although we may find it comprehensible to imagine that "facts," specifically the Pauline Gentile mission, "forced" the Twelve to give up their earlier position, nevertheless, we ought not to forget that a "necessity" is not a "decision," and that "the Twelve" could not escape a "decision," because their own existence as "Apostles" depended on it.

23. It is not enough to derive the technical linguistic usage of *ekklēsia* from the Septuagint. To clarify its meaning, we need to look instead to the new situation in which the apostles found themselves. [This is an allusion to a long-running dispute between Peterson and the New Testament scholar Karl Ludwig Schmidt (1891–1956) on the derivation of the Christian concept of the Church. Schmidt believed that the concept of the community as an assembly (*ekklēsia*) needed to be understood in the light of its use in the Septuagint; he saw the Christian "people of God" as analogous to the Jewish people of God, the two existing alongside each other. Peterson held a stronger view of Christianity's relation to Judaism: "The Church is not a Jewish eschatological sect; it does not exist *along with* the continuing existence of the Old Testament people of God. No, as the Old Testament migrated with the Twelve to the Gentiles, so too did the predicate 'people of God' . . ." (cited in Nichtweiß, *Erik Peterson*, 522 n. 221; see Excursus 19 on Peterson and Karl Ludwig Schmidt, ibid., 522–523). On the question of Schmidt and Peterson's disagreement on the derivation of *ekklēsia* from Greek political terminology, Helmut Koester has spoken in support of Peterson's position. While recognizing that *ekklēsia* is the Septuagint's translation of Hebrew *qhl*, Koester says, "It must be noted, however, that ancient Judaism preferred the term *synagōgē*, and that in the Greek world the term *ekklēsia* is used exclusively in the political realm. It never occurs as a designation for a religious association." See Helmut Koester, "Writings and the Spirit: Authority and Politics in Ancient Christianity," *Harvard Theological Review* 84 (1991): 354–372, at 358 n. 18.—Ed.]

24. It can be shown in various ways that the *laos* of the Christian *ekklēsia* is the successor of the ancient *dēmos*. I am thinking not merely of the acclamations, which passed over from the *dēmos* to the *laos*, but would also like to draw attention to a connection discovered by Josef Partsch, according to which manumission in the Christian *ekklēsia*, in the form of a proclamation, goes back to a practice of the secular *ekklēsia*. See Jos. Partsch, *Mitteilungen aus der Freiburger Papyrussammlung*, 2: *Juristische Texte der römischen Zeit* = Sitzungsberichte der Heidelberger Akad-

emie der Wissenschaften, Phil.-histor. Klasse, Abhandlung 10 (1916), 44f. Also Ulrich Wilcken in J. Partsch, *Juristische Papyri der Ptolemäerzeit*, 106.

25. That the citizens of the "Heavenly City" assemble in worship has the result that the liturgy on earth corresponds to a celebration in heaven. The correspondence of heavenly and earthly liturgy in the Masses of old is no fantastic invention of the "embellishment" of divine worship, but rather a necessary component of the liturgy, and is entailed in the essence of the very concept of the Church. [Peterson develops this theme more fully in "The Book on the Angels."—Ed.]

26. [Peterson's denial that the Church's worship was a "celebration of the mysteries" reflects his deep disagreement with Odo Casel, the Benedictine sacramental theologian from Maria Laach, whose influential scholarship helped shape the liturgical movement. The disagreement had to do with Casel's fascination with the history-of-religions school of Richard Reitzenstein and others. Under their influence, Casel saw the sacraments in terms of the pagan mystery religions and understood the meaning of the sacraments to be a mystical identification with the death and resurrection of Jesus. Peterson, who, as noted, had studied with Reitzenstein and had admired his approach, had by 1925 distanced himself from it. He insisted that the sacraments should be understood above all from an eschatological perspective, as the sacramental performance here and now of what would be fully accomplished at the End. The sacraments were not an "experience" analogous to the mysteries; they were par excellence the way in which the New Age had broken in with Jesus' death and resurrection. Because they had legal and public force, they were also crucial to the Church's "public" (*öffentlich*) character as a religious-political community: the sacraments were the binding cultic acts of the Christian assembly of the heavenly city—hence Peterson's sharp rejection of the "voluntaristic" aspects of the mystery religion model. He develops these ideas much more fully in "The Book on the Angels." On the controversy with Casel, see Nichtweiß, *Erik Peterson*, 414–426.—Ed.]

27. [The German text reads, "So lange sie verstockt bleiben . . ."; the "stubbornness," "obduracy," or "hardening" of the Jews is language taken from Romans 11:7 and 11:25, which speak of their "hardening" (Gk. *pōrōsis*) against God. The concept has had an unhappy role in the history of Christian anti-Judaism, but it was particularly provocative in the context of the increasing anti-Semitism of post–World War I Germany. Peterson's essay puts special stress on this *pōrōsis*, because for him it is the precondition for the very existence of the Church in lieu of the deferral of the Kingdom. In others' hands, Jewish "hardening" was sometimes described as a virtual second Original Sin, a second Fall. Although that concept is missing in "The Church," its currency elsewhere did not make acceptance of the essay any easier. See Nichtweiß, *Erik Peterson*, 848–849, in particular her comments on the concept and the language of a "second Fall" in the writings of no less a figure than Romano Guardini, who was probably influenced by Peterson, she suggests, although she contends that Guardini's speculations were "much more reckless" than his.—Ed.]

CHAPTER 4: THE CHURCH FROM JEWS AND GENTILES

All biblical translations are from the Revised Standard Version—see http://quod
.lib.umich.edu/r/rsv/browse.html (accessed January 8, 2011).

1. [This prefatory note appeared in the first publication of *Die Kirche aus Juden
und Heiden*, three lectures given in the summer of 1932 in the Salzburg Hochschulwochen and published a year later, but was omitted from later editions.—Ed.]

2. Aponius, *Aponii in Canticum canticorum explanatio* 1.2 (Aponius's Commentary on the Song of Songs), ed. Bottino and Martini (Rome, 1843).

3. Matthias Joseph Scheeben, *Die Mysterien des Christentums* (Freiburg im Br.,
1912). The seventh major portion has the heading "The Mystery of the Church
and Its Sacraments."

4. Humbert Clérissac, O.P., *Le mystère de l'église* (Paris, 1925).

5. Rom. 11:33–36.

6. [Frequently in this commentary, in place of the German word *Kirche*, Peterson uses the transliterated Greek *ekklēsia*, "church" or "assembly," to stress its etymol-
ogy, "[those] called out." I have retained the transliterated Greek wherever it appears,
reserving "Church" for *Kirche*.—Ed.]

7. Is. 6.

8. Matt. 5:20.

9. Christian worship cannot be understood as the "spiritualizing" of the Jewish cultus, for it is marked by a "cancellation" of animal sacrifice by the sacrifice of
the "Son of Man." The *logikē latreia* of the Christians must thus be fundamentally
distinguished from the so-called "spiritualizing" sublimation of Jewish or other
ancient worship by Greek philosophy.

10. Vis-à-vis Judaism, this stipulates a completely changed attitude to wealth.
If the New Testament speaks of "wealth" in a positive fashion, it is always in terms
of the "richness" of God's grace (Eph. 1:7, 2:7) or the "richness" of his glory (Rom.
9:23; Eph. 3:16) and similar passages. In a Syriac poem on the Church and the Synagogue (an apologetic poem), the Synagogue says:

Strophe 11:

The earth is mine, and should I not inherit
An inheritance that comes to me?
With Abraham he concluded a covenant,
That he would give me the whole earth.

[To which the Church answers:]

Strophe 12:

You are supposed to have my land, be still;
You are supposed to inherit it totally; it doesn't make me jealous.
For I need no land,
But to my bridegroom I raise myself on high.

See "Alfabetische Acrosticha in der syrischen Kirchenpoesie," ed. Bruno Kirschner, *Oriens Christianus* 6 (1906): 26–27. Here we see not only the diverse attitudes to property, but also the possibility of a turning to mysticism that results from these attitudes.

11. In a fragment of Diodore of Tarsus, Abraham is even called "the father of the Church" (*ho patēr tēs ekklēsias*): see Joseph Deconinck, *Essai sur la chaîne de l'Octateuque* (Paris, 1912), p. 112, 16. Cf. also Irenaeus, *Adversus Haereses* (Against Heresies) 4.15: "Abraham et semen eius, quod est ecclesia (Abraham and his seed, which is the Church)."

12. The following passage from Diodore of Tarsus seems important to me. Diodore asks, in connection with Rom. 5:21–22: "Where has sin now abounded? Where the law is. But if the law is with the Jews, then there too has 'grace abounded.' For from there come the evangelists and the apostles and our sacred Head, Christ" (*pou oun epleonasen hē hamartia; hopou ho nomos. Ei de para Ioudaiois ho nomos, ekei kai "hypereperisseusen hē charis." Ekeithen gar euaggelistai kai apostoloi kai to tēs sōtērias kephalaion, ho Christos.* In K. Staab, *Paulus-Kommentare aus der griechischen Kirche* (Commentaries on Paul from the Greek Church) (= Neutestamentliche Abhandlungen, 15; Münster, 1933), pp. 85, 7ff.

13. [The RSV translation is here amended to reflect Peterson's exegesis, which depends on a debated punctuation of the Greek text of the benediction in Rom. 9:5. Peterson follows a punctuation that places "God" in direct apposition to "Christ."—Ed.]

14. The genuine sting of this is often ignored in definitions of the concept of the apostle—as if the apostles could have been spared faith and the anguish of faith.

15. The wealth of the patriarchs has a symbolic meaning as pointing to the wealth of divine grace. But the wealth of the Jews since the coming of Christ is without any promise, and is therefore regarded like the silver coins in the betrayal of Jesus. Because the wealth of the Jews can only be understood "theologically" as blessing or curse, it will always remain problematic from a natural point of view.

16. Among the fatuities of modern thought is the notion that a decision of God (such as the election of Israel) could be corrected by so-called history. [This note shows that Peterson is positing the opening theses of the paragraph only in order to overturn them.—Ed.]

17. In Sermon 32 (= "On the Solemnity of the Epiphany" no. 3), [Pope] Leo the Great has very nicely emphasized how Abraham's descendants are shown to him in the stars (Gen. 15:5): "ut . . . non terrena, sed coelestis progenies speraretur" (that he might hope not for an earthly but a heavenly offspring) (*Sancti Leonis Magni . . . Opera omnia* [Venice, 1748]), 31. By the look up at the stars, the focus is drawn away from the body and bodily offspring.

18. [German *pneumatisch* rendered here and elsewhere as "spiritual," is occasionally found as "pneumatic."—Ed.]

19. Of the many possible sources, I cite only Aponius's commentary on the Song of Songs 1.13, ed. Bottino and Martini, p. 7: "baptismatis . . . ubi gloriosa copula

Christi, filii Dei et ecclesiae celebratur ([through the water] of baptism, where the glorious wedding of Christ, the Son of God, and of the Church is celebrated)." The idea is prominently displayed in Syriac literature; cf., e.g., the dialogue poems of Narsai, in *Syrische Wechsellieder von Narses*, ed. Franz Feldman (Leipzig, 1896), p. 18.

20. Here too a great many sources could be cited. I mention only the Gelasian Sacramentary, ed. H. A. Wilson, *The Gelasian Sacramentary: Liber Sacramentorum Romanae Ecclesiae* (Oxford, 1894), 85: "ab immaculato divini fontis utero [from the immaculate womb of the divine font]." Ibid., p. 84: "ad creandos novos populos, quos tibi fons baptismatis parturit [for the creation of new peoples, whom the baptismal font has borne for you]." In Sermon 24 (*Sancti Leonis Magni . . . Opera omnia* [1748], 22), [Pope] Leo the Great drew a parallel between the womb of the Mother of God and the baptismal font: "Originem quam sumpsit in utero virginis, posuit in fonte baptismatis. Dedit aquae, quod dedit matri [The origin that he assumed in the womb of the Virgin, he placed in the baptismal font. He gave to the water what he gave to (his) mother]," etc.

21. Thus we have the following prayer from the Gelasian Sacramentary: "praesta ut in Abrahae filios et in Israeliticam dignitatem totius mundi transeat plenitudo [grant that the fullness of the whole world may cross over to the sons of Abraham and to the dignity of Israel]" (ed. Wilson, p. 82f.). Compare with this what [Pope] Leo [I] says in Sermon 32 (*Sancti Leonis Magni . . . Opera omnia* [1748], 31): "Intret, intret in patrarcharum familiam gentium plenitudo et benedictionem in semine Abrahae, qua se filii carnis abdicant, filii promissionis accipiant [May the fullness of the gentiles enter into the family of the patriarchs, and may the sons of the promise receive the blessing in the seed of Abraham, which (his) sons by the flesh renounce]."

22. Whoever regards the relationship of the Church to the synagogue simply as a historical and not a theological problem inevitably ends up repeating the gnostic gambit by trying to eliminate the Old Testament and the Messiah "after the flesh." To that extent, it is not an accident that Harnack the "historian" should align himself theologically with Marcion the "gnostic."

23. The Church's so-called proof-text method, based on the stories of the patriarchs, plays a great role in patristic literature. Cf. the collected materials in Nathanael Bonwetsch, *Der Schriftbeweis für die Kirche aus den Heiden als das wahre Israel bis auf Hippolyt* (The Biblical Proof for the Church from the Gentiles as the True Israel, up to Hippolytus) (= *Theologische Studien, Th[eodor] Zahn dargebracht*) (Leipzig, 1908). For Hippolytus, see Adolf Hamel, *Der Kirchenbegriff Hippolyts* (Hippolytus's Concept of the Church) (diss., Bonn, 1929), 13ff. Reference may at least be made to Gregory the Great's Homily 22, "On the Gospels," which does not take the patriarchal narratives as its point of departure.

24. Caesarius of Arles's little treatise *De comparatione ecclesiae vel synagogae* (On the Comparison of the Church and the Synagogue), ed. G[ermain] Morin, *Revue bénédictine* 23 (1906): 31ff., assembles all the Old Testament examples of the

younger being preferred to the elder. If we were to read just one or two examples from patristic literature, Caesarius explains, we might mistakenly think they could be interpreted in some other way: "cum vero toties iuniores senioribus legamus fuisse praepositos [but since we read so many times that the younger have been preferred to the elder]," we must necessarily conclude that "haec divinitus dispensata esse [this has happened by divine dispensation]" (lines 108ff.).

25. Cf. also Carlo Passaglia, *De ecclesia Christi: commentariorum libri quinque* (On the Church of Christ: Five Books of Commentaries) (Regensburg, 1853), 1: 10. I consider this patristic interpretation of the word *ekklēsia*, which serves to distinguish the constitutional forms of *ekklēsia* and synagogue, to be more meaningful than the modern assertions that in the Septuagint the words *ekklēsia* and *synagōgē* are used interchangeably. It is not the mere citation but the specific situation in which a word is used that is decisive for its meaning.

26. The concept of the "fleshly" in Pauline theology can't be understood either from the Old Testament or from Greek philosophy; it is, rather, a "polemical" concept for illuminating its contrast with the concept of the spiritual-supernatural in its specifically Christian form.

27. Voluntary celibacy in the Church thus became a characteristic feature over against Judaism, a necessary existential expression of the spiritual-supernatural over against the "fleshly" Jewish sphere, just as voluntary poverty stands in contrast to the Jewish esteem for wealth. On these points Luther overlooked essential elements of the earliest Christian life.

28. Gal. 4:26.

29. Rom. 8:2.

30. The grotesque example of [Karl] Künstle, *Ikonographie der Christlichen Kunst* (Freiburg im Br., 1926–1928), 1: 81f., shows just how little the theological significance of these figures in medieval art of the synagogue and the *ekklēsia* is grasped today. Künstle argues that they embody the *concordia veteris et novi testamenti*, an ancient theological principle: "The conflictual posture of both in medieval art does not contradict the assumption that they are symbols of the *concordia veteris et novi testamenti*, for the result of the conflict is always the *concordia*, meaning that the synagogue always recognizes that the Old Testament has found its fulfillment in the New." Any critique of these assertions would be superfluous.

31. The synagogue has become not just constrained but barren. Aponius's commentary (12.29) neatly applies Songs 8:8 to the synagogue: "soror nostra parva, et ubera non habet" (our sister is little, and she has no breasts) (ed. Bottino and Martini, p. 227f.).

32. The fates of the Jews in the political world are in the final analysis to be understood not in terms of the political but the theological sphere.

33. The concept of "election" is naturally defined first of all by the Jewish understanding of it. But it takes on its specific meaning only after it is incorporated into the complex of ideas of Christian eschatology.

34. By "eschatological time," I mean the time that begins with the first coming of Christ and ends with his second coming. I give it this name because this age is in a specific sense oriented toward the end (the *eschaton*). On the concept of eschatological time, I refer to Heb. 1:1, according to which God *ep eschatou tōn hēmerōn toutōn elalēsen hēmin en huiōi* (in these last days he has spoken to us by a Son). The Gelasian Sacramentary (ed. Wilson, p. 82) speaks similarly: "quod in fine saeculorum pascha nostrum immolatus est Christus [because at the end of the ages Christ our Passover (lamb) has been sacrificed]." Examples could easily be multiplied.

35. Luke 13:7–8: "And he said to the vinedresser, 'Lo, these three years I have come seeking fruit on this fig tree, and I find none. Cut it down. . . .' And he answered him, 'Let it alone, sir, this year also. . . .'"

36. It is therefore theologically perfectly justified when, for example, the *Ludus de Antichristo* has the figures of the synagogue and the *ekklēsia* appear in the days of the Antichrist. Cf. Gottfried Hasenkamp's translation, *Das Spiel vom Antichrist* (The Play on the Antichrist) (Münster, 1933).

37. Transcendence and eschatology are correlative concepts. This is what distinguishes the Christian from the Greek concept of transcendence.

38. Luke 14:16ff.

39. Eusebius *Church History* 4.5.2.

40. This "playing dumb" of the Jews appears to be a reason in the Middle Ages for occasionally forcing them to listen to a Christian sermon.

41. So says Leo the Great: the zeal of the Jews has turned into *invidia* (jealousy), cf. Sermon 35, in *Sancti Leonis Magni . . . Opera omnia* (1748), p. 35. The problem this poses for the Jews is especially painful because it touches directly their sense of legitimacy. Cf. Leo's exposition in Sermon 34, ibid., p. 34: "haereditatem Domini ante saecula praeaparatam accipiunt adoptivi et perdiderunt, qui videbantur esse legitimi." (Those who were adopted receive the Lord's inheritance prepared before the ages, while the ones who seemed to be legitimate have lost it.)

CHAPTER 5: MONOTHEISM AS A POLITICAL PROBLEM

1. *Ta de onta ou bouletai politeuesthai kakōs; "ouk agathon polykoiraniē, heis koiranos estō"* (Arist. *Metaphysics* Λ 12.1076a 3ff.).

2. Werner Jaeger, *Aristoteles: Grundlegung einer Geschichte seiner Entwicklung* (Berlin, 1923), p. 228 (Aristotle: Foundation of a History of His Development). Likewise Hans Friedrich von Arnim, *Die Gotteslehre des Aristoteles* (Aristotle's Doctrine of God), Sitzungsberichte der Wiener Akademie, no. 212 (Vienna, 1931), 31.

3. The impact is clearly evident in Simplicius, whose commentary on Aristotle's *Physics* refers repeatedly to this conclusion (ed. Hermannus Diels, 9: 250.26, 256.21; 10: 1254.13—all citations in this note are from the Berlin edition of the *Commentaria in Aristotelem graeca* [Greek Commentaries on Aristotle] [Berlin, 1882–1909]). Alexander of Aphrodisias paraphrases the text in Aristotle's *Metaphysics* in this fashion:

Polyarchia (polyarchy) is *ataxia* (disorder). Then he continues: *epeidē ta eph' hēmin hyp' allēlōn synergoumena ou kakōs politeutetai all' aristōs, ouk an eien archai pollai. Ou gar agathon polykoiraniē, all' heis koiranos, mia archē, heis theos esti* (since our affairs are conducted cooperatively under one another and we are governed not badly but very well, there would not be many first principles. For the rule of many is not good, rather there is one lord, one principle, one god.) (ed. Michael Hayduck, 1: 721.28ff.). Syrianus poses the question in his commentary of whether the Seasons who stand next to Zeus are able to serve as independent *archai* (principles) and denies that they can by citing the passage from Homer (ed. Guilelmus Kroll, 6, 1: 194.9).

4. *Epeisodiōdēs* (a series of episodes) Λ 10, 1076a.1 and N 1, 1090b.19. Cf. Theophrastus *Metaphysics* 1.1: *mē epeisodiōdes to pan* (the universe is not a mere series of episodes) (ed. W. D. Ross and F. H. Fobes, 2.14).

5. The revival of Aristotelian doctrines by Andronicus occurred in the first century BC.

6. *Aristotelis de mundo* (Aristotle's On the World], ed. Lorimer (Nouvelle collection de textes et documents publiée sous le patronage de l'Association Budé). W. Capelle, *Die Schrift von der Welt* (The Treatise on the World] (Leipzig, 1905) is important for the understanding of this text.

7. We may put aside here the question whether the treatise *On the World* has a connection with Posidonius, so, e.g., Paul Wendland, *Philos Schrift über die Vorsehung* (Philo's Treatise on Providence) (Berlin, 1892), 10.2; Capelle, *Schrift von der Welt*, passim; Eduard Norden, *Agnostos Theos: Untersuchungen zur Formengeschichte religiöser Rede* (The Unknown God: Researches in the Form-History of Religious Address) (Berlin, 1913), 26. But see Karl Reinhardt, *Kosmos und Sympathie* (Munich, 1926), 151 n. 3 ("Its appearance in *Peri Kosmou* [*On the World*] is in no way a guarantee that something comes from Posidonius"), and id., *Posidonios* (Munich, 1921), 174f.

8. It would be fruitful to analyze how the treatise *On the World* tries to solve *aporiai* (problems) in Aristotelian metaphysics without, for once, focusing on the question of dependency.

9. Let me emphasize here that I am thinking of the substantive intellectual connection. Of course, I am naturally well aware, that the designation of Zeus as *basileus* is old. See, e.g., Ulrich von Wilamowitz-Moellendorff, *Der Glaube der Hellenen* (The Faith of the Greeks), 2 vols., (Berlin, 1931–1932), 1: 140.1. On *Kronos basileus*, see Max Pohlenz in *Neue Jahrbücher für das klassische Altertum* 39 (1916): 559. For the usage in Plato, see *Epistula* (Letter) 2.312E and *Ep.* 6.323D. (Cf. *Philebus* 28C and 30D.)

10. It is quite likely that the author of the treatise *On the World* had already encountered the application of the image of the Persian Great King to the Aristotelian God in the literature. See, e.g., Zeller, *Ursprung* etc., 12. I don't believe that, as Yizhak Heinemann, *Posidonios' metaphysische Schriften* (Posidonius's Metaphysical Writings) (Breslau, 1921–1928), 1: 126ff., appears to assume, Posidonius in-

vented the image. It is probably early Hellenistic. On the use of the concept of the "Great King" in the diatribe, see Rudolf Helm, *Lucian und Menipp* (Lucian and Menippus) (Leipzig, 1906), 55.

11. In his Latin translation of the treatise *On the World*, Apuleius emphasized a particular interpretive possibility of the word *dynamis* (see, e.g., *Cod. Justinian.* 1.1.5.1, and 1.1.6.4, where the *mia dynamis* of the three-in-one God stands for the common *potestas*) by interchanging it with *potestas*. In this fashion, he was able to disclose the ambiguity, of both a physical and a political sort, of the concept of *dynamis*, similar to the way in which Aristotle had disclosed the double meaning of the concept of *archē*.

12. It should not be overlooked that Aristotle gave a *polemical* twist to the metaphysical concept of unity in the twelfth book of the *Metaphysics*: the tragedy metaphor and the citation from the Iliad are both meant *polemically*.

13. "The unity of God with the world (according to Aristotle) is established neither by God's immanence in the world, nor by his enclosure within himself of the totality of its forms as the intelligible world; rather the world 'depends' (*ērtētai*) on him: he *is* its unity, although he is not in it," Jaeger argues (*Aristoteles*, 411). In the image of the Persian Great King, we have the rather one-sided conception that God is not in the world, which therefore also means the appropriation of the image of the puppeteer.

14. In the formulation of his monarchic ideal within the metaphysical order, did not Aristotle reveal a prior decision in favor of Alexander the Great's shaping of Hellenistic monarchy? Cf. Jaeger, *Aristoteles*, 121, on the "symbolic" connection between Aristotle and Alexander the Great.

15. [Ambrosiaster?] *Pseudo-Augustini quaestiones veteris et novi testamenti CXXVII* (Pseudo-Augustine's 127 Questions on the Old and New Testament), ed. Alexander Souter, *CSEL*, 50 (Vienna, 1908; reprint, New York, 1963) 272.22ff., 273.2f. On the contrasting of *basileus* and *dēmiourgos* in Numenius, see H.-Ch. Puech, "Numénius d'Apamée et les théologies orientales au second siècle . . . ," in *Mélanges Bidez* = Annuaire de l'Institut de philologie et d'histoire orientales, 2 (Brussels, 1933–1934), 763; cf. 762, 765. Of Numenius's *prōtos theos*, Eusebius *Praeparatio evangelica* (Preparation for the Gospel) 11.18.8 says *argon einai ergōn xympantōn kai basilea* (the First God is free from work of all kinds and is king); see Puech, 757. In addition, it is characteristic that the Marcionite Lucan was an Aristotelian (see Adolf von Harnack, *Marcion: Das Evangelium vom fremden Gott* (Marcion: the Gospel of the Alien God), 2nd ed. [Leipzig, 1924], 401ff.).

16. To my knowledge the political consequences of a gnostic or dualistic worldview have never been explored in a larger context.

17. *Sama teas, despoina, monarcheias* (the sign, O queen, of your monarchical rule), *Inscriptiones graecae* 12, 5, no. 739, line 6 = Werner Peek, *Der Isishymnus von Andros und verwandte Texte* (Berlin, 1930), 15.6. Peek does not comment on the word (cf. pp. 26 and 28).

18. Ulrich Wilcken, *Urkunden der Ptolemäerzeit* (Berlin, 1922), 1: 29 and n. 3.

19. Thus in the prose hymn in his oration on Poseidon, Aelius Aristides speaks of the monarchy of Poseidon over the sea, but at the same time of the co-rulership of Leukothea (*Oratio* 46.38 [ed. Keil, 374.12]).

20. For the language of prayer, cf. 3 Macc. 2:2, *hagie en hagiois monarche* (holy among the holy ones, only ruler); *Constitutiones apostolicae* (Apostolic Constitutions) 8.11.2, *anarche, monarche* (without beginning, only ruler); Pap. Berolinensis Nr. 13415, see Carl Schmidt in *Neutestamentliche Studien für G. Heinrici* (Leipzig, 1914), 68, *mon[arche hagie]* (king, holy one). "You the only sole ruler (*monarchēs*)," in an unknown ancient Gnostic work in *Koptisch-Gnostische Schriften* (Coptic Gnostic Writings), ed. Carl Schmidt (Leipzig, 1905), 1: 359.13. On the prayerful invocation *monarche*, Suitbert Beckmann, *Die Gottesanrede im Ante-Sanctus* (Divine Address in the Prayer Before the Sanctus) (diss., Münster, 1932), has nothing to say.

21. *Papyri graecae magicae: Die griechischen Zauberpapyri* (Greek Magical Papyri), ed. Karl Preisendanz, 2 vols. (Leipzig, 1928–1931), 1: 180–198, Pap. V; Pap. VIII, line 17 reads: *kata Hellēnas: ho pantōn monarchos basileus* (among the Greeks: the royal monarch of the universe) (ed. Dieterich, p. 809 [Editor's note: the original Dieterich edition cited by Peterson was unavailable to me; I have used the subsequent 1928–1931 Preisendanz edition, in which, however, I could not verify the quotation from Papyrus VIII]. In Egyptian *akoē* means sole ruler (see Pap. VII, lines 591f. [ed. Preisendanz, 2: 27]), see Schmidt, *Göttingische gelehrte Anzeigen* (1934): 178, and cf. also the name of the god *Pneoubas* = the only lord (*theai megistēi*); see Friederich Preisigke, *Sammelbuch griechischer Urkunden aus Ägypten* (Collection of Greek Documents from Egypt) (Wiesbaden, 1900), 1: 172.

22. The word *monarchia* is predominantly in Euripides but also occurs in Aristophanes, Sophocles, and Aeschylus.

23. For hymnic language reference may be made to the Sybilline Oracles 3.11, *heis theos esti monarchos* (the one God is monarch) (cf. frgm. 1.7, *heis theos, hos monos archei*) (God is one, he alone rules) and 3.704 (from the oldest Jewish Sybilline book, as is frgm. 1), all in Johannes Geffcken, ed., *Die Oracula Sibyllina* (Leipzig, 1902), pp. 47, 227, and 84 respectively. See as well the section in the *Constitutiones apostolicae* (Apostolic Constitutions) 7.35.9 (in the opinion of many, stemming from a Hellenistic Jewish agenda), *adiadochos hē monarchia* (his monarchy is perpetual). Finally we may mention Gregory of Nazianzus *Hymn on Christ* line 1, *Se ton aphthiton monarchēn* (You, the immortal King) (*Anthologia graeca carminum christianorum* [Greek Anthology of Christian Hymns], ed. Christ-Paranickas [Leipzig, 1871]), 23, and line 25f., *Triada zōsan erō se. Hena kai monon monarchēn* (I will proclaim you, living Trinity, one and only monarchy).

24. *Trepteon d' epi tous kata meros ēdē nomous kai prōtous, aph' hōn archesthai kalon, tous peri monarchias horisthentas.*

25. Similarly, the heading describing the content of the First Commandment

in *De decal.* 51: *peri monarchias hēi monarcheitai ho kosmos* (concerning the monarchy by which the cosmos is ruled). Similar sounding is *De spec. leg.* 2.224. Further: *De decal.* 155: *ho men prōtos* (sc. *nomos*) *tōn peri monarchias* (the [first] law, which concerns monarchy); *De virtut.* 220, *tēn peri monarchias epistēmēn, hēi monarcheitai ho kosmos* (the knowledge concerning monarchy, by which the cosmos is ruled). Further: *Quis rerum divinarum heres sit* (Who Is the Heir of Divine Things?) 169; *De spec. leg.* 2.256.

26. Cf., e.g., Josephus *Antiquities* 5.57, *theos heis kai to Hebraiōn genos* (one God and the people of the Hebrews). The juxtaposition of "One people [*Volk*], one God" that is found in Josephus is consistent with rabbinic tradition, see the examples of von Grünbaum in *Zeitschrift der deutschen Morgenländischen Gesellschaft* 21 (1867): 594 n. 4, cf. 616 n.

27. Cf. also *De spec. leg.* 2.163, 165f. Further, *De vita Mosis* (On the Life of Moses) 1.149, (Israel . . .) *hoper emellen ex hapantōn tōn allōn hierasthai tas hyper tous genous tōn anthrōpōn aei poiēsomenon euchas* (which before all others was going to be dedicated to offer perpetual prayers on behalf of the peoples of the human race). In the light of this text, Yizhak Heinemann, *Philons griechische und jüdische Bildung* (Philo's Greek and Jewish Education) (Breslau, 1932), speaks of "Jewish self-confidence." But in doing so he psychologizes and moralizes the underlying problem. This "Jewish self-confidence" has its ultimate root in the transformation of the concept of God into a cosmic "monarchy."

28. This "self-confidence" of the Hellenistic Jew, who is confident "of being a guide to the blind, a light in darkness, an educator of the ignorant, a teacher to the immature" (translation by Lietzmann) appears to me to be contested by St. Paul in Rom. 2:19. Cf. also Norden, *Agnostos Theos*, 296f., who emphasizes the Hellenistic character of the *rēseis* (utterances) cited here.

29. It does not always seem possible to me to distinguish clearly in the tradition between *megas basileus* meaning "Great King" as an actual title or simply meaning a "great king." *Megas basileus* in Philo as a designation for God: *De vita Mos.* 166; *De agricultura Noe* (On the Agriculture of Noah) 51, 78; *De opificio mundi* (On the Creation of the World) 88; *De confus.* 170; *De plantatione Noe* (On the Planting of Noah) 33; *De somniis* (On Dreams) 1.140; *De decal.* 61.178.

30. On the word *hyparchos* (subordinates or legates), see Philo *De agric.* 51 for the relationship of the Logos to God, the *megas basileus*; *De opif. m.* 88 on man in relation to the *megas basileus*; *De somn.* 1.140 on souls (demons). On astral spirits and angels: Philo *De spec. leg.* 1.14, 19; *De vita Mos.* 1.166; *De Abrah.* 115. On the Logos: *De somn.* 1.241. The word belongs to the Hellenistic tradition. Zeus gives the gods the four regions *hoion hyparchoi tines kai satrapai* (like subordinates and satraps) (Aelius Aristides *Eis Dia* [On Zeus] 43.18 [ed. Keil, 343.26]). Likewise Celsus in Origen *Contra Celsum* (Against Celsus) 8.36, where the word is similarly linked with *satrapai*, as in Philo *De decal.* 61 (*tois hyparchois satrapais*) (the subordinate satraps). We may probably suspect that in many cases the word *hyparchos* was

simply an equivalent for the foreign word *satrapēs*. It is worth noting that the old title *satrapēs* had become obsolete in Persia even before the Sassanid period. See A. Christensen, *L'empire des Sassanides* (The Empire of the Sassanids), Mémoires de l'académie de Copenhague, 7th ser., 1.1 (Copenhagen, 1907), 42.

31. *Kathaper oun tou megalou basileōs tas timas ei tis tois hyparchois satrapais apeneimen, edoxen an ouk agnōmonestatos monon alla kai ripsokindynotatos einai, charizomenos ta despotou doulois, ton auton tropon [an] tois autois ei tis gerairei ton pepoiēkota tois gegonosin, istō pantōn aboulotatos ōn kai adikōtatos* etc. (Philo *De decal.* 61). Somewhat different is the image used in Philo's treatise *On Providence*: human beings do not for the most part crowd around the king, the *nous*, but remain standing among the gatekeepers, that is, the external goods. (See the text in Eusebius *Praeparatio evangelica* [Preparation for the Gospel] 8.14 [*PG* 21: 657]; cf. Wendland, *Philos Schrift von der Vorsehung*, 53 and 92.)

32. *Hypodiakonos* in Philo *De spec. leg.* 1.66, 1.116, 3.201 (next to *hypēretēs*) (minister); *De Abrah.* 115 (next to *hyparchos*). In both cases used of angels. For the association with *pylōroi* (gatekeepers), I refer to *Passio Romani Antiocheni* (Passion of Romanus of Antioch) 1, *tois eis tas thyras kathēmenois hypodiakonois* (to the subordinates who are seated at the doors), *Analecta Bollandiana* 50 (1930): 249, and *Acta Cypriani et Justinae* (Acts of Cyprian and Justina) F. 1 *hypodiakonos kai thyrōros* (doorkeeper) in Ludwig Radermacher, *Griechische Quellen zur Faustsage* (Greek Sources on the Faust Saga) (Vienna, 1927), 110.7.

33. The *pylōroi* are also mentioned in chap. 6 of the *Peri kosmou* (On the World). Originally, these were probably the *eisangeleis* (ushers) stationed at the *prothyra* (vestibule) of the heavenly court of whom Maximus of Tyre speaks (*Oratio* 11.12 [ed. Hobein, 145.5]), reduced from their high official rank at the Persian and Ptolemaic courts to simple gatekeepers (*pylōroi*). The court service of the *derandarjbedh* (*organisateur de la "Porte"* [keeper of the "gate"] [perhaps = *maître des cérémonies?*]) is documented. See Christensen, *L'empire des Sassanides*, 40.

34. §31 is more unclear: (God . . .) *tou presbytatou kai pantōn aitiou* (of the most ancient cause of everything). The uncertainty in the formulation is due both to the sources used and to Philo's ambiguities in his concept of creation.

35. The opinion has often been expressed that the treatise *On the World* was composed by a Hellenistic Jew or written under Jewish influence (see, e.g., Marie-Joseph Lagrange, *Revue thomiste*, n.s., 10 (1927): 201f.). But I believe that no Hellenistic Jew, in dealing with the image of the king of the gods and his officials, could have resisted a polemic against the worship of many gods, as we find for example in Philo.

36. If, as I suspect (see n. 33 above), the high-ranking *eisangeleis* declined into lowly *pylōroi*, the linguistic formulation of the polemic suggests a Cynic model.

37. *Eis Dia* (On Zeus) 43.15: *hōste kai theōn hosa phyla aporroēn tēs Dios tou pantōn patros dynameōs hekasta echei* (and so each of the many races of gods has its emanation from the power of Zeus, the father of all) (ed. Keil, 343.1ff.). On

this Julius Amann, *Die Zeusrede des Ailios Aristeides* (Aelius Aristides's Oration on Zeus), Tübingen Beiträge zur Altertumswissenschaft, 12 (Stuttgart, 1931), 75. In 43.17, Aelius Aristides describes the activity of the other gods as an administrative work assigned by Zeus. (Zeus . . .) *proedrian men kai archas kai prostasias didōsi theois* (he gives preeminence, rule, and hegemony to the gods) (ed. Keil, 343.16f.). When Celsus says, "Probably the parts of the earth were from the beginning apportioned to one or another of the overseers, divided in the ordering of certain dominions and governed in this fashion" (Theodor Keim, *Celsus' wahres Wort* [Celsus's True Word] [Zurich, 1873], 67 = Origen *C. Cels.* 5.25), he is referring—with the help of Plato, *Politicus* (Statesman) 15—to the same cosmic division of duties as Aristides.

38. *Korē kosmou* (Maiden of the Cosmos) in Walter Scott, ed., *Hermetica* (Hermetic Corpus), 496.7 = Johannes Stobaeus *Anthologium* (Anthology) (ed. Wachsmuth, 1: 407.30–408.1): *kai eisin hoi archontes tou basileōs aporroiai* (and the archons [governors] are emanations of the king).

39. *De virtutibus* (On the Virtues) 179f. and 220 clearly show the connection between the concept of the *monarchia* and proselyte instruction. E. R. Goodenough, "Philo's Exposition of the Law and his *De vita Mosis*," *Harvard Theological Review* 26 (1933): 109ff. (cf. 117), has shown that Philo wrote expositions for proselytes, including *On the Virtues*. I shall show later that Christian usages in baptismal instruction continued Jewish practice in the instruction of proselytes.

40. *De virtut.* 179.

41. *De decal.* 155.

42. *De fuga et inventione* (On Flight and Discovery) 10; *De decal.* 155; *De opif. mundi* 171.

43. *Hoi noun ephasan elthonta panta diakosmēsai tēn ex ochlokratias en tois ousin ataxian eis archēs nomimou, basileias, taxin agagonta* (they say that Mind comes to govern everything, by bringing the disorder wrought by mob rule into the order of lawful authority, meaning kingship). For Zeus = *nous*, see Maximus of Tyre *Or.* 4.8 (ed. Hobein, 50.3f.); Diogenes Laertius *Lives of the Eminent Philosophers* 8.135 (Posidonius); Porphyry *Peri agalmatōn* (On Images) frgm. 3.8, in Joseph Bidez, *Vie de Porphyre, le philosophe néo-platonicien: avec les fragments des traités* Peri agalmatōn *et* De regressu animae (Gand, 1913); Seneca *Naturales quaestiones* (Natural Questions) 2.45 (*Iovem . . . animum ac spiritum mundi* [Jupiter . . . soul and spirit of the world]). Also see Wendland, *Philos Schrift über die Vorsehung*, 10f. n. 2.

44. *Monarchias alēthous hetairos* (adherent of the true Monarchy).

45. Recall the meaning of the doctrine of *isotēs* (equality) for Philo.

46. *Eis taxin auto ēgagen ek tēs ataxias, hēgēsamenos auto toutou pantos ameinon* (out of a disordered state, he [God] brought it [the world] into an ordered condition, since he thought that the one was wholly superior to the other).

47. Émile Bréhier, *Les idées philosophiques et religieuses de Philon* (The Philosophical and Religious Ideas of Philo), 2nd ed. (Paris, 1925), 33 n. 7, refers on this

passage to Alexandre Moret, *Caractère religieux de la royauté pharaonique* (Religious Character of Pharaonic Kingship) (Paris, 1902), 297: "Le roi égyptien est au même titre que le dieu un createur (The Egyptian king is at the same time a deity and a creature)." But I doubt that Philo could have been aware of these connections. Wilhelm Weber, *Der Prophet und sein Gott* (The Prophet and His God) (Leipzig, 1925), 155ff., is of the opinion that the paragraph in which this turn of phrase occurs has been adopted by Philo from a hymn to Augustus. Not political is the formulation for the act of creation found in *De spec. leg.* 187: *ta gar mē onta ekalēsen eis to einai, taxin ex ataxias* (for things that did not exist he called into being, order out of disorder) (cf. also *De plantatione* 3 and *De somn.* 1.241). That corresponds to Platonic tradition, cf., e.g., Albinos *Eisagoge* (Introduction) 13 (167.12ff.): *hēn* [= *hylēn*] *ataktōs kai plēmmelōs kinoumenēn pro tēs ouranou geneseōs ek tēs ataxias paralabōn pros tēn aristēn ēgage taxin* (he took it [= matter], as it moved in disordered and irregular fashion before the creation of heaven, and brought it out of its disorder toward the best order). Perhaps comparable to Philo's political interpretation of creation, however, are the expositions of Celsus in Origen *C. Cels.* 6.212 (= 94, ed. Keim).

48. *Taxis* synonymous with *politeia*: see Egon Weiss, *Griechisches Privatrecht* (Greek Private Law) (Leipzig, 1923), 1: 57 n. 82.

49. *Pro tēs Dios archēs hapanta staseōs kai thorybou kai ataxias einai mesta, elthontos de epi tēn archēn Dios panta dē katastēnai, kai tous Titanas eis tous katōtatous mychous tēs gēs apelthein* . . . *houtōs an tis kai peri tōn pro hymōn te kai eph' hymōn pragmatōn logizomenos hypolaboi* . . . [after the Romans' seizure of power] *taxis de pantōn kai phōs lampron eisēlthe biou* . . . [a] *koinē* . . . *adeia dedotai* (Before the reign of Zeus, the world was filled with revolt and uproar and disorder. But after he became sovereign, the world came to rest, and the Titans went away to the deepest recesses of the earth . . . one ought to think in similar fashion when considering events before our time and during our time . . . [after the Romans' seizure of power] life experienced universal order and a bright light shone . . . a universal . . . amnesty has been granted). Aelius Aristides *Eis Rōmēn* (On Rome), *Or.* 26.163 (ed. Keil, 121f.)—on this oration on Rome, see Wilhelm Sieveking, *De Aelii Aristidis oratione* Eis Rōmēn (On the Oration *On Rome* by Aelius Aristides) (diss., Göttingen, 1919). It is evident that Aristides' encomium on Rome is connected both formally and materially with imperial encomia, as shown with special clarity in the celebrated inscription dedicated to Augustus from Priene (*Orientis graeci inscriptiones selectae* [Selected Inscriptions from the Greek East], ed. W. Dittenberger, 2 vols. (Leipzig, 1903–1905), 2, no. 458).

50. On Callimachus's *Hymn to Zeus*, cf. Emile Cahen, *Les hymnes de Callimaque* (The Hymns of Callimachus) (Paris, 1930), 7ff.

51. The Latin text reads: "quod si non aliam venturo fata Neroni invenire viam magnoque aeterna parantur regna deis caelumque suo servire Tonanti non nisi saevorum potuit post bella Gigantum, iam nihil, o superi, querimur" (But if the fates could find no other way for Nero to come, nor an eternal realm be gained

for the gods and heaven serve its Thunderer [Jupiter] save after the wars with the savage Giants, then, O heavens, we make no complaint). See Sieveking, *Aelii Aristidis*, 51 n. 1. We may also recall Martial *Epigrammata* (Epigrams) 8.49.1ff., where the emperor's entertainment of the people after the victorious conclusion of the Sarmatian war is juxtaposed with the victory banquet of Zeus after the victory over the giants; or Horace *Carmina* (Poems) 3.1.5ff. Finally, there is the celebrated inscription on the Rosetta Stone, on which the deeds of Ptolemy V are made parallel to the deeds of the gods, except that it lacks a reference to Greek myth. (The Rosetta inscription is in *Orientis graeci inscriptiones selectae*, ed. Dittenberger, 1, no. 90.)

52. Cf. Hesiod *Theogony* 96: *ek de Dios basilēes* (kings are from Zeus). The Roman imperial period often repeated this idea. Cf., e.g., Dio Chrysostom 1.45 (ed. v. Arnim, 8.27f.); Themistius *Or.* 11 (ed. Dindorf, 170.21ff.). On the coins of Hadrian, which show him exercising dominion jointly with Jupiter, see Paul Strack, *Untersuchungen zur römischen Reichsprägung des zweiten Jahrhunderts* (Studies of Roman Imperial Coinage), 3 vols. (Stuttgart, 1931), 2: 44f., 97f. See further the Senate's coin minted for Hadrian in AD 119, in which Jupiter's eagle is shown granting Hadrian the scepter (Strack, ibid.). See further Wilhelm Weber, *Untersuchungen zur Geschichte des Kaisers Hadrianus* (Studies in the History of the Emperor Hadrian) (Leipzig, 1907), 102–103 n. 344, and esp. Andreas Alföldi in *25 Jahre römisch-germanische Kommission* (25 Years of the Roman-Germanic Commission) (Berlin, 1930), 21 and n. 79. On the triumphal arch in Benevento, there is a representation of Jupiter giving Trajan his lightning bolt, see, e.g., Domaszewski in *Österreichische Jahreshefte* 2: 176f., and Ferdinand Noack in *Vorträge der Bibliothek Warburg* 5 (1925–1926): 198. Already in Ovid we read: "caelo tonantem credidimus Jovem regnare, praesens divus habebitur Augustus" (We believe that thundering Jupiter reigns in heaven, here below Augustus will be held divine) (*Carm.* 3.5.1ff.); also his *Fasti* 2.131f. See Lily Ross Taylor, *The Divinity of the Roman Emperor* (Middletown, Conn., 1931), 70. In Franz Sauter, *Der römische Kaiserkult bei Martial und Statius* (The Roman Imperial Cult in Martial and Statius) (Stuttgart, 1934), 74, passages from Latin authors are cited in which it is said that the emperor rules as the representative of Jupiter. In the same book, chapter discusses the emperor as Jupiter. On the idea in Plato and the Neoplatonists that the *politikon* (the political) belongs to Zeus, cf. Karl Mras, *Des Makrobius Kommentar zum Somnium Scipionis* (Macrobius's Commentary on the Dream of Scipio), Sitzungsberichte der Berliner Akademie (1933), 27 and 32. On the parallel between the emperor and Zeus (Jupiter), cf. also Samson Eitrem in *Symbolae Osloenses* 10 (1932): 54; Arthur Darby Nock in *Journal of Hellenic Studies* 48 (1928): 34, and Josef Kaerst, *Studien zur Entwicklung und theoretischen Begründung der Monarchie im Altertum* (Studies in the Development and Theoretical Foundation of Monarchy in Antiquity) (Leipzig, 1898), 66.

53. Cf. Heinemann, *Philons griechische und jüdische Bildung*, 55; id., *Poseido-*

nios 1: 126ff., 2: 308ff.; Paul Wendland, *Jahrbuch für die klassische Philologie*, suppl. no. 21, 707.1; Gunnar Rudberg, *Forschungen zu Poseidonios* (Uppsala, 1918), 194.

54. According to Sterling Tracy, "III Maccabees and Pseudo-Aristeus: A Study," *Yale Classical Studies*, no. 1 (1928), 247, 3 Maccabees originated in the second century BC.

55. Dio Chrysostom 12.22: *koinos anthrōpōn kai theōn basileus te kai archōn kai prytanis kai patēr, eti de kai eirēnēs kai polemou tamias* (The universal king of men and gods, and archon and president and father, and also the dispenser of peace and war).

56. Ael. Aristides *Or.* 43.29 (ed. Keil, 346.20ff.): *houtos hapantōn euergetēs kai prostatēs kai ephoros, houtos prytanis kai hēgemōn kai tamias* (He [Zeus] is the provider of everthing, and protector and overseer, he is president and ruler and dispenser). Amann, *Die Zeusrede des Ailios Aristides*, 163, says correctly, "Because the cosmos is commonly compared to a polis, these names are appropriate for the supreme leader, to whom everything belongs."

57. The polis took great satisfaction in passing resolutions for the bestowal of honorary titles and in shouting acclamations. This led naturally to the conferral of the polis's honorary titles and acclamations on God as a form of honor. It is thus easy to understand, e.g., that God is called *prostatēs* (protector), *epikouros* (helper), *tamias* (dispenser), *phylax* (guardian), *teichos* (wall), in *Constit. apost.* 8.11.5. This expression of God's "honor" in the political language of the polis is in need of a comprehensive study. In passing, it is noteworthy that Maximus of Tyre *Oratio* 4.9 (ed. Hobein, 51.1ff.), compares the activity of Zeus with that of both the Persian Great King and the Athenian *dēmos* (citizen body). This may also express the belief that actual government belongs to Zeus, as well as sovereignty, while the Stoics limit God's activity for the most part to administration. Especially instructive: Epictetus *Dissertationes* (Discourses) 1.12.7, cf. also Wendland, *Philos Schrift von der Vorsehung*, 72.

Finally, that the king is "honored" by the polis and that correspondingly too the polis's honorary titles can be conferred on "the King of the world" (God), is connected with the federal character (speaking in political and legal terms) of Hellenistic monarchy, on which see Paola Zancan, *Il monarcato ellenistico nei suoi elementi federativi* , Pubblicazioni della Facoltà di lettere e filosofia, no. 8 (Padua, 1934).

58. I should think that the relation between the early Christian *didaskalos* (teacher) and the *ekklēsia* (church) was similar to that between the Jewish *didaskalos* (Philo) and the *synagōgē* (synagogue). I do not believe that the "schools" of these *didaskaloi* would have had a "private" character, as, e.g., B. D. van den Eyde, *Les norms de l'enseignement chrétien* (The Norms of Chistian Instruction) (diss., Louvain, 1933), 61, appears to assume. On the other hand, these "teachers" need not yet have become ecclesiastical "officials." Perhaps baptismal instruction (and Jewish proselyte instruction) was partially or completely entrusted to such teachers depending on place and circumstance. Such an assumption makes it easier to grasp

the later status of the *didaskalos*, as represented, e.g., in Jerusalem—see Klaudius Jüssen, *Die dogmatischen Anschauungen des Hesychius von Jerusalem* (The Dogmatic Views of Hesychius of Jerusalem) (Münster, 1931), 1: 7.

59. Eusebius *Historia ecclesiastica* (Church History) 4.18.4: *peri tou monarchias, hēn ou monon ek tōn par' hēmin graphōn, alla kai tōn Hellēnikōn synistēsin bibliōn.*

60. I do not regard as decisive all the objections with which it is customary to deny to Justin the treatise contained in MS. Parisinus 450. Aimé Puech, *Histoire de la littérature grecque chrétienne* (History of Greek Christian Literature) (Paris, 1928), 2: 223, seeks to deny that the writing is Justin's on the basis of the style of the introduction and the conclusion, but I would like to object that stylistic criteria make definite conclusions impossible when we are dealing with this type of "school literature," in which little original material is normally found.

61. On Ps.-Hecataeus, see Emil Schürer, *Geschichte des jüdischen Volkes im Zeitalter Jesu Christi* (History of the Jewish People in the Age of Jesus Christ), 3rd ed. (Leipizig, 1898), 3: 433 and 461.

62. *Hymeis, Ō Hellēnes . . . tēn polykoiraniēn mallon ēper tēn monarchian exēskēsate kathaper ischyrois nomizontes [tois] daimosin katakolouthein.* The predication of the *daimones* (demons) as *ischyroi* (strong) is supposed to evoke the *archē* (sovereign) character of the pagan gods.

63. In Zachary of Mytilene's *Disputatio de mundi opificio* (Disputation on the Creation of the World) (*PG* 85: 1053), the verse from the Iliad is deployed against Neoplatonic dualism. The verse is appropriated into the philosophical literature because it was already a traditional citation in the rhetorical and constitutional literature. In Stobaeus (ed. Wachsmuth-Hense, 4: 239) it serves as a proof text for the thesis: *hoti kalliston hē monarchia* (that monarchy is best). Celsus quotes the verse against the Christians in order to urge them to obey the emperor (Origen *C. Cels.* 8.68). A Greek inscription from Egypt reads: *Heis kaisar, megas autokratōr, heis koiranos estō* (One is caesar, great is the sole ruler, let one be king), etc., in J. G. Milne, *Greek Inscriptions* (Oxford, 1905), no. 9267, cf. J. G. Milne, "Greek Inscriptions from Egypt," *Journal of Hellenic Studies* 22 (1901): 286, and *Archiv für Papyrusforschung* 2 (1903): 568f., no. 142. (See also Jerzy Manteuffel, *De opusculis graecis Aegypti e papyris, ostracis lapidibusque collectis* [Short Greek Texts from Egypt, Collected from Papyri, Ostraca, and Stone] [Warsaw, 1930], 8.) Homer was always quoted in speeches to kings. See the *Technē rētorikē* (Rhetorical Method) of Dionysius of Halicarnassus 2.1 [This reference seems erroneous—Ed.], 8.4, and 8.11 (ed. H. Usener and L. Radermacher, *Dionysii Halicarnasei quae exstant*, vol. 6, 2: *Opuscula* (Stuttgart, 1985; reprint of 1929 edition), 298.4 and 310.23–311.3). Cf., too, *Mitteilungen aus der Papyrussammlung der Staatsbibliothek in Wien* 1: 119. According to Martin Nilsson, *Das Homerische Königtum* (Homeric Kingship), Sitzungsberichte der Berliner Akademie (1927), 27, the verse was generally targeted at the high command in the leadership of the army. The Iliad verse also played a role in the medieval conflict between emperor and pope on the relationship between

church and state, see Martin Grabmann, *Studien über den Einfluss der aristotelischen Philosophie auf die mittelalterlichen Theorien über das Verhältnis von Kirche und Staat,* Sitzungsberichte der bayerischen Akademie der Wissenschaften (Munich, 1934), no. 2, pp. 105, 114, 118, 121). In Dante's *Monarchia* 1.10 (ed. Bertalot [Florence, 1920], 21.19f.) it is quoted as a passage from Aristotle.

64. The translation of *To Autolycus* in J. Leitl, *Frühchristliche Apologeten und Märtyrakten* (Early Christian Apologists and Martyr-Acts), Bibliothek der Kirchenväter, ser. 1, no. 14 (Munich, 1913), 29, translates *monarchia* as "absoluteness."

65. Cf. *Ad Autol.* 3.7: *Platōn de, ho tosauta eipōn peri monarchias theou kai psychēs anthrōpou* (ed. Otto, 204).

66. Ibid. 2.18: *kai plēthyn eisēgagon, kai monarchian eipon* (ed. Otto, 74).

67. Cf. also the exposition in ibid. 2.38 (ed. Otto, 184).

68. Cf. ibid. 2.35. All of the prophets speak: *peri te monarchias theou kai tēs tou kosmou geneseōs kai tēs anthrōpou poiēseōs* (about the monarchy of God and the origin of the cosmos and the creation of humanity) (ed. Otto, 160).

69. See Adolf von Harnack, *Marcion* (Leipzig, 1921), 97; cf. 2nd ed. (1924), 104, 273. On Theophilus's treatise against Marcion, see Harnack, ibid., 315.

70. Harnack (*Marcion,* 2nd ed., 318 n. 3) also found a polemical reference to Marcion's *Antitheses* in Theophilus *Ad Autol.* 2.25.

71. Friedrich Loofs, *Theophilus von Antiochien adversus Marcionem und die anderen theologischen Quellen bei Irenaeus* (Theophilus of Antioch *Against Marcion* and the Other Theological Sources in Irenaeus) (Leipzig, 1930), 74, also assumes that the treatise against Marcion was written before the apology.

72. Further research should examine the extent to which the repetition of Marcionite doctrines in the Pseudo-Clementine literature goes back to Theophilus of Antioch's treatise against Marcion. I think, e.g., that *Homily* 16.6 (ed. Lagarde, 152) in the Pseudo-Clementines, in which the majority of the gods are traced back to the original sin (in lines 20f. Adam and Eve become "like one of us"; cf. Gen. 3:22), points back literarily to Theophilus's lost treatise. It is only this passage from the Pseudo-Clementines that actually enables us to understand the terse allusion in *Ad Autolyc.* 2.28. So when, in Ps.-Clem. *Hom.* 16.12, the creation of humanity by the *one* God is bought into relation with God's Wisdom, which was always with God and "is stretched out like a hand in order to create everything," both this Sophia (Wisdom) doctrine and the thought that Sophia is the "hand" of God should be seen as the characteristic contribution of Theophilus (see Loofs, *Theophilus,* 46, 51 and n. 6). Given these inferences, it is worth considering whether the keyword *monarchia* in Ps. Clem. *Hom.* 16 is also attributable to Theophilus. It should not be a surprise that material in the Pseudo-Clementines stems from Theophilus, since the Pseudo-Clementines too originated in Antioch. On this see Eduard Schwartz in "Unzeitgemäße Beobachtungen zu den Clementinen" (Untimely Meditations on the Clementines), *Zeitschrift für die Neutestamentliche Wissenschaft* 31 (1932): 178. Kellner's argument (*Theologische Revue* 2 [1903]: 421) on the

concept of the divine monarchy in the Pseudo-Clementines is false, because he contends that this idea is an invention of the author of the collection.

73. On Florinus see above all Anton Baumstark in *Zeitsch. f. Neutest. Wissen.* 11 (1912): 306f., and Felix Haase, *Altchristliche Kirchengeschichte nach orientalischen Quellen* (Early Christian Church History According to Oriental Sources) (Leipzig, 1925), 354ff. Cf., too, H. Koch, *Zeitsch. f. Neutest. Wissen.* 11 (1912): 69ff.

74. One need only place the formulation in *Ref.* 9.10.11 (*houtōs gar dokei monarchian synistan* [for he thinks he proves a monarchy]) alongside that in *Contra Noetum* (Against Noetus) (ed. Lagarde, 44.6), *houtō phaskousin synistan hena theon* (they assert that this proves one god), to see that there can be no talk of Hippolytus as a witness to the usage of *monarchia* as a technical term. As a rule the verb *synistan* (*synistasthai*) in the phrase *monarchian synistan* (to establish a monarchy) is a conventional usage. See, e.g., Eusebius *Hist. eccl.* 4.18.4, Socrates *Historia ecclesiastica* (Church History) 2.19.16 (ed. Hussey, 224), ibid. 2.19.27 (ed. Hussey, 228), Gregory of Nazianzus *Fifth Theological Oration* 17 (ed. Mason, 166.7). Cf. *monarchiam tenemus* (we hold the monarchy) in Tertullian *Adv. Prax.* 3. In the later tradition, the keyword *monarchia* appears apparently in tandem with Sabellius. See Gregory of Nazianzus *In laudem Heronis Philosophi* (In Praise of Hero the Philosopher), *Or.* 25 (*PG* 35: 1208C); Epiphanius *Adversus Haereses* (Against Heresies) 62.3 (*PG* 41: 1053B); Marius Mercator, Append. 18.

75. Adolf von Harnack, *Dogmengeschichte*, 3rd ed. (Freiburg im Br., 1898), 1: 657 n. 1, has rightly pointed to the fact that the word—even in Tertullian—is not actually the name of a heresy but only an ironic turn of phrase.

76. Tertullian *Adv. Prax.* 7 (ed. Kroymann., 236.21).

77. See, too, Alexander Beck, *Römisches Recht bei Tertullian und Cyprian* (Roman Law in Tertullian and Cyprian), Schriften der Königsberger Gelehrten Gesellschaft, Geistesw. Kl., no. 7, 2 (Halle, 1930), 69f. The arguments of Martin Kriebel, *Studien zur älteren Entwicklung der abendländischen Trinitätslehre* (Studies on the Ancient Development of the Western Doctrine of the Trinity) (diss., Marburg, 1932), 36f., do not advance understanding of the Monarchian doctrine in *Against Praxeas*.

78. Interpreted differently in Isidore of Seville *Origines* (Etymologies) 9.3.23: "monarchae sunt, qui singularem possident principatum (Monarchs are those who possess a singular power of rule)."

79. Cf. the arguments in *Adv. Prax.* 4 (232.19ff.).

80. "Trinitas per consertos et connexos gradus a patre decurrens et monarchiae nihil obstrepit" (ibid. 8 [239.11ff.]). On this sentence, see Karl Müller in *Zeitschr. f. Neutest. Wissens.* 24 (1925): 284.

81. Cf. the ironic comment in *Adv. Prax.* 27: "Talem monarchiam apud Valentinum fortasse didicerunt" (Perhaps they learned about such a monarchy in the company of Valentinus) (280.6).

82. It should thus be understood that the ideas developed in *Against Praxeas* did not exercise an influence on Novatian.

83. It is found in Maximus of Tyre in the treatise: *Tis ho theos kata Platōn* (According to Plato, who is God?). Theophilus of Antioch can therefore say: *Platōn de ho tosauta eipōn peri monarchias* (Plato is someone who has a great deal to say about monarchy) (*Ad Autolyc.* 3.7). In the same way it says in Lactantius's *Divinae Institutiones* (Divine Institutes) 1.5.23 (cf. *Epitome* 4): "Plato . . . monarchian plane aperteque defendit (Plato plainly and openly defends monarchy)." That Plato taught there was only *one* God belongs to solid doxographical tradition in pagan education (Apuleius *De Platone* [On Plato] 1.5 [ed. Thomas, 86.13]) and among Christians too (Hippolytus *Refut.* 1.19.6 [ed. Wendland]; Eusebius *Praep. evang.* 11.13 [*PG* 21: 880C]; Cyprian *Quod idola dei non sint* [That Idols Are Not Gods] [ed. Hartel, 24.5]).

84. *Koinōnous tēs archēs pollous men horatous theous, pollous de aphaneis, tous men peri ta prothyra auta heilomenous, hoion eisangeleas tinas kai basileas syngenestatous, homotrapezous autous kai synestious, tous de toutōn hypēretas, tous de eti toutōn katadeesterous* (ed. Hobein, 155.3ff.).

85. Maximus of Tyre *Oratio* 11.12: *hoti theos heis pantōn basileus, kai patēr, kai theoi polloi, theou paides, synarchontes theou. Tauta kai ho Hellēn legei, kai ho barbaros legei.*

86. Aelius Aristides *On Zeus* 18 [ed. Keil, 343.26). On this passage see: Amann, *Die Zeusrede des Ailios Aristides*, 85, and Otto Weinreich, *Menekrates Zeus and Salmoneus: Religionsgeschichtliche Studien zur Psychopathologie des Gottmenschentums in Antike und Neuzeit* (Menekrates Zeus and Salmoneus: Religious-Historical Studies on the Psychopathology of Divinized Humanity in Antiquity and Modernity) (Stuttgart, 1933), 10.

87. Origen *Against Celsus* 8.35; Pseudo-Clementine *Homilies* 10.14: *Honper gar tropon heis estin ho kaisar, echei de hyp' auton tous dioikētas, hypatikous, eparchous, chiliarchous, hekatontarchous, dekadarchous, ton auton tropon henos ontos tou megalou theou hōsper kaisaros kai houtoi kata ton tōn hypokeimenōn exousiōn logon theoi eisin, hypokeimenoi men ekeinōi, dioikountes de hēmas.* Cf. too Ps.-Clem. *Recognitions* 5.19f., among other passages. Maximus of Turin is thus dependent on this text; see A. Spagnolo and C. H. Turner, "Maximus of Turin Against the Pagans *Contra Paganos*," *Journal of Theological Studies* 17 (1916): 321–337, at 333f.

88. This concept is certainly not of Stoic origin, as Johannes Geffcken, *Zwei griechische Apologeten* (Two Greek Apologists) (Leipzig, 1907), 186 n. 2, maintains. Heinemann, *Poseidonios' metaphysische Schriften*, 1: 128 n. 1, concedes that the concept is "to be attributed to a Peripatetic." Note the following examples:

(a) Orosius *Adversus Paganos* (Against the Pagans) 6.1.3: "non se plures deos sequi, sed sub uno deo magno, plures ministros venerari fatentur" (They say they do not follow many gods but venerate many ministers under one great god).

(b) Konstantinus Diaconus, who composed an interesting encomium on the martyrs, has the pagans say: *kai par' hēmin . . . en diairesei prosōpōn mia theotēs gnōrizetai* (And among us . . . one godhead is recognized in a distinction of persons) (*PG* 88: 501C).

(c) *Sancti Pachomii Vitae graecae* (Greek Lives of Saint Pachomius), ed. Francois Halkin, Subsidia hagiographica, 19 (Bruxelles, 1932), 161.10ff.

(d) Arnobius *Adversus Nationes* (Against the Nations) 1.28, 3.2–3, 7.35.

(e) Athanasius? *De Diabolo* (On the Devil): *epangellontai theon kai theous* (they [the pagans] proclaim [both] god and gods), in "An Early Homily on the Devil Ascribed to Athanasius of Alexandria," *Journ. Theol. Stud.* 36 (1935): 9.37; *oikeioi, phēsi, tou theou* (they say that [the gods] are kinsmen of the [one] god), ibid., 9.20f.

89. Tertullian *Apology* 24.3. R. Heinze, *Tertullians Apologeticum* (Tertullian's *Apology*), Sitzungsberichte der Sächsischen Gesellschaft der Wissenschaften, no. 62 (Leipzig, 1910), 348 n. 1, has pointed to a parallel in Seneca. Cf., too, the note in the edition of the *Apology* by J. Martin, *Florilegium Patristicum* 6 (Bonn, 1933): 104.

90. The gods are described as "satraps": Philo *De Decal.* 61; Aelius Aristides *On Zeus* 18 (ed. Keil, 343.18); Celsus, in Origen *C. Cels.* 8.35; Michael Psellus in *Catalogue des manuscrits alchimiques grecs*, ed. Joseph Bidez et al., 8 vols. (Brussels, 1924), 6: 185.4, 9 (also see p. 179).

91. *Theou paides kai philoi* (Maximus of Tyre 11.12a [ed. Hobein, 144.4]); Athanasius? *De Diabolo: oikeioi tou theou* (kinsmen of the god)—see n. 88 (e) above.

92. The terms for the "official" character of the lower gods are especially instructive. I shall address this subject shortly.

93. God as "Great King": besides texts already cited, see too Maximus of Tyre 17.12 (cf. 14.8); Dio Chrysostom *De Regno* (On Kingship), *Or.* 2.75 (ed. v. Arnim, 33.1). Also see Geffcken, *Zwei griechische Apologeten*, 191 with n. 6. It is to be noted that *megas basileus* (great king) can also designate the Roman emperor (Plotinus 5.5.3; Dio Chrysostom *Or.* 32.32; *Martyrium Cononis* 3.2 (ed. Musurillo, 188.12); Apuleius *Metamorphoses* 11.17), in addition see Andreas Alföldi in *Römische Mitteilungen des Deutschen Archäologischen Instituts* 49 (1934): 101f. On the use of *megas basileus* in Byzantium, see Franz Josef Dölger, *Byzantinische Zeitschrift* 33 (1933): 204.

94. Ps.-Clem. *Hom.* 10.15: *hōs ouk exesti to kaisaros onoma heterōi tini . . . houtōs . . . to theou onoma heterōi dothēnai ouk exestin.* The formulation in the Ps.-Clementines is strikingly close in its content to Tertullian's. Somewhat different are the following: Ambrosiaster's commentary on Rom. 1:22: The pagans say that one can come to God through the gods, "sicut per comites pervenitur ad regem. Age, numquid tam demens est aliquis, aut salutis suae immemor, ut honorificentiam regis vindicet comiti" (as one approaches the king through his companions. But come now, no one is so mad or so heedless of his welfare as to claim the king's honor for [the king's] companion) (*PL* 17: 60C). Further: Ps. Augustinus *Questiones Veteris et Novi Testamenti* (Questions on the Old and the New Testament) 114.2 (ed. Souter, 304): "ad contumeliam pertinet conditoris, ut contempto domino colantur servi et

spreto imperatore adorentur comites" (the result of insulting the creator is that the servants are venerated, the master having been held in contempt, and the emperor having been scorned, his companions are worshiped) (cf. also 113.9 [307.17f.], 45.1 [81.24ff.]); Lactantius *Div. Instit.* 2.16.7.—see Franz Cumont in *Monuments et mémoires de la Fondation Eugène Piot* 26 (1923): 30f.; id., *Les religions orientales dans le paganisme romain*, 4th ed. (Paris, 1929), 299; Geffcken, *Zwei griechische Apologeten*, 186, 191, 241, 251, 276, 293, 297; Joseph Bidez, *La cité du monde et la cité du soleil chez les Stoïciens* (The Earthly City and the City of the Sun According to the Stoics) (Paris, 1932), 8 and n. 1.

95. One only need read the material on the secondary co-rulership in Th. Mommsen's *Abriß des römischen Staatsrechts* (Outline of Roman State Law), 2nd ed. (Leipzig, 1907), 201f., to realize the theological impossibility of Tertullian's construction.

96. It is worth noting that Faustus the Manichee asserts to St. Augustine that Jews and Christians had taken their concept of monarchy from pagans (Augustine *Contra Faustum Manichaeum* (Against Faustus the Manichee) 20.4 (538.4.15). Augustine denies it but adds that pagans had not completely lost the knowledge of the one and only God (20.19 [559.20ff.]). That is a very interesting discussion. There is reason to think that Faustus adopted this reproach against the Catholics from an older tradition. In the *Acts of Archelaus*, Mani says: "Ego duas naturas esse dico, unam bonam et alteram malam . . . Si enim dicimus monarchiam unius naturae et omnia deum replere et nullam esse extraneum locum, quis erit creaturae susceptor?" (*Acta Archelai* 16 [ed. Beeson, 26.5–6, 12–14]) This passage proves that the "monarchy" was a contested point between Catholics and Manicheans, and that, on the other hand, both among the Manicheans (recall the *carmen amatorium* [love song] in Augustine *C. Faust.* 15.5, among other passages) and among the Mandeans, the court of the "Light King" is described in a way that reminds one of the court of the Persian "Great King." That in general the idea of a heavenly official court of God originated not as a theme in Greek literature but was actually known in Persia, is witnessed to by Mazdak, who according to Shahrastani (as translated by Theodor Haarbrücker, *Abu-'al-Fath' Muh'ammad asch-Schahrastani's Religionspartheien und Philosophenschulen* [Halle, 1850–1851], 1: 292) represented God as sitting on a throne in the manner of the Persian king. The four highest dignitaries who stand by the throne of the Persian king are also found in heaven. Cf. Christensen, *L'empire des Sassanides*, 31. It is also known that the six Amesha-Spentas figure as viziers of the highest King; see A. V. Williams Jackson, *Zoroastrian Studies* (New York, 1928), 42.

97. Eduard Zeller, *Die Philosophie der Griechen in ihrer geschichtlichen Entwicklung* (The Philosophy of the Greeks in Its Historical Development), 5th ed. (Leipzig, 1923), 3, pt. 2: 123 n. 4.

98. Harnack has included the text currently under discussion in his collection of Porphyry fragments; see *Porphyrios Gegen die Christen* (Porphyry Against the

Christians), Abhandlungen der königlichen preussischen Akademie der Wissenschaften, Phil.-Hist. Kl., no. 1 (Berlin, 1916), 91f. no. 75. Also see Harnack's *Kritik des Neuen Testaments von einem griechischen Philosophen des dritten Jahrhunderts* (Critique of the New Testament by a Greek Philosopher of the Third Century), Texte und Untersuchungen zur Geschichte der altchristlichen Literatur, 37, no. 4 (Leipzig, 1911), 128f. The question whether this pagan's fragments are attributable to Porphyry or to someone else is discussed in standard literary histories, cf. most recently Pierre de Labriolle, *La reaction païenne* (The Pagan Reaction) (Paris, 1934), 245ff., where the polemic over the "monarchy" is discussed, but with no new insights.

99. If I am not mistaken, the *Korē Kosmou* of Hermes Trismegistos agrees with the terminological usage that Porphyry advocates (in Stobaeus *Anthol.* 1 [ed. Wachsmuth, 1: 394.13 and 21, 395.16, 397.4, 403.10, 407.9]). J. Kroll, *Die Lehren des Hermes Trismegistus* (The Teachings of the Thrice-Great Hermes), Beiträge zur Geschichte der Philosophie des Mittelalters, 12, nos. 2–4 (Münster, 1914), 31, did not examine the meaning of the word *monarchos* in these passages. It is quite likely to be understood differently when the Coptic Gnostic *Apocryphon of John* describes the original being as "a *monarchia*, over which no one rules"; see Carl Schmidt in *Philotesia: Paul Kleinert zum LXX Geburtstag* (Berlin, 1907), 320. Still other presuppositions are involved when the reworking of the *Kata meros pistis* (Brief Exposition of Doctrine) that was available to Leontius attributes the *monarchēs* predicate only to God the Father. See Hans Lietzmann, *Apollinaris von Laodicea und seine Schule: Texte und Untersuchungen* (Tubingen, 1904), 176. The older form of the confession of faith runs: *homologoumen hena theon alēthinon, mian archēn* (We confess one true God, one First Principle); see C. P. Caspari, *Alte und neue Quellen zur Geschichte des Taufsymbols* (Old and New Sources on the History of the Baptismal Creed) (Christiania, 1879), 18 (cf. 20), and also 136.

100. It may be regarded as probable that Neo-Pythagoreanism's critique of monotheism has its roots in Pythagorean teaching. The tradition of the schools speaks of Pythagoras having assumed two *archai* (first principles), the *monas* (monad) and the *aoristos duas* (infinite dyad). Cf. Hermannus Diels, ed., *Doxographi graeci* (Berlin, 1879), 302.17–21; Pseudo-Plutarch *De vita et poesi Homeri* (On the Life and Poetry of Homer) 2.145, etc.

101. That the emperor Hadrian is named in the example may need an explanation. Is it perhaps to be found in Porphyry's dependence on a Pythagorean sophist of Hadrian's time?

102. Lactantius has a different explanation for why the angels cannot be interpreted in a polytheistic sense, which for him is denied by their status as God's servants (*Divin. instit.* 2.16.6, cf. 8).

103. Cf. Karl Müller, "Dionysios von Alexandrien im Kampf mit den libyschen Sabellianern" (Dionysius of Alexandria in His Struggle with the Libyan Sabellians), *Zeitschr. f. Neutest. Wissen.* 24 (1925): 278ff.

104. Letter in Athanasius *De decretis Nicenae Synodi* (On the Decrees of the Council of Nicaea) 26 (*PG* 25: 461D = C. L. Feltoe, ed., *The Letters and Other Remains of Dionysius of Alexandria* [Cambridge, 1904], 177.1ff.).

105. Ibid.: *pros tous diairountas kai katatemnontas kai anairountas to semnotaton kērygma tēs ekklēsias tou thou, tēn monarchian, eis treis dynameis tinas kai memerismenas hypostaseis kai theotētas treis.*

106. Athanasius, ibid. (*PG* 25: 464A): *Markiōnos gar . . . didagma eis treis archas tēs monarchias tomēn kai diairesin.* Also see Harnack, *Marcion*, 2nd ed., 336.

107. *Houtō gar an kai hē theia trias kai to hagion kērygma tēs monarchias diasōzoito.* Athanasius, ibid. (*PG* 25: 465A = Feltoe, ed., 182.7f.).

108. In Didymus *De trinitate* (*PG* 39: 865B) *monarchia* is once placed next to *monas*, but that association is conditioned by the interpretation of 1 Tim. 1:17 and similar passages. In any case, the immediately following occurrence of *polykoirania* (lordship of many) betrays the allusion to the Iliad verse. When Dionysius of Alexandria speaks of the *monarchia*, in my view that reflects the influence of Dionysius of Rome and not, as Karl Müller, *Zeitschr. f. Neutest. Wissen.* 24 (1925): 284, assumed, and is not to be attributed to Tertullian's influence.

109. The passages in Athanasius in which the word appears are either citations from Dionysius of Rome (*PG* 25: 461D, 464A, 465A), are in documents having to do with the fifth formula of faith (*PG* 26: 732A, 735C), or occur in a spurious work (*Contra Arianos* [Against the Arians], *Oratio* 4 [*PG* 26: 468]). I owe the collection of *monarchia* citations to the courtesy of Rev. Guido Müller, S.J., in Feldkirch, who has prepared a concordance to Athanasius.

110. The reproach of "hatred of humanity" that pagans raised against Jews and Christians (see the testimonies in Adolf von Harnack, *Die Mission und Ausbreitung des Christentums* [The Mission and Expansion of Christianity], 4th ed. [Leipzig, 1924], 1: 281f.) is obviously related to the concept of a divine "election" of a people. It is interesting that Celsus interprets Jewish-Christian monotheism "sociologically."

111. It is at least possible that the formulation of the Christian understanding that one ought not to serve several lords but one Lord only, is conditioned not only by biblical passages such as Matt. 6:24 and 1 Cor. 8:6, but also by the Iliad verse: *ouk agathon polykoiraniē, heis koiranos estō.*

112. Celsus has words of recognition for the national character of the Jewish religion (5.24). Insofar as the Jews adhere to their national worship, they do not act any differently from other peoples (*patrion d' oun phylassontes homoia tois allois anthrōpois drōsin, hoti hekastoi ta patria, hopēi pot' an tychēi, periepousin*). The concept of the *patrion* (ancestral custom), in conjunction with *thrēskeia* (worship) and *eusebeia* (piety), needs a monographic treatment—it also plays an important role in Porphyry's polemic against the Christians. See frgms. 1 and 66, ed. Harnack.

113. Careful attention needs to be given to the special twist given here to the idea that we have met again and again: the highest God rules, but the national deities govern.

114. In my opinion modern scholarship doesn't give enough emphasis to the political character of anti-Christian polemics in antiquity, or just ignores it completely. (Cf. Geffcken's expositions of Celsus's polemic in *Zwei griechische Apologeten*, 260f.)

115. The concept of *nomos* in this ethnogaphic speculation of the ancients needs a careful and comprehensive investigation. In chap. 9, *peri nomōn*, of Theodoret's *Ellēnikōn therapeutikē pathēmatōn* [Remedy for Hellenic Maladies] (ed. Räder, 219ff.), there is a discussion of how the *nomos* Christi has supplanted the *nomos* of the peoples. But this was no new discovery of Theodoret's—it belonged to the Christian tradition from the beginning—see the polemic against the plurality of the *nomos* in the individual *poleis* in Tatian's *Apology* (28 [ed. Schwartz, 29.17ff.]). It would then have to be shown to what extent the Christian unification of the *nomos* corresponded to the Stoic ideal of a single *nomos*.

116. Because of the abrupt formulation of "he who thinks this knows nothing" (*ho touto oiomenos oiden ouden*), there has been speculation that a sentence of Celsus's may have fallen out of Origen's citation (Keim, 139 n. 1). But I prefer to think that Celsus has worded this sentence so abruptly because, as his ultimate "pagan" conviction, it stood in no need of justification. To be sure, Anna Miura-Stange, *Celsus und Origenes* (Gießen, 1926), 114, makes Celsus into a "monotheist," while for her "Origen's worldview is polytheistically oriented" (117, cf. 119). I do not think one could have more completely misunderstood the truth of the matter.

117. It appears that Celsus has philosophically exploited the pagan demand against the Christians to adhere to their ancestral religion. So too Geffcken, *Zwei griechische Apologeten*, 258 (cf. G. Glöckner in *Philologus* 82 [1927]: 343f.). However, it would still be worth investigating whether the theory that the individual nations are apportioned to divine "overseers" (*epoptai*) was not developed even earlier, on the basis of Plato's *Politikos* (Statesman) 15 (Plato himself does not have this theory, but Porphyry as preserved in Proclus, *Procli Diadochi in Platonis Timaeum commentaria* [Commentary on the Timaeus of Plato], ed. Ernst Diehl, 1: 152.20f., knows, e.g., gods of the *ethnē* and *poleis* [nations and cities]). Miura-Stange (91) gives the name of *Epimelētai* (caretakers) to these divine "overseers" of the nations, although Celsus's text gives no justification for this. She says further, "The highest officials by the throne of God are the angels of the nations" (ibid.). Of this too there is not a word in Celsus. The pagan philosopher nowhere speaks specifically of "angels of the nations" who stand by the throne of God. Although the substance of the idea admittedly suggests bringing Celsus's "overseers" of the nations into connection with the angels of the nations in the book of Daniel (so already Oecumenius, who compares the *ethnarchous theous* [gods with national oversight] with the angels in *Kommentar zur Apokalypse* [Commentary on Revelation] [ed. Hoskier, 204]), it would nevertheless be difficult to prove a historical basis for this connection. Even if Celsus read the book of Daniel (*Against Celsus* 7.53 shows that he was familiar with the story of Daniel's rescue), it is unlikely that

he adopted his theory of the "overseers" of the nations from it. As for Daniel itself, the origin of the doctrine of the angels of the nations has been too little explored. (On this see now Bertholet in *Oriental Studies in honour of Cursetji Erachji Pavry* [Oxford, 1934], 34ff.) Geffcken shows (*Zwei griechische Apologeten*, 305, 317 n. 4) that Julian the Apostate and Symmachus, like Celsus, but not in precisely the same way, also spoke of the gods of the individual nations in their opposition to Christianity. Symmachus's formulation sounds very "Roman": "Varios custodes urbibus cunctis mens divina distribuit. Ut animae nascentibus ita populis fatales genii dividuntur [The divine Mind distributes various protectors to all cities. Just as souls [are imparted] to individuals when they are born, so predestined guiding spirits are divided among peoples]" (*Relatio* [Report] 8). The idea of the *genius* of the nations is probably derived from the idea of a *genius loci*. On the *Genius Pannoniae* or *Illyrici* (Spirit of Pannonia or Illyricum) on the coins of Decius, see Alföldi in *25 Jahre römisch-germanische Kommission*, 12.

118. The text from Zephaniah is also discussed by Eusebius in his *Eclogai propheticae* (Prophetic Selections) 3.20 (ed. Gaisford, 120) and his *Demonstratio evangelica* (Proof of the Gospel) 2.2.9 (ed. Heikel, 58.12ff.), 2.3.38 (67.21 and 23), 2.3.157 (88.18ff.). It belongs to the traditional body of proof texts for the calling of the Gentiles and for the second coming of Christ. Isidore of Seville uses the text in this sense in his writing *De fide catholica contra Judaeos* (On the Catholic Faith, Against the Jews) 2.1.11 (*PL* 83: 502A). This is not the place to explore how far Zephaniah's teaching on the *one* language that all people will speak after the world conflagration can be related to Iranian teaching. Jerome (*Comm. Zeph.* [Commentary on Zephaniah] 3.9 [*PL* 25: 1444A]) knew—perhaps from Origen?—a Jewish interpretation according to which everyone would speak Hebrew. Franz Cumont, "La fin du monde selon les mages occidentaux (The End of the World According to the Western Magi)," *Revue de l'histoire des religions* 103 (1931): 63, cites the report of Theopompus (?) in Plutarch *De Iside* (On Isis) 47, on Iranian teaching: (At the end of the world . . .) *tēs de gēs epipedou kai homalēs genomenēs, hena bion kai mian politeian anthrōpōn makariōn kai homoglōssōn genesthai* (when the earth becomes flat and level, there will be one way of life and one government of human beings, who will be blessed and will speak the same language). As a parallel Cumont adduces from the *Bundahish* 30.23 (p. 126): "All men become of one voice and administer loud praise to Aûharmazd" (cf. also Carl Clemen, *Die griechischen und lateinischen Nachrichten über die Persische Religion* [Greek and Latin Reports on Persian Religion] [Gießen, 1920], 168), while H. Windisch, *Die Orakel des Hystaspes* (The Oracle of Hystaspes), Verhandelingen Akademie te Amsterdam, Afd. Letterkunde, N.R. 28, 3 (1929), 29, refers to Mandaean literature (*Ginza* [Treasure], ed. Lidzbarski, 45.30f.): "All will call out in *one* voice and *one* song of praise, which I have brought into this world for them to use in praise," although the passage in the *Ginza* is not clear.

119. On the theological-political significance of the confusion of languages,

see now Anselm Stolz, "Theologie der Sprache" (Theology of Language), *Benediktinische Monatsschrift* 17 (1935): 121ff.

120. Origen phrases his formulation very carefully—no doubt intentionally: *kai tacha alēthōs adynaton men tō toiouto tois eti en sōmasi, ou mēn adynaton tois apolytheisin autōn* (ed. Koetschau, 2: 290.13f.). When Labriolle, *Réaction païenne*, rehearses the point at issue between Celsus and Origen in the following fashion, his abbreviated reference is not only false but is even responsible for introducing new misunderstandings today: "Cette unité, Celse la considère comme une utopie: Origène croit fermement qu'elle est possible et qu'elle se réalisera quelque jour [Celsus considers this unity as a utopia: Origen firmly believes it is possible and that some day it will be realized]" (150).

121. The Greek text is in Koetschau's edition [of Origen], *Gegen Celsus*, ed. Paul Koetschau, in *Origenes Werke*, 12 vols. (Leipzig, 1899–1955), 1: 158.2–20.

122. See A. von Ungern-Sternberg, *Der alttestamentliche Schriftbeweis "De Christo" und "De Evangelio" in der alten Kirche bis zur Zeit Eusebs von Caesarea* (The Old Testament Biblical Proof *De Christo* and *De Evangelio* in the Early Church up to the Time of Eusebius of Caesarea) (Halle, 1913), passim.

123. To answer this would require analyzing Origen's attitude to political life. Guilelmo Massart's *Società e stato nel cristianesimo primitivo: La concecione di Origene* (Society and State in Early Christianity: The Conception of Origen) (Padua, 1932) is without value. A short description of Origen's apolitical character is found in Labriolle, *Réaction païenne*, 169.

124. On this theme, cf. Geffcken, *Zwei griechische Apologeten*, 92f. A further reference should be added to Hippolytus's commentary on Dan. 4:9: *epi Augoustou kaisaros gegennētai ho kyrios, aph' houper ekmase to tōn Rōmaiōn basileion* (In the time of Augustus Caesar the Lord was born, and since that time the kingdom of the Romans has flourished) (206.11f.). Hippolytus's terse formulation corresponds in substance to Melito's observation, but Melito is more rhetorical. When Adolf von Harnack, *Reden und Aufsätze* (Lectures and Essays) (Gießen, 1906), 1: 305, supposes that Melito is dependent on an inscription in Sardis dedicated to Emperor Augustus (like those found in Priene and Halicarnassus), that is certainly incorrect. Melito received a rhetorical education, as did the composers of imperial dedications. Imperial birthday orations and orations on Rome were obviously a necessary element in every rhetorical education, especially in Asia Minor: recall what St. Augustine says in his *Confessions* (6.6.9): "How wretched I was . . . when I had to get ready to recite speeches in praise of the emperor" (Quam ergo miser eram . . . cum pararem recitare imperatori laudes).

125. In his *Commentary on Matthew* (Matt. 24:37), Origen likewise cites Ps. 72:7 and interprets it politically. The name of Augustus, of course, is not mentioned directly, but he had him in mind (69.21ff.). The Matthew commentary must fall in about the same time as *Against Celsus* (after 244). See the notices in Eusebius *Church History* 6.36.1–2.

126. See Ungern-Sternberg, *Alttestamentliche Schriftbeweis*, passim. In his *Prophetic Selections*, Eusebius speaks similarly on this text (*Ecl. Proph.* 1.8 [ed. Gaisford, 24.25ff.]).

127. Herod's foreignness is similarly emphasized in Eusebius's *Prophetic Selections* (ed. Gaisford, 25.20) and elsewhere as well. The same topos is presumed by Bar Hebraeus in his interpretation of Matt. 2:1: "When the manifestation of our Lord approached, the scepter had departed from Judah, forasmuch as the kingdom had passed away from the Jews, and the Gentiles held sway over them" (*Commentary on the Gospels from the Horreum mysteriorum / Gregory Abu'l Faraj, Commonly Called Bar-Hebraeus*, ed. Wilmot Eardley Carr [London, 1925], 9). St. Cyril of Alexandria cites the familiar biblical text of Gen. 49:10 when commenting on Luke 2:1, but he does not have a genuine "Augustus theology" (*A Commentary to St. Luke*, ed. Payne Smith, 1: 7; cf. also the Greek text in *PG* 72: 484).

128. In the *Selections*, the apologetic viewpoint of the scriptural "proof" against the Jews, to the effect that the Messiah has come, receives more emphasis: *dēlon hōs elēlythen ho peprophēteumenos Sōtēr hēmōn* (it is plain that our Savior, who was prophesied, has come) (ed. Gaisford, 25.25f.). That is naturally the older and more traditional approach.

129. This point of view on the understanding of the "historian" Eusebius is usually ignored; for example, Ad. Bauer, in his analysis of Jewish and Christian historical writing, says not a word about it (*Vom Judentum zum Christentum* [From Judaism to Christianity] [Leipzig, 1917]).

130. In the work of P. J. Koets, *Deisidaimonia* (Superstition): *A Contribution to the Knowledge of the Religious Terminology in Greek* (Purmerend [Netherlands], 1929), what is trivial here has been duly noted, but precisely this original formulation is not mentioned.

131. I note in passing that the preceding arguments of 8.3.7 have their parallels in 6.13.18, but that Eusebius has adapted two different sources, as the different interpretation of the word *koilades* (valleys) proves. One would first have to pursue Eusebius's use of sources before placing the *Proof* in a "history" of the Old Testament proof from Scripture, as Ungern-Sternberg has done.

132. Eusebius concludes his arguments with this sentence: *anamphilekton hēgoumai tēn apodeixin eilēphenai ton chronon tēs thespizomenēs eis anthrōpous tou kyriou parousias* (I consider [this] an irrefutable proof that the time has come when the Lord's prophesied appearance among men took place) (ed. Heikel, 394.6f.).

133. I quote the following texts:

(a) *Praep. evang.* 1.4: *syn tēi peri monarchias henos tou epi pantōn theou probeblēmenēi didaskaliai autou, homou kai tēs polyplanous kai daimonikēs energeias, homou kai tēs tōn ethnōn polyarchias eleutheron katastēnai to tōn anthrōpōn genos* (along with the spread of his teaching about the sole sovereignty of the one God of the universe, at the same time the human race was liberated both from diverse and demonic activity, and from the diversity of rulers among the nations)

(*PG* 21: 37A). There follows a description of humanity suffering under wars, in turn followed by the prophecy in Is. 2:4ff. Eusebius goes on to say: *akoloutha tais prorrēsesin epēkolouthei ta erga, pasa men autika periēireito polyarchia, Augoustou kata auto tei tou Sōtēros hēmōn epiphaneiai monarchēsantos* (the events that followed matched what had been prophesied: all diversity of government was overcome, when Augustus gained sole power at the same time as the appearance of our Savior) (*PG* 21: 37C). Since then, up to the present day, there has been peace among the nations. War is connected with the pagans' worship of the demons (ibid.).

(b) *Hist. eccl.* 1.5.2: Christ is born under Augustus, when the national dynasties had ceased. The *allophylos* (foreigner) Herod becomes king of the Jews (1.6.1f., esp. 1.6.4).

(c) *Syriac Theophany* 2.76 (ed. Gressmann, 114f.): Universal peace, since all confess "the One Helmsman of the universe" (ed. Gressmann, 144.34). The demons, who love war, no longer trouble the cities (115.1). With the cessation of belief in Fate, the necessity that leads to war also ceases (115.7, cf. 114.9). In *Theophany* 2.77, it is explained how many dominions existed before the appearance of our Savior (115f.). *Theophany* 3.1 says: "The entire error of polytheism was destroyed, and at once all the works of the demons were extinguished. There were no longer (city) fathers, power mongers, tyrants and national governments." There was no more war, "rather One God was preached to all and One Kingdom of the Romans flourished over all; totally abolished was the eternally violent and irreconcilable enmity of the nations. But when the teaching of our Savior passed on to all human beings the knowledge of the One God and One Ethic of justice and respect, there also appropriately existed One King, at one and the same time, over the entire kingdom of the Romans. And deep peace suffused everything" (126). The Roman Empire and the Church are therefore "two offshoots of the Good," which sprang up at God's bidding (127.1).

(d) *Tricennial Oration* 16: The nations were divided. The causes were to be found in the error of polytheism (ed. Heikel, 249.2). After the resurrection of Christ *ouk et' ēsan toparchiai kai polyarchiai, tyrannides te kai dēmokratiai* (there were no longer district or national governments, tyrannies and democracies) (249.7f.). There were no more wars. *Theos men <heis> eis pantas ekērytteto; en tautōi de kai basileia mia tois pasin hē Rōmaiōn epēnthei* (One God was proclaimed to all; at the same time the one kingdom of the Romans flourished among all) (249.9ff.). At the same time two *blastoi* (shoots) sprang up, the Romans' hegemony and the pious teaching, etc.

134. It would be worth investigating whether Eusebius's attribution of war to demons is aimed at a quite specific teaching on demons (perhaps Porphyry's). There is also a connection between polytheism and war in Pseudo-Justin *Cohortatio ad Graecos* (Exhortation to the Greeks) (*PG* 6: 273C) and in Constantine's oration (ed. Heikel, 155.15; cf. 157.12). Lactantius *Div. instit.* 5.5 is original (also see the *Epitome* 20.1ff.): polytheism and war are the results of Jupiter's rebellion against Saturn; the golden age under Saturn, which then came to an end, was monotheistic and free

of wars. In the Ps.-Clementines, *Hom.* 9.2 (ed. Dressel, 198.5f.) has: *hē men monarchia homonoias esti parektikē, hē de polyarchia polemōn exergastikē* (monarchy leads to peace; polyarchy produces wars). It would also be worth investigating to what extent the topos that the divine monarch guarantees peace derives from a topos of ancient rhetoric, according to which (earthly) monarchy is a guarantor of peace.

135. The idea that the One King on earth corresponds to the One King in heaven is an adaptation of the old idea that the king imitates God. See the Pythagorean Diotogenes and Sthenidas in Stobaeus *Anthol.* 4.7.61 and 4.7.63 respectively (ed. Wachsmuth, 4: 265 and 270). Cf. on this idea E. R. Goodenough, "The Political Philosophy of Hellenistic Kingship," *Yale Classical Studies* 1 (1928): 55–102 (not accessible to me); N. H. Baynes, "Eusebius and the Christian Empire," in *Mélanges Bidez* (Brussels, 1934), 1: 13f., reprinted in Norman H. Baynes, *Byzantine Studies and Other Essays* (London, 1955), 168–172; W. W. Tarn, *Alexander the Great and the Unity of Mankind* (London, 1933), 8; Vlad. Valdenberg, "Les idées politiques dans les fragments attribués à Pierre le Patrice," *Byzantion* 2 (1925), 57, 62, 64; Heinemann, *Philons griechische und jüdische Bildung*, 187, 190 n. 1, 193ff., 195, 198 and n. 2; Kroll, *Lehren des Hermes Trismegistus*, 324.

136. Probably, Eusebius's formulation of the idea that the Roman Empire had improved the apostles' access to all nations (especially clear in the Syriac *Theophany* [ed. Gressmann, 128.7ff.]), is also shaped by the rhetorical topos in the encomia on Rome, according to which the Roman Empire had made free commerce possible. See, e.g., Aelius Aristides *On Rome, Or.* 26.106 (121.1ff.). The further idea in Eusebius, that everyone in the Roman Empire had become one family, also stems from rhetoric, cf. W. Gernentz, *Laudes Romae* (The Praises of Rome) (diss., Rostock, 1918), 136, who also discusses (142) the topos that the Roman Empire had enabled freedom of trade (see also Harald Fuchs, *Augustin und der antike Friedensgedanke: Untersuchungen zum neunzehnten Buch der "Civitas Dei"* (Augustine and Ancient Thought on Peace: Studies in the Nineteenth Book of the *City of God*) (Berlin, 1926), 197 n. 4). Eusebius the "rhetorician" deserves a special monograph. His treatise *Against Hierocles* shows that Eusebius even mastered the language of the Second Sophistic.

137. Cf., too, Fuchs, *Augustin und der antike Friedensgedanke*, 162, 163 n.

138. *Ou gar oikothen, ou de par' heautou tote ho Augoustos to dogma touto exepempsen, alla tou theou kinountos autou tēn psychēn, hina kai akōn hypēretēsētai tēi tou Monogenous parousiai* (For Augustus did not get the idea of promulgating this decree from his financial department or from his own initiative, rather it was God who moved his soul, so that even unwittingly he would assist the coming of the Only-begotten One). Cf. also John Chrysostom *Homiliae in Matt.* (Homilies on Matthew) Hom. 8.4 (*PG* 57: 87): *kai ho Augoustos hypēreteitai tōi en Bēthleem tokōi dia tou prostagmatos tēs apographēs* (And Augustus assisted the birth in Bethlehem by his decree of the census).

139. Diodore on Rom. 13:1, in Karl Staab, *Pauluskommentare aus der griechischen*

Kirche (Commentaries on Paul from the Greek Church), Neutestamentliche Abhandlungen, no. 15 (Münster, 1933), 107: *Hē de ge tōn Rōmaiōn archē kai oikonomias exairetou para tou theou tetychēken. Mellontos gar tou sōtēros epiphainesthai tois anthrōpois, mikron prolabōn ho theos eis hypēresian heautou tēn Rōmaïkēn proseballeto, di' hēs hēmeron kai eirēnikōteron tōn anthrōpōn ton bion katestēsen. Tōn men ep' allēlōn polemōn apallaxas autous, tosautēn de scholēn dous tēs heautou epignōseōs* (The Roman Empire has come into being through the excellent dispensation of God. When the Savior was about to appear among men, God conscripted the Roman Empire into his service, and thereby rendered human life gentle and more peaceful. He took human beings away from their wars and gave them instead the great school of the knowledge of himself). There follow two citations from Ps 46: 9f. and 11: *anelontos toinun tou theou tous synecheis polemous kai dontos epimixian polesi te kai ethnesi dia to tēs eusebous politeias kērygma, syneōrakōs ho apostolos tēn oikonomian tēn peri tas basileias, parainei hypotassesthai tais exousiais. Tou gar theou taxantos autas to mē peitharchein asebes meta tou kai en tōi paronti biōi epikindynon echein tēn aponoian* (Since God has canceled the ceaseless wars and brought sociability to cities and nations by the preaching of the pious way of life, the Apostle Paul, aware of the providential dispensation for kingdoms, counsels [his readers] to be subject to the powers that be. Since it is God who orders them, disobedience is impious and is dangerous madness both in the present life and afterwards).

140. Theodoret *in Danielem* (On Daniel) 2 (*PG* 81: 1308f.) and esp. *Jesajakommentar* (Commentary on Isaiah), ed. Möhle (14.7,16 and 83.32ff.).

141. Let me cite Titus of Bostra on Luke 2:1: *syntrechei hē monarchia tēs gēs tēi tou dogmatos eusebeiai* (Sole rule over the earth correlates with the piety of doctrine) (*Titus von Bostra: Studien zu dessen Lukashomilien* [Titus of Bostra: Studies on His Homilies on Luke], ed. Joseph Sickenberger, Texte und Untersuchungen zur Geschichte der altchristlichen Literatur, n.s., 6, 1, pt. 1 [Leipzig, 1901]). Cyril of Alexandria also emphasizes God's providence over the Romans in his book *Against Julian* 7 (*PG* 76: 833). In his commentary on the prophet Micah, he applied the peace prophecy to the peace of the Roman Empire, although without mentioning monotheism. The same point of view recurs in his interpretation of Is. 2:4 (*PG* 70: 72–73). See further Pseudo-John Chrysostom (*PG* 50: 795 and 799).

142. Richard Delbrück, *Spätantike Kaiserporträts von Constantin Magnus bis zum Ende des Westreichs* (Late Antique Imperial Portraits of Constantine the Great up to the End of the Western Empire) (Berlin, 1933), 15, holds the opinion that the growing resemblance of Constantine to Augustus, which is visible in representational art, has no literary parallel, "perhaps because the orations delivered in Rome at that time have not survived." But Eusebius basically lets us see this parallel.

143. On Augustus as the model for Roman emperors, cf. besides ibid., 12, 15, 37, 38, also [Paul] Strack, *Römische Reichsprägung* 2: 13, 53, 104f., 106f.; Andreas Alföldi, *Zeitschrift für Numismatik* 38 (1928): 197ff.; id. in *25 Jahre römische-germanische Kommission*, 31,36; Jean Gagé in *Mélanges de l'École française de Rome*

49 (1932): 81ff.; Gerhart Rodenwaldt, *Archäologischer Anzeiger* (1931): 318ff.,320f.; Ernst Hohl, "Vopiscus und die Biographie des Kaisers Tacitus," *Klio* 11 (1911): 221 n. 3. On the image of Augustus as the model for Emperor Henry II, see Percy Schramm, "Das Herrscherbild in der Kunst des frühen Mittelalters (The Image of the Ruler in the Art of the Early Middle Ages)," *Vorträge der Bibliothek Warburg* 2 (1924): 148 n. 5.

144. *Prudentius*, trans. H. J. Thomson (London, 1949–1953), 2: 53–57 (translation slightly revised). Also see Prudentius *Peristephanon* (Crowns of Martyrdom) 2.417ff. (ed. Bergman, 311).

145. The rhetorical description of the civil wars is missing (perhaps because of a gap in the manuscript tradition) in Eusebius's *Commentary on the Psalms*, though it is in any case found in St. Jerome's interpretation of Mic. 4:2 (*PL* 25: 1188). One scarcely needs to posit a literary forebear for Ambrose and Jerome (that would naturally be Origen); it is more likely that this *ekphrasis* of the civil wars derived from the rhetorical tradition. An influence on St. Ambrose from St. Basil does not in this instance need to be considered, because Basil interpreted this psalm verse without considering the political situation. See *PG* 29: 425D–428C. Whether a dependence on Origen is present, as Viktor Stegemann, *Augustins Gottestaat* (Augustine's City of God), Heidelberger Abhandlungen zur Philosophie und ihrer Geschichte, no. 15 (Tübingen, 1928), 30, assumes, I would not presume to decide, until it can be determined whether the text printed in the *Selecta in psalmos* (Selections on the Psalms) (ed. Lommatzsch, 12: 331f.) is really Origen's. That Ps. 46:9f. was also understood politically by Diodore is shown by the text in Staab, *Pauluskommentare*, 107. In his interpretation of the psalm verse, St. John Chrysostom (*PG* 55: 207), and likewise Theodoret (see *PG* 80: 1205C), have references to the political circumstances in the Roman Empire. Cassiodorus on Ps. 46:9 similarly makes reference to the political situation, although with a different accent (*PL* 70: 331). Pseudo-Ambrose, *Breviarium in Psalmos* (Short Commentary on the Psalms), comments on this verse: "Omnia bella in adventu Domini quievisse, multorum narrant historiae" (As many [authors'] histories tell us, all wars had ceased at the coming of the Lord) (*PL* 26: 1019B).

146. Thus Stegemann, *Augustins Gottestaat*, 26 (although note the reservations on p. 30). On Ambrose's interpretation of Ps. 46, see finally Jean-Rémy Palanque, *Saint Ambroise et l'Empire romain* (Paris, 1934), 334, 335 and n. 54, also 291 and 551.

147. In his *Commentary on Isaiah*, St. Jerome comments (*PL* 24: 46A): "usque ad vicesimum octavum annum Caesaris Augusti . . . in toto orbe terrarum fuisse discordiam. . . . Orto autem Domino salvatore . . . et Evangelicae doctrinae pax Romani imperii praeparata, tunc omnia bella cessaverunt (Up to the twenty-eighth year of Caesar Augustus, discord had prevailed throughout the whole world. But when our Lord the Savior appeared and the peace of the Roman Empire was prepared for the Gospel teaching, then all wars ceased)" People return to agriculture, and only professional soldiers are used in war against the barbarians. This last idea

is also found in Cyril of Alexandria's *Commentary on Isaiah* (*PG* 70: 73A) and is not unimportant for defining the concept of the Pax Romana. War still exists only against "barbarians," and such warfare can be reserved for the standing army (cf., too, Fuchs, *Augustin und der antike Friedensgedanke*, 197 n. 3).

148. Remarkably, virtually nothing has been written on Orosius. Several short notices on him are found in Elisabeth Pfeil, *Die fränkische und deutsche Romidee im frühen Mittelalter* (The Frankish and German Idea of Rome in the Early Middle Ages) (Munich, 1929), 36ff. See too [Sergio] Mochi Onory, *Vescovi e città (sec. IV–VI)* (Bishops and City in the Fourth and Sixth Centuries) (Bologna, 1933), 92f.

149. According to the ancient tradition (*Corpus inscriptionum Latinarum*, 2nd ed., 1: 231) this occurred on January 11 (see *Paulys Realencyclopädie der classischen Altertumswissenschaft* [Berlin, 1894–1972], 10: 338.18ff.). To fit his theology of history, Orosius changes that date to January 6, the day of Epiphany. Aponius, *In Cantica canticorum explanatio* (Commentary on the Song of Songs), ed. Bottino and Martini (Rome, 1843), 237, knows of a return of Augustus on Epiphany.

150. The rejection of *dominus* as a form of address was from an early date noted by both Jews (Philo *The Embassy to Gaius* 23) and Christians (Tertullian *Apology* 34). That took place in AD 3 (see *Paulys Realencyclopädie*, 10: 369.2ff.).

151. The association of the angels' cry of "Peace" with the imperial peace of Augustus is also found in St. Jerome, *Commentary on Isaiah* (*PL* 24: 46B).

152. The comparison of the Roman Empire with the Babylonian and Persian Empires is a rhetorical topos; see Gernentz, *Laudes Romae*, 99ff. Here it is applied in a Christian sense.

153. The mention of the *pauperrimus status pastoris* likewise is attributable to a rhetorical topos of the panegyrics on Rome; see ibid., 38. One has the impression that for Orosius the "poor shepherds" who founded Rome parallel the "poor shepherds" of Christ's infancy narrative.

154. Cf. also Orosius 3.8.5: "sub Augusto . . . universum terrarum orbem positis armis abolitisque discordiis generali pace et nova quiete conpositum Romanis paruisse legibus." Fuchs, *Augustin und der antike Friedensgedanke*, pays as little attention to Orosius's definition of the Pax Romana—according to which war has been abolished—as he does in general to the patristic view that national pluralism has been overcome in the Pax Romana. In general, Orosius explicitly emphasizes that the peace of Augustus was not the emperor's doing but that of the Son of God (e.g. 3.8.8; likewise Cassiodorus on Ps. 46 [*PL* 70: 331C] and already Origen *Commentary on Matthew* [ed. Klostermann-Benz, 69.21f.], in open contradiction to the phrase "Pax Augusta," which attributed the establishment of peace to the emperor himself. See Franz Altheim, *Römische Religionsgeschichte* (History of Roman Religion) (Berlin, 1933), 3: 59. On the mythologizing of the peace ideology of Augustus and his successors, cf. Alföldi in *Zeitschrift für Numismatik* 38 (1928): 184f.

155. Orosius is thus ultimately the presupposition for the origin of the Ara Coeli legend. On the medieval Augustus legend, see E. von Frauenholz, "Impera-

tor Augustus in der Geschichte und Sage des Mittelalters (The Emperor Augustus in the History and Legends of the Middle Ages)," *Historisches Jahrbuch der Görresgesellschaft* (1926): 86ff.

156. Geffcken, *Zwei griechische Apologeten*, 300 n. 2, provides some information about pagan charges that Christianity was incompatible with the Roman Empire and politically harmful, but more detailed treatment is needed.

157. Pseudo-Alcuin, *De divinis officiis* (On the Divine Offices) 1 (*PL* 101: 1174B–C), a tenth-century text (see L. Eisenhofer, *Handbuch der katholischen Liturgik* [Freiburg im Br., 1932], 1: 121), reiterates Orosius's ideas: At the birth of Christ "congruum erat, ut pax per totum orbem constituta esset, et homines perduelles cessarent a bellis et inimicitiis. Viae quoque publicae tunc tutae fieri sunt iussae, quia verissima via debebat nasci (it was fitting that peace should be established throughout all the world, and bellicose humankind should cease from wars and hostilities. Public highways were then ordered to be made safe, because the truest Way had to be born)." An account of the miracles of Augustus follows, which resembles Orosius's, although an intermediate source should probably be presumed.

158. *Sōizomenēs en hapasi pantote tēs hyperochēs tou theou kai monarchias.*

159. M. Albertz, *Untersuchungen über die Schriften des Eunomius* (Investigations into the Writings of Eunomius) (diss., Halle, 1908), 14, assumes that chap. 27 is the fragment of a sermon by Eunomius.

160. Ibid. 36ff. [The citation of *Constit. apost.* 7.4.1 is incorrect; probably *Constit. apost.* 7.41 was meant. See *Les constitutions apostoliques*, ed. Marcel Metzger, Sources chrêtiennes, 336 (Paris, 1987), 99.—Ed.]

161. *plērōsanta pasan tēn gēn, syntribonta polyarchian toparchiōn kai polytheïan atheōn, kēryssonta de ton hena theon kai cheirotonounta tēn Rōmaiōn monarchian* (filling the whole world, crushing the polyarchy of local governments and the polytheism of the godless, proclaiming the one God and ordaining the monarchy of the Romans). The word *monarchia* is also in *Const. apost.* 3.5.4 (the *Didascalia*; cf. *Didascalia Apostolorum* [Teaching of the Apostles], ed. Connolly [Oxford, 1929], 132.15) and 5.15.3. The same in 6.9.1, which stems from the Ps.-Clementines. On 5.20.11, cf. in general Adolf von Harnack, *Die Lehre der zwölf Apostel nebst Untersuchungen zur ältesten Geschichte der Kirchenverfassung und des Kirchenrechts* (The Teaching of the Twelve Apostles, with Investigations into the Earliest History of the Church's Constitution and Church Law) (Leipzig, 1884), 248.

162. In Eusebius's *De ecclesiastica theologia* (On the Ecclesiastical Theology), he has given his own speculations on the divine monarchy: *alla phobēi, ō anthrōpe, mē dyo hypostaseis homologēsas, dyo archas eisagagois kai tēs monarchikēs theotētos ekpesois: manthane toinyn hōs, henos ontos anarchou kai agennētou theou tou de hyiou ex autou gegennēmenou, mia estai archē monarchia te kai basileia mia* (But beware, sir, that in confessing two entities, you do not introduce two first principles and thereby deviate from the monarchical godhead: learn, then, that since there is one God who is without beginning and unbegotten, while the Son has been begotten from him,

there will be one first principle, and one monarchy and kingdom) (2.7; cf. also ibid. 1.11.3).

163. Basil *De spiritu sancto* (On the Holy Spirit) 45: *menomen epi tēs monarchias, eis plēthos apeschismenon tēn theologian mē skedannyntes* (we hold to the monarchy and do not reduce the mystery of God to a pile of fragments) (ed. Johnston, 91.18f.), and ibid., 47: *hai hypostaseis homologountai kai to eusebes dogma tēs monarchias ou diapiptei* (the individual persons are confessed without the pious dogma of the monarchy collapsing) (ed. Johnston, 95.21f.); Gregory of Nazianzus *Third Theological Oration* 2 (ed. Mason, 74.12–75.7) and *Fifth Theological Oration* 17 (ed. Mason, 166.7); Epiphanius in his polemic against Tatian: *anachthēsetai ta panta eis tēn mian monarchian* (everything will be referred back to the one sole principle) (*Adv. Haeres.* 46.2.6 [ed. Holl, 2: 206.8f.]), his polemic against Saturnilus: *epi tēn monarchian <dein> to pan agein* (everything must be attributed to the sole principle) (*Adv. Haeres.* 23.4.8 [ed. Holl, 1: 253.5f.]), and also this text: *ou polytheïan eisēgoumetha, alla monarchian kēryttomen. Monarchian de kēryttontes ou sphallometha, alla homologoumen tēn triada* (we do not introduce polytheism, but rather we proclaim monarchy. In proclaiming monarchy, we do not commit error but we confess the triad) (*Adv. Haeres.* 62.3.2f. [ed. Holl, 2: 391.22ff.]); John of Damascus *De fide orthodoxa* (On the Orthodox Faith) 1.8 (*PG* 94: 830B); Ed. Bratke, *Das sogennante Religionsgespräch am Hof der Sassaniden* (The Alleged Religious Discussion at the Court of the Sassanids), in Texte und Untersuchungen, no. 19, 3 (Leipzig, 1899), 2.24; Pseudo-Caesarius *Dialogi: Quaestiones et responsiones* (Dialogues: Questions and Responses) 1, qu. 4 (*PG* 38: 864).

164. *Treis hai anōtatō doxai peri theou. Anarchia kai polyarchia kai monarchia. Hai men oun dyo paisin Hellēnōn epaichthēsan kai paizesthōsan. To te gar anarchon atakton, to de polyarchon stasiōdes kai houtōs anarchon kai houtōs atakton. eis tauton gar amphotera pherei, tēn ataxian. Hē de eis lysin. Ataxia gar meletē lyseōs. hēmin de monarchia to timōmenon. Monarchia de, ouch hēn hen perigraphei prosōpon (esti gar kai to hen stasiazon pros heauto polla kathistasthai.), all' hēn physeōs homotimia synistēsi kai gnōmēs sympnoia kai tautotēs kinēseōs kai pros to hen tōn ex autou synneusis, hoper amēchanon epi tēs gennētēs physeōs* (There are three predominant opinions about God: anarchy, polyarchy, and monarchy. The first two were the playthings of the Greeks, and let them play their games with them. The anarchic principle is disordered and the polyarchic principle is subversive, hence both anarchic and disordered. Both of them tend to the same end, disorder, which is dissolution, for disorder is preparation for dissolution. But with us it is monarchy that is honored. A monarchy, however, that is not limited to one person, for a single person can produce [divisive] plurality if he rebels against himself. We honor a monarchy that is constituted by a natural equality of honor, a harmony of mind, an identity of movement, and a convergence of its elements toward unity, something that is impossible for created nature). *Third Theological Oration* 2 (*PG* 36: 76A–B; ed. Mason [Cambridge Patristic Texts], 74.12–75.7). On the syllogism in this passage,

see Johs. Focken, *De Gregorii Nazianzeni argumentandi ratione* (On Gregory of Nazianzus's Method of Argumentation) (diss., Berlin, 1912), 8ff.

165. Gregory of Nyssa *Catechetical Oration* 3.2 (ed. Srawley, 16.6ff.): *Hē tēs physeōs henotēs ton diamerismon ou prosietai, hōs mēte to tēs monarchias schizesthai kratos eis theotētas diaphorous katatemnomenon, mēte tōi Ioudaïkōi dogmati symbainein ton logon, alla dia mesou tōn dyo hypolēpseōn chōrein tēn alētheian* (The unity of nature does not admit of division, so that the power of the sole sovereignty is not divided and fragmented into distinct divinities, nor does the doctrine agree with the Jewish teaching; rather,it reaches the truth by passing in between the two conceptions). Cf. too Ps.-Athanasius *Quaestiones ad Antiochum ducem* (Questions to General Antiochus) Qu. 1 (*PG* 28: 597E): *eis monarchian pisteuontes Ioudaïzomen; eis de palin treis theous, prodēlon hoti Hellēnizomen* (if we believe in one divine principle [monarchy], we become Jews; but if on the other hand we accept three gods, we have plainly become pagans); Pseudo-John Chrysostom *Contra Judaeos, gentiles, et haereticos* (Against Jews, Gentiles, and Heretics): *epeidē Hellēnes polytheïan esebonto, hoi Iudaioi de monarchian, hina dē kai tēn polytheïan anelēi kai tēn monarchian, dia touto elegen: "Eite gar eisi theoi polloi kai kyrioi polloi, eite en ouranōi, eite epi gēs, all' hēmin heis theos ho patēr." Kai eipōn to "heis" aneile tēn polytheïan. Hopou gar heis, ouk eisi polloi. Kai eipōn "Patera" aneile tēn monarchian, hopou gar patēr, dēlon hoti kai hyios* (Since Greeks worship many gods but Jews one divine principle [monarchy], so that he might overturn both polytheism and a single divine principle, he therefore said, "For there are many gods and many lords, be they in heaven or on earth; but for us, one God is father." And by saying "father," he overturned monarchy, for if he is father, plainly there is a son) (*PG* 48: 1080). On this idea cf. Karl Holl, *Amphilochius von Ikonium* (Tübingen, 1904), 143, and Johannes Leipoldt, *Didymus der Blinde* (Didymus the Blind) (Leipzig, 1905), 129; Jakob Bilz, *Die Trinitätslehre des hl. Johannes von Damascus* (The Trinitarian Doctrine of St. John of Damascus), Forschungen zur christl. Literatur und Dogmengeschichte, no. 9, 3 (Paderborn, 1909), 39. (See John of Damascus *De fide orthodoxa* 1.7 [*PG* 94: 805C-808A]). One might also cite Nicetas: "nec more gentilium potestatum diversitates opinemur . . . nec Judaeorum scandalum succumbamus [we neither hold to a diversity of powers, in the manner of the Gentiles, nor do we succumb to the scandal of the Jews]" (ed. A. E. Burn, *Niceta of Remesiana: His Life and Works* [Cambridge, 1905], 37.11ff.). W. A. Patin, *Niceta von Remesiana* (diss., Munich, 1909), 36, therefore compares §23 of the decisions of the fourth synod of Damasus (see Denzinger, *Enchiridion Symbolorum*, 10th ed. [Freiburg im Br., 1928], 34): "omnes haeretici de Filio Dei et Spiritu sancto male sentientes, in perfidia Judaeorum et gentilium inveniuntur [all heretics who think wrongly about the Son of God and the Holy Spirit are found in the perfidy of the Jews and the Gentiles]."

166. On St. Augustine's critical judgment of the Pax Augusta (the traditional understanding is found in *On the City of God* 18.22,46), see Stegemann, *Augustins Lehre vom Gottesstaat*, 40, and Fuchs, *Augustin und der antike Friedensgedanke*, 52f. In this

context it is significant that Augustine also does not collaborate in the Church Fathers' usual glorification of Augustus. For him, Augustus is the one who "iam enervem ac languidam libertatem omni modo extorsisse Romanis [who had already in every way wrenched a limp and exhausted liberty from the Romans]" (*De civitate Dei* 3.21). See also Heinrich Scholz, *Glaube und Unglaube in der Weltgeschichte* (Belief and Unbelief in World History) (Leipzig, 1911), 181. On the ancient source of this perception, see Klingner in *Hermes* 63 (1928), 190, and Matthias Gelzer in *Philologus* 86 (1931): 274. The profound difference between Orosius and Augustine is inadequately emphasized in the standard literary histories.

167. A theology essentially linked to the Imperium Romanum had to imperil the universality of the Christian proclamation. From the newly discovered Coptic papyrus text of Mani, we see how Christianity appeared to him to be a religion restricted to the west, in contrast to which he now emphasizes the true universalism of his teaching (*Kephalaia* 1 [Stuttgart, 1935], 65.7ff., 12.26f., 7.18f.). Cf. also Carl Schmidt, *Neue Originalquellen des Manichäismus aus Ägypten* (New Original Sources of Manicheism from Egypt) (Stuttgart, 1935), 19f. It was certainly not an accident that it was St. Gregory the Great, schooled theologically in Augustine, who undertook the mission to the Germans. And Augustine's legacy is also discernible when the author of the treatise *De vocatione gentium* (On the Calling of the Gentiles) 2.16(*PL* 51: 704) represents the opinion that the *latitudo imperii* (which St. Augustine had regarded with misgivings) did indeed have providential significance, but that Christianity was nevertheless not limited to the Imperium Romanum. This quite general sense of a preparation for the Gospel by the Imperium Romanum is reflected in a prayer in the *Gelasian Sacramentary*: "Deus, qui praedicando aeterni regni evangelio Romanum imperium praeparasti [O God, you who have prepared the Roman Empire for the preaching of the Gospel of the eternal kingdom]" (ed. Wilson, 277). Today this prayer is still found in the *Missale Romanum* among the *Orationes diversae*. It is just as free of any "political theology" (on the attempt of the Franks to "nationalize" this prayer text, cf. Gerd Tellenbach, *Römischer und christlicher Reichsgedanke in der Liturgie des frühen Mittelalters* (Roman and Christian Imperial Ideology in the Liturgy of the Early Middle Ages), Sitzungsberichte Heidelberger Akad. der Wissenschaften, Phil.-Histor. Klasse [1934–1935], 21) as is the notice in the *Martyrologium Romanum* for December 25, according to which Our Lord was born "anno imperii Octaviani Augusti quadragesimo secundo, toto orbe in pace composito [in the forty-second year of the Emperor Octavian Augustus, when the whole world was composed in peace]." This was a fixed topos in both historiography (e.g., Caesar Baronius, *Annales ecclesiastici* [Rome, 1597–1612], 1: 3f.) and exegesis (e.g., Antonius de Escobar y Mendoza, *Ad evangelia sanctorum et temporis commentarii* [Lyon, 1642], 1: 51: "vigente pace Christum exortum [Christ appeared when peace reigned]").

168. To my knowledge, the concept of "political theology" was introduced into the literature by Carl Schmitt, *Politische Theologie* (Political Theology) (Munich,

1922). His brief arguments at that time were not systematic. Here we have tried to show by a concrete example the theological impossibility of a "political theology."

CHAPTER 6: THE BOOK ON THE ANGELS

1. [Dedication to St. Benedict in the original 1935 publication.—Ed.]

2. "Toutes les creatures visible et invisibles sont quelque chose à l'église. Les anges sont ministres de son salut, et par l'église se fait la recrue de leurs légions désolées par la désertion de Satan et de ses complices; mais dans cette recrue, ce n'est pas tant nous qui sommes incorporés aux anges que les anges qui viennent à notre unité, à cause de Jésus, notre commun chef, et plus le nôtre que le leur." Jacques Bénigne Bossuet, *Correspondance de Bossuet*, ed. Eugène Levesque and Charles Urbain, new ed., 15 vols. (Paris, 1909–1925), 1: 61. [The quotation from Bossuet was in the original 1935 publication but omitted in 1951 and 1994 editions. Peterson quotes it in note 130 below and credits an article by Yves Congar for having brought it to his attention.—Ed.]

3. "Coepit enim haec Ecclesia ab Jerusalem, ista terrena, ut gaudeat inde Deo in illa Jerusalem coelesti: Ab hac enim incipit, ad illam terminat." (For this Church begins from Jerusalem, the earthly one, that she may then rejoice in God in that other Jerusalem which is heavenly: it begins from the one, it ends in the other.) Augustine, *Enarrationes in psalmos* (Explanations of the Psalms) 147 (*PL* 37: 1929).

4. The apostles' departure from the earthly Jerusalem is a dogmatically decisive event.

5. The expression *polis menousa* (lasting city) in Heb. 13:14 should be understood in the context of the earthly city's claim to "endure." Ancient people pray for the *diamonē* (permanence) of sovereignty. See Erik Peterson, *Heis Theos* (Göttingen, 1926), 174. Further Matthias Gelzer in *Philologus* 86 (1931): 292f. The Letter to the Hebrews denies the possibility of a permanent sovereignty, the possibility of a *polis menousa*. Only God's royal sovereignty is "unshakeable" (*asaleutos*—Heb. 12:28).

6. The verb *proserchesthai* has here the technical meaning "to approach the cultic shrine / the gods of the cult" (see James Hope Moulton and George Milligan, *Vocabulary of the Greek Testament* [London, 1930], s.v.).

7. So I believe *apographesthai* in the Greek text should be interpreted. See H. G. Liddell and R. Scott, *A Greek-English Lexicon*, s.v. Cf. Gregory the Great, *Homilies on the Gospels*, 1.15: "in illa superna angelorum curia adscribi festinate."

8. The Greek has *panēgyris*.

9. The term *politeuma* in itself is capable of various interpretations. See W. Ruppel, "*Politeuma*: Bedeutungsgeschichte eines staatsrechtlichen Terminus," *Philologus* 82 (1927): 268ff., and Schönbauer, *Zeitschrift der Savigny-Stiftung, Romanistische Abteilung* 46 (1929): 354ff., among others. The translation I've given [*Stadtgemeinde*] appears to me to be the most probable. Tertullian *Adversus Marcionem* (Against Marcion) 3.24, and Jerome *In Jeremiam* (On Jeremiah) 3.76.3 (CCL 74: 168.21),

renders *politeuma* in Phil. 3:20 with *municipatum*. The suggestion of Paul Perdrizet, *Graffites grecs du Memneion d'Abydos* (Nancy, 1919), p. xii, that *politeuma* means "foreigners' quarter" seems wrong to me, for Christians are aliens not in heaven but on earth (1 Pet. 2:11 and 1:1; Heb. 11:13).

10. *Sōtēr* = savior. I have intentionally left the Greek word untranslated. Perhaps the connection between the relative clause and the preceding clause is to be seen in the fact that Christ is the *sōtēr* of the polis. That would correspond to ancient linguistic usage.

11. Erik Peterson, *Die Kirche* (Munich, 1929), 14. ["The Church," p. 38, in this volume.—Ed.]

12. In Heb. 12:23, *apographesthai* appears to mean the enrollment in the citizen list of the heavenly city.

13. That the legal enactments of the Church are also cultic acts has been shown by Rudolf Sohm, *Das altkatholische Kirchenrecht und das Dekret Gratians* (The Old Catholic Canon Law and the *Decretum* of Gratian) (Leipzig, 1918), though he uses the somewhat misleading term "sacramental law."

14. That for St. Augustine the concepts of the *civitas Dei* and *ecclesia catholica* are not simply coterminous is also evident in the analysis of Fritz Hofmann, *Der Kirchenbegriff des heiligen Augustinus* (St. Augustine's Concept of the Church) (Munich, 1933), cf. 492, 496ff.

15. In St. Augustine and even more strongly in Gregory the Great, *civis* means almost the equivalent of "angel." Cf., e.g., *supernorum civium numerus* (the number of heavenly citizens), in *Moralia in Job* (Moral Reflections on Job) 17.13.18 (*PL* 76: 20C), *illis supernis civibus* (to those heavenly citizens), in *Homiliae in Ezechielem* (Homilies on Ezekiel) 2.5.4 (*PL* 76: 986C), and many other places.

16. The Seer only weeps because no one is judged worthy to open the seals of the book.

17. The theological correctness reflected in the literary composition of Revelation is the inner proof of the "reality" of the Johannine visions, i.e., of the fact that they issue from the Holy Spirit.

18. As otherwise polis and temple are parallel concepts, so here ruler and cult.

19. Jewels are symbolic of every genuine dominion and therefore play an important role on the garments, weapons, etc., of the Roman emperors. Cf., e.g., Andreas Alföldi in *Acta Archaeologica* 5 (Copenhagen, 1934): 108; also in *Römische Mitteilungen* 49 (1934): 16f.

20. Cf. the analogous usage in the imperial cult. On this, Franz Cumont, *Revue d'histoire et de littérature religieuse* 1 (1896): 441ff.; also in his *Les religions orientales dans le paganisme romain* (Eastern Religions in Roman Paganism), 4th ed. (1929), 127; W. Otto in *'Epitymbion, Heinrich Swoboda dargebracht* (Reichenberg, 1924), 194ff.; finally, Andreas Alföldi in *Römische Mitteilungen* 49 (1934): 111ff.

21. The detailed description of the heavenly throne room in chap. 4 corresponds with the detailed account of the heavenly Jerusalem in chap. 21. To express

the power of the dominion, be it in the symbol of the throne or in the symbol of the city, the Seer has to go into great detail.

22. In the Thrice Holy of the synagogue's prayer liturgy, the Qedusha, Ezek. 3:12 is combined with Is. 6. Nevertheless, a formal synthesis does not occur. On Trisagion and Qedusha, see A. Baumstark, "Trishagion und Qeduscha," *Jahrbuch für Liturgiewissenschaft* 3 (1923): 18ff.

23. If I understand correctly, this emphasis on the unceasing nature of the praise of the angels, even outside of Holy Scripture, is not current in Judaism. (R. H. Charles sees it differently in his commentary on the Apocalypse [*A Critical and Exegetical Commentary on the Revelation of St. John*, 2 vols. (New York, 1920)], 1: 125f., though he invokes texts that have been partly subjected to Christian re-working.) When Enoch 39:12 says, "Those who do not sleep praise you," that is a circumlocution for the so-called *egrēgoroi* angels ["Watcher-angels"] and does not yet have anything to do with the representation of a ceaseless praising. The Jewish perception, as it is expressed in the Pseudo-Jonathan Targum on Gen. 32:26, is rather that the angels in their praise are following a division of time defined by Jewish ritual. According to the tractate Hagiga 12b, the angels (in the fifth heaven) praise God by night but are silent by day because of the praises of Israel. Even the crude explanations in the tractate Hullin 91b on the Thrice Holy do not admit of any sense that the Thrice Holy is unceasing. See Hermann Strack and Paul Biller-beck, *Kommentar zum Neuen Testament aus Talmud und Midrasch*, 4 vols. (Munich, 1922–1956), 2: 177; nor is anything comparable shown (ibid., 4: 799).

24. Cf. Cassiodorus *Expositio psalmorum* (Explanation of the Psalms), *in Ps.* 148: "Nam sicut sunt immortalia [= ista de coelis], ita nec eorum laudes aliquo fine clauduntur (For as [the things of heaven] are immortal, so too their praises have no end)" (*PL* 70: 1042D).

25. The expressive richness of the "praise, honor, and thanksgiving" corresponds to the similar richness of the "sing, cry out, glorify, shout, and speak" in the liturgy of Mark. See F. E. Brightman, *Liturgies Eastern and Western*, vol. 1: *Eastern Liturgies* (Oxford, 1896), 131. This subject will be addressed later.

26. This is evident in the way *eucharistia* is used in Greek votive inscriptions giving thanks for a rescue or a healing.

27. On the angels' knowledge of supernatural mysteries, cf. Matthias Joseph Scheeben, *Handbuch der katholischen Dogmatik* (4 vols.; Freiburg im Br., 1873–1903), bk. 3 §181.2.4 (nos. 1134, 1135), 2: 486.

28. On obeisance in Revelation, cf. Johannes Horst, *Proskynein* (Gütersloh, 1932), 253 ff.

29. That the throne room becomes a temple is explained in that the heavenly Jerusalem becomes the temple of God. Rev. 21 and 22 say explicitly that the heavenly Jerusalem has no temple because God the Lord, the Almighty and the Lamb, *is* the temple of the heavenly city. In general in the Near East, temple and palace are usually closely associated. Cf., e.g., Kurt Möhlenbrink, *Der Tempel Salomos: eine*

Untersuchung seiner Stellung in der sakralarchitektur des alten Orients (The Temple of Solomon: An Investigation of its Position in the Sacred Architecture of the Ancient Near East) (Stuttgart, 1932), 48ff.; Hermann Thiersch in *Orientalistische Literaturzeitung* 36 (1933): 535.

30. The commentaries on Revelation stress that this is an oriental mode of homage, but the homage of Tiridates before Nero is any case to be interpreted differently. See on this Franz Cumont, *Rivista di filologia* 61 (1933): 148.

31. See Rev. 1:6, 20:6, 22:5, and 1 Pet. 2:9.

32. This is why the phrase "our Lord and God" (*dominus et deus noster*), the usage customary for the Roman emperors, is here said of God.

33. Because the Church's worship has this original relationship to the political sphere, ceremonies taken from the imperial cult are appropriately adopted in the Mass. I include here processions during Mass (whether with the Gospel or with the Eucharistic elements), in which thurifers are swung and candles carried. I consider an influence from the ceremonies of the imperial cult to be highly probable. Interesting, e.g., is the commentary of Pseudo-Sophronius on the Mass, which says, "The candles and wax tapers are a type of the eternal light," or "The wax tapers carried as an escort in the procession show the divine light" (in Angelo Mai, *Spicilegium Romanum*, 10 vols. [Rome, 1839–1844], 4: 35, 42). Here we feel reminded of the ceremonies in the imperial cult.

34. In 1929, using a formulation that admittedly lent itself to various misunderstandings, I wrote in my little treatise "Die Kirche": "But something of the Kingdom clings to the Church, both of the political desire of the Jews for the Kingdom of God, as well as of the claim to sovereignty of "the Twelve" in the Kingdom of God" [p. 38 in the present volume; *Theologische Traktate*, 423; *AS* 1: 254—Ed.]. Perhaps what I said then becomes more understandable in the light of the present exposition. The political relationship consists in the fact that the heavenly Jerusalem is not only a temple but also a polis. Thus Rev. 20:6 and 22:5 speak of a "ruling" with Christ. This co-ruling with Christ became a well-known topos in the literature on martyrdom, but the Church Fathers, too, among them St. Augustine, have given attention to the concept. For Augustine, see, e.g., Hofmann, *Kirchenbegriff des hl. Augustinus*, 498.

35. See Peterson, *Heis Theos*, 176ff., on the relationship of the *axios* acclamation to the political sphere.

36. Cf. Rev. 6:15 and Ps. 2:2ff. The phrase "kings of the earth" is eschatological vocabulary. Cf. also Acts 4:25f.

37. On this phrase, cf. also 7:9.

38. See the testimonies assembled in Adolf von Harnack, *Die Mission und Ausbreitung des Christentums*, 4th ed. (Leipzig, 1924), 1: 259ff. And see also Ambrose *De mysteriis* (On the mysteries) 4.23 (*unus solus populus Christianus*); Lactantius *Divine Institutes* 7.15 ("*populus dei ex omnibus linguis congregatus* [the people of God, gathered from all languages]"); Cassiodorus *in Ps.* 137 ("*populus catholicus*

. . . qui est collectus de universo orbe [the Catholic people . . . who have been gathered from the whole world]," *PL* 70: 979B); Augustine *Ep.* 54.1.1 ("sacramentis numero paucissimis . . . societatem novi populi colligavit [with the number of a very few sacraments . . . he has bound together the fellowship of a new people]," *PL* 33: 200); etc. Also, phrases like *regnante domino nostro Jesu Christo* (when our Lord Jesus Christ was reigning) (see, e.g., *Acts of Carpus* 7 in *Ausgewählte Märtyrerakten*, ed. G. Krüger and G. Ruhbach, 4th ed. (Tübingen, 1965), 13.24; *Acts of Maximus*, ibid., 61.36–37, *Acts of Cyprian*, ibid., 64.6–7; *Acts of Marcellus*, ibid., 89.28; *Martyrdom of Irenaeus*, ibid., 105.2), as well as the corresponding Greek phrase (*Martyrdom of Dasius* 12, ibid., 94.39; *Martyrdom of Agape*, ibid., 100.2; *Martyrdom of Pionius*, ibid., 57.13; *Martyrdom of Apollonius*, ibid., 35.14–15), assert that Christ has created a new people for himself, who bear the name of their ruling Lord.

39. On the parallelism between "royal priesthood" and "holy people," see 1 Pet. 2:9. Cf. also Rev. 7:9.

40. To this degree, then, the "eschatological" knowledge of the Church is set over against the "historical" knowledge that derives from the concrete political situation of a people.

41. For this reason it is only the theological and not the political writing of history that is truly capable of interpreting "history."

42. Cf. Augustine: "post captivitatem vetustatis cantans canticum novum [singing a new song after the captivity of old age]" (*Enchiridion* 56, *PL* 40: 258f.).

43. Greek *phōnē* can be a technical term for "acclamation." See Peterson, *Heis Theos*, 148.

44. We may observe that in St. Paul too (Phil. 2:11), the returning Christ is greeted, as in Rev. 5:13 and Heb. 12:23, by the threefold divided spiritual world with the acclamation "Jesus Christ is Lord." The eschatological acclamation of Christ by the entire spiritual world is apparently a common faith tradition among all the apostles. On the eschatological praise of God, see also Cassiodorus *in Ps.* 148:13 (*PL* 70: 1064A). Irenaeus (*Against Heresies* 1.10.1) also demonstrates the relationship of Phil. 2:10f. to the second coming of the Lord, likewise Romanos in his hymn on the second coming of Christ—see strophe 3 of the hymn "On the Last Day," in Karl Krumbacher, "Studien zu Romanos," Sitzungsberichte der königlichen bayerischen Akademie der Wissenschaften zu München, Philos.-Philol. und Hist. Cl., no. 2 (1898,), 165.62–166.69. Perhaps too a fragment of Hippolytus *Pros Hellēnas* (Against the Greeks) in Karl Holl, *Fragmente vornizänischer Kirchenväter aus den Sacra parallela* (Fragments of the Pre-Nicene Church Fathers from the Sacred Parallels), Texte und Untersuchungen, 20, no. 2 (Leipzig, 1899), 143, with its tripartite *angeloi, pneumata, anthrōpoi* (angels, spirits, human beings), should be set in this context.

45. The Jewish *bērakha* is intended here. There is no reason to reject the translation of *eulogia* as "blessing," as some recent commentators do.

46. On the animals' homage to Christ after his rejection of the temptation,

and on the eschatological homage of the animals, some good references are found in Horst, *Proskynein*, 216f.

47. Compare the "great throng" dressed in white garments and standing with palm branches in hand, who cry out, "Salvation belongs to our God, who sits on the Throne, and to the Lamb" (Rev. 7:9f.). Probably they correspond to "the souls of the just who have been made perfect" (*pneumata dikaiōn teteleiōmenōn*) who in Heb. 12:23 appear in the heavenly festal gathering. Hippolytus *Against the Greeks* likewise names the *pneumata* along with the *angeloi* (Holl, *Fragmente*, 143).

48. It is not my task here to explain the entire set of connections that link Revelation to worship or to any particular liturgy. On worship in Revelation, see J. C. W. Augusti, *Beiträge zur christlichen Kunstgeschichte und Liturgik*, 2 vols. (Leipzig, 1841–1846), 1: 82ff.; Weizsäcker in *Jahrbücher für deutsche Theologie* 21 (1876): 480ff.; Eduard Alexander von der Goltz, *Das Gebet in der ältesten Christenheit* (Prayer in Earliest Christianity) (Leipzig, 1901), 136f. and passim.

49. With this perspective in mind, one could explore whether the symbolic cultic acts in Rev. 4 and 5 don't also stand in some type of connection with political symbolism. Horst's investigation of obeisance in his instructive book *Proskynein* thus warrants further examination. Also worth considering is whether the thurifer and the zither in the hands of the elders come from the political world or at least in some way are related to it. On *turibula* in the imperial cult, see most recently Andreas Alföldi in *Römische Mitteilungen* 49 (1934), 114f. On the zither, note that under Theodoric, acclamations in Rome were offered "sub quadam harmonia citharae (under a certain harmony of the zither)" (Cassiodorus *Variae* [Various Letters] 1.31).

50. The *Corpus Christi* says: "mea lingua est graeca, mea est syra, mea est hebraea, mea est omnium gentium, quia in unitate sum omnium gentium [my language is Greek, it is Syriac, it is Hebrew, my [language] is that of all the nations, because I am in the unity of all the nations]" (Augustine, *in Ps.* 147, *PL* 37: 1919). Cf. Pacianus *Ep.* 2.4: "omnes linguas spiritus sanctus intelligit [the Holy Spirit understands all languages]." The opposite of this transcending of every language by the Holy Spirit is the Jewish understanding, as reported by Jerome, in his commentary on Zephaniah 3:9. The Jews say: "sicut ante aedificationem turris fuit, quando una lingua omnes populi loquebantur, ita conversis omnibus ad cultum veri Dei, locuturos Hebraice, et totum orbem Domino serviturum [as it was before the building of the tower, when all peoples spoke the same language, so they will all speak Hebrew once they have been converted to the worship of the true God, and the whole world will serve the Lord]" (*PL* 25: 1444A). On Hebrew as a "sacred language" according to the rabbis, see Strack and Billerbeck, *Kommentar*, 2:443f.

51. The wording of the Thrice Holy in the Jewish Qedusha is, as Baumstark, "Trishagion und Qeduscha," emphasizes, strictly biblical. I therefore believe that the formula *pasa hē ktisis* (all of creation), as found in 1 Clem. 34:6 is already a

Christian interpretation and not, as Baumstark (p. 29) assumes, of Jewish origin. Cf. the *pan ktisma* (every creature) in Rev. 5:13.

52. Greek text in Brightman, *Eastern Liturgies*, 131.

53. According to Acts 1:2, the apostles are described as losing sight of Christ in the course of his ascension to heaven.

54. I consider the enumeration of choirs of angels in *Constitutiones apostolicae* (Apostolic Constitutions) 7.35.3—where according to Bousset, Baumstark, and Lietzmann a fragment of the Jewish Qedusha is supposed to have survived—to be a product of Christian rewriting. If I am not mistaken, Judaism is acquainted with a military but not a specifically hierarchical segmentation of the angelic world. In general, I think the main argument for the Jewish origin of *Constit. Apost.* 7.35—the connection between Ezek. 3:12 and Is. 6—is problematic. Although it has not previously been noticed, we find the same association in Ps.-Dionysius *De caelesti hierarchia* (On the Celestial Hierarchy) 7.4. It would be difficult to presuppose a Jewish Qedusha for Ps.-Dionysius.

55. Dan. 7:10 is also used in Rev. 5:11, as well as in the Sanctus of the Letter of Clement 34:6. Perhaps the *myriades angelōn* (innumerable angels) of Heb. 12:22 also come from Dan. 7:10, in which case a recollection of a cultic Sanctus would probably underlie Heb. 12:22–23.

56. In *Doxa: Eine bedeutungsgeschichtliche Studie* (Glory: a Historical Study of Its Meaning) (Gütersloh, 1932), Johannes Schneider has completely ignored this concrete posing of the question.

57. Interesting too is Theodoret *in Jesajam* (On Isaiah) (ed. Möhle, 32.13): Israel *tēs proteras gymnothēsetai doxēs kai anti tou theiou phōtos tou Rōmaikou pyros eisdexetai ton kapnon* (Israel will be stripped of its former glory, and instead of the divine light it will get the smoke of the Roman fire). In general, this is good textual evidence for the thesis advanced vigorously by Schneider, *Doxa*, that *doxa* has the meaning of shining light.

58. Once we have become clear about the concrete development of the *doxa* concept, it no longer seems possible to derive the Trisagion in the Church's usage from a purely coincidental adoption from Jewish synagogal worship, as Baumstark, "Trishagion und Qeduscha," and Lietzmann, *Messe und Herrenmahl*, 258ff., have tried to do. It should further be noted that the demonstration by Jewish scholars of the late date of the Qedusha in the synagogal liturgy (see most recently Marmorstein in *Revue des études juives* [1934]) makes this adoption by the Church hardly conceivable.

59. Baumstark, "Trishagion und Qeduscha," seeks to demonstrate that the expansion "Heaven and earth" was of Jewish origin, but the passage from the Targum on the Prophets that he quotes (p. 30) does not seem to me to confirm what he wants to see in it. Noteworthy is the Trisagion in Enoch 30:12: "Holy, holy, holy is the Lord of the spirits, who fills the earth with spirits." Mention of heaven is thus missing here too.

60. That appears to me to be the methodological error of Baumstark and Lietzmann in the books just cited.

61. Cf. John 2:19–21, also Matt. 26:61.

62. Compare the words in the text of the liturgy: "All things forever declare your holiness."

63. The use of substantive rather than verbal forms reflects Semitic linguistic preferences. Unfortunately, the commentaries don't address this question. Manichean literature has parallels to the linguistic usage in Revelation. On this see Peterson, *Heis Theos*, 324f., the addendum to p. 226 n. 2.

64. So also Johannes Schneider, *Doxa*, 126. I realize, of course, that both Jewish apocalyptic literature (cf. Enoch 61:9) and the Qedusha show the same preponderance of verbs. But in my view, it fills another function in the Christian liturgy, because the Sanctus cry in Christian worship is *theologia*, i.e., singing inspired by the Holy Spirit. Thus already Cyril of Jerusalem *Mystagogical Catecheses* 5.6; the Syrian Liturgy of James (in Brightman, *Eastern Liturgies*, 86.6); the Liturgy of Basil (ibid., 323.25f.); and the Index in Brightman, s.v. Cf. also Lietzmann, *Messe und Herrenmahl*, 153. This "mystical" significance of the Sanctus will be treated later.

65. According to Baumstark, "Trishagion und Qeduscha," 25, the Hosanna formula in the Sanctus is supposed to have spread from the worship of the Church in Jerusalem to the other liturgies. If so, it must have arisen rather late, since it is known neither to Cyril of Jerusalem and the Antiochene Liturgy (*Apost. Const.* 8.12.27) nor to Theodore of Mopsuestia (see Lietzmann, *Die Liturgie des Theodor von Mopsuestia* [Berlin, 1933], 20).

66. It is naturally also structured differently from the Holy Cry (Qedusha) in Jewish worship, something not sufficiently noticed by Baumstark and Lietzmann, I think. Rudolf Otto's attempt to construct a universal category of "the Holy" naturally also strikes me as pointless.

67. See Brightman, *Eastern Liturgies*, 1:50.17ff.

68. Ps.-Cyprian, *Oratio* 1, in G. Hartel, ed., *Cypriani Opera, CSEL*, 3, pt. 3 (Vienna, 1871), 145.1–5.

69. [See the prefaces for the first Sunday in Lent—also known as Quadragesima Sunday—and the one used for the feast of the Holy Cross in the preconciliar Mass of the Roman Rite, as printed in *The Saint Andrew Daily Missal*, ed. Gaspar Lefebvre (St. Paul, Minn., 1940), 971.—Ed.]

70. The contrast between the angel and the creation, which praise God unceasingly, and humanity, which is lazy as regards divine praise, is expressed eloquently by St. Basil in his commentary on Ps. 28 (*PG* 29: 301D).

71. On the "dignum et justum est" as a legally binding acclamation, cf. Peterson, *Heis Theos*, 178 n. 4. Also cf. St. Augustine: "Et vos adtestamini: 'Dignum et iustum est' [And you bear witness: "It is right and just"]" (Sermon 227). Cf. id.: "Respondetis. 'Habemus ad Dominum.' Laborate ut verum respondeatis, quia

apud acta Dei respondetis [You answer: "We have lifted [them] to the Lord." Be careful to answer truthfully, since you answer in the presence of the acts of God]" (*Sancti Augustini Sermones, post Maurinos reperti* [Sermons of Saint Augustine, Discovered after the Maurists], ed. Germanus Morin, in *Miscellanea Agostiniana*, 2 vols. [Rome, 1930–1931], 1: 31.6–8). Also see Cyril of Jerusalem *Myst. Catech.* 5.4: *"echomen pros ton kyrion." Toutōi synkatatithemenoi, di' hōn homologeite* ("We have lifted [them] up to the Lord." Assenting to this, by these words you express your agreement).

72. Cf. Clement of Alexandria *Stromateis* (Miscellanies) 4.8.66.1 (ed. Stählin, 278.10ff.): *eikōn de tēs ouraniou ekklēsias hē epigeios, hoper euchometha kai "epi gēs genesthai to thelēma hōs en ouranōi."* (The image of the heavenly Church is the earthly one, as we pray "your will be done on earth as in heaven.") Further, Hilary *Tractatus super psalmos* (Tractate on the Psalms), *in Ps.* 134:22, "ut, sicut voluntati eius in caelis ab indefessis et caelestibus virtutibus paretur, ita et a nobis parea-tur, ne corporalis nos infirmitas ab exequenda eius voluntate deflectat, in caelis enim indefessis cotidie vocibus dicitur: sanctus, sanctus, sanctus, Dominus Deus Sabaoth, pleni sunt caeli et terra gloria tua [so that, as it is offered to his will in heaven by the unwearying and heavenly powers, so too it may be offered by us, let bodily weakness not divert us from following his will, for in heaven is said daily by unwearying voices: Holy, holy, holy, Lord God of Hosts, heaven and earth are full of your glory]" (ed. A. Zingerle, *CSEL*, 22 [Vienna, 1891], 708.22–27). Tertullian *De Oratione* (On Prayer) 3 already links the Our Father's "hallowing" of the name of God with the angels' Sanctus.

73. This is an Augustinian idea. Cf. *Enchiridion* 62.16: "Instauratur quippe quae in caelis sunt, cum id, quod in angelis lapsum est, ex hominibus redditur [What belonged to heaven is restored, when what the angels lost is given back from humankind]." See further Augustin, *City of God* 22.1; *Augustini Sermones*, ed. Morin, 1: 480.20–21. According to Gregory the Great, the ninety-nine sheep that in Jesus' parable stay with the shepherd are the angels, while humanity is the one sheep that strays away (*PL* 76: 1247B–C; cf. 76: 1252 B–C).

74. Also instructive is Nicetas of Remesiana *De symbolo* (On the Creed) 10: "Etiam angeli, etiam virtutes et potestates supernae in hac una confoederantur ecclesia [The angels too, and also the heavenly virtues and powers, are joined to-gether in this one Church]" (*PL* 52: 871B = C.P. Caspari, *Kirchenhistorische Anec-dota, nebst neuen Ausgaben patristischer und kirchlich- mittelalterlicher Schriften* (Church-Historical Narratives, with New Editions of Patristic and Ecclesiastical-Medieval Writings) (Christiania [Oslo], 1883], 1: 355f. On this whole complex of ideas, cf. also J. P. Kirsch, *Die Lehre von der Gemeinschaft der Heiligen im christli-chen Altertum* (The Doctrine of the Communion of Saints in Christian Antiquity) (Mainz, 1900).

75. On the concept of the heavenly hierarchy, cf. Scheeben, *Dogmatik*, bk. 3 §142.3.3 (no. 237), 2: 89. The angels are "not simply different groups juxtaposed

next to one another, but different orders structured vertically, like the several estates of a kingdom and the several ranks in an army." To support his thesis, Scheeben could have cited the following interesting passage from Gregory the Great *Epistolae* (Letters) bk. 5, *Letter* 54 (*PL* 77: 786A): "Quia vero creatura in una eademque aequalitate gubernari vel vivere non potest, coelestium militarium exemplar nos instruit, quia dum sunt angeli, et sunt archangeli, liquet quod non sunt aequales, sed in potestate et ordine, sicut nostis, differt alter ab altero [That creation cannot live or be governed in one and the same equality, the example of the heavenly ranks teaches us that inasmuch as some are angels and others archangels, clearly they are not equal, but, as you know, one differs from the other in power and rank]."

76. That the monks imitate the existence and the liturgy of the angels in their ordering means that they become similar to the angels through their participation in the angels' life and their office—it does not meant that they *become* angels.

77. On the Sanctus as the prayer of the people, cf., e.g., G. Nickl, *Der Anteil des Volkes an der Meßliturgie im Frankenreich von Chlodwig bis auf Karl den Grossen* (The Participation of the People in the Celebration of the Mass in the Frankish Kingdom from Clovis to Charlemagne) (Innsbruck, 1930), 24f.

78. The "cry" of the Seraphim is perhaps to be interpreted as a symbolic expression for *alalazein*, which is an archaic cultic cry. In another context, it could then be interpreted as a mystical *krazein*. On the latter, cf. Peterson, *Heis Theos*, 191f., n. 3. On the "cry" of the angels, there is a short note in Scheeben, *Dogmatik*, bk. 3 § 141.1.2 (no. 219), 2: 83.

79. *Epinikios hymnos* (Victory Hymn) in the Liturgy of St. John Chrysostom: see Brightman, *Eastern Liturgies*, 313.24; further, the Liturgy of St. James, ibid., 50.29. The designation *epinikios ōidē* for the Thrice Holy is found in John Chrysostom *On the Baptism of Christ* 4 (*Opera*, 2: 374C). In the designation of the angels' Sanctus cry as a "victory hymn," reference is made to the "victory of the Lion of Judah," Christ, who has ascended into heaven and sits at the right hand of the Father. The interpretation that Johannes Brinktrine, *Der heilige Messe* (The Holy Mass) (Paderborn, 1931), 148 n. 1, gives to the expression ("this designation refers to the idea that the angels fight for God"), seems inappropriate to me, because it is "the Lion of Judah" who has "conquered," not the angels.

80. See the Greek text in J. B. Pitra, *Analecta sacra*, 8 vols. (Paris, 1876–1891), 3: 314. Whether this text actually comes from Origen could only be established by a study of the history of patristic exegesis of the psalms. Strangely, research on a topic so important to early Church piety has hardly begun.

81. Besides Origen, this is an idea that can also be found, for example, in Didymus (?) *In Ps.* 4 (*PG* 39: 1165A). Cf. the same on Ps. 146, where the higher activity, in comparison with the psalm, is called *theologia* (*PG* 39: 1612A). See also Gregory of Nyssa in the *Psalms Catena* (*PG* 69: 708B). In Origen (?) *in Ps.* 39:4 (see Pitra, *Analecta sacra*, 3: 35), *hymnos*, as compared to *asma kainon* (new song), stands for a yet higher level.

82. Cf. the text in J. B. Pitra, *Hymnographie de l'église grecque* (Hymnography of the Greek Church) (diss., Rome, 1867), 43, where it is asserted that the singing of *troparia kai kanones kai ēchoi* (troparia, canons, and modes) is fit for secular priests and laypeople, but for monks often harmful.

83. *Hoi psalmoi panta echousin, hoi de hymnoi palin ouden anthrōpinon . . . hate theioteron pragma. Hai gar anō dunameis hymnousin, ou psallousin* (The psalms have everything, but hymns have nothing human . . . inasmuch as their subject is more divine. For the powers above sing hymns, not psalms) (John Chrysostom *in epistulam ad Colossianos* [On the Letter to the Colossians] 3.9.2).

84. The substantive distinction of the literary genres, which precedes Christianity, did not yet lead to a ranking of religious singing conditioned via transcending.

85. That the angels sing with *one* voice is often said in the literature of antiquity.

86. Franz Leitner, *Der gottesdienstliche Volksgesang im jüdischen und christlichen Altertum* (Liturgical Popular Music in Jewish and Christian Antiquity) (Freiburg im Br., 1906), 257ff., tries to explain ancient Christianity's rejection of instrumental music in terms of the reaction against the pagan sacrificial cult and a "spiritual understanding of the Christian life" (260). I believe that the thesis of our treatise leads to a theological understanding of the early Church's rejection of instrumental music. Leitner rightly says (258): "Because the churches of both East and West originally agreed on this, while for example there was variation in singing practices at least until near the end of the fourth century, reasons of principle must have been decisive." I would like to suggest that these "reasons of principle" were laid down by the apostles when they cut their link with the Temple in Jerusalem, along with its music, in order to draw near to the heavenly temple, in which the angels alone sing. See also Zonaras, *Expositio canonum Damasceni* (Exposition of the Canons of John of Damascus) (*PG* 135: 425C). It is noteworthy that today even the Benedictines do not renounce the use of the organ at Mass.

87. On the symbolic interpretation of the musical instruments, cf. Th. Gérold, *Les pères de l'église et la musique* (The Fathers of the Church and Music) (Paris, 1931), 123ff.

88. For example, Regino of Prüm (d. 915) in Martin Gerbert, *Scriptores ecclesiastici de musica sacra*, 3 vols. (Sankt Blasien im Schwarzwald, 1784), 1: 235a, who appeals to Macrobius, but also to Christian writers who agree *in hac coelesti harmonia* (about this heavenly harmony). On the doctrine of the harmony of the spheres in Macrobius, see now Karl Mras, *Der Kommentar des Macrobius zu Ciceros Somnium* (Macrobius's Commentary on Cicero's *Dream*) (Berlin, 1933), 35ff. Cassiodorus *On the Arts and Disciplines of the Liberal Arts* (*PL* 70: 1209A and 1212B) speaks without reservation of the harmony of the spheres. In his commentary on Ps. 148, he deals with a theological correction of this doctrine: "Sed nos obsequia naturalium rerum ad auctoris referamus imperium [But let us refer the obedience of natural things back to the command of (their) author]" (*PL* 70: 1047C). In his exposition of Ps. 1, Ambrose unhesitatingly juxtaposes the harmony

of the spheres with the angels' song of praise (*PL* 14: 96A). In his treatise *De Isaac vel anima* (On Isaac or the Soul) 7 (ed. C. Schenkl, *Sancti Ambrosii Opera, CSEL* 32, pt. 1 [Vienna, 1897], 686.21–687.3), he speaks of the harmony of the spheres. In *De Abrahamo* (On Abraham) 2.8 (ibid., 608.7f.), on the other hand, the polemic against the music of the spheres runs parallel with the polemic against Plato (*Timaeus* 36B–40A).

89. "Dicat aliquis: Quomodo sol et luna et stella laudant Deum? In eo, quod a suo officio et servitio non recedunt. Servitium ipsorum laus Dei est (Someone may say: "How do the sun and moon and stars praise God?" In this sense, that they do not diverge from their duty and their service)": Jerome on Ps. 148, in *Commentarioli in Psalmos*, Anecdota Maredsolana, ed. Germain Morin(1895–1903), 3.2: 307.28–30.

90. Cf. inter alia Plotinus 6.9.8, on the circular motion of the divine stars. Elsewhere we read too of the *periphora* (revolution) of the stars (or spheres): Plato *Phaedrus* 246f. and *Republic* 8.546; Ps.-Plato *Axiochos* 370B; Maximus of Tyre 41.2b; Hippolytus *Refutation* 7.32. The *periphora* ultimately becomes the *choros* (dance).

91. On the *jubilus*, see Gérold, *Les pères de l'église et la musique*, 120ff. The passage cited in the text is from Augustine *in Ps.* 46 ("Ascendit Deus in jubilatione" [God goes up with a joyful shout]). The passages that Gérold cites from Jerome and Augustine could easily be multiplied from other authors, such as, e.g., Cassiodorus *in Ps.* 32 (*PL* 70: 226D, *in Ps.* 46 (*PL* 70: 334C and 333B), *in Ps.* 65 (ibid., 451C), *in Ps.* 88 (ibid., 633B), *in Ps.* 94 (ibid., 672A), *in Ps.* 97 (ibid., 689D), *in Ps.* 99 (ibid., 697D); Gregory the Great *Moralia* (*PL* 76: 292A and 856A). In general, it is noteworthy that in Christian antiquity, the *jubilus* is felt—in completely unromantic fashion—as a defect in contrast to the pure singing of the angels. Cf. especially the contrast between the imperfect *jubilatio* of humanity and the praise of the angels in Gregory *Moralia* bk. 28.15 §§ 34, 35 (*PL* 76: 468).

92. Cf., e.g., Ambrose *De mysteriis* 4.22 and *De sacramentis* (On the Sacraments) 2.2. The latter passage shows that the text from the Gospel of John was part of the scriptural reading in the Mass for the baptized. It is still found today in the Mass at Milan. (See Ballerini in the edition of the works of St. Ambrose, 4: 466.)

93. See J. Amann, "L'ange du baptême dans Tertullien" (The Baptismal Angel in Tertullian), *Revue des sciences religieuses* 1 (1921): 208f.

94. Also see the Sacramentary of Autun (*PL* 72: 274D).

95. See also the prayer for the blessing of the water on the feast of Epiphany: *Idou gar ho tēs heortēs hēmin kairos kai angeloi meta anthrōpōn heortazousi kai choros hagiōn plēsiazetai hēmin* (for behold, the time of your feast is upon us, and angels celebrate along with humankind and the chorus of the saints draws near to us), in Alexi Dmitriewski, *Beschreibung der liturgischen Handschriften in den Bibliotheken des rechtgläubigen Ostens* (Description of the Liturgical Manuscripts in the Libraries of the Orthodox East), vol. 2: *Euchologia* (Prayerbooks) (Kiev, 1901), 8.

96. Cf. Ambrose *De sacramentis* 4.6.27: "ut hanc oblationem suscipias in sub-

limi altari tuo per manus angelorum tuorum, sicut suscipere dignatus es [that you would accept this offering your sublime altar by the hands of your angels, just as you deigned (to accept)]."

97. On the Mozarabic prayers in which angels are named as bearers of sanctification, see Lietzmann, *Messe und Herrenmahl*, 103. Lietzmann's effort to reconstruct the development remains very hypothetical.

98. This is true even though the mention of the *archangelikē latreia* (archangelic worship) is missing in the (previously unnoticed) oldest citation of this prayer from the Liturgy of St. Mark in Cosmas Indicopleustes. See my article "Die Alexandrinische Liturgie bei Cosmas Indicopleustes (The Alexandrian Liturgy in Cosmas Indicopleustes)," in *Ephemerides Liturgicae* 46 (Rome, 1932): 66–77. I doubt that Lietzmann is right when he interprets the prayer in the Roman canon as an ancient incense prayer that only later was added to the Eucharistic elements (*Messe und Herrenmahl*, 120).

99. In this context, the whole question can naturally only be touched on. Cf. elsewhere Paul Cagin, *Te Deum ou Illatio? Contributions à l'histoire de l'Euchologie latine à propos des origines du* Te Deum (*Te Deum or Illatio?* Contributions to the History of the Latin Euchologia a propos of the Origins of the *Te Deum*) (Oxford, 1906), 220f.; Maurice de la Taille and A. d'Alès, "La sacrifice céleste et l'Ange du Sacrifice," in *Recherches de science religieuse* 13 (1923): 218f.; Bernard Botte, "L'ange du sacrifice," in *Cours et conferences des Semaines liturgiques* 7 (1929): 209f.; id., "L'ange du sacrifice et l'épiclèse au moyen âge" (The Angel of Sacrifice and the *Epiclesis* [Invocation Prayer] in the Middle Ages), *Recherches de théologie ancienne et médiévale* 1 (1929): 285f.

100. The notion of the angels gazing upon the newly baptized as they move toward the altar, attested to by Ambrose *De sacramentis* 4.2.5, is different. Recital of the baptismal creed *coram angelis* (before the angels) follows, according to Nicetas *De symbolo* (see *PL* 52: 873A).

101. Text of the translation from John Chrysostom according to August Nägle, *Johannes Chrysostomus: Sechs Bücher über das Priestertum* (Six Books On the Priesthood), Bibliothek der Kirchenväter, series 1, no. 27 (Munich, 1916), 227. Nägle quotes parallel passages in *Die Eucharistielehre des heiligen Johannes Chrysostomus des Doctor Eucharistiae* (The Eucharistic Doctrine of St. John Chrysostom, Doctor [= Teacher] of the Eucharist), Straßburger theologische Studien 3, no. 4–5 (Freiburg im Br., 1900), 104–105.

102. From the German translation by Simon Weber in *Ausgewählte Schriften der armenischen Kirchenväter*, ed. id., Bibliothek der Kirchenväter, ser. 1, no. 58 (Munich, 1927), 226. Cf. also the anonymous citation in *Makarius Magnes*, ed. Schalkhauser, II.16–17: *epi ta theia dōra katerchomenon to pur kai meta to pur plēthos angelōn* (upon the divine gifts fire descends, and after the fire a throng of angels); ibid., II.19: *kai hoi men angeloi hestēkan kuklōi tēs hagias trapezēs* (and the angels stand in a circle around the holy table). And see in general also *The Liturgical Hom-*

ilies of Narsai, ed. R. H. Connolly, Texts and Studies: Contributions to Biblical and Patristic Literature, 8, no. 1 (Cambridge, 1909), 7. From this perspective, it becomes understandable why the priest in the Greek Church prays: *angelon de phōtos, sulleitourgounta kai enischuonta me, katapempson* (send down the angel of light, who concelebrates and confirms me), in the holy Mass (Dmitriewski, *Euchologia,* 171). A well-known inscription from Syria should then be understood on the basis of the same set of ideas: *Theou gegonen oikos to tōn daimonōn katagōgion . . . hopou thusiai eidōlōn, nun choroi angelōn* (The residence of the demons has become the house of God . . . where [once were] sacrifices to idols, now [there are] choirs of angels) (from AD 515). See William Kelly Prentice, *Greek and Latin Inscriptions* (New York, 1908), no. 437a = Dittenberger, *Orientis graeci inscriptiones selectae,* 2, no. 610.

103. Cf. *Zeitschrift für systematische Theologie* 7 (1929–1930), 682ff.

104. It is instructive to compare the application of the passage in Ps. 137:1 in St. Benedict with the interpretation of the psalms in the early Church. As far as I can see, nowhere does one find a similarly straightforward interpretation. I cite the following texts in which the psalm verse is expounded: Augustine, *PL* 37: 1775, 1776; Hilary, *CSEL* 22: 736.27–737.24; Jerome, in *Anecdota Maredsolana,* ed. Morin, 3, 2: 266.9ff.; Arnobius, *PL* 53: 542D; Eusebius, *PG* 24: 37C. Cassiodorus, *PL* 70: 980A, comes the closest to Benedict.

105. Paul Warnefrid [more commonly known as Paul the Deacon, author of other monastic writings and an important history of the Lombards—Ed.] was copied by Hildemar (*PL* 66: 473A). In his commentary on the holy Rule, Smaragdus does not touch on the angels (*PL* 102: 839). The interpretation of the English Benedictines in the *Regula Benedicti cum declarationibus et constitutionibus congregationis Anglicae* (Rule of Benedict, with Declarations and Constitutions of the English Congregation) (Stanbrook, 1909), 44 ("cum primarium officium nostrum sit in terra praestare, quod angeli in coelo [since our primary duty is to perform on earth what the angels do in heaven]"), endorsed by E. C. Butler, *Benedictine Monachism: Studies in Benedictine Life and Rule* (London, 1919), trans. as *Benediktinisches Mönchtum: Studien über benediktinisches Leben und die Regel St. Benedikts* (St. Ottilien, Oberbayern, 1929), 31, introduces a foreign idea into the text of the holy Rule.

106. On this see Gougaud in *Ephemerid. Liturg.* 41 (1927): 188.

107. Ibid., 188 n. 1. Cf. also Saint Bernard, Sermon 7, *in Canticum Canticorum* (On the Song of Songs): "Doleo aliquos vestrum gravi in sacris vigiliis deprimi somno, nec coeli cives revereri, sed in praesentia principum tamquam mortuos apparere [I grieve that some of you are sunk in deep sleep during the sacred vigils, nor do you reverence the citizens of heaven, but in the presence of princes, you look as though you are dead]."

108. Bernard of Clairvaux, *Sermon 7, in Cant.* (*PL* 183: 808) also says: "Credimus angelos sanctos astare orantibus (We believe the holy angels stand by our side as we pray)."

109. Cf. Elias of Nisibis in the edition of L. Horst, *Des Metropoliten Elias von Nisibis Buch vom Beweis der Wahrheit des Glaubens* (The Metropolitan Elias of Nisibis's Book on the Proof of the Truth of the Faith) (diss., Colmar, 1886), 90: "There[= in the church] a person enjoys security, there the angels stand by." The reference is to the church building. On this basis we can understand why Pachomius in his vision sees the whole church full of angels (*Pachomii Vitae*, ed. Halkin, 104.16ff.). The Gargano legend—according to which the emperor Henry II sees the angels with Christ going to holy Mass in the church at night (*Monum. Germ. Scriptores*, 4: 818)—also belongs in this context; see now J. Bernhart, *Der Engel des Deutschen Volkes* (The Angel of the German People) (Munich, 1934), 73–74.

110. [Ger., *Weckholz*, Grk., *sēmantron*; the reference is to the sounding-board that is struck with a mallet at the beginning of the service in Byzantine churches.—Ed.]

111. The *bēma* recalls the *epouranion thusiastērion* (heavenly sacrificial altar) (Mai, *Spicilegium Romanum*, 4: 33), and when the priests give the body of the Lord to the people, they handle it as did the Seraphim that laid the burning coals on the lips of Isaiah (ibid.). Cf. also, e.g., Germanus on the correspondence of the heavenly and the earthly *thusiastērion* (N. Borgia, *Il commentario liturgico di S. Germano* [The Liturgical Commentary of St. Gemanus] [Grottaferrata, 1912], 12.26ff.); on the *sēmantron* he speaks (10.26) as does Ps.-Sophronius. Germanus's interpretation of the *Cheroubikos hymnos* (Cherubic Hymn) (29.34ff.) is important. Note also that in the blessing for the consecration of a deacon in the *Gelasian Sacramentary*, the service of the deacon is apparently placed in parallel with the service of the angels (ed. Wilson, 28).

112. This doctrine of the angels of the Church (based on Rev. 2 and 3) has especially been explored by Origen, though we do not need to touch on that here, nor on the concept of the ship of the Church, in which the angels are the rudders: Hippolytus *De antichristo* (On the Antichrist) 59, ed. H. Achelis, in *Hippolytus Werke*, vol. 1, pt. 2: *Hippolyt's kleinere exegetische und homiletische Schriften* (Leipzig, 1897), 40.3f.; *Opus imperfectum in Matthaeum* (Unfinished Work on Matthew) (*PG* 56: 753). Cf. John Chrysostom, *in synaxim archangelorum* (On the Assembly of the Archangels) (*PG* 59: 756): *kath' hekastēn de ekklēsian epestēsen angelous phulakas ho Christos* (Christ has appointed guardian angels over every church).

113. Mariano San Nicolò, *Ägyptisches Vereinswesen zur Zeit der Ptolemäer und Römer* (Egyptian Associations in the Ptolemaic and the Roman Periods), Münchener Beiträge zur Papyrusforschung, no. 2 (Munich, 1913–1915), 2: 99, remarks:

Aristotle identifies the state as an acting subject with the assembled citizens, and in the documents of the Greek and also the Egyptian associations this idea can be traced with still greater clarity, in that in no association does the assembly of the members appear as "a collegial organ of a corporate unity that is distinct from it" [Otto von Gierke, *Das deutsche Genossenschaftsrecht*, 4 vols. (Berlin, 1868–1913), 2: 485]; it is rather the society itself, which voluntarily appears, secures rights, and enters into obligations. The Greek standpoint is much more concrete than ours: it is the truly visible society, which in the assembly and not through the assembly wills and acts as its organ.

San Nicolò's arguments, especially the last sentence, are equally valid for the early Church *ekklēsia*.

114. Because the synods in their original forms just change the appearance of the liturgical *ekklēsia*, it is not surprising that they too speak of the angels. I recall here the letter of the Council of Arles to Silvester of Rome: "Placuit ergo, praesente Spiritu sancto et angelis eius" (J. D. Mansi, ed., *Sacrorum conciliorum, nova et amplissima collectio*, 54 vols. [Paris, 1901–1927]) 2: 469).

115. Yet to be investigated is the question of the extent to which the ancient practice of conducting legal business in the presence of the gods is analogous to the Christian conception of conducting legal business in the presence of the angels. In any case, "before the gods" in actuality means in the presence of the gods' statues. See the manumission documents from Hyampolis (*Inscriptiones graecae*, 9, pt. 1, ed. W. Dittenberger [Berlin, 1897], no. 86) and from Thespiai (*Inscriptiones graecae*, 7, ed. W. Dittenberger [Berlin, 1892], no. 1779 [cf. 1780]). On which, see Adolf Wilhelm, *Neue Beiträge zur griechischen Inschriftenkunde* (New Contributions to Greek Epigraphical Sources), Sitzungsberichte der Wiener Akademie, 1 (1910), 1–2. A related concept is the occasional practice of drafting the marriage contract before the image of a member of the imperial family. See Ulrich Wilcken, *Zeitschrift der Savigny-Stiftung, Romanistische Abteilung* 30: 504ff., and Wilhelm, *Neue Beiträge*.

116. See Peterson, "Zur Bedeutungsgeschichte von *parrēsia*" (On the History of the Meaning of *parrēsia* [free speech]), in W. Koepp, ed., *Festchrift für Reinhold Seeberg* (Leipzig, 1929), 1:283ff.

117. St. Gregory the Great describes the "mystical" life of the angels in the following way: "In hac aeternitate angeli sancti vino sapientiae inebriantur, dum ipsum Deum facie ad faciem videntes, omni voluptate spiritali satiantur" (*In Cantica* [On Songs] 2.4 [*PL* 79: 459D]). According to the Church's tradition, the name of the "seraph" expresses the glow of ecstatic and loving union with God. See Scheeben, *Dogmatik*, bk. 3 §142.3.4a (no. 240), 2: 90.

118. *Kephalaia gnōstika* 67, in Diadochus Photicensis, *Diadoque de Photicé: Oeuvres spirituelles*, ed. Édouard Des Places, S.J., Sources chrétiennes 5, 3rd ed. (Paris, 1966), 127.10–19. See Richard Reitzenstein, *Historia monachorum und Historia Lausiaca* (Göttingen, 1916), 133 n. 4.

119. On the teaching of Evagrius Ponticus, see Wilhelm Bousset, *Apophthegmata: Studien zur Geschichte des ältesten Mönchtums* (Sayings [of the Fathers]: Studies in the History of the Earliest Monasticism) (Tübingen, 1923).

120. On the choirs of angels and the mystical ascent in St. Augustine, see Cuthbert Butler, *Western Mysticism* (London, 1922), 33. It is also obviously a theme in the Ps.-Areopagitic corpus.

121. We need to mention these simple truths explicitly because Protestant the-

ology in Germany—especially under Ritschl's influence—no longer recognizes such distinctions.

122. So, e.g., Orpheus serves as a *theologos*.

123. See, e.g., *The Christian Topography of Cosmas Indicopleustes*, ed. E. O. Winstedt (Cambridge, 1909), 83.28ff.: *hoi men gar tōn angelōn ton aera kinein epetreponto, hoi de ton hēlion, hoi de tēn selēnēn, alloi ta astra, heteroi nephelas kai brochas ergazomenoi kai hetera polla* (Some of the angels were given charge of moving the air, others the sun, others the moon, others the stars, and still others control the clouds and the rains and many other things). See too the citation from Epiphanius, ibid., 309.1ff. That the angels move the stars is a doctrine of the Nestorians. See Heinrich Kihn, *Theodor von Mopsuestia und Junilius Africanus als Exegeten* (Theodore of Mopsuestia and Junilius Africanus as Exegetes) (Freiburg im Br., 1880), 425. See further Slavic Enoch 4 (stars), 5 (snow and clouds), 6 (dew), 19 (seasons and years, rivers and seas, fruits and grass, all have their angels).

124. Ps.-Dionysius, *Celestial Hierarchy* 7.1, also expresses this idea.

125. The Christian doctrine of the angels is, as various expositions have shown, especially closely linked with the doctrine of Christ's Ascension. Apart from Sacred Scripture, see, e.g., ibid., 7.3.

126. Cf. Gal. 1:8.

127. Cf. 1 John 3:2.

128. The virtues of someone "like an angel" are metaphysical and not moral.

129. The appearance of the seraph in the stigmatization of St. Francis is not a coincidence but reflects an intrinsic theological connection. Cf. Bonaventure in his *Life of St. Francis*.

130. Cf. Gregory the Great, *Homilies on Ezechiel* 1.8.28: "in omne quod ab angelis amatur per omne quod ab hominibus desideratur, unus est, qui in cordibus ardet amantium [in everything that is loved by the angels, through everything that is desired by human beings, there is one [person] who burns in the hearts of those who love]" (*PL* 76: 867). In the same text it says further: "eius membra sunt electi angeli in coelo, eius membra sunt conversi homines in terra [his (Christ's) members are the elect angels in heaven, his members are converted human beings on earth]." In John of Damascus: *di' emou [Christ] angelōn kai anthrōpōn mia ekklēsia genēsetai* (through me [Christ] one Church of angels and human beings comes into being) (*Homily on the Withered Fig* [*PG* 96: 584D]). Cf., too, the epigraph from Bossuet that I have placed at the beginning of this little book, which I found in a noteworthy article by Père Yves Congar, O.P., "Sur les saints Anges" (On the Holy Angels), *La Vie spirituelle* 37 (1933), 18–28 , who quotes the passages in St. Thomas that discuss the holy angels' affiliation to the Church.

131. *Angeloi met' anthrōpōn syneortazousi*, Sophronius in the *Euchologion to mega* (The Great Euchologion) (Rome, 1873), 221.18. Ps.-Gregory of Nyssa, *On the Presentation of the Lord* (*PG* 46: 1156B): *hē tōn anō pneumatōn hagia panēguris tēi tōn anthrōpōn sōtēriai lian ephēdetai. Houtō gar koinēi panegurizein syn tois epigeiois ta*

ourania eiōthen, tēn angeloprepē politeian tōn epi gēs aspazomenōn (The holy assembly of the spirits above rejoices greatly at the salvation of human beings. For the heavenly [spirits] are thus accustomed to hold festal assembly jointly with those on earth, when they embrace the way of life fit for the angels). In the Post Sanctus of the fifth Sunday of Lent in the Mozarabic liturgy, it says: "vere hec illa preclara et admirabilis supernarum creaturarum eterna laudatio: que celestibus sine defectu psallitur ab angelis: et hic solenniter decantatur a populis. Illic conclaudant celestia, hic adorant terrestria [truly, this excellent and admirable praise of the creatures on high is eternal: it is sung without ceasing by the heavenly angels: and here is chanted by the people. There the heavenly powers join together in praise, here those on earth adore]" (Marius Férotin, *Le Liber Mozarabicus sacramentorum et les manuscrits mozarabes* [The Mozarabic Sacramentary and the Mozarabic Manuscripts], Monumenta ecclesiae liturgica, 6 [Paris, 1912], 542ff. [1190]). See also St. Bernard of Clairvaux: "Laudem ergo cum coeli cantoribus in commune dicentes, utpote cives sanctorum et domestici dei, psallite sapienter [Since you are therefore joined with the singers of heaven in giving praise, inasmuch as you are citizens with the saints and household servants of God, sing wisely]" (*Sermon 7, On the Song of Songs*).

132. We may recall the legend about St. Ignatius of Antioch, who is supposed to have heard the angels singing in antiphony; cf. Socrates *Hist. eccl.* 6.8 (*PG 67*: 689C–692A), Cassiodorus *Historia Tripartita* (Three-part History) 10.9 (PL69: 1171D), and Nicephorus 13.8 [Nicephorus Callistus Xanthopulus *Historia ecclesiastica* 13.8 (*PG* 146: 978A)]. The story was very widespread in the Middle Ages—see, e.g., the *Tonarius* of Regino of Prüm in Charles Edmond Henri de Coussemaker, *Scriptores de musica medii aevi*, n.s., 2: 1 (Paris, 1867), and Rupert of Deutz *in Regulam Sancti Benedicti* (On the Rule of St. Benedict) 2.5 (*PL* 170: 502C). The significance attributed to the Alleluia of the "heavenly" singing is noteworthy. Nicetas concludes from this that if the Alleluia song "is sung with appropriate faith and devotion, it is joined with the angels [digna fide et devotione celebretur, angelis esse coniunctum]" (G. Morin in *Rev. bénéd.* 14 [1897]: 396.187ff.). Remarkable too—and apparently not yet noticed—is that Isidore of Seville *De ecclesiasticis officiis* (On the Ecclesiastical Offices) 1.13 (*PL* 83: 750B) speaks of the Alleluia song in the exactly the same words. Cf. further Cassiodorus *in Ps.* 145 (*PL* 70: 1629B).

133. Especially instructive on this is the *Cheroubikos hymnos* in the Byzantine liturgy. I cite from the version *Sigēsatō pasa sarx* (Let all flesh be silent) (on the various forms of the *Cheroubikon*, see Brightman, Index, 573) the following lines: *ho gar basileus tōn basileuontōn Christos ho theos hemōn proerchetai* (for the king of kings, Christ our God, is coming) [i.e. in the Great Entrance], *sphagiasthēnai kai dothēnai eis brōsin tois pistois, proēgountai de toutou hoi choroi tōn angelōn meta pasēs archēs kai exousias* (to be sacrificed and given as food for the faithful, before him advance choirs of angels with every power and dominion), etc. (Brightman, 41.30–42.3).

134. In these notes, occasional reference is made to the pseudo-Areopagitic writings, which correspond in the dogmatic frame of reference to a tradition that radiates from primitive Christianity throughout the entire ancient Church; philosophically speaking, they are, of course, Neoplatonic.

135. It is noteworthy that the *Te Deum* addresses God as *Pater immensae majestatis* (Father of immense majesty) and the Son as *Rex gloriae* (King of glory). Thus the *Te Deum* too testifies to the religio-political language of the Christian cultus.

CHAPTER 7: CHRIST AS *IMPERATOR*

1. Adolf von Harnack calls this "a designation that I have not encountered elsewhere" ("Die Pfaff'sche Irenäus Fragmente als Fälschungen Pfaffs nachgewiesen, Patristische Miscellen," in Texte und Untersuchungen, 20, no. 3 [1900], 144).

2. In this particular Sibylline oracle, the subject is God, who is called *hēgētēs* (Leader) (frgm. 1, v. 6).

3. Cf. *Augustini Sermones*, ed. Morin, 1: 532.6: "a duce, rege, imperatore . . . Jesu Christo [by our general, king, and emperor]."

4. So Louis Bayard in his edition of the letters of St. Cyprian: *Saint Cyprien. Correspondance* (Paris, 1925), 1: 43 and 80.

5. This passage from Vergil was often repeated in the literature; see Gernentz, *Laudes Romae*, 41f.

6. The Introit for the Sunday within the octave of Epiphany reads: "In excelso throno vidi sedere virum, quem adorat multitudo angelorum, psallentes in unum: ecce, cuius imperii nomen est in aeternum [On a throne on high, I saw a man sit, whom a multitude of angels adored, singing in unison: 'behold (him), the name of whose empire is forever']."

7. See the analysis of the *Notitia dignitatum* (List of Offices) by Andreas Alföldi in *Römische Mitteilungen* 49 (1934): 115.

8. [The collection of lives of the emperors known variously as the *Scriptores Historiae Augustae* or the *Historia Augusta* is a pagan compilation of uncertain historical value dating from the late fourth or early fifth centuries.—Ed.]

9. Alföldi in *Röm. Mitt.*, 134.

10. Ibid., 94ff. On representations of imperial vestment, cf. now André Grabar, *L'empereur dans l'art byzantin* (Paris, 1936), 88ff.; on the gesture of the twenty-four elders as a contrast to the official submission ceremony of foreign kings, see ibid., 232f.

11. This polemical symbolism is still recognizable in Ambrose's *Sermo contra Auxentium* (Sermon Against Auxentius) (*PL* 16: 1018), in which it is said that Christ is the Imperator of the Church.

12. It is characteristic for the Book of Revelation that the "Salvation" acclamation is made jointly to God and to the Lamb in 7:10 (likewise 19:1: "salus et gloria et virtus Deo nostro est"), even though in any literal sense it is meaningless to

offer the "Salvation" acclamation to God and to the Lamb as though they were distinct and contrasting.

13. Alföldi in *Röm. Mitt.*, 78f.

14. The formula for taking an oath is thus politicized. We know that Christians omitted mention of *tychē* in the pagan oath formula (Ulrich Wilcken, *Mitteilungen aus der Würzburger Papyrussammlungen* [Berlin, 1934], 90) but retained the reference to *Salus* (ibid., 104); this shows that they recognized and rejected the pagan political worldview in which the emperor's *tychē* held sway.

15. This acclamation was Christianized by associating it with the victory of the Cross; see Peterson, *Heis Theos* (Göttingen, 1926), 153 and n. 1. Cf. too Jean Gagé in *Revue d'histoire et de philosophie religieuses* 12 (1932): 370ff.

16. The hostile attitude of Herod and the Herodians to Jesus needs to be explained *theologically*, by means of a comprehensive theological treatment of the kingdom of Christ. When the heresiologists speak of the Herodians as a sect, they are not as far off the mark as it seemed to nineteenth-century historians.

17. Where oath taking was concerned, the acute question for the early Christians was whether it was possible to recognize a historical and political worldview that was not Christian.

18. The designation of *dominica caena* (*deipnon kyriakon*, Lord's supper) in 1 Cor. 11:20 would not even have been possible had the Eucharist been only a mystery celebration. There is a political and juridical expression underlying the adjective in the Greek which emphasizes the public character of this meal rather than its connection to the mysteries. [A dig at Odo Casel, O.S.B., and his sacramental theology.—Ed.]

19. Harnack's translation in *Militia Christi*, 33 n. [English translation of Sr. Emily Joseph Daly in *Tertullian: Apologetical Works*, Fathers of the Church, no. 10 (New York, 1950), 123, considerably revised.—Ed.]

20. In depicting Christ as *imperator*, early Christian and Byzantine art also expressed the imperial Church's sense of itself as the Church of the Martyrs; on this see Grabar, *L'empereur dan l'art byzantin*, passim; cf. also Johannes Kollwitz in *Römische Quartalschrift* 44 (1936): 57ff. This is not, however, the place to explore the question of the inner connection between the divine election of Christian kings and Christian eschatology.

CHAPTER 8: WITNESS TO THE TRUTH

1. Ernst Lohmeyer in his commentary on the letter to the Philippians.

2. Cf. Hans von Campenhausen, *Die Idee des Martyriums in der alten Kirche* (The Idea of Martyrdom in the Early Church) (Göttingen, 1936). This carefully written book transcends confessional prejudices in its comprehensive understanding of the early Christian concept of the martyr.

3. The concept of the martyr belongs to the eschatological proclamation of

primitive Christianity. Contemporary discussion has not always grasped its eschatological origin with sufficient clarity.

4. It seems to me to be a mistake in inter-confessional discussion to begin, as one always does, with the concept of the saint instead of the martyr. The martyr is the paradigmatic category for what constitutes a "saint" in the Catholic sense.

5. Because martyrdom exists only for the mystical body of Christ, church teaching says that heretics, who are separated from this body, cannot become martyrs, even though they may lack nothing in the way of religious zeal.

6. It is remarkable that in the numerous works in recent years on the body of Christ, the place of the martyrs has not been treated in any detail.

7. The fact that baptism by blood does not have status as a sacrament ([Aquinas] *Summa Theologiae* 3.66.12 *ad* 1) should not suggest the mistaken inference that baptism by blood is a mere "substitute" for baptism by water (cf., e.g., [Leonhard] Atzberger in Scheeben's *Dogmatik*, 4, pt. 2: 535, and the commentary of the German edition of Thomas Aquinas, 29: 515).

8. Cyril of Jerusalem, *Catechetical Homilies* 3.57.

9. Cf. the relevant teaching of St. Ambrose. See [Johann] Niederhuber, *Die Lehre des Ambrosius vom Reiche Gottes auf Erden* (The Teaching of Ambrose on the Kingdom of God on Earth) (Mainz, 1904), 148.

10. *Against the Arians* 3.57.

11. This is how St. Damasus puts it.

12. Recall Hippolytus's use of apocalyptic, or Cyprian's paraenetic exploitation of the same (e.g., *Letters* 12.1, 58.7, 65.1, or *On the Good of Patience* 21. Especially frequent in *To Fortunatus*, etc.).

13. The orientation of St. Augustine's book to the time of the martyrs and also to the time of the Empire's collapse has in each instance has a substantial rooting in the Book of Revelation.

14. On the differentiation of the concept of the martyr and the confessor, see [Hippolyte] Delehaye, *Sanctus: Essai sur le culte des saints dans l'antiquité*, Subsidia hagiographica, 17 (Brussels, 1927), 74ff.

15. The New Testament does not use the word "apocalypse" (in the sense of revelation) to refer to the first coming of Jesus.

16. 2 Cor. 1:5–7, 4:17; Rom. 5:3–5, 8:17f.

17. The community of suffering, through which the Church's concept of community gets formed, is not a sociological concept rooted in the sphere of the historical but an eschatological phenomenon that transcends every natural concept of a community.

18. In contrast to my earlier translation in *Hochland*, I use the term "participation" rather than "comradeship" here, because the concept of "comradeship" is unable to express the eschatological and transcendent sense intended.

19. The "cosmic" concept in primitive Christianity is closely linked with eschatology.

20. Rom. 8:24; Phil. 1:20.

21. Cf. Phil. 1:20.

22. Only in this context does one grasp why the reports of the martyrs' sufferings have been published as trial records.

23. It makes no sense for Protestants to set the "theology of the cross" over against the "theology of glory." The "theology of glory" that the Gospel of John proclaims has its roots in the "theology of the cross" that St. John preaches in Revelation.

24. "Non ergo nobis erubescenda est ignominia crucis Christi, quam contra omnia humana opprobria, in eminentiori corporis parte, id est in fronte gestamus [We are therefore not put to shame by the ignominy of the cross of Christ, which against all human reproaches we bear on the more prominent part of the body, that is, on our brow]." Amulo, *Liber contra Judaeos* (Book Against the Jews) (*PL* 116: 158D).

25. Just as the suffering is not only human tribulation but a cosmic suffering as well, so too not just humanity but the whole cosmos will become revealed.

26. Think, e.g., of the Arianism of antiquity or of medieval Averroism.

27. It is therefore a given that over against Christ, the "neutrality" of liberalism can only be a transitional arrangement to something else.

28. That the cosmos in all its dimensions, and not just humanity, is "punished," fits with the correspondence between cosmos and humanity already noted.

29. It is added explicitly that the two witnesses suffered in the great city, "where also their Lord was crucified."

30. Cf. 2 Thess. 2:7. It is significant that 2 Thess. 2:3ff. speaks of the "revealing" (*apokalyptein*) of the "man of sin" (= Antichrist).

31. Only the Gnostics, who avoid martyrdom, can speak ill of God's creation.

32. See the homily of Leo the Great in the fourth reading of the Office for Epiphany.

33. The Prayer for the Feast of the Holy Innocents on December 28 says: "Martyres non loquendo, sed moriendo confessi sunt(The martyrs made their confession not by speaking but by dying)."

34. In the encyclical of Pius XI establishing the Feast of Christ the King (*Quas primas*, from December 28, 1925), this hymn is cited as *perbelle* (very beautiful). See *Acta Apostolicae Sedis* 17 (1925), 600.

35. The text of John 18:33–37 is well known as a reading for the feast of Christ the King.

36. Cf. Acts 4:27: "For in this city, in fact, both Herod and Pontius Pilate, with the Gentiles and the peoples of Israel, gathered together against your servant Jesus, whom you anointed."

37. The attempt of [Ferdinand] Kattenbusch, *Das apostolische Symbol: Seine Entstehung, sein geschichtlicher Sinn, seine ursprüngliche Stellung im Kultus und in der Theologie der Kirche* (The Apostles Creed: Its Origin, Its Historical Meaning,

Its Original Status in the Worship and the Theology of the Church) (Leipzig, 1894–1900), 2: 631, to explain the inclusion of Pilate's name as the incorporation of a formula of exorcism is in reality the denial of an explanation. The arguments of von Campenhausen, *Die Idee des Martyriums*, 50f., do not make sense to me. It seems certain to me that the *martyria* of Jesus in 1 Tim. 6:13 (more exactly: *martyrōn homologian*) is the eschatological *martyrion* that Jesus requires his disciples to practice in the commission address (Mark 6:11).

38. Ignatius, *Letter to the Magnesians* 11, emphasizes that the resurrection occurred under the governorship of Pontius Pilate.

39. The striking conceptual agreements between the gospel and Revelation appear to me to exclude entirely the possibility that they had different authors.

40. The universality of the kingdom of Christ has also been emphasized in the texts for the feast of Christ the King and in Pius XI's encyclical that inaugurated the observance of this feast (*Quas primas* of December 11, 1925).

41. Cf. *Christus als Imperator*, p. 149.

42. Cf., e.g., Fritz Kern, *Gottesgnadentum und Widerstandsrecht im früheren Mittelalter* (By the Grace of God and the Right of Resistance in the Early Middle Ages) (Leipzig, 1915), 113. Something similar also occurred in Byzantium; cf., e.g., Heinrich Gelzer, "Das Verhältnis von Staat und Kirche in Byzanz" (The Relationship of State and Church in Byzantium), *Historische Zeitschrift* 86 (1901): 202f. Also cf. Gerd Tellenbach, *"Libertas": Kirche und Weltordnung im Zeitalter des Investiturstreites* (Freedom: Church and World Order in the Age of the Investiture Conflict) (Stuttgart, 1936), 42, 45. (Related argumentation is already found in the letter of Pope Gelasius.)

43. Cf. Fritz Hofmann, *Der Kirchenbegriff des heiligen Augustinus* (St. Augustine's Concept of the Church) (Munich, 1933), 158f. and 275, and further, Damasus Zähringer, *Das kirchliche Priestertum nach dem heiligen Augustinus* (The Ecclesiastical Priesthood According to St. Augustine), Forschungen zur christlichen Literatur und Dogmengeschichte, no. 17, 1, 2 (Paderborn, 1931), 201ff. The question of whether baptism or confirmation confers participation in the priesthood of Christ need not be discussed here.

Cultural Memory in the Present

Sara Guyer, *Romanticism After Auschwitz*

Alison Ross, *The Aesthetic Paths of Philosophy: Presentation in Kant, Heidegger, Lacoue-Labarthe, and Nancy*

Gerhard Richter, *Thought-Images: Frankfurt School Writers' Reflections from Damaged Life*

Bella Brodzki, *Can These Bones Live? Translation, Survival, and Cultural Memory*

Rodolphe Gasché, *The Honor of Thinking: Critique, Theory, Philosophy*

Brigitte Peucker, *The Material Image: Art and the Real in Film*

Natalie Melas, *All the Difference in the World: Postcoloniality and the Ends of Comparison*

Jonathan Culler, *The Literary in Theory*

Michael G. Levine, *The Belated Witness: Literature, Testimony, and the Question of Holocaust Survival*

Jennifer A. Jordan, *Structures of Memory: Understanding German Change in Berlin and Beyond*

Christoph Menke, *Reflections of Equality*

Marlène Zarader, *The Unthought Debt: Heidegger and the Hebraic Heritage*

Jan Assmann, *Religion and Cultural Memory: Ten Studies*

David Scott and Charles Hirschkind, *Powers of the Secular Modern: Talal Asad and His Interlocutors*

Gyanendra Pandey, *Routine Violence: Nations, Fragments, Histories*

James Siegel, *Naming the Witch*

J. M. Bernstein, *Against Voluptuous Bodies: Late Modernism and the Meaning of Painting*

Theodore W. Jennings, Jr., *Reading Derrida / Thinking Paul: On Justice*

Richard Rorty and Eduardo Mendieta, *Take Care of Freedom and Truth Will Take Care of Itself: Interviews with Richard Rorty*

Jacques Derrida, *Paper Machine*

Renaud Barbaras, *Desire and Distance: Introduction to a Phenomenology of Perception*

Jill Bennett, *Empathic Vision: Affect, Trauma, and Contemporary Art*

Ban Wang, *Illuminations from the Past: Trauma, Memory, and History in Modern China*

James Phillips, *Heidegger's* Volk: *Between National Socialism and Poetry*

Frank Ankersmit, *Sublime Historical Experience*

István Rév, *Retroactive Justice: Prehistory of Post-Communism*

Paola Marrati, *Genesis and Trace: Derrida Reading Husserl and Heidegger*

Krzysztof Ziarek, *The Force of Art*

Marie-José Mondzain, *Image, Icon, Economy: The Byzantine Origins of the Contemporary Imaginary*

Cecilia Sjöholm, *The Antigone Complex: Ethics and the Invention of Feminine Desire*

Jacques Derrida and Elisabeth Roudinesco, *For What Tomorrow . . . : A Dialogue*

Elisabeth Weber, *Questioning Judaism: Interviews by Elisabeth Weber*

Jacques Derrida and Catherine Malabou, *Counterpath: Traveling with Jacques Derrida*

Martin Seel, *Aesthetics of Appearing*

Nanette Salomon, *Shifting Priorities: Gender and Genre in Seventeenth-Century Dutch Painting*

Jacob Taubes, *The Political Theology of Paul*

Jean-Luc Marion, *The Crossing of the Visible*

Eric Michaud, *The Cult of Art in Nazi Germany*

Anne Freadman, *The Machinery of Talk: Charles Peirce and the Sign Hypothesis*

Stanley Cavell, *Emerson's Transcendental Etudes*

Stuart McLean, *The Event and Its Terrors: Ireland, Famine, Modernity*

Beate Rössler, ed., *Privacies: Philosophical Evaluations*

Bernard Faure, *Double Exposure: Cutting Across Buddhist and Western Discourses*

Alessia Ricciardi, *The Ends of Mourning: Psychoanalysis, Literature, Film*

Alain Badiou, *Saint Paul: The Foundation of Universalism*

Gil Anidjar, *The Jew, the Arab: A History of the Enemy*

Jonathan Culler and Kevin Lamb, eds., *Just Being Difficult? Academic Writing in the Public Arena*

Jean-Luc Nancy, *A Finite Thinking*, edited by Simon Sparks

Theodor W. Adorno, *Can One Live after Auschwitz? A Philosophical Reader*, edited by Rolf Tiedemann

Patricia Pisters, *The Matrix of Visual Culture: Working with Deleuze in Film Theory*

Andreas Huyssen, *Present Pasts: Urban Palimpsests and the Politics of Memory*

Talal Asad, *Formations of the Secular: Christianity, Islam, Modernity*

Dorothea von Mücke, *The Rise of the Fantastic Tale*

Marc Redfield, *The Politics of Aesthetics: Nationalism, Gender, Romanticism*

Emmanuel Levinas, *On Escape*

Jean-François Lyotard, *Soundproof Room: Malraux's Anti-Aesthetics*

Jan Patočka, *Plato and Europe*

Hubert Damisch, *Skyline: The Narcissistic City*

Isabel Hoving, *In Praise of New Travelers: Reading Caribbean Migrant Women Writers*

Richard Rand, ed., *Futures: Of Jacques Derrida*

William Rasch, *Niklas Luhmann's Modernity: The Paradoxes of Differentiation*

Jacques Derrida and Anne Dufourmantelle, *Of Hospitality*

Jean-François Lyotard, *The Confession of Augustine*

Kaja Silverman, *World Spectators*

Samuel Weber, *Institution and Interpretation: Expanded Edition*

Jeffrey S. Librett, *The Rhetoric of Cultural Dialogue: Jews and Germans in the Epoch of Emancipation*

Ulrich Baer, *Remnants of Song: Trauma and the Experience of Modernity in Charles Baudelaire and Paul Celan*

Samuel C. Wheeler III, *Deconstruction as Analytic Philosophy*

David S. Ferris, *Silent Urns: Romanticism, Hellenism, Modernity*

Rodolphe Gasché, *Of Minimal Things: Studies on the Notion of Relation*

Sarah Winter, *Freud and the Institution of Psychoanalytic Knowledge*

Samuel Weber, *The Legend of Freud: Expanded Edition*

Aris Fioretos, ed., *The Solid Letter: Readings of Friedrich Hölderlin*

J. Hillis Miller / Manuel Asensi, *Black Holes / J. Hillis Miller; or, Boustrophedonic Reading*

Miryam Sas, *Fault Lines: Cultural Memory and Japanese Surrealism*

Peter Schwenger, *Fantasm and Fiction: On Textual Envisioning*

Didier Maleuvre, *Museum Memories: History, Technology, Art*

Jacques Derrida, *Monolingualism of the Other; or, The Prosthesis of Origin*

Andrew Baruch Wachtel, *Making a Nation, Breaking a Nation: Literature and Cultural Politics in Yugoslavia*

Niklas Luhmann, *Love as Passion: The Codification of Intimacy*

Mieke Bal, ed., *The Practice of Cultural Analysis: Exposing Interdisciplinary Interpretation*

Jacques Derrida and Gianni Vattimo, eds., *Religion*